This book provides a state-of-the-art overvie
methods, and applications. It is a must read
transdisciplinary understanding of people's e
places, and how those are shifting in response to contemporary patterns of
climate change, disease pandemics, rapid urbanization, and enforced migration.

Daniel Stokols, Chancellor's Professor Emeritus, School of Social Ecology,
University of California, Irvine, USA, and author of *Social Ecology in the
Digital Age*.

Place Attachment

Following on from the ground-breaking first edition, which received the 2014 EDRA Achievement Award, this fully updated text includes new chapters on current issues in the built environment, such as GIS and mapping, climate change, and qualitative approaches.

Place attachments are powerful emotional bonds that form between people and their physical surroundings. They inform our sense of identity, create meaning in our lives, facilitate community, and influence action. Place attachments have bearing on such diverse issues as rootedness and belonging, placemaking and displacement, mobility and migration, intergroup conflict, civic engagement, social housing and urban redevelopment, natural resource management, and global climate change.

In this multidisciplinary book, Manzo and Devine-Wright draw together the latest thinking by leading scholars from around the globe, including contributions from scholars such as Daniel Williams, Mindy Fullilove, Randy Hester, and David Seamon, to capture significant advancements in three main areas: theory, methods, and applications. Over the course of fifteen chapters, using a wide range of conceptual and applied methods, the authors critically review and challenge contemporary knowledge, identify significant advances, and point to areas for future research.

This important volume offers the most current understandings about place attachment, a critical concept for the environmental social sciences and placemaking professions.

Lynne C. Manzo is an environmental psychologist and Professor in the College of Built Environments and an Adjunct Professor in the School of Social Work at the University of Washington in Seattle. Her research focuses on people–place relationships, particularly place attachment, displacement, and socio-spatial justice.

Patrick Devine-Wright is a Professor in the Geography department at the University of Exeter, UK. His research combines environmental psychology and human geography perspectives to focus on the role of place attachment in relation to climate change and energy transitions. He is the lead author of the Intergovernmental Panel on Climate Change and Chair of the Devon Net Zero Task Force.

Edited by Lynne C. Manzo and
Patrick Devine-Wright

Place Attachment

Advances in theory, methods
and applications

2nd edition

LONDON AND NEW YORK

First published 2021
by Routledge
2 Park Square, Milton Park, Abingdon, Oxon OX14 4RN

and by Routledge
52 Vanderbilt Avenue, New York, NY 10017

Routledge is an imprint of the Taylor & Francis Group, an informa business

British Library Cataloguing-in-Publication Data
A catalog record for this book is available from the British Library

Library of Congress Cataloging-in-Publication Data
Names: Manzo, Lynne, editor. | Devine-Wright, Patrick, editor.
Title: Place attachment : advances in theory, methods and applications / edited by Lynne C. Manzo and Patrick Devine-Wright.
Description: 2nd Edition. | New York : Routledge, 2020. | Revised edition of Place attachment, 2014. | Includes bibliographical references and index.
Identifiers: LCCN 2020027857 (print) | LCCN 2020027858 (ebook) | ISBN 9780367223472 (hardback) | ISBN 9780367223496 (paperback) | ISBN 9780429274442 (ebook)
Subjects: LCSH: Place attachment–Psychological aspects. | Attachment behavior. | Environmental psychology.
Classification: LCC BF353 .P55 2020 (print) | LCC BF353 (ebook) | DDC 155.9/1–dc23
LC record available at https://lccn.loc.gov/2020027857
LC ebook record available at https://lccn.loc.gov/2020027858

ISBN: 978-0-367-22347-2 (hbk)
ISBN: 978-0-367-22349-6 (pbk)
ISBN: 978-0-429-27444-2 (ebk)

Typeset in Frutiger
by KnowledgeWorks Global Ltd.

Contents

List of figures

List of tables

Acknowledgements

As we wrap up this second edition, we are each in our respective homes in lockdown from the COVID-19 pandemic. Ironically, when finishing the first edition, I was still reeling from the aftermath of superstorm Sandy that destroyed many of the beloved places of my childhood. These circumstances, then and now, remind us of the power of places and our attachments to them. This book is dedicated to the people and places that are special to me, and to the tender and nebulous anchors we find in each other. To my partner, Rick Katterman, and the precious emotional "home" he has provided for me over the years, who is with me in heart although in lockdown thousands of miles away. My thanks to Patrick Devine-Wright for continuing this intellectual journey with me, and for years of collegiality and friendship. And to my dear colleagues whose work comprises this volume. You are each an inspiration.

-Lynne Manzo

Seattle, May 2020

To my co-editor, Lynne Manzo, I wish to acknowledge your drive and passion for research on place attachment, which has driven this book project from beginning to end. Some years ago now, we decided to come together to act on an absence – the two decades that had passed since the 1992 Altman and Low book on Place Attachment without a follow-up volume. At that stage, we could not have expected to present our own follow-up volume, a 2nd edition textbook that recognises the sweeping changes in global scholarship on place attachment over the past six years. Now, we finish this book during another sweeping change – the Covid 19 pandemic. Surely, this is an opportunity for a future volume assessing its impacts on people-place relations? To all of the contributing authors of this book, many old friends from the first edition but also several new ones, I wish to acknowledge your responses faithfully and patiently to the many and repeated requests from both editors for updates and revisions. To staff at Routledge, for editorial guidance and to the wider, global community of researchers working in this area who have all contributed to this volume through their collective efforts to deepen understanding of place attachment. Finally, I wish to dedicate this book to all of those whose lives have been disrupted by the pandemic, for whom matters of place are not academic abstractions but crucial elements of everyday significance and survival.

Patrick Devine-Wright

Exeter, May 2020

Notes on contributors

Marino Bonaiuto is a Full Professor of Social Psychology, Faculty of Medicine and Psychology, Sapienza University of Rome; Ph.D. board member at Department of Psychology of Socialization and Development Processes; CIRPA Director (Inter-university Centre for Research in Environmental Psychology); President of the Master Course in Psychology of Communication and Marketing; awarded Research Fellow IAAP (International Association of Applied Psychology).

Mirilia Bonnes is the founder of CIRPA (Centre for Inter-university Research on Environmental Psychology) and former professor of social and environmental psychology at Sapienza University of Rome. Long-time collaborator of UNESCO Program of Ecological Sciences, Man and Biosphere (MAB), also as Chair of the Italian MAB Committee.

Giuseppe Carrus, PhD, is aFull Professor of Social Psychology at the Department of Education Sciences, Roma Tre University, Italy. He received national and EU grants. He has been Secretary of the International Association of People-environment Studies (IAPS). He is currently Chief Specialty Editor of Frontiers in Psychology—Environmental Psychology.

Patrick Devine-Wright is a Professor in the Geography Department at the University of Exeter, UK. His research combines environmental psychology and human geography perspectives to focus on the role of place attachment in relation to climate change and energy transitions. He is the lead author of the Intergovernmental Panel on Climate Change and Chair of the Devon Net Zero Task Force.

Andrés Di Masso Tarditti, Ph.D., is a Full Professor in applied social psychology, political psychology, qualitative methods, and epistemology at the University of Barcelona (Spain). His research focuses on the micropolitics of place and the ideological construction of people-place relations, across socially sensitive topics such as public space and the right to the city, urban transformations, racism, migration, nationalism, gender, and mobilities.

John Dixon is a Professor of Social Psychology at the Open University, having worked previously at Lancaster University and the University of Worcester in the UK and at the University of Cape Town in South Africa. Among other themes, his work explores the relationship between place identity, segregation, and social change.

Kevin Durrheim is a Professor of Psychology at the University of KwaZulu-Natal. He writes on topics related to racism, segregation, and social change. His publications include *Qualitative Studies of Silence* (Murray & Durrheim (Eds.) 2019 Cambridge), *Race Trouble* (Durrheim, Mtose & Brown, 2011, Lexington Press), and *Racial Encounter* (Durrheim & Dixon, 2005, Routledge).

Ferdinando Fornara is an Associate Professor of Social and Environmental Psychology at the University of Cagliari, Italy. He is member of the editorial board of the *Journal of Environmental Psychology* and board member of the IAPS (International Association of People-environment Studies). His research interests include lay evaluation of design attributes and normative influence on pro-environmental choices.

Mindy Thompson Fullilove, MD, is a Social Psychiatrist who has published 100 papers and 8 books examining the connection between upheaval and disease. Her most recent work, examining the role of Main Streets in creating mental health, is reported in *Main Street: How a City's Heart Connects Us All*.

Robert Gifford is a Professor of Psychology and Environmental Studies at the University of Victoria, a Fellow of the American Psychological Association, the Canadian Psychological Association, the Association for Psychological Science, the International Association of Applied Psychology and was recently inducted into the Royal Society of Canada.

Sarah Gottwald (M.Sc.) is a Doctoral Student in the PlanSmart research group at Leibniz University Hannover, Germany. In her research, she applies deliberative and instrumental participatory mapping methods to assess sense of place and perceived environmental problems and codesign nature based solutions in river landscapes. https://www.umwelt.uni-hannover.de/gottwald.html

Bernardo Hernández is currently a Full Professor of Social Psychology in the Department of Cognitive, Social, and Organizational Psychology at University of La Laguna, Spain. His research interests include place attachment and place identity, ecological beliefs, pro-environmental behaviors, and environmental crime. He was the editor of *PsyEcology* until 2018.

Randolph T. Hester is a Director of the Center for Ecological Democracy, Durham, North Carolina; Professor Emeritus, University of California, Berkeley; and a founder of SAVE, International. An award-winning designer, Hester's built works set precedents for participatory design, place attachment, conservation biology, and environmental justice. His writing includes classic books on democratic design.

M. Carmen Hidalgo is currently a Professor of Environmental Psychology in the Department of Social Psychology, Social Work, AS & EAO at University of Málaga,

Spain. Her current research interest focus on place attachment, benefits of natural environments, and climate change awareness.

Maria Lewicka is a Professor of Social and Environmental Psychology, Head of the Institute of Psychology, Nicolaus Copernicus University in Toruń, Poland. Her research includes relationships between urban settings and people's behaviors, emotions, and cognitions, in particular place attachment, place identity, and place memory.

Lynne C. Manzo is an Environmental Psychologist and Professor in the College of Built Environments and an Adjunct Professor in the School of Social Work at the University of Washington in Seattle. Her research focuses on people-place relationships particularly on place attachment, displacement, and socio-spatial justice.

Nikolay L. Mihaylov is a Community Psychologist and Assistant Professor of Sociology at the Faculty of Public Health, Medical University Varna, Bulgaria. He researches social and environmental movements, community organizing, empowerment, school-based community building, citizen expertise, and grassroots democracy.

Brett Alan Miller is an Environmental and Natural Resource Sociologist who collaborates on transdisciplinary research on complex and contested social-ecological systems. By examining the conjoint constitution of the environment, he focuses on dynamic interactions between the social constructions and material consequences of place, community, and ecosystem services for different stakeholders.

Tara Quinn is a research fellow at the University of Exeter working on risk perception, place attachment, and the well-being impacts of climate change adaptation. Tara is particularly interested in how place attachment develops, its relationship to a sense of security and how place attachment relates to individual and collective responses to environmental climate change.

Douglas D. Perkins is a community/environmental psychologist and founding director of the Program in Community Research & Action, Vanderbilt University. He researches citizen participation, empowerment, community organization, and local democracy; and urban disorder, fear and violence; plus the global development of applied community studies across 12 disciplines and 105 countries.

Laís Pinto de Carvalho is a psychologist and Postdoctoral Researcher in University of Valparaíso, Chile. Her research topics revolve around critical environmental psychology, with a focus on place attachment and the psychosocial processes of home making and unmaking in contexts marked by the violation of the right to adequate housing.

Christopher Raymond (PhD Philosophy) is a Professor in Sustainability Science (Sustainability Transformations and Ecosystem Services) at the Helsinki Institute of Sustainability Science, University of Helsinki, Finland. He develops novel concepts and methods for assessing place attachment, the multiple values of nature, and the co-benefits of nature-based solutions. www.hn-transformations.com

Clare Rishbeth, PhD, is a Senior Lecturer in the Department of Landscape Architecture, University of Sheffield, UK. Her research focuses on migration histories and the experiential qualities of place, developing a landscape-specific contribution within a broad field of literature encompassing belonging and isolation, conviviality, racism, and transnational connections.

Deni Ruggeri is an Associate Professor at the Norwegian University of Life Sciences. His research/teaching focuses on place attachment and participatory community development. He holds a PhD from UC Berkeley and Master's Degrees from Cornell. He practices landscape architecture and participatory design internationally and coordinates the first EU-funded online course on Landscape Democracy.

Cristina Ruiz is currently a Professor in the Department of Cognitive, Social, and Organizational Psychology at University of La Laguna, Spain. Her research interests include human environment interactions, place attachment and place identity, and their relations with psychological wellbeing, likewise environmental crime and the impact of tourism on the environment.

Carmen Sarich graduated from the University of Victoria in 2019 with a Bachelor of Science Major Combined in Biology and Psychology with a Minor in Slavic Studies. She is currently completing a Master of Science in Audiology at the University of British Colombia.

Dr. Leila Scannell's primary research focus is on place attachment. She is a Research Associate at the University of Victoria and an Associate Editor for the *Journal of Environmental Psychology*. A fond place of interpersonal and place attachment is her home on Elwood Avenue where her son was born.

Massimiliano Scopelliti is an Associate Professor of Social Psychology at LUMSA University in Rome, Italy. He is author of several scientific publications in international journals and book chapters. His research interests include different areas in environmental psychology, such as restorative environments, pro-environmental behavior and biodiversity protection, urban environmental quality, and place attachment.

David Seamon is a Professor of Environment-Behavior and Place Studies in the Department of Architecture at Kansas State University in Manhattan, Kansas, USA. His writings focus on a phenomenological approach to place, architecture, and environmental design as place making. His most recent book is *Life Takes Place: Phenomenology, Lifeworlds and Place Making* (Routledge, 2018).

Richard C. Stedman is a Professor and Associate Chair of the Department of Natural Resources at Cornell University. His work uses as sense of place framework to understand multiple phenomena; current projects in this area emphasize energy transitions, human-wildlife conflict, and water quality/fishery systems.

Daniel R. Williams is a Research Social Scientist with the USDA Forest Service, Rocky Mountain Research Station in Fort Collins, Colorado. His research focuses on the human dimensions of landscape change and, in particular, the use of place-based inquiry and practice to inform the adaptive governance of complex social-ecological systems.

Elizabeth Williams is completing doctoral studies in environmental psychology at the University of Victoria. Her research centers on sustainability, conservation, and inter-species relationships. She holds an M.Sc. in resource management and environmental studies from the University of British Columbia, and a BA (Honors) in psychology from the University of Winnipeg.

Introduction

In the seven years since the first edition of this book was published, the literature on place attachment has continued to grow and move our comprehension of the way we relate to place forward. At the same time, the need to understand place attachment has magnified as we face increased socio-spatial precarity—from the global climate crisis, increased migration, displacement, rapid urbanization, and even pandemics (see also Raymond et al, forthcoming 2021, for consideration of changing senses of place in the context of these global challenges). As we finalize this book manuscript, we are in the midst of the COVID-19 pandemic. People worldwide are anchored in place as entire countries are in lockdown. We find ourselves both emplaced and displaced in ways we did not previously imagine possible. Scholars have begun exploring the "ecology of disease" in earnest drawing on connections already identified between epidemics and place, particularly linkages between disease, environmental change, and ecosystem breakdown (Robbins, 2012). Thus, the pandemic is one of a number of global challenges that call us to reconsider yet again our relationships to place—to ponder the entanglements of emplacement and the dynamism of place, community, and connection all while being sequestered in place. Our current circumstances prod us to understand our relationships to place with even greater urgency.

In such a context, we can appreciate the complexities, nuances, and dynamism of our attachments to place even more. The writings on place attachment gathered from the scholars in this volume attest to its complexity by the sheer diversity of perspectives on how to conceptualize the construct, how to study it, and how to apply it. Generally, it is agreed that place attachments are emotional bonds to places at varying scales, and that they form and change over time. Beyond that, despite more than four decades of scholarship, much is still debated. For example, while some scholars focus on individual-level attachments and examine its emotional and cognitive components (e.g., Fornara et al., in this volume; Hernandez et al., in this volume), others address community-level attachments (e.g., Mihaylov et al., this volume) or view place attachments as socially constructed and discursively negotiated among groups of people (as illustrated by Di Masso et al., Chapter 5, this volume). And while there is still a tendency to see place attachments as positive affective bonds, there is continued evidence that, at least in some cases, emotional responses are multivalent, also involving negative and ambivalent feelings and experiences (e.g., Fullilove Chapter 11 ; Manzo & Pinto de Carvalho, Chapter 7 this volume). Similarly, debate continues about whether there is a single center of attachment with the residence at the core (Lewicka, 2011), whether people can be strongly attached to places at larger scales extending outwards to neighborhood, city/town, region up to and including the global (Devine-Wright, 2013; Raymond & Gottwald, Chapter 9 this volume) or to multiple, geographically scattered places simultaneously that together create a web of meaning (Di Masso et al., 2019; Gurney et al., 2017; Manzo, 2003; Williams & van Patten, 2006).

It seems, then, that the discourse on place attachment has grown even more divergent since the publication of the first edition. This stems, in part, from the growing popularity of the subject and its application in a range of contexts by scholars from various disciplines. While some might advocate for making territorial claims and to "defend their turf" (Smith, 2015, p. 390), our view is that multiple disciplinary explorations will move our understanding of place attachments forward in vital ways. The fact that different disciplines have different points of entry can enrich our understanding. For example, Smith's (2018) volume on place attachment through a geographical lens leads with the characteristics of places themselves, with the volume organized around categories of place qualities (e.g., secure places, restorative places, validating places) and each chapter focuses on a single geographic locale. In contrast, psychologists tend to begin with, or foreground, the experiences of people who feel attachments to those places and examine the dynamics between them and the places to which they are attached. And while the legacy of psychological research has influenced a trend toward examining the emotive-cognitive aspects of attachments at the individual level as noted earlier (see, e.g., Scannell et al., Chapter 3, this volume), this is not always the case, as community psychologists and sociologists (e.g., Mihaylov et al., Chapter 10, this volume) shift the scale of attachments to the group or community level. In addition, urban designers and landscape architects who study and engage place attachments in their practice bring a perspective that emphasizes both physical places as sites of attachment and the community scale of these attachments with an eye toward how these attachments can inform socially responsive and participatory design practice (Hester, Chapter 13; Rishbeth, Chapter 8; Ruggeri, Chapter 15, this volume).

The onto-epistemological frameworks that researchers use also strongly influence the ways that place attachments are studied. As Lynne Manzo and Lais Pinto de Carvalho note in Chapter 7 of this volume, there are quite divergent approaches to research based on whether a researcher is operating within a positivist, post-positivist, or more subjective, or critically reflexive paradigm. This multiplicity of paradigmatic approaches—which cut across disciplinary boundaries—has provoked controversy as well, as some might regard multiple and divergent approaches to place attachment as a weakness rather than a strength, seeking instead to establish a singular, overarching framework for the body of place attachment research (Raymond, 2013). In developing this volume, we took a different position, one that sees singularity as an impossibility given the multiple disciplinary and onto-epistemological frameworks and geopolitical contexts in which researchers operate. We accept, and even wish to celebrate, the plurality of visions and voices, as Dan Williams advocates in the first and now this second edition of the book (with Brett Miller, Chapter 1, this volume). This diversity is evident in the collection of arguments across the chapters including several new chapters added to round out the discourse further.

In this second edition, we have elected to continue the three-pronged structure of the first edition based on theories, methods, and applications of place attachment research, as a still useful way of structuring contributions on the topic. In our view, each of these three aspects remains essential components of a thriving literature on place attachment, equally important in furthering our understanding of this important topic. This volume also retains a predominant review orientation, focusing on the literature as a whole rather than offering a series of specific case studies. In this way, it serves as a useful introduction and guide to particular aspects of place attachment theory, method, and application. However, many authors do offer specific studies and cases as a way to ground their broader arguments about place attachment. Below we identify new developments in the area of theory, methods, and applications as explored in this second edition.

WHERE HAS THE DISCOURSE GONE?

Theory

The diversity of perspectives on place attachment, its meaning, and relation to other concepts remain a hallmark of the literature and perhaps even more so currently. At the same time, it can be argued that place attachment theory has not radically shifted over the years, as many researchers have proceeded with empirical studies without clarifying or expanding the concept. This has sometimes led to the perpetuation of more restricted notions of place attachment that do not account for key aspects including memory, mobility, multiple and multiscalar place attachments, the political dimensions of place relationships, and the ways a range of emotions and experiences contribute to place attachments. There are, however, some exceptions. As is evident in this volume, there is a growing interest in how place attachment might intersect with mobility (Lewicka; see also Di Masso et al., 2019) and place change either through changes in a physical space over time (Ruggeri) or through the cultivation of transnational ties among immigrants (Rishbeth). Although the latter two chapters are situated in the methods and applications section of the volume, respectively, they still speak to the dynamics of place attachments in the context of change and offer valuable empirical grounding to advance place attachment theory in this regard. Together, these are important developments in the literature that respond to the increased uncertainty of our relationships to place, although they still must make their way more fully into place attachment theory.

The dynamism and plural aspects of place attachments are also tackled in this volume by Dan Williams (now with Brett Miller), Maria Lewicka, David Seamon, and Mindy Fullilove—scholars who have long been thinking about place and our attachments to it. As Williams and Miller point out in the first chapter, this plurality is best understood in the context of successive waves of intellectual currents across the social sciences, from modernist to systemic approaches, which have influenced understandings of place and attachments to those places. This is an important new contribution to this second edition that contextualizes current work within broader trajectories of scholarly discourse on place over time, identifying key "metatheoretical moments" along the way. In Chapter 2, David Seamon grounds us in the phenomenological roots of place attachment, while at the same time exploring new dimensions and potentialities for our understanding of place attachments when they are understood holistically, dialectically, and generatively. In Chapter 3, Leila Scannell et al. update the connections between the main principles of interpersonal attachment theory and place attachment theory emphasizing the processes and dynamics of attachments to people and place as parts of a stabilizing system. In Chapter 4, Maria Lewicka extends the explorations of people-place dynamics by considering the role of continuity in place attachments in a mobile world, furthering the theoretical developments regarding attachment and mobility as put forward by Per Gustafson in the first edition. In Chapter 5, Andres Di Masso, John Dixon, and Kevin Durrheim finish out the theory section by outlining a discursive perspective on human-environment relations, with a particular focus on the process of place attachment as socially and linguistically negotiated. In doing so, they challenge current place attachment theory to consider the ways that attachments to place are socially constructed. Given the post-modern, post-structuralist turn in the social sciences in the past several decades, this is a particularly important line of inquiry.

As noted earlier, chapters in the methods and applications sections also have substantial insight for the development of place attachment theory. For example, in her examination of forced serial displacement of African-American communities through US history, Mindy Fullilove offers the "frayed knot hypothesis" that can inform theorization of how attachments draw on the agency of displaced people as they rebuild new attachment by drawing on "the-place-that-was" to recreate "the beloved community." Similar theoretical implications are offered by Clare Rishbeth's examination of transnational place attachments among immigrants in the methods section. All of the theory chapters underscore the dynamic and processual aspects of place attachment, reflecting a deepening awareness and appreciation of these dimensions of the phenomenon that have emerged over time in the literature, a point also stressed by Patrick Devine-Wright and Tara Quinn in Chapter 14.

Methods

In the Methods section of this book, scholars explore the onto-epistemological foundations and methodological possibilities and challenges to studying place attachment, sometimes suggesting novel approaches hitherto neglected in the literature. These newer contributions are a critical departure from a strong historical trend in place attachment research that focuses on developing scales to measure the various dimensions of the concept quantitatively using questionnaires (see, especially, Williams & Roggenbuck, 1989 and Williams & Vaske, 2003; also discussed in Lewicka, 2011). At the same time, another research thread that has developed for some time but has been less dominant in the discourse employs more diverse and qualitative approaches to place attachment (see, e.g., Manzo, 2019a; Mazumdar & Mazumdar, 2004). The nature and value of this line of work is more directly called out in a new chapter by Lynne Manzo and Lais Pinto de Carvalho.

We treat these separate methodological approaches in new detail in this updated volume. In Chapter 6, Bernardo Hernandez, M. Carmen Hidalgo, and Cristina Ruiz offer a critical review of the quantitative approaches that have developed in the research to characterize emotional bonds between humans and places, organizing them into three different models. This is followed by the first comprehensive treatment of the application of qualitative methods to the study of place attachments, and in particular the ontological and epistemological bases that underlie them. Lynne Manzo and Lais Pinto de Carvalho underscore the ways that methods are grounded in underlying presumptions about the world that are often glided over, emphasizing the value of qualitative methods to explore the less well-understood and emergent aspects of place attachment that are not captured in existing measurement tools.

Newer methodological explorations are provided by landscape architect Clare Rishbeth in Chapter 8, which offers a compelling update to both visual (photographic and filmic) and interview techniques for exploring the complex and nuanced nature of transnational attachments among immigrants. The two projects she presents here offer possibilities for "a richer and more responsive research environment specifically appropriate to researching place attachment." Similarly, in Chapter 9, Christopher Raymond and Sarah Gottwald offer a new exploration of the methodologies that can be used to examine place attachment at local, regional, national, and global scales, reflecting an emergent interest in how place attachment beyond the local can be captured using a variety of approaches including participatory mapping and spatial navigation methods.

The interconnected nature of place attachment scholarship is well illustrated in this methods section where the chapters, out of necessity, engage in critical exploration of place attachment concepts and theories as a way to understand methodologies and forge new ways of studying place attachments. For example, both Hernandez et al. and Manzo and Pinto de Carvalho trace different methodological approaches to the particular ways that place attachment has been conceptualized, and the former chapter further situates place attachment in relation to other similar constructs such as place identity and place dependence.

Applications

The application of place attachment in various fields and to diverse topics is arguably the most thriving aspect of the literature over the past decade. One of the areas of significant development in place attachment work is its application to various contexts, environmental challenges, and areas of inquiry. This work has responded to the critical challenges of contemporary society, from global climate change to urban restructuring programs proliferating in the US and Western Europe, to increased mobility in a context of globalization. Recent years has seen place attachment applied to the study of natural resource management (Masterson, Enqvist, Stedman, & Tengö, 2019), community responses to the siting of renewable energy technologies (Devine-Wright & Wiersma, 2019), pro-environmental behavior (Larson et al., 2018; Meloni, Fornara, & Carrus, 2019), tourism (Cheng & Wu, 2015; Han, Kim, Lee, & Kim, 2019), responses to disasters and flood preparedness (Haney, 2018), housing policy and displacement (Lee & Evans, 2020; Manzo, 2019b), and socially responsive community design (Ruggeri, 2018).

In the Applications section of the book, we hear from an array of scholars and practitioners who apply place attachment concepts in their work, revealing how an understanding of people's attachment to place can influence research, policy, and design practice. The section opens with Chapter 10 by Nikolay Mihaylov, Douglas Perkins, and Rich Stedman who build on theories of place attachment at the community level to consider how these processes are involved in response to controversial energy developments, drawing on case studies of a critical environmental concern—the extraction of shale gas using hydraulic fracturing or "fracking"—in the United States and Bulgaria. In Chapter 12, Fernando Fornara et al. also draw out associations between place attachment and environment-related behavior. Their broad scope includes pro-environmental behavior, tourist-related activities, and actions that could be considered anti-environmental (e.g., objections to the designation of rural areas as protected spaces or to the siting of renewable energy projects). In yet another connection to environmental concerns, Patrick Devine Wright and Tara Quinn articulate the relevance of place attachments to climate change in Chapter 14, noting that place attachments can enable or constrain both adaptation and mitigation depending on the interactions between attachment bonds and the meanings associated with particular places impacted by climate change. Together, these application chapters offer significant insights to inform environmental policies, management strategies, and pro-environmental behavior.

Other critical applications offered in this section are related to the nature of place change and people's agency in adapting to, participating in, or resisting that change. In particular, psychiatrist Mindy Fullilove has updated her examination of what happens to place attachments in the context of serial forced displacement in the African-American community. This work has important applications to public health and planning policy as well as social justice advocacy. Similarly, Randy Hester offers an update to his work through the concept of "endemic design" developed from decades of applying place attachment ideas to community design work. His chapter also calls out issues of race and the political dimensions of place meaning that must be considered in participatory design. Finally, Deni Ruggeri's chapter, another new addition to this second volume, connects place attachments to participatory design and landscape democracy. This work draws on two cases of local change and identity in Italy and Norway, linking place attachment with stewardship and resilience in a way that recognizes the empowering nature of attachments to reclaim and revitalize place.

WHERE TO GO FROM HERE

Going forward, we see at least four promising avenues for explorations in place attachment theory, methods, and applications: (1) a deepening realization of how unexpected societal upheavals such a global health crises can teach us critical lessons about the way we relate to place to survive, heal, and move onward; (2) the need to further develop theory in order to better reflect the complex and multifaceted nature of place attachments; (3) the need for greater inter- and transdisciplinary explorations of place attachments for a more nimble use of the construct in addressing contemporary societal challenges; and (4) further explorations of emerging aspects of place attachments including their political dimensions, how place intersects with power, and how a greater appreciation of place attachments can possibly have an emancipatory role in advocating for greater socio-spatial justice.

If the current pandemic is teaching us anything about place, it is underscoring the inevitability of change and uncertainty, and the extent to which our relationships to place are implicated in this. It further reminds us of the powerful connection between place, health, and well-being. And as we begin to see the differential effects of the pandemic on those with wealth and privilege and those without, we are reminded of the intensely political nature of place and our connections to it. Our way forward is to embrace our interconnectedness with each other and with place, to use our growing knowledge of the power of place, and our attachments to it, for the greater good of ourselves and our planet.

REFERENCES

Cheng, T., & Wu, H. C. (2015). How do environmental knowledge, environmental sensitivity, and place attachment affect environmentally responsible behavior? An integrated approach for sustainable island tourism. *Journal of Sustainable Tourism*, *23*, 557–576.

Devine-Wright, P. (2013). Think global, act local? The relevance of place attachments and place identities in a climate changed world. *Global Environmental Change*, *23*, 61–69.

Devine-Wright, P., & Wiersma, B. (2019). Understanding community acceptance of a potential offshore wind energy project in different locations: An island-based analysis of 'place-technology fit'. *Energy Policy*, *137*, 111086.

Di Masso, A., Williams, D. R., Raymond, C. M., Buchecker, M., Degenhardt, B., Devine-Wright, P., ...von Wirth, T. (2019). Between fixities and flows: Navigating place attachments in an increasingly mobile world. *Journal of Environmental Psychology*, *61*, 125–133. https://doi.org/10.1016/j.jenvp.2019.01.006

Gurney, G., Blythe, J., Adams, H., Curnocke, M., Faulkner, L., James, T., & Marshall, N. A. (2017) Redefining community based on place attachment in a connected world. *Proceedings of the National Academy of Sciences*, *114*, 10077–10082.

Han, J. H., Kim, J. S., Lee, C., & Kim, N. (2019). Role of place attachment dimensions in tourists' decision-making process in Cittáslow. *Journal of Destination Marketing & Management*, *11*, 108–119.

Haney, T. J. (2018). Paradise found? The emergence of social capital, place attachment, and civic engagement after disaster. *International Journal of Mass Emergencies & Disasters*, *36*(2), 97–119.

Larson, L. R., Cooper, C. B., Stedman, R. C., Decker, D. J., & Gagnon, R. J. (2018). Place-based pathways to proenvironmental behavior: Empirical evidence for a conservation–recreation model. *Society & Natural Resources*, *31*, 871–891.

Lee, B. A., & Evans, M. (2020). Forced to move: Patterns and predictors of residential displacement during an era of housing insecurity. *Social Science Research*, 87, 102415.

Lewicka, M. (2011). Place attachment: How far have we come in the last 40 years? *Journal of Environmental Psychology*, *31*(3), 207–230. https://doi.org/10.1016/J.JENVP.2010.10.001.

Manzo, L. C. (2019a). Qualitative data and design: Understanding the experiential qualities of place. *Technology: Architecture and Design*, *3*(2), 142–145.

Manzo, L. C. (2019b). The experience of place and displacement in 21st century cities. In K. Bishop, & N. Marshall (Eds.), *The Routledge handbook on people and place in the 21st century city* (pp. 125–134). London: Routledge.

Manzo, L. C. (2003). Beyond house and haven: Toward a revisioning of emotional relationships with places. *Journal of Environmental Psychology*, *23*(1), 47–61.

Masterson, V. A., Enqvist, J. P., Stedman, R. C., & Tengö, M. (2019). Sense of place in social–ecological systems: From theory to empirics. *Sustainability Science*, *14*, 555–564.

Mazumdar, S., & Mazumdar, S. (2004). Religion and place attachment: A study of sacred places. *Journal of Environmental Psychology*, *24*(3), 385–397.

Meloni, A., Fornara, F., & Carrus, G. (2019). Predicting pro-environmental behaviors in the urban context: The direct or moderated effect of urban stress, city identity, and worldviews. *Cities*, *88*, 83–90.

Raymond, C. (2013). Review of place attachment: Advances in theory, methods and applications. *Estudios de Psicologia*, *34*(23), 345–348.

Raymond, C., Manzo, L., von Wirth, T., Di Masso, A., & Williams, D. (Eds.). (Forthcoming, 2021). *Changing senses of place: Navigating global challenges*. Cambridge: Cambridge University Press.

Robbins, J. (July 14, 2012). The ecology of disease. New York Times. https://www.nytimes.com/2012/07/15/sunday-review/the-ecology-of-disease.html

Ruggeri, D. (2018). Storytelling as a catalyst for democratic landscape change in Modernist utopia. In S. Egoz, K. Jørgensen, & D. Ruggeri (Eds.), *Defining landscape democracy: The search for spatial justice*. Glos, UK: Edward Elgar Publishing.

Smith, J. S. (2018). *Explorations in place attachment*. Routledge research in culture, space, and identity series. London: Routledge.

Smith, J. S. (2015). Review of place attachment: Advances in theory, methods, and applications. *Journal of Cultural Geography*, *32*, 389–390.

Williams, D. R., & Roggenbuck, J. W. (1989, October). *Measuring place attachment: Some preliminary results*. In NRPA Symposium on Leisure Research, San Antonio, TX (Vol. 9).

Williams, D. R., & van Patten, S. (2006). Home and away? Creating identities and sustaining places in a multi-centered world. In N. McIntyre, D. Williams, & K. McHugh (Eds.), *Multiple dwelling and tourism: Negotiating place, home and identity* (pp. 32–50). Wallingford: CABI.

Williams, D. R., & Vaske, J. J. (2003). The measurement of place attachment: Validity and generalizability of a psychometric approach. *Forest Science*, *49*(6), 830–840.

PART I

Theory

Chapter 1: Metatheoretical moments in place attachment research: Seeking clarity in diversity

Daniel R. Williams and Brett Alan Miller

INTRODUCTION

Over fifty years of progress in place attachment research has produced many important insights as well as many competing senses of place attachment as a theoretical construct. Place constructs range from fairly specific terms such as place dependence and place identity to more general terms such as rootedness and sense of place, which all attempt to describe some aspect of place experience and attachment. These constructs are often used interchangeably, which adds to the confusion resulting from different and contested place definitions and relationships (Lewicka, 2011; Relph, 2008). Consequently, the literature abounds with expressions of concern for the apparent lack of theoretical coherence (Hernández, Hidalgo, & Ruiz, 2014). However, as Patterson and Williams (2005) have argued, such consternation over the state of conceptual development in place attachment research represents a flawed quest for unity given the underlying diversity of the many research programs involved, which are often marked by very different substantive goals and conflicting ontological, epistemological, and axiological commitments.

In this chapter, we attempt to demonstrate that, rather than being a single body of literature, research on *place attachment* forms, and benefits from, a diverse and multidisciplinary inquiry. We focus on the specific construct of place attachment as it has developed across time and disciplines as illustrative of both the richness and braided quality of place research. As an interdisciplinary boundary object, place attachment can facilitate fruitful discussion across different disciplines. But without some kind of orienting guide, the multifaceted evolution of this construct appears chaotic and incomprehensible. Going forward, for place attachment to remain relevant, an even greater awareness of the diverse origins of place concepts and constructs seems necessary.

Unfortunately these diverse origins also propagate controversies over the disciplinary ownership of place attachment as a theoretical construct. For instance, one cultural geographer reviewing the first edition of *Place Attachment* commented that: "Once again … the vast literature on people and place published by cultural geographers [was] overlooked (more likely ignored)" (Smith, 2015, p. 389–390).

Smith even calls on "geographers to step up and defend their turf by publishing solid research on place attachment" (p. 390), such as his own subsequent anthology, *Explorations in Place Attachment* (Smith, 2018) where all of the contributions are authored by geographers. One could argue, however (e.g., Devine-Wright, 2015), that there is a surprising lack of cross-boundary interest in place attachment in geographical works. For example, Cresswell's (2015) updated (and excellent) primer on the study of place highlights different branches of a genealogy of place rooted in geography but generally omits a vast literature on place published in cognate disciplines, notably environmental psychology (Lewicka, 2011), sociology (Gieryn, 2000; Trentelman, 2009), and environmental and natural resource management (Patterson & Williams, 2005; Stedman, 2003).

Whereas Cresswell's genealogy underrepresents this disciplinary diversity, the rich variety of different perspectives and purposes driving place research also prevents place attachment research from fulfilling Low and Altman's (1992) predicted path of theoretical constructs to progress toward consensus. There are many disciplinary and interdisciplinary perspectives on place attachment where scholars borrow freely across disciplines to support a specific construct in their place attachment research. The progression of ideas around place has ebbed and flowed, interweaving rather than strictly branching. The result is that various disciplines interested in place attachment have coevolved an assorted array of competing concepts that have split-off and merged back together into a morphology that looks more like a braided stream than a coherent body of work.

To reflect this reality we present the development of place attachment, not as a branching genealogy and not as headed toward convergence, but as a braided stream flowing from common origins and inspirations. And just as Denzin and Lincoln (1994) organized the history of qualitative methods into a sequence of "moments," we attempt to demonstrate how the progression of six important metatheoretical moments shaped the complex, braided course of place attachment research (see Figure 1.1). The aim is to better illustrate the punctuated coevolution of the construct and the various substantive differences, attendant epistemologies, and metatheoretical influences of place attachment across a variety (but by no means an exhaustive list) of disciplines.

Across this interdisciplinary landscape, we represent some of the main branches of the place attachment literature through time as interconnected and cross-influenced (i.e., braided). Brief descriptions of the broader research paradigms affecting particular moments of place attachment research are listed across the top of the figure and across the bottom are brief descriptions of these moments. These moments represent the confluence of larger paradigm shifts occurring across empirical disciplines and the progression of place attachment to meet evolving research interests. Through this process, different research traditions influence place attachment, and in turn, research on place attachment influences the development of other subdisciplines (represented as white spaces in the figure). These branches are also reacting to a larger social landscape and major social-political developments such as globalization.

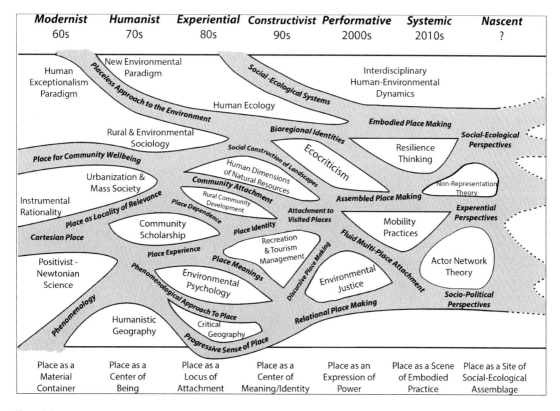

Modernist 60s	Humanist 70s	Experiential 80s	Constructivist 90s	Performative 2000s	Systemic 2010s	Nascent ?
Place as a Material Container	Place as a Center of Being	Place as a Locus of Attachment	Place as a Center of Meaning/Identity	Place as an Expression of Power	Place as a Scene of Embodied Practice	Place as a Site of Social-Ecological Assemblage

Figure 1.1
Metatheoretical moments
shaping place attachment
research.

The dates are, of course, approximate. Our goal is not to provide a taxonomy of concepts and definitions. Rather, it is to interrogate how place attachment has both shaped and responded to larger metatheoretical trajectories of social science over the past half century. Although these trajectories are also influenced by parallel developments in the spatial sciences and in the humanities, we focus largely on a subset of the social sciences. Obviously, our training and positionality as US-based scholars inevitably affects how we select and organize these moments and corresponding braids. Consequently, rather than attempting to present an exhaustive depiction, we focus on how key fields were inspired by various epistemological shifts that then propelled place attachment research along. Further, a key to understanding this evolution is not to think of these moments as necessarily replacing or overriding previous ideas but more often augmenting existing ideas and adding to the diversity and complexity of place attachment research.

SIX KEY MOMENTS IN PLACE ATTACHMENT RESEARCH

Modernist metatheory

Before the 1970s, place was often little more than a passive container of material reality and social action (Cresswell, 2013). At its apex in the early post–WWII era, the modernist metatheoretical moment comprised a constellation of hegemonic ideas about human-environment relations that effectively minimized place as a factor in human affairs. The significance for this chapter is that this forms a common point of departure for a variety of disciplinary and cross-disciplinary discourses focused on the power of place as a social science concept, which, in the modernist metatheory, had been under-theorized, marginalized, and devalued (Agnew, 1989). Across different disciplines, the term *place* was almost completely absent from the intellectual landscape. Instead, the focus was directed toward the *environment* as something that could be decomposed into separable, substitutable, and fungible qualities each having some independent impact on perception, behavior, experience, or wellbeing (Stokols, 1990).

Modernist geographical practice was dominated by formalized spatial science, quantitative modeling (e.g., central place theory), and logical positivism fixated on location and distance. Simultaneously, interest in place was eclipsed by the transition from small-scale local communities to a larger scale "mass society" (Agnew, 1989). Additionally, modernism promoted a technocratic view of planning, development, and management in which human satisfaction and wellbeing could be managed scientifically using instrumental means-ends logic (Gee, 1994). During this period, rural sociology and community sociology defined places as social spaces where people met their daily needs with little thought to sentiment and attachments (Loomis, 1958). Likewise in anthropological writing, "places [were] equated with ethnographic locales" (Rodman, 1992, p. 640). Taken together, the modern understanding of place was to look "at the world and the people in it as objects rather than subjects" (Cresswell, 2009, p. 171).

Modernism also minimized the role of the environment in human action and wellbeing (Stokols, 1990) and regarded human civilization as both largely exempt from the limitations of nature and yet widely capable of molding the environment to meet human needs (Dunlap & Catton, 1979). However, as societal concern over environmental issues accelerated, a concomitant desire developed to interrogate environmental problems through the lens of social science. Dunlap and Catton (1979) describe this major shift in thinking as a rejection of the "human exceptionalism" paradigm[1] while proposing a "new environmental paradigm". Ironically, this new paradigm retained a mostly monolithic view of the environment with little significant focus on specific places (Buttel, 2002).

In psychology, growing concern for the environment led scholars to reject laboratory settings as artificial and instead examine the role of larger, naturalistic settings on human behavior (Proshansky, Ittelson, & Rivlin, 1970). But in keeping with modernist metatheory, early work on environment and behavior tended toward functional (instrumental) framings (Wohwill, 1970). Modernist metatheory held that humans were rational actors operating within a rational world. Thus, environmental psychology drew heavily from cognitive information processing and utilitarian metaphors of rational actors as a way to refute the idea of humans as passive stimulus processors. Much of this early work focused on decomposing these settings into attributes and quantifying human perceptions, preferences, and behaviors relative to these attributes (Wohwill, 1970). A pervasive way of operationalizing this was to adopt some form of a multi-attribute model for the assessment and evaluation of places (Gee, 1994).

A few early voices of discontent pushed back against this modernist metatheory of environment to offer a different view of place. One of the very first was Firey (1945) who documented the "retentive influence" of sentiment and symbolic properties of urban spaces such as friendship and family ties. These findings challenged what he saw as the prevailing instrumental view of space, which assumed "the only possible relationship that locational activities may bear to space is an economic one" (p. 140). Another early critique of instrumental thinking about place was Fried's (1963) widely cited study of grieving for homes lost to urban renewal projects. Fried found that the depth of grief was primarily related to the loss of local social relationships and spatial orientations. However, it is not until the 1970s and the emergence of a humanist backlash that place starts to become more widely conceived as a particular, valued space imbued with meanings and attachments (Tuan, 1977).

Humanist metatheory

The humanist moment represents perhaps the most germinal and impactful theoretical development in place attachment research. In fact the origins of place attachment are almost universally traced to the onset of the phenomenological perspective in the 1970s, particularly within humanistic geography and "Tuan's (1977) now classic work [examining] the ways in which people attach meaning to place" (Manzo & Perkins, 2006, p. 337). Place in this moment is described phenomenologically as a center of "being-in-the-world" (Tuan, 1977). To counteract modernist reductionism concerning place, humanistic geographers in particular sought to elevate their understanding of place to a central role in human awareness of being in the world. Building on existential philosophy (e.g., Heidegger and Husserl), these scholars began to consider humans as subjects with intentions, feelings, emotions, and attachments to the world. Essential to this awareness was the concept of place and the recognition that people were always "somewhere" (Relph, 1976). "Geography informed by phenomenology would not simply be about the world or about people but about people-in-the-world" (Cresswell, 2013, p. 112).

This humanist moment also surfaced as a critique of global capitalism's role in eroding the diversity and distinctiveness of places, commodifying "authentic" places, and producing "placelessness." For instance, humanistic geographers such as Relph (1976) and architectural phenomenologists such as Norberg-Schulz (1980) were critical of expert-driven rational approaches to environmental management and design that dominated the post–WWII period. They advanced the notion that place attachment was a fundamental human need—"a secure point from which to look out on the world, a firm grasp of one's own position in the order of things, and a significant spiritual and psychological attachment to somewhere in particular" (Relph, 1976, p. 38). In the end, humanistic geography grappled with many issues that would subsequently shape place attachment scholarship and play a central role in human geography and cognate fields. Among these are the ideas of experience, emotion and affect, body and performance, as well as interest in interpretive and qualitative methods (Cresswell, 2013).

Cognate environmental scholarship, also motivated by disenchantment with instrumental understandings of the environment and an emerging placelessness, began investigating the role of attachment to places and communities on residential satisfaction and sense of belonging (Stokols & Shumaker, 1982). Some of these scholars were explicitly concerned about the loss of communities as systems of informal connections between community members within a "locality of relevance" (place) that was threatened by the homogenizing process of urbanization and the placeless influence of global capitalism (Warren, 1978). In this effort, community scholars and rural sociologists began refining concepts such as "neighboring" that would later be developed into concepts such as community attachment and place attachment (Trentelman, 2009).[2]

In retrospect, the impact of this early humanist metatheoretical moment centered as much on the importance of spatial awareness (place as a center-of-being) and the essential (invariant) structure of place experience as it did on the particular experience or sense of a given place as a locus of attachment. That is not to say actual experiences were ignored (see Seamon, 1980), but this metatheoretical turn was at least partly about the fundamental ontological nature of place in human experience. As Relph (2008, p. 36) argued (citing Malpas): "'Place is integral to the very structure and possibility of experience' ... and not just a product of what is encountered in experience... [and is] certainly not susceptible to quantitative excavation." But it is this fixed, bounded, essentialist view of place that would later generate intense criticism from a social constructionist perspective (Harvey, 1996).

The experiential metatheory

The experiential moment began toward the end of the 1970s and represents an elaboration of the humanist idea, but with a stronger empirical focus on characterizing the experience of particular places, both place as a locus of attachment and as a center of meaning (Williams, 2014). The earlier humanistic turn in geography and architecture opened up new avenues of theorizing about human-environment relationships across a range of disciplines. During the 1980s various cognate disciplines, inspired by the humanist moment, were conducting empirical assessments of the subjective experience of places, particularly residential place attachment. These scholars wanted to understand the underlying psycho-social processes that produced place attachments and meanings and how they influenced satisfaction and wellbeing. But when they looked to humanist geographers, they did not find much methodological guidance (Buttimer, 1976).[3]

In a review from environmental psychology, Giuliani (2003) identified three contexts driving residential place attachment research during this period. The first dealt with the search for environmental quality measures sensitive to inhabitants' needs, which is closely aligned with place dependence (Stokols & Shumaker, 1982).

This begins to differentiate place attachment from mere positive regard for a place to a "bond, with enduring quality, directed toward a specific target, not interchangeable with the same functional quality" (Giuliani, 2003, p. 148). Second, Giuliani described how the confluence of attachment and identity built on Proshansky's (1978) concept of place-identity comprised cognitions about the physical environment that help to define the self. The third context examined territorial attachment as a "feeling of possessiveness" toward a particular place because of its association with self-image or social identity through such mechanisms as personalization of space that intensifies affective bonds (Brown, 1987).

By the end of the 1980s, environmental psychology and human geography were both well-established fields researching place attachments. Insights from these fields and research on place more broadly also influenced the emergence of new environmental social sciences. For instance the topic of natural resource sociology in the US emerged toward the end of the 1980s with a focus on relationships between rural communities and proximate natural resource values that are inextricably place-based, along with other burgeoning natural resource social sciences (Field & Burch, 1991). Pulling as well from humanistic roots, these scholars began engaging the topic of place attachment by focusing on the relationship between specific communities and their particular places.

These different interdisciplinary braids set the stage for a significant expansion in the literature around quantitatively measuring place attachments, examining the attachment process, and more clearly articulating the antecedents and consequences of attachments, which today dominates the larger body of place attachment research (Lewicka, 2011). Although a diverse braid of qualitative work persisted throughout this period (Altman & Low, 1992; Manzo, 2003), much of this early interdisciplinary work focused on developing quantitative measurements. For example, drawing inspiration from Tuan's (1977) distinction between space perceived as a territory for activity versus place as a locus for feelings of attachment and belonging, Williams, Patterson, Roggenbuck, and Watson (1992) developed a psychometric measure of the place attachments held by recreational visitors to parks, forests, and other wildland and tourist destinations.[4] This approach, which measured place dependence and place identity as two facets of place attachment, would strongly shape the way place attachment was understood and measured, including embedded assumptions about its composition and expression (Lewicka, 2011).

A lack of common definitions and the interdisciplinary nature of this moment made it difficult for scholars to take full advantage of work from outside their respective fields. When scholars coalesced around certain specific terms, they often meant parallel but slightly different things based on disciplinarily specific epistemologies or assumptions (Patterson & Williams, 2005). The dominance of quantitative approaches not only would continue through the 1990s and beyond but also lead to the constructivist critique that forms the next major theoretical development in place literature.

Critical-constructivist metatheory

Across academic literature, there was increased consideration of the social construction of social facts and material realities starting around the late 1980s and into the early 2000s. Although this shift does not define all place attachment literature during this time, it is a major metatheoretical moment where many new disciplines exhibit interest in place attachment research. For instance, "ecocritical" approaches to the humanities and environmental ethics (Glotfelty & Fromm, 1996) promoted explicitly place-focused concepts such as bioregional identity. Also and more generally, the humanities began to grapple with the social construction of place bonds in narratives (Lippard, 1997). A similar focus on narratives in place attachment research showed how place identities and sense of belonging to a place result in important social differences in how people view, enact, and ultimately shape and control place narratives (Dixon & Durrheim, 2000).

The narrative (discursive) approach to place attachment intersects with critical (relational) theories in geography about the politics of place. Where the phenomenological approach to place venerated place as something universally experienced, felt, and sensed (Cresswell, 2009), "critical" geographies, also born from a critique of positivist spatial science, began to point out the neglected role of social position and power in the construction of contested places (Harvey, 1996). These insights inspired some environmental psychologists to recognize that "it is not possible to adequately consider emotional relationships with places without recognizing the significant political implications of such phenomena" (Manzo, 2003, p. 54). Focusing on discursive strategies is one way to demonstrate how place meanings are socially constructed and therefore embedded in the structures of power in everyday life (Dixon & Durrheim, 2000). This added a more discursive approach that augmented cognitive views (relying on surveys and self-reports) with more narrative approaches (Stokowski, 2002).

Focusing on the way places are made and remade (socially constructed) promoted a relational view of place (Massey, 1994). In this framing, social practices and narratives produce psychological accounts of relationships, which carry normative, relational, political, and material consequences (Di Masso, Dixon, & Hernández, 2017). This shift in thinking inevitably supported consideration of the social construction of physical landscapes as well. For instance, rural and community sociology began to consider how the physical environment (previously treated as an immutable anchor) was also socially constructed (Greider & Garkovich, 1994). This influenced place attachment as well as the development of natural resource sociology and environmental sociology (Field, Luloff, & Krannich, 2013). Also, this recognition led to critical, place-based topics in environmental sociology and interdisciplinary fields such as political ecology to examine the struggle for place (Yung, Freimund, & Belsky, 2003; Pellow & Nyseth Brehm, 2013).

The constructivist moment also promoted increased interdisciplinary engagement on the use and definition of place constructs such as sense of place, place attachment and identity, and community attachment (Williams & Stewart, 1998).

In cognate fields place attachment provided insights on the relationship between community and place in stakeholder environmental concerns (Eisenhauer, Krannich, & Blahna, 2000), and the challenges of disentangling "place" from "community" (Trentelman, 2009). However, the recognition of the socially constructed nature of places triggered critical impasses in attempts to consolidate terms. In this moment, the unexamined origins of particular terms and disciplinary-specific discourses were adding to confusion and inconsistency surrounding place attachment research (Patterson & Williams, 2005).

In sum, the critical-constructive moment refigured place attachment research to recognize that from the relational perspective, place does not have singular unique identities, but multiple contested ones that are continually reproduced through discourse and practice. However, two additional features suggested by Massey's relational view of place were not as prominent in place attachment research of the 1990s. One was the recognition that place is not a fixed entity but produced through flows and mobilities, in addition to power relations. The second was that places are not bounded localities (as was typical of humanistic phenomenology), but permeable entities constituted from constellations or networks of local and global connections grounded in concrete places, practices, and performances. The constructivist (post-structural) emphasis on meaning via text, language, and discourse often overlooked the significance of material practice, movement, flow, and emotional embodiment in constituting place attachment. Also, some scholars began to question whether place was *just* a social construction uninfluenced by material reality (Stedman, 2003). Others were starting to consider the active ways that places are "conjointly constituted" through social construction and material reality (Freudenburg, Frickel, & Gramling, 1995). These concerns contributed to the next major metatheoretical moment shaping place attachment literature where *lived* performances of place are considered.

The performative metatheory

Performative metatheory takes place attachment in an even more relational and fluid direction from the critical-constructivist moment. This was in part driven by increasing awareness of how globalization was impacting relationships to place including migration (Williams & McIntyre, 2001) and underscored a view in which global flows of people, things, and ideas required a re-theorization of place attachment based less on fixed place attachment and more on how people navigate multiple, fluid attachments (Di Masso et al., 2019). The focus was not on intentionality as with phenomenology, but on the production of meaning through habitual interaction with places. In this case, place becomes a scene or venue of embodied practice. As Cresswell (2015, p. 63) notes, some humanistic geographers were interested in bodily mobility rather than rootedness to understand place, for example, recalling how routine movements produce a "place-ballet" that generates a strong sense of place and feeling of belonging (Seamon, 1980).

One of those embodied practices is mobility itself. As the new century begins some social scientists describe a "new mobilities paradigm" (Sheller & Urry, 2006), which shows up in studies of attachment to multiple places and especially second homes (Gustafson, 2014). This work challenged the notion among "[h]uman geographers, environmental psychologists, and community sociologists [who] often regarded place attachment as good [while associating mobility] with uprootedness and social disintegration" (Gustafson, 2014, p. 38). In adapting to living in a globalized and mobilized world, identities and attachments may be multi-centered and deployed more like rhizomes than roots for constructing a coherent identity narrative across multiple places over one's life-course (Williams & McIntyre, 2001).

The recognition of multi-centered place identities leads some to reconsider the treatment of the power and politics of place. For instance, Di Masso and Dixon (2015) build on the discursive framework to consider how the production of public space in Barcelona was "entwined with other kinds of material and embodied practices – practices through which place meanings were actively performed, reproduced, and contested" (p. 46). By highlighting how "place making [is] relational, political and performative" Buizer and Turnhout (2011) describe the everyday subpolitics of "how [citizens] perform a place in discursive and material practices" in their effort to create a "protected area" (p. 532).

Within human geography, another example of performative thinking relevant to place attachment research is the development of so-called non-representational theory (Thrift, 2007 as cited in Cresswell, 2015). Non-representation theory does not dismiss interpretation and representation but emphasizes events, emotions, and practices. Since place attachment is an embodied relationship to the world, places are constituted by people doing things in place and thus are constantly being performed and are never finished. For example, posting trip blogs on social media offers new online venues for people to perform leisure-related place attachments by presenting public narratives recounting their experience of and relationship to particular outdoor recreation places (Champ, Williams, & Lundy, 2013). Non-representation theory seems to sidestep the realist/constructionist divide by reframing places as moments and events of performance actively creating material reality in a constant state of becoming.

By extending the consideration of performance and agency to nonhuman entities, actor-network theory (Latour, 2005) is a more overt attempt to resolve the divide between realism/constructionism as well as other binaries (e.g., structure/agency, culture/nature, and mind/body) that continue to reemerge and weave through these metatheoretical moments. By recognizing nonhuman agency, scholars naturally began to expand their focus on agency as the product of networks and "connectedness rather than either atomistic humans or systematic structures" (Cresswell, 2013, p. 251). The nature of these connections is emergent, changing, and complex and thus place attachment is recast as an emergent phenomenon as well. Since places are an assemblage of things, agents, and connections in a complex system, a transdisciplinary approach has developed that incorporates a larger focus on both the biophysical and social aspects of place. While many scholars still investigate place attachment using quantitative scales, notions of assemblage, networks, embodiment, and systems of attachments take on greater significance in the next moment.

Systems thinking and assemblage theory

As we write this chapter, a new metatheoretical moment grappling with the implications of systems thinking spanning the natural and social sciences is influencing the literature on place attachment. Increasingly, scholars interested in environmental issues think of place as a site of social-ecological assemblage. For instance, with the ascendancy of social-ecological systems, relational ideas of place and place-making have been heralded as ways to understand and organize sustainable conservation and other environmental practices (Masterson, Enqvist, Stedman, & Tengö, 2019; Williams, 2018) with place attachment playing a potentially important role in how people adapt to social-ecological system change (Fresque-Baxter & Armitage, 2012).

Social-ecological systems thinking arose in the late 1980s with the seminal work of Ostrom and colleagues examining collaborative place-based governance of common-pool (collective) resources (Ostrom, 1990). By the 2000s, environmental governance concepts were increasingly linked to place making in the context of social-ecological systems and polycentric governance approaches to specific places (Williams, 2018). Seeking to bridge the social-ecological divide through systems-oriented lenses of ecological psychology, Raymond, Giusti, and Barthel (2018) applied perceptual affordance theory and embodied ecosystems to argue that human-environment connections are not exclusive to the mind but include a web of relations among mind, body, culture, and the biophysical environment.

In psychology and human geography, systems thinking also shows up in assemblage theory. Originating from the philosophy of Deleuze and Guattari (1987) and the "thrown-together-ness" of Massey's (1994) relational sense of place, assemblage theory conceptualizes place as a complex, dynamic constellation of materiality, representations, and performative practices (Cresswell, 2015). It emphasizes the interrelated socio-spatial processes of gathering, collective or distributed agency, emergence, and provisonality (Anderson & McFarlane, 2011; Di Masso & Dixon, 2015). For example, Anderson (2012) used assemblage theory to examine a "surfed wave" as a relational place. He shows how surfers, boards, and waves are "connected" together to form one coherent unit for the duration of the ride. This surfed wave becomes a place whose constituent parts are blurred into a converged entity/process. Ultimately, assemblage theory has particular relevance to place attachment because places are "gathering[s] of things, memories, stories and practices" (Cresswell, 2015, p. 53).

In the constructivist moment, the focus was on whose representation of place prevailed. Later on, the ways that those representations are performed received greater attention. Now scholars are increasingly recognizing that in a complex world, the struggle over place is inextricably connected to larger and smaller connected systems that distribute power and resources across scales (Williams, 2018). Not only are places affected by larger environmental processes (e.g., local consequences of global change) but also by people who are embedded in local and extra-local institutional structures. Thus, place attachment is increasingly of interest for the study of social-ecological resilience, since place attachments are not only threatened by environmental and economic change but can also facilitate adaptation strategies (Fresque-Baxter & Armitage, 2012).

From a systems perspective, many of the different braids of place attachment research have renewed relevance now. For instance, much of the early work on community and place attachment in the context of mass society in the 1970s was about the loss of local communities as systems (Warren, 1978). This view also underscores the relational idea of place from Massey as a constellation of local and more distant (global) processes. Even the earliest roots of place attachment in the phenomenological tradition revealed place as a complex ballet (Seamon, 1980). Moreover, in such systems we can still consider the agency of individuals to actively remain stationary or be mobile, to consume and produce place-based narratives and performances, and to assemble and reassemble places in rhizomatic networks. As Di Masso et al. (2019, p. 131) state:

> In this way, place attachment can be viewed as an emergent property of a complex system wherein the bond at a given point in time has properties not reflected in the individual components of a system or assemblage.

CONCLUSION

In this chapter, we have tried to document the diverse origins and complex developmental path of place attachment research. Contrary to earlier suggestions that place attachment is or ought to be converging into a singular theory, we find that the domain of place attachment has and will continue to be ontologically, epistemologically, and axiologically pluralistic, with different developments splitting off and coming back together much like a braided stream. While other interpretations of the same literature could lead to legitimately different portrayals, there is value in considering the different braids and how they intersect across the interdisciplinary landscape of place attachment research.

Having taken stock of the past, we sense some incipient structure to the nascent moment. Current place attachment research still retains key elements of the humanist and experiential tradition while adding insights on social difference and power relations, as well as assemblage and social-ecological systems thinking. Put another way, we see three major currents embedded in what is otherwise a complex, braided flow: experiential perspectives on place attachment focused on identities and emotional bonds formed from social-psychological processes; sociopolitical perspectives emphasizing structure and power relations in the ways that places are made, contested, and remade through local and global processes; and social-ecological perspectives where place attachment is conjointly constituted through human and nonhuman agency in complex, nested systems.

In the space available in this chapter, it is difficult to do justice to all the various metatheoretical moments shaping place attachment. For example, there are innumerable rivulets intersecting the main branches of place attachment literature over time, and reasonable arguments could be made to position some confluences at different moments in time. Taking this metaphor even further, eddies form around debates in the literature that seem to never resolve and there are points where the literature either stagnates or deposits ideas along the way that provide fruitful soil for other disciplines. Of course all metaphors impose limitations, but we hope scholars find our attempt to unravel some of the braids useful in their own attempts to make sense of place attachment and develop new lines of research including non-western understandings of place. We intended this overview to provide a provisional roadmap (or perhaps a canoe?), for scholars to navigate and explore the intellectual terrain through which this braided steam has flowed. We think that occasionally looking back (up-stream so to speak) will make navigating the waters ahead a little easier.

NOTES

1 The human exceptionalist paradigm that dominated social science in the modernist era treated the physical environment as mostly irrelevant to understanding social facts and phenomena.
2 Despite neglecting the importance of place, early environmental sociology drew heavily from rural and community sociology and environmental psychology (cf. Dunlap & Catton, 1979).
3 Buttimer (1976, p. 278) noted how phenomenology lacked "clear operational procedures to guide the empirical investigation and should not be understood as a method but as a perspective."
4 Relph (2008) regards such efforts as antithetical to the phenomenological view.

REFERENCES

Agnew, J. A. (1989). The devaluation of place in social science. In J. A. Agnew, & J. S. Duncan (Eds.), *The power of place: Bringing together geographical and sociological imaginations* (pp. 9–29). London: Unwin Hyman.

Altman, I., & Low, S. (Eds.). (1992). *Place attachment*. New York: Plenum.

Anderson, B., & McFarlane, C. (2011). Assemblage and geography. *Area, 43*, 124–127.

Anderson, J. (2012). Relational places: The surfed wave as assemblage and convergence. *Environment and Planning D: Society and Space, 30*, 570–587.

Brown, B. (1987). Territoriality. In D. Stokols, & I. Altman (Eds.), *Handbook of environmental psychology* (pp. 505–31). New York: Wiley.

Buizer, M., & Turnhout, E. (2011). Text, talk, things and the subpolitics of performing place. *Geoforum, 42*, 530–538.

Buttel, F. H. (2002). Environmental sociology and the sociology of natural resources: Institutional histories and intellectual legacies. *Society & Natural Resources, 15*, 205–211.

Buttimer, A. (1976). Grasping the dynamism of the lifeworld. *Annals of the Association of American Geographers, 66*, 277–292.

Champ, J. G., Williams, D. R., & Lundy, C. M. (2013). An on-line narrative of Colorado wilderness: Self-in-"cybernetic space." *Environmental Communication, 7*, 131–145.

Cresswell, T. (2009). Place. *International Encyclopedia of Human Geography, 8*, 169–177.

Cresswell, T. (2013). *Geographic thought: A critical introduction*. Chichester: Wiley-Blackwell.

Cresswell, T. (2015). *Place: An introduction* (2nd ed.). Chichester: Wiley-Blackwell.

Deleuze, G., & Guattari, F. (1987). *A thousand plateaus: Capitalism and schizophrenia*. Minneapolis: University of Minnesota Press.

Denzin, N. K., & Lincoln, Y. S. (1994). Introduction: History of the field of qualitative research. In Denzin, N., & Lincoln, Y. (Eds.), *Handbook of qualitative research* (pp. 1–7). Thousand Oaks: Sage.

Devine-Wright, P. (2015). Local attachments and identities: A theoretical and empirical project across disciplinary boundaries. *Progress in Human Geography, 39*, 527–530.

Di Masso, A., & Dixon, J. (2015). More than words: Place, discourse and struggle over public space in Barcelona. *Qualitative Research in Psychology, 12*(1), 45–60.

Di Masso, A., Dixon, J., & Hernández, B. (2017). Place attachment, sense of belonging and the micro-politics of place satisfaction. In G. Fleury-Bahi, E. Pol, & O. Navarro (Eds.), *Handbook of environmental psychology and quality of life research* (pp. 85–104). Dordrecht: Springer.

Di Masso, A., Williams, D. R., Raymond, C. M., Buchecker, M., Degenhardt, B., Devine-Wright, P., … & von Wirth, T. (2019). Between fixities and flows: Navigating place attachments in an increasingly mobile world. *Journal of Environmental Psychology, 61*, 125–133.

Dixon J., & Durrheim, K. (2000). Displacing place identity: A discursive approach to locating self and other. *British Journal of Social Psychology, 39*, 27–44.

Dunlap, R. E., & Catton, W. R. J. (1979). Environmental sociology. *Annual Review of Sociology, 5*, 243–273.

Eisenhauer, B. W., Krannich, R. S., & Blahna, D. J. (2000). Attachments to special places on public lands: An analysis of activities, reason for attachments, and community connections. *Society & Natural Resources, 13*, 421–441.

Field, D. R., & Burch, W. R. (1991). *Rural sociology and the environment*. Boulder, CO: Social Ecology Press.

Field, D. R., Luloff, A. E., & Krannich, R. S. (2013). Revisiting the origins of and distinctions between natural resource sociology and environmental sociology. *Society & Natural Resources, 26*, 211–225.

Firey, W. (1945). Sentiment and symbolism as ecological variables. *American Sociological Review, 10*, 140–148.

Fresque-Baxter, J., & Armitage, D. (2012). Place identity and climate change adaptation: A synthesis and framework for understanding. *WIREs Climate Change, 3*, 251–266.

Freudenburg, W. R., Frickel, S., & Gramling, R. (1995). Beyond the nature/society divide: Learning to think about a mountain. *Sociological Forum, 10*, 361–392.

Fried, M. (1963). Grieving for a lost home. In L. J. Duhl (Eds.), *The urban condition* (pp. 151–171). New York: Basic Books.

Gee, M. (1994). Questioning the concept of the 'user'. *Journal of Environmental Psychology, 14*, 113–124.

Gieryn, T. G. (2000). A space for place in sociology. *Annual Review of Sociology, 26*, 463–496.

Giuliani, M. V. (2003). Theory of attachment and place attachment. In M. Bonnes, T. Lee, & M. Bonaiuto (Eds.), *Psychological theories for environmental issues* (pp. 137–170). Hants: Ashgate.

Glotfelty, C., & Fromm, H. (Eds.). (1996). *The ecocriticism reader: Landmarks in literary ecology*. Athens, GA: The University of Georgia Press.

Gustafson, P. (2014). Place attachment in an age of mobility. In L. Manzo, & P. Devine-Wright (Eds.), *Place attachment: Advances in theory, methods and applications* (pp. 37–48). London: Routledge.

Greider, T., & Garkovich, L. (1994). Landscapes: The social construction of nature and the environment. *Rural Sociology, 59*(1), 1–24.

Harvey, D. (1996). *Justice, nature and the geography of difference*. Oxford: Backwell.

Hernández, B., Hidalgo, C. M., & Ruiz, C. (2014). Theoretical and methodological aspects of research on place attachment. In L. Manzo, & P. Devine-Wright (Eds.), *Place attachment: Advances in theory, methods and applications* (pp. 125–137). London: Routledge.

Latour, B. (2005). *The politics of nature. How to bring the sciences into democracy*. Cambridge, MA: Harvard University Press.

Lewicka, M. (2011). Place attachment: How far have we come in the last 40 years? *Journal of Environmental Psychology, 31*, 207–230.

Lippard, L. (1997). *The lure of the local: Senses of place in multicentered society*. New York: New York Press.

Loomis, C. P. (1958). El Cerrito, New Mexico: Changing village. *New Mexico Historical Review, 22*, 53–75.

Low, S., & Altman, I. (1992). Place attachment: A conceptual inquiry. In I. Altman, & S. Low (Eds.), *Place attachment* (pp. 1–12). New York: Plenum.

Manzo, L. C. (2003). Beyond house and haven: Toward a revisioning of emotional relationships with places. *Journal of Environmental Psychology, 23*, 47–61.

Manzo, L. C., & Perkins, D. D. (2006). Finding common ground: The importance of place attachment to community participation. *Journal of Planning Literature, 20*, 335–350.

Massey, D. (1994). A global sense of place. *space, place and gender* (pp. 146–156). Minneapolis: Blackwell.

Masterson, V. A., Enqvist, J. P., Stedman, R. C., & Tengö, M. (2019). Sense of place in social-ecological systems: From theory to empirics. *Sustainability Science, 14*, 555–564.

Ostrom, E. (1990). *Governing the commons: The evolution of institutions for collective action*. Cambridge, UK: Cambridge University Press.

Norberg-Schulz, C. (1980). *Genius loci: Towards a phenomenology of architecture*. New York: Rizzoli.

Patterson, M. E., & Williams, D. R. (2005). Maintaining research traditions on place: Diversity of thought and scientific progress. *Journal of Environmental Psychology, 25*, 361–380.

Pellow, D. N., & Nyseth Brehm, H. (2013). An environmental sociology for the twenty-first century. *Annual Review of Sociology, 39*, 229–250.

Proshansky, H. M. (1978). City and self identity. *Environment and Behavior, 10*, 147–169.

Proshansky, H., Ittelson, W., & Rivlin, L. (1970). *Environmental psychology: Man and his physical setting*. Oxford: Holt, Rinehart & Winston.

Raymond, C. M., Giusti, M., & Barthel, S. (2018). An embodied perspective on the co-production of cultural ecosystem services: Toward embodied ecosystems. *Journal of Environmental Planning and Management, 61*, 778–799.

Relph, T. (1976). *Place and placelessness*. London: Pion Limited.

Relph, T. (2008). Sense of place and emerging social and environmental challenges. In J. Eyles, & A. Williams (Eds.), *Sense of place, health and quality of life* (pp. 31–44). Aldershot: Ashgate.

Rodman, M. (1992). Empowering place: Multilocality and multivocality. *American Anthropologist, 94*, 640–656.

Seamon, D. (1980). Body-subject, time–space routines, and place-ballets. In A. Buttimer, & D. Seamon (Eds.), *The human experience of space and place* (pp. 148–165). New York: St. Martin's Press.

Sheller, M., & Urry, J. (2006). The new mobilities paradigm. *Environment and Planning A*, *38*, 207–226.

Smith, J. S. (2018). *Explorations in place attachment*. New York: Routledge.

Smith, J. S. (2015). Place attachment: Advances in theory, methods, and applications. *Journal of Cultural Geography*, *32*, 389–390.

Stedman, R. C. (2003). Is it really just a social construction? The contribution of the physical environment to sense of place. *Society & Natural Resources*, *16*, 671–685.

Stokols, D. (1990). Instrumental and spiritual views of people-environment relations. *American Psychologist*, *45*, 641–646.

Stokols, D., & Shumaker, S. A. (1982). The psychological context of residential mobility and wellbeing. *The Journal of Social Issues*, *38*(3), 149–171.

Stokowski, P. (2002). Languages of place and discourses of power: Constructing new senses of place. *Journal of Leisure Research*, *34*, 368–382.

Trentelman, C. K. (2009). Place attachment and community attachment: A primer grounded in the lived experience of a community sociologist. *Society & Natural Resources*, *22*, 191–210.

Tuan, Y.-F. (1977). *Space and place: The perspective of experience*. London: University of Minnesota Press.

Warren, R. L. (1978). *The community in America* (3rd ed.). Chicago: Rand McNally.

Williams, D. R. (2002). Leisure identities, globalization, and the politics of place. *Journal of Leisure Research*, *34*, 351–367.

Williams, D. R. (2014). 'Beyond the commodity metaphor' revisited: Some methodological reflections on place attachment research. In L. Manzo, & P. Devine-Wright (Eds.), *Place attachment: Advances in theory, methods and applications* (pp. 89–99). London: Routledge.

Williams, D. R. (2018). Spacing conservation practice: Place-making, social learning, and adaptive governance in natural resource management. In T. Marsden (Ed.), *The SAGE handbook of nature, v3* (pp. 285–303). London: Sage.

Williams, D. R., & McIntyre, N. (2001). Where heart and home reside: Changing constructions of place and identity. *Trends 2000: Shaping the future* (pp. 392–403). Lansing, MI: Michigan State University.

Williams, D. R., Patterson, M. E., Roggenbuck, J. W., & Watson, A. E. (1992). Beyond the commodity metaphor: Examining emotional and symbolic attachment to place. *Leisure Sciences*, *14*, 29–46.

Williams, D. R., & Stewart, S. I. (1998). Sense of place: An elusive concept that is finding a home in ecosystem management. *Journal of Forestry*, *96*(5), 18–23.

Wohwill, J. F. (1970). The emerging discipline of environmental psychology. *American Psychologist*, *25*, 303–312.

Yung, L., Freimund, A., & Belsky, J. M. (2003). The politics of place: Understanding meaning, common ground and political difference on the Rocky Mountain Front. *Forest Science*, *49*, 855–866.

Chapter 2: Place attachment and phenomenology: The dynamic complexity of place

David Seamon

As a phenomenologist, I face a dilemma in contributing to a volume on place attachment, which can be defined as the emotional bonds between people and a particular place or environment (Lewicka, 2011; Manzo and Devine-Wright, 2014; Scannell and Gifford, 2017; Smith, 2018). An important phenomenological question is whether place attachment is a phenomenon unto itself or only one dimension of a more comprehensive lived structure identified as *place* and the *experience of place* (Casey, 2009; Cresswell, 2014; Donohoe, 2014, 2017; Gieryn, 2018; Malpas, 2018; Williams, 2014). In this chapter, I consider place, place experience, and place attachment as they might be understood phenomenologically from three perspectives: first, *holistically*; second, *dialectically*; and third, *generatively*. I argue that each of these three perspectives points to a spectrum of complementary experiences, situations, actions, and meanings that remain faithful to the lived comprehensiveness of place and place experience. I suggest that each of these three perspectives offers a range of useful ways for thinking about and understanding place attachment.

Phenomenologically, place can be defined as any environmental locus that gathers human experiences, meanings, and actions spatially and temporally (Seamon, 2018a, p. 2). Malpas (2018) described this space-time gathering quality of place as "an open and interconnected region within which other persons, things, spaces, and abstract locations, and even one's self, can appear, be recognized, identified, and interacted with" (p. 36). In this sense, places are spatial-temporal fields that integrate, activate, and interconnect things, people, experiences, meanings, and events. Places can range in scale from a furnishing or some other environment element to a room, building, neighborhood, city, landscape, or region. One important phenomenological concern is identifying kinds of physical environments and spaces that facilitate positive place attachment (Tilley, 2012; Tilley and Cameron-Daum, 2017). For example, geographer Jeff S. Smith (2018) identified six broad categories of places with which humans experience supportive emotional involvement: (1) *secure places*, where one feels safe and in control; (2) *socializing places*, involving positive interpersonal encounters; (3) *transformative places*, relating to locales associated with personal growth and significant events for a person or group; (4) *restorative places*, associated with environments that strengthen human wellbeing; (5) *validating places*, which celebrate and reinforce personal and group identity; and (6) *vanishing places*, involving environments that have disappeared or may disappear because of destruction, depletion, or encroachment. As a geographer, Smith emphasized that his typology highlights "types of places to which people become attached" and offers a language for considering how "specific human activity lends itself for the emotional bonding with place" (pp. 3, 6).

Though particular kinds of environments may support different modes of place experience, meaning, and attachment, a phenomenology of place insists that, existentially, place is not the physical environment apart from the people associated with it but, rather, the *indivisible, normally unnoticed phenomenon of person-or-people-experiencing-place* (Casey, 2009; Janz, 2017; Malpas, 2018; Seamon, 2018a; Stefanovic, 2008). This phenomenon of people/place enmeshment is typically complex, multivalent, and dynamic, incorporating generative processes through which a place and its experiences and meanings, including place attachment, shift or stay more or less the same. One phenomenological aim is generalizations about place and lived emplacement that respect the physical and lived specificity of particular places, place experiences, and place meanings but also generate broader conceptual frameworks, including those grounded in the holistic, dialectic, and generative aspects of place.

WHOLENESS, BODY-SUBJECT, AND PLACE ATTACHMENT

As indicated by the definitions of place above, a central phenomenological assumption about place is that people and their worlds are integrally intertwined experientially and ontologically (Moran, 2000; van Manen, 2014). As one descriptive means for understanding this lived interconnectedness accurately, phenomenologists have increasingly turned to the phenomenon of place (Casey, 2009; Donohoe, 2017; Janz, 2005, 2017; Malpas, 2018; Seamon, 2018a). As a phenomenological concept, place is powerful both theoretically and practically because it offers a way to articulate more precisely the experienced wholeness of people-in-world, which phenomenologists call the *lifeworld*, the everyday world of taken-for-grantedness normally unnoticed and thus concealed as a phenomenon (Finlay, 2011; van Manen, 2014).

Place and lived emplacement are phenomena integral to human life and hold lifeworlds together environmentally, marking out centers of human meaning, intention, and comportment that, in turn, help make place (Casey, 2009; Relph, 1976; Malpas, 2018). For research in place attachment, the lived fact that human being always necessarily involves human-being-in-place (Casey, 2009, pp. 15–16) suggests that any emotional bond between people and environment requires a descriptive language arising from and accurately portraying this lived emplacement (or *displacement* in the case of negative place situations such as domestic abuse, forced relocation, or neighborhoods of social dissolution). To interpret place attachment in subjectivist terms of affective or cognitive representations, or in the objectivist terms of external social, cultural, political, or environmental factors is, from a phenomenological perspective, a reductive rendition of the wholeness of the relationship (Kogl, 2008; Malpas, 2018; Seamon, 2018a).

In this sense, one cannot, on one hand, readily identify and measure some degree of place attachment and, then, on the other hand, look for correlations with so-called predictor factors like age, social status, physical features, time spent with place, and so forth (Lewicka, 2011, pp. 216–219). Rather, place attachment is interdependent with other aspects of place—for example, geographical and cultural qualities, rootedness in place, degree of personal and social involvement, quality of life, environmental aesthetics, individual and group identity with place, and so forth. As Malpas (2018, p. 166) explained, "place cannot be reduced to any one of the elements situated within its compass but must instead be understood as a structure comprising spatiality *and* temporality, subjectivity *and* objectivity, self *and* other. These elements are established only in relation to each other and thus only within the topographical structure of place." From a phenomenological perspective, place attachment is part of a broader lived synergy in which the various human and environmental dimensions of place reciprocally impel and sustain each other (Malpas, 2018; Seamon, 2018a). One phenomenological aim is to provide a range of conceptual and real-world perspectives from which to view the synergism of place and to clarify the relative role of place attachment within this dynamic complexity (Donohoe, 2014, 2017; Freestone and Liu, 2017; Jacobson, 2009; Janz, 2017; Malpas, 2015).

One phenomenological thinker who has made a preeminent contribution toward better understanding the dynamic complexity of place is French philosopher Maurice Merleau-Ponty (1962). One of his foundational concepts is *body-subject*, which refers to the precognitive, normally unnoticed, facility of the lived body to smoothly integrate its actions with the world at hand. Body-subject is the pre-reflective corporeal awareness manifested through everyday actions and behaviors and typically in synchronicity with the spatial and physical environment in which the action unfolds (Hünefeldt and Schlitte, 2018; Jacobson, 2010; Moran, 2014; Seamon, 2014). Drawing on the concept of body-subject, phenomenological researchers have pointed to its environmental versatility as expressed in more complex bodily routines and ensembles extending over time and space and contributing to the lived dimensions of place, including attachment grounded in habitual regularity (Atkinson and Duffy, 2019; Jacobson, 2010; Middleton, 2011; Seamon, 2018a, 2018b; Toombs, 2000).

Perhaps most pertinent to research on place attachment is the possibility that individuals involved in their own bodily routines can come together in time and space, thereby contributing to and participating in a larger scale environmental ensemble that can be called a *place ballet*—an interaction of individual bodily routines rooted in a particular environment that may become an important place of interpersonal and communal exchange, meaning, and attachment (Pearce, 2019; Seamon, 1979; van Eck and Pijpers, 2016). Examples include a well-used student lounge, a lively urban plaza, a robust city street, or a thriving city neighborhood

(Fullilove, 2004, 2011; Jacobs, 1961; Mehta, 2013; Oldenburg, 2013; Watson, 2009). In relation to place attachment, place ballet may be significant in that everyday habitual routines regularly happening in place are one important foundation for longer term involvement and identity with place, which in turn sustain and are sustained by feelings of attachment to that place. In studies of coffeehouses in Portland, Oregon, and Minneapolis, Minnesota, Broadway, Legg, and Broadway (2018) and Broadway and Engelhardt (2019) considered how intensity of place attachment relates to such other place qualities as social engagement, environmental design, and the use of digital technology and media. In a study of daily encounters among older people visiting a park in the Dutch city of Eindhoven, van Eck and Pijpers (2016) determined that many park users had daily walking routines characterized by a "clockwork precision" that included customary meetings with other park regulars. These researchers found that these taken-for-granted engagements in place facilitated "an atmosphere of fellowship" that encouraged users to "notice and care for each other" (van Eck and Pijpers, 2016, p. 166). These studies indicate how attachment to place may be propelled by regular environmental actions and routines that, in turn, are maintained and strengthened through that attachment (Fullilove, 2004; Lager, Van Hoven, and Huigen, 2016; Middleton, 2011).[1]

PLACE AND PLACE ATTACHMENT AS LIVED DIALECTICS

If place can be portrayed phenomenologically as a space-time whole in which people and place are intimately interconnected, it can also be described in terms of lived dialectics that arise from that wholeness. Partly, phenomenologists are interested in dialectical aspects of place because environmental and place experiences often involve some continuum of lived opposites—for example, inside and outside (Relph, 1976; Seamon, 2008); dwelling and journey (Bollnow, 2011; Jager, 1975); parochialism and cosmopolitanism (Kossoff, 2019; Tomaney, 2012, 2014); and fixity and flow (Di Masso et al., 2019; Williams and McIntyre, 2012). Here, I highlight two lived dialectics and consider their relevance for place attachment: first, *movement and rest*; and, second, *inwardness and outwardness*.

Place attachment as involving movement and rest

In considering how bodily dimensions of our human constitution contribute to the nature of human experience, one immediately realizes that our existence as physical bodies involves the typical situation of moving, on one hand, and remaining in place, on the other (Bollnow, 2011; Casey, 2009; Seamon, 2018b). Drawing on Merleau-Ponty's work, one can argue that, at their most basic lived level, movement and rest are founded in pre-predicative awareness and the unself-conscious actions of body-subject: Everyday movement patterns and places of rest are part of a habitual time-space lattice composed in part of bodily routines often intermingling in places of rest and paths of movement (Bollnow, 2011; Seamon, 1979). Because of the unself-conscious facility of body-subject, life just happens, and we follow a more or less regular regimen of actions, experiences, situations, and occasions all grounded in particular places and paths of movement along those places (Casey, 2009; Moores, 2012; Rowles, 2017; Seamon, 2014).

Through conscious decision, including self-reflective awareness of body-subject, human beings can shift habitual patterns of movement and rest. They can act in, encounter, and reshape place in new, intentional ways. On one hand, therefore, the habitual regularity and routine often associated with place does not negate individual choice, environmental change, or a good amount of flexibility and freedom in person, group, and place dynamics. On the other hand, this habitual regularity contributes to environmental, social, and personal order and continuity. Relph (1976, p. 55), for example, identified the deepest mode of place experience as *existential insideness*, a situation where one feels so completely at home and immersed in place that the importance of that place in the person's everyday life is usually unnoticed unless the place dramatically shifts in some way—for example, one faces a progressively debilitating illness (Seamon, 2014; Toombs, 2000); or one's home and community are undermined or destroyed by natural or human-generated disruption (Bormanis, 2019; Cox and Holms, 2000; Million, 1992). In these instances, one suddenly realizes how integral habitual regularity and routine are to his or her day-to-day life. Because the taken-for-grantedness of one's place has changed in some way, he or she may experience some degree of emotional distress ranging from momentary annoyance to sadness, regret, worry, depression, anger, fear, or grief (Fullilove, 2004; Klinenberg, 2002; Simms, 2008). I have termed this immediate, normally unself-conscious field of emotional presence and awareness *feeling-subject*—a matrix of positive (and sometimes negative) emotional intentionalities extending in varying intensities to the places, spaces, routes, and typical routines comprising a person's lifeworld (Seamon, 1979, p. 76).

For research on place attachment, the phenomenological interpretation of movement and rest is important because, in everyday life, the emotional ambience and resonance of places, routes, and routines typically run beneath the lived surface of the lifeworld and, much of the time, are pre-reflective and unnoticed. Many studies of place attachment ask respondents to describe or evaluate their environmental feelings explicitly through words, drawings, or measuring instruments (Lewicka, 2011). If much of the emotional fabric soldered to place is pre-reflective and thus typically beneath the level of conscious awareness, then developing a language and methodology for self-conscious elicitation is a formidable task.

One essential methodological component for gaining accurate, explicit accounts of place attachment is bringing deeper, more empathetic attention to the research process (Finlay, 2011; van Manen, 2014). For example, urban planner John Forester (2006) considered practical ways whereby interviewing can become "astute listening" and a more potent vehicle for comprehensively understanding "situations full of conflict, ambiguity, posturing, and differences of culture, class, race, gender, and values" (Forester, 2006, p. 126). In phenomenological research, one approach for gaining explicit accounts of place attachment is narratives of individuals and groups who have come to realize firsthand the importance of place attachment in their lives because they have experienced loss of or dramatic shifts in place—for example, the forced displacement of Albertan ranchers because of dam destruction (Million, 1992), the disruption of an Australian rural community by bushfires (Cox and Holms, 2000), the post–WWII destruction of African-American neighborhoods in major American cities because of urban renewal (Fullilove, 2004, this volume; Simms, 2008), or the displacement and rehousing of lower income families because of gentrification and urban regeneration (Lewis, 2017; Manzo, 2008). In addition, one can explore and compare how specific modes of movement and rest as experienced vary individually, socially, culturally, and place-wise—for example, mobility (Arp Fallov, Jørgensen, and Knudsen, 2013; Moores, 2012; Pearce, 2019), migration (Barcus and Brunn, 2009; Easthope, 2009; Lems, 2014; Moores, 2012), homelessness (Moore, 2007), agoraphobia (Jacobson, 2011), homes of divorce (Anthony, 1997) and domestic violence (Goldsack, 1999; McMahon, 2014), lived-place differences for lifestyle groups living in the same physical place (Seamon, 2008, 2019; Sowers, 2010), and lived differences between real and digital places (Greenfield, 2017; Meyrowitz, 2015; Relph, 2015, 2018).[2]

In relation to place attachment, one important phenomenological recognition is that movement and rest are *always present as an existential dialectic* in human lifeworlds. Because of their lived, binary nature, movement and rest each constitute aspects of the other. Through movement-as-journey, people leave the taken-for-grantedness of their homeplace and extend their horizons, geographically and existentially (Bollnow, 2011; Jager, 1975). Through rest-as-dwelling, people return to their homeplace and restore themselves for future ventures outward (Jager, 1975; Seamon, 1979). Recent research on place attachment has clarified the movement/rest dialectic in several innovative ways (Arp Fallov et al., 2013; Easthope, 2009; Lems, 2014). In their study of place attachment and mobility in rural Appalachia, for example, Barcus and Brunn (2009) pinpointed three modes of relationship as identified via questionnaires collected from attendees of family reunions in rural eastern Kentucky: first, *rooted-in-place* respondents, who lived in their home place their entire lives, had strong place attachments and expressed little interest in moving away from their home county; second, *mobile-but-attached* respondents, who had strong place attachments but had moved within-country, within-region, or out-of-region because of employment or education opportunities; and, third, *tied-to-place* respondents, who had weaker place attachments and higher rates of mobility "characteristic of impoverished rural households" facing economic, social, or health crises that required them "to move from one home to another" (Barcus and Brunn, 2009, p. 42).

One of the most thorough, recent efforts to think through the lived relationship between movement and rest is a study by Di Masso et al. (2019, p. 125), who considered "how place attachments are forged and become dynamically linked to increasingly common mobility practices". Describing the movement/rest dialectic in terms of *fixity* and *flow*, these researchers identified six "modes of interrelationship": (1) *fixity*, (2) *fixity OR flow*, (3) *fixity and flow*, (4) *fixity FROM flow*, (5) *flow in fixities*, and (6) *flow*. *Fixity*, for example, relates to deep place attachment incorporating "a maximum degree of spatial stasis and temporal stability," just as *flow* refers to a "maximum degree of movement, corporal distance, and territorial disconnection extended in time" (Di Masso et al., 2019, p. 130). In between fixity and flow, Di Masso et al. (2019, p. 130) describe four other dialectical modes—for example, *fixity and flow*, relating to a mode of place attachment that accommodates both a local sense of belonging as well as enjoyment of "rich mobile experiences;" and *flow in fixities*, in which attachment is associated with a nexus of shifting connections among a network of places "configured as a web of meaningful nodes". These six modes of fixity/flow relationship are significant for research on place attachment because they illustrate how individuals and groups may have "different types, valences, and intensities of place attachments depending on varying and overlapping modes of interrelation between mobility and immobility" (Di Masso et al., 2019, p. 131).

Place attachment as involving inward and outward aspects of place

Besides movement and rest, places typically involve a dialectic incorporating *inward* and *outward* aspects (Seamon, 2018a). On one hand, place is a world unto itself and within itself. For example, the typical home in contemporary Western societies is a realm of personal and familial privacy mostly insulated from the larger public world; its occupants are typically in control of what aspects of the larger world have entry into the home (Donohoe, 2014, 2017; Jacobson, 2009, 2010; Seamon, 2018a). On the other hand, the home requires relationship with that larger public world in terms of basic needs and wider social and communal relationships (Bollnow, 2011; Moore, 2007). The inward aspect of any place relates to its being apart from the rest of the world, while it's more outward, externally oriented aspects relate to the larger world of which it is part. These two significances of place are often different and may even contradict each other, but both are integral aspects of most place experience. One way phenomenologically to explore the inward/outward dialectic of place is to examine situations that "overstate" one lived pole over the other—for example, the inhospitable home that turns its back to the world and thereby exaggerates the inward dimension of place experience, or the "showcase" home that mostly exists only for visitors and thereby exaggerates the outward dimension.

It is important to clarify that, phenomenologically, the inward/outward dialectic of place is different experientially from the inside/outside dialectic that has received considerably more attention in the phenomenological literature, partly because of Relph's work (Relph, 1976; Schnell, 2018; Seamon, 2008). Place as defined by insideness and outsideness refers to the degree of comfort and "in-place-ness" or discomfort and "out-of-placeness" felt by the experiencer. In contrast, place as defined by its inward and outward aspects requires consideration of the possible range of ways in which a place *does or does not connect itself to the larger world of which it is part*. One example is the insular environmental mosaics springing up today in cities throughout the world and identified by gated communities, commercial developments, and private streets and plazas, all regularly monitored by surveillance technology and designed to make a profit by allowing "insiders" of these places to feel undisturbed, safe, and privileged (Minton, 2009; Seamon, 2018a, p. 61). In these defensive developments, the inward aspects of place dominate to such a degree that outward interconnections are thwarted or blocked entirely. At the same time, "outsiders' to these restricted developments, while "insiders" to their own places, may see these fortress-like enclaves as symbols of unfairness, inequity, and injustice. Rather than drawing the inward and outward aspects of place together, these developments fracture urban wholeness, intensify civic frustrations, and undermine place attachment for the larger city fabric of which these developments are a part (Allen and Crookes, 2009; Minton, 2009; Rae, 2003).

One of the most perplexing aspects of the inward/outward dialectic today relates to digital technology and cyberspace, which blur the inward and outward qualities of place in that worlds beyond a particular place may become readily accessible to that place, at least vicariously and virtually, and thus potentially shift its inward nature (Seamon, 2018a, p. 62). If the inward dimension of physical place is largely superseded by the "outward" presence and pull of virtual places, what does lived emplacement and place attachment become? If virtual places come to be experienced as "real" as their real-world counterparts, is emotional attachment to these virtual places possible and is it of the same mode and quality as attachment to real places? Does the development of virtuality point toward the eventual demise of many real-world places and the emotional ties that users feel for those real-world places? (Freestone and Liu, 2017; Greenfield, 2017; Meyrowitz, 2015; Miller, 2016; Relph, 2009, 2018).

PLACE ATTACHMENT AND PLACE PROCESSES

Place attachment is rarely static. In considering how places and feelings for place shift over time, one brings attention to the *generative aspects of place*—in other words, identifying underlying lifeworld processes that impel ways that places are what they are and what they become (Lewicka, 2011, pp. 224–225). Elsewhere (Seamon, 2018a), I argued that places can be interpreted phenomenologically in terms of six interconnected processes that each contribute to supporting or eroding the lived structure and dynamics of the particular place. Here, I describe these six processes in their place-sustaining and place-undermining modes. I then point to some ways in which these six place processes might have significance for better understanding place attachment.

Place interaction

Place interaction refers to the typical goings-on in place. It can be related to "a day in the life of a place" and involves the constellation of more or less regular actions, behaviors, situations, and events that unfold in the typical days, weeks, and seasons of a place. Interaction is important to place because it is the major engine through which its users carry out their everyday lives and the place gains activity and a sense of environmental presence. Place ballet is one mode of place interaction whereby individual actions and interpersonal exchanges merge together spatially through bodily co-presence and social encounters grounded in place (Jacobs, 1961). Place interaction as process undermines place when certain actions, situations, and events disrupt the co-presence of users and generate distress, fragmentation, and decline. Typical interactions become fewer or destructive in some way—for example, a busy stretch of sidewalk and street become empty of users; regular interpersonal exchanges in place become fewer and less friendly; the convenience of daily place interactions devolves into a situation of inefficiency, nuisance, worry, conflict, or fear (Fullilove, 2004; Klinenberg, 2002; Mehta, 2013; Minton, 2009; Simms, 2008).

Place identity

Place identity relates to the process whereby people living in or otherwise associated with a place take up that place as a significant part of their world. One unself-consciously and self-consciously accepts and recognizes the place as integral to his or her personal and communal identity and self-worth.[3] Place identity and place interaction are reciprocal processes in the sense that, through place interaction, participants actively engage with place. They come to feel a part of place and associate their personal and group identity with the identity of that place. Place identity as process undermines place when individuals and groups become isolated from the place of which they are a part. They mistrust or feel threatened by other people or events of the place and may consider moving elsewhere to a safer or more accepting situation. If offensive action is not possible, the person or group may withdraw defensively into minimal interaction with and exposure to the place (Klinenberg, 2002; Simms, 2008). Alternately, out of anger or frustration, the person or group may actively work to undermine or harm the place in some way, thereby contributing to a vicious circle of devolving interaction and identity (Fullilove, 2004; Klinenberg, 2002; Simms, 2008).

Place release

Place release involves an environmental serendipity of unexpected encounters and events. Examples of place release are meeting an old friend accidentally on the sidewalk; enjoying the extemporaneous performance of an itinerant street musician; or becoming friendly with, dating, and eventually marrying the checkout clerk who just happened to take your take-out lunch order each work day. Through unexpected experiences, situations, and surprises relating to place, "life is good" (Jacobs, 1961; Oldenburg, 2013). Place release as process undermines place when the pleasure of the place becomes unsettled and unsettling in some way. The place less often or no longer offers enjoyable surprise and unexpectedness; users feel less a zest for daily life to which the place formerly contributed. In a more crippling mode, release as undermining place can involve unexpected, disruptive situations whereby one is upset or hurt—for example, one happens by chance to be mugged in front of the apartment house where he or she lives.

Place realization

Place realization refers to the palpable presence of place. The environmental ensemble of the place (its particular physical constitution as a landscape, building, furnishings, or otherwise), coupled with that place's human activities and meanings, evokes a distinctive place ambience, character, and atmosphere that seem as real as the human beings who know, encounter, and appreciate that place. In short, place is "realized" as a unique phenomenal presence as substantive as its environmental and human parts—for example, the "London-ness" of London or the "Istanbul-ness" of Istanbul. Place realization as process undermines place when the ambience of place deteriorates in some way or is shattered entirely through inappropriate policy, insensitive design, lack of care, or a destructive event like war or natural disaster. The place may devolve into shabbiness, decrepitude, disorder, distress, violence, or some other entropic quality that works against place interaction and identity.[4]

Place intensification

The first four processes of interaction, release, and realization describe what places are and how they work. In contrast, the two remaining processes—*intensification* and *creation*—speak to how positive human effort and well-crafted making can improve places or, through inappropriate understandings and constructions, can activate place decline. *Place intensification* identifies the independent power of befitting policy, design, and fabrication to revive and strengthen place. In this sense, place is *active* in relation to human beings, since physical and spatial changes in the place reconfigure human actions and experiences. Place intensification sheds light on how the physical and designed environments, though they may be only massive material "stuff," can be an active contributor to enhancing place quality and character (Gieryn, 2018; Johnson Coffin and Young, 2017). The result is that place becomes better or more durable in some way—for example, drawing many more users to a plaza by adding well-designed seating (Whyte, 1980); stimulating greater sidewalk traffic by creatively redesigning storefronts (Mehta, 2013); or dramatically enhancing street life by making an urban district's street grid more connected and permeable for pedestrians (Hillier, 2008). Place intensification as process undermines place through poorly conceived designs, policies, and constructions that enfeeble or squelch the life of the place—for example, urban megastructures that provide little physical or visual connectedness to sidewalk and street (Mehta, 2013; Whyte, 1980); or low-density, auto-dependent suburban development that separates functions spatially and incorporates a street system that inhibits walking, pedestrian co-presence, and interpersonal encounters in place (Hillier, 2008; Minton, 2009).

Place creation

In *place creation*, human beings are *active* in relation to place. Concerned people responsible for a specific place draw on their commitment to and empathetic knowledge of the place to envision and make creative shifts in policy, planning, advocacy, and design so that place interaction, identity, release, and realization are enhanced in positive ways (Alexander, 2012; Johnson Coffin and Young, 2017; Mehta, 2013). For example, a team of designers, residents, and community leaders work out practical ways to generate more positive street and sidewalk activity in their urban neighborhood. Place creation as process unsettles place when it leads to thinking, envisioning, and making that misunderstand, ignore, or intentionally undermines the real needs of place. The result is arbitrary or thoughtless policies, designs, and actions that weaken place by misinterpreting what it is and thereby negating its core features and qualities. Examples include inserting constructions and functions inappropriate for the place or introducing environmental disruptions such that people who are a part of the place face difficulties or dissatisfaction in remaining associated with it (Alexander, 2012; Jacobs, 1961; Minton, 2009; Seamon, 2018a).

PLACE ATTACHMENT AND THE SIX PLACE PROCESSES

In relating the six place processes to place attachment, one must emphasize that, in well-used and well-liked places, all six processes are typically present and involved in an intricate, robust give-and-take that is largely unpredictable. None of the six processes are more important than the others, though for particular places and historical moments, the dynamic of the six processes may involve different generative combinations and different gradations of intensity, quality, and duration (contrast, e.g., a big-box, corporate-retail mega-mall with a pedestrian-friendly, mixed-use neighborhood of dwellings and locally owned stores, eateries, and workplaces). In synergistic fashion, one process activates and is activated by others in a vibrant dynamism that Jane Jacobs (1961) identified as "organized complexity"—a sophisticated synergy of intricately intertwined elements, process, and relationships always in flux, sometimes evolving and sometimes devolving in their degree of connectedness, coherence, resonance, and life (Seamon, 2018a).

In relation to place attachment, all six processes contribute to the modes and intensity of emotional bonds with place. Place interaction and place identity relate to place attachment in that one becomes affectively involved with the regularity and familiarity of actions and encounters that contribute to who one is and what his or her life routinely is in relationship with place. Place release and place realization relate to place attachment in that planning and design most appropriate for place is most probable if generated by individuals who care for the place they hope to make better. Similarly, place intensification relates to place attachment in that users are more likely to feel fondness for a place incorporating spatial, material, and fabricated elements and qualities that sustain and enhance everyday user needs as well as the ambience and character of the place.

As Di Masso et al. (2019), Lewicka (2011), and Relph (1976, 2009) pointed out, the feelings for place can range from disinterest and minimal cognitive awareness to superficial fondness, stronger devotion, or attachment so powerful that people are willing to defend and even sacrifice their lives for a place. This spectrum of potential place attachments is at least partly understood through the six place processes, which can unfold at an extensive range of intensities to sustain, on one hand, strong place attachment (committed people, an integrated physical and spatial environment, and a strong place ambience) or, on the other hand, dissipated or moribund place attachment (disinterested or alienated people, a dysfunctional physical and spatial environment, and an unpleasant, weak, or nonexistent place ambience).

What ultimately seems most important for activating and sustaining positive place attachment is a steady, exuberant, ever-shifting interplay and exchange among the six place processes in their constructive modes (Seamon, 2018a). The result, in terms of place, is a robust environmental synergy. The result, in terms of place experience and meaning, is a spectrum of emotional engagement that ranges from appreciation, pleasure, and fondness to concern, respect, responsibility, care, and deep love for place.

NOTES

1 As lived experience, place attachment is a complex, multivalent phenomenon that can vary individually, socially, culturally, environmentally, temporally, and historically. This complexity of attachment can involve such lived qualities as time—for example, newcomers/long-time residents (Allen and Crookes, 2009; Lewis, 2017); spatial scale—for example, house/neighborhood/city/region (Hillier, 2008; Kossoff, 2019); individual differences—for example, abled/less-abled (Moore, Carter, and Sheikh, 2013; Toombs, 2000); social and cultural differences—for example, groups of varying ethnic, racial, or occupational backgrounds associated with the same geographical locale (Klinenberg, 2002; Sebastien, 2019); structural and economic shifts—for example, disappearance of small, locally owned places (e.g., Davis, 2012; Oldenburg, 2008); and life-course shifts—for example, aging and place (e.g., Raymond, Kyttä, and Stedman, 2017; Rowles, 2017). Though there is a wide range of negative place attachments (Manzo, 2014), I mostly emphasize positive place attachment in this chapter because care for and love of place is crucial for positive, robust place making.

2 Also see the chapters in this volume by Fullilove and Devine-Wright and Quinn.

3 There is a considerable research literature on "place identity" as defined by the ways that environmental and spatial qualities contribute to how a person or group describes and understands individual or collective self (Devine-Wright and Clayton, 2010). In their review of place research, Patterson and Williams (2005, pp. 368–369) associate much of this work with a "psychometric paradigm" that requires precisely defined concepts measured empirically. As I interpret place identity here, I emphasize the phenomenological contention that "structural, holistic understanding cannot be accomplished through the types of concise operational definitions employed in psychometric epistemology" (Patterson and Williams, 2005, pp. 369–370). Instead, I argue that place identity is one of six generative processes all intimately enmeshed and interconnected. I contend that place identity (and place attachment) can only be understood in terms of this integrative six-fold structure that, in turn, is subsumed by the more comprehensive lived structure of place and place experience (Seamon, 2018a).

4 One important aspect of place realization is a sense of place and environmental and architectural atmospheres (see Borch, 2014; Griffero and Tedeschini, 2019; Riedel, 2019; Seamon, 2018a, pp. 87–91).

REFERENCES

Alexander, C. (2012). *Battle for the life and beauty of the earth*. New York: Oxford University Press.

Allen, C., & Crookes, L. (2009). Fables of the reconstruction: A phenomenology of 'place shaping' in the North of England. *Town Planning Review, 80*, 455–480.

Anthony, K. (1997). Bitter homes and gardens. *Journal of Architectural and Planning Research, 14*, 1–19.

Arp Fallov, M., Jørgensen, A., & Knudsen, L. B. (2013). Mobile forms of belonging. *Mobilities, 8*, 467–486.

Atkinson, P., & Duffy, M. (2019). Seeing movement. *Emotion, Space and Society, 30*, 20–26.

Barcus, H. R., & Brunn, S. D. (2009). Toward a typology of mobility and place attachment in rural America. *Journal of Appalachian Studies, 15*(1/2), 26–48.

Bollnow, O. (2011). *Human space*. London: Hyphen Press.

Borch, C. (Ed.) (2014). *Architectural atmospheres*. Basil: Birkhäuser.

Bormanis, E. (2019). Spaces of belonging and the precariousness of home. *Puncta, 2*(1), 19–32.

Broadway, M. J., & Engelhardt, O. (2019). Designing places to be alone or together: A look at independently owned Minneapolis coffeehouses. *Space and Culture, 22*, 1–18.

Broadway, M. J., Legg, R., & Broadway, J. (2018). Coffeehouses and the art of social engagement: An analysis of Portland coffeehouses. *Geographical Review, 108*(3), 433–456.

Casey, E. S. (2009). *Getting back into place*. Bloomington: Indiana University Press.

Cox, H. M., & Holms, C. A. (2000). Loss, healing, and the power of place. *Human Studies, 23*, 63–78.

Cresswell, T. (2014). *Place: A history*. Oxford: Blackwell.

Davis, H. (2012). *Living over the store*. London: Routledge.

Devine-Wright, P., & Clayton, S. (2010). Place, identity and environmental behaviour, *Journal of Environmental Psychology, 30*, 267–270.

Di Masso, A., Williams, D.R., Raymond, C.M., Buchecker, M., Begenhard, B., Devine-Wright, P., Hertzog, A., Lewicka, M., Manzo, L., Shahrad, A., Stedman, R., Verbrugge, L. & von Wirth, T. (2019). Between fixities and flows: Navigating place attachments in an increasingly mobile world. *Journal of Environmental Psychology, 61*, 125–133.

Donohoe, J. (2014). *Remembering places*. New York: Lexington Books.

Donohoe, J. (Ed.) (2017). *Place and phenomenology*. New York: Roman & Littlefield.

Easthope, H. (2009). Fixed identities in a mobile world? The relationship between mobility, place, and identity. *Identities, 16*, 61–82.

Finlay, L. (2011). *Phenomenology for therapists*. Oxford: Wiley-Blackwell.

Forester, J. (2006). Policy analysis as critical listening. In M. Moran, M. Rein, & R. E. Goodin (Eds.), *Oxford handbook of public policy* (pp. 124–151). New York: Oxford University Press.

Freestone, R. L., & Liu, E. (Eds.) (2017). *Place and placelessness revisited*. London: Routledge.

Fullilove, M. T. (2004). *Root shock*. New York: Ballantine Books.

Fullilove, M. T. (2011). *Urban alchemy*. New York: New Village Press.

Gieryn, T. F. (2018). *Truth-spots: How places make people believe*. Chicago: University of Chicago Press.

Goldsack, L. (1999). A haven in a heartless world? In T. Chapman, & J. Hockey (Eds.), *Ideal homes?* (pp. 121–132). London: Routledge.

Greenfield, A. (2017). *Radical technologies: The design of everyday life*. London: Verso.

Griffero, T., & Tedeschini, M., (Eds.) (2019). *Atmosphere and aesthetics*. London: Palgrave Macmillan.

Hillier, B. (2008). The new science and the art of place. In T. Hass (Ed.), *New urbanism and beyond* (pp. 30–39). New York: Rizzoli.

Hünefeldt, T., & Schlitte, A. (Eds.) (2018). *Situatedness and place*. Cham, Switzerland: Springer.

Jacobs, J. (1961). *The death and life of great American cities*. New York: Vintage.

Jacobson, K. (2009). A developed nature: A phenomenological account of the experience of home. *Continental Philosophy Review*, *42*, 355–373.

Jacobson, K. (2010). The experience of home and the space of citizenship. *The Southern Journal of Philosophy*, *48*(3), 219–245.

Jacobson, K. (2011). Embodied domestics, embodied politics: Women, home, and agoraphobia. *Human Studies*, *34*, 1–21.

Jager, B. (1975). Theorizing, journeying, dwelling. In A. Giorgi, C. Fischer, & E. Murray (Eds.), *Duquesne studies in phenomenological psychology* Vol. 2 (pp. 125–160). Pittsburgh, PA: Duquesne University Press.

Janz, B. B. (2005). Walls and borders. *City & Community*, *4*(1), 87–94.

Janz, B. B. (Ed.). (2017). *Place, space and hermeneutics*. Cham, Switzerland: Springer.

Johnson Coffin, C., & Young, J. (2017). *Making places for people*. New York: Routledge.

Klinenberg, E. (2002). *Heat wave*. Chicago: University of Chicago Press.

Kogl, A. (2008). *Strange places*. New York: Rowman & Littlefield.

Kossoff, G. (2019). Cosmopolitan localism. *Cuaderno*, *73*, 51–66.

Lager, D., Van Hoven, B., & Huigen, P. (2016). Rhythms, ageing and neighbourhoods. *Environment and Planning A*, *48*, 1565–1580.

Lems, A. (2014). Placing displacement. *Ethos*, *42*, 1–23.

Lewicka, M. (2011). Place attachment: How far have we come in the last 40 years? *Journal of Environmental Psychology*, *31*, 207–230.

Lewis, C. (2017). Turning houses into homes. *Environment and Planning A*, *49*, 1324–1340.

Malpas, J. E. (Ed.) (2015). *The intelligence of place*. London: Bloomsbury.

Malpas, J. E. (2018). *Place and experience* (2nd ed.). Cambridge: Cambridge University Press.

Manzo, L. C. (2008). The experience of displacement on sense of place and well-being. In J. Eyles, & A. Williams (Eds.), *Sense of place, health and quality of life* (pp. 87–104). Aldershot, Hampshire, UK: Ashgate.

Manzo, L. C. (2014). Exploring the shadow side: Place attachment in the context of stigma, displacement, and social housing. In L. C. Manzo, & P. Devine-Wright (Eds.), *Place attachment* (pp. 178–190). London: Routledge.

Manzo, L. C., & Devine-Wright, P. (Eds.). (2014). *Place attachment: Advances in theory, methods and research* (1st ed.) New York: Routledge.

McMahon, L. (2014). Home invasions. *Journal of Speculative Philosophy*, *28*, 358–369.

Mehta, V. (2013). *The street*. London: Routledge.

Merleau-Ponty, M. (1962). *The phenomenology of perception*. New York: Humanities Press.

Meyrowitz, J. (2015). Place and its mediated re-placements. In J. Malpas (Ed.), *The intelligence of place* (pp. 93–128). London: Bloomsbury.

Middleton, J. (2011). I'm on autopilot, I just follow the route. *Environment and Planning A*, *43*, 2859–2877.

Miller, V. (2016). *The crisis of presence in contemporary culture*. London: Sage.

Million, M.L. (1992). "It was home": A phenomenology of place and involuntary displacement as illustrated by the forced dislocation of five southern Alberta families in the Oldman River Dam flood area. Doctoral dissertation, Saybrook Institute Graduate School and Research Center, San Francisco, California..

Minton, A. (2009). *Ground control*. London: Penguin.

Moore, A., Carter, B., & Sheikh, K. (2013). Space, place and notions of home in lived experiences of hospice day care. *Health & Place*, *19*, 151–158.

Moore, J. (2007). Polarity or integration? *Journal of Architectural and Planning Research*, *24*(2), 143–159.

Moores, S. (2012). *Media, place and mobility*. Basingstoke, UK: Palgrave Macmillan.

Moran, D. (2000). *Introduction to phenomenology*. New York: Routledge.

Moran, D. (2014). The ego as substrate of habitualities. *Phenomenology and Mind*, *6*, 26–47.

Oldenburg, R. (2008). The third place: A belated concept. In T. Haas (Ed.), *New urbanism and beyond* (pp. 234–237). New York: Rizzoli.

Oldenburg, R. (2013). The café as a third place. In A. Tjora, & G. Scambler (Eds.), *Café society* (pp. 7–22). New York: Palgrave.

Rae, D. W. (2003). *City: Urbanism and its end*, New Haven: Yale University Press.

Patterson, M., & Williams, D. (2005). Maintaining research traditions on place. *Journal of Environmental Psychology*, *25*, 361–380.

Pearce, L. (2019), *Mobility, memory and the lifecourse in twentieth-century literature and culture*. London: Palgrave Macmillan.

Raymond, C. M., Kyttä, M., & Stedman, R. (2017). Sense of place, fast and slow. *Frontiers in Psychology*, *8*,1674. DOI:10.3389/psyg.2017.01674.

Relph, E. (1976). *Place and placelessness*. London: Pion.

Relph, E. (2009). A pragmatic sense of place. *Environmental and Architectural Phenomenology*, *20*(3): 24–31.

Relph, E. (2015). Place and connection. In J. Malpas (Ed.), *The intelligence of place* (pp. 177–204). London: Bloomsbury.

Relph, E. (2018). Speculations about electronic media and place. *Environmental and Architectural Phenomenology*, *29*(1), 14–18.

Riedel, F. (2019). Atmosphere. In J. Slaby, & C. von Scheve (Eds.), *Affective societies* (pp. 20–32). New York: Routledge.

Rowles, G. D. (2017), Identity and place attachment in late life. In M. W. Skinner, G. J. Andrews, & M. P. Cutchin (Eds.), *Geographical Gerontology* (pp. 203–215). London: Routledge.

Scannell, L., & Gifford, R. (2017). The experienced psychological benefits of place attachment. *Journal of Environmental Psychology*, *51*, 256–269.

Schnell, S. M. (2018). Exploring place attachment and the immigrant experience in comics and graphic novels: Shaun Tan's *The arrival*. In J. S. Smith (Ed.), *Explorations in place attachment* (pp. 97–113). New York: Routledge.

Seamon, D. (1979). *A geography of the lifeworld*. New York: St. Martin's.

Seamon, D. (2008) Place, placelessness, insideness, and outsideness in John Sayles'. *Sunshine State, Aether*, *3*, 1–19.

Seamon, D. (2014). Physical and virtual environments. In B. Schell, G. Gillen, & M. Scaffa, (Eds.), *Willard & Spackman's Occupational Therapy* (12th ed.) (pp. 202–214). Philadelphia: Wippincott, Williams & Wilkens.

Seamon, D. (2018a). *Life takes place*. London: Routledge.

Seamon, D. (2018b). Merleau-Ponty, lived body, and place. In T. Hünefeldt, & A. Schlitte (Eds.), *Situatedness and Place* (pp. 41–79). Cham, Switzerland: Springer.

Seamon, D. (2019). Glimpses of place spirituality in American filmmaker John Sayles' *Limbo*: Authenticity, inauthenticity, and modes of place engagement. In V. Counted, & F. Watts (Eds.), *The psychology of religion and place* (pp. 239–259). London: Palgrave Macmillan.

Sebastien, L. (2019). The power of place in understanding place attachments and meanings. *Geoforum*, *107*, 1–13. https://doi.org/10.1016/j.geoforum.2019.11.001.

Simms, E. (2008). Children's lived spaces in the inner city. *The Humanistic Psychologist*, *36*, 72–89.

Smith, J. S. (Ed.) (2018). *Explorations in place attachment*. New York: Routledge.

Sowers, J. (2010). *A phenomenology of place identity for Wonder Valley, California*. Doctoral Dissertation, Department of Geography, Kansas State University, Manhattan, KS.

Stefanovic, I. L. (2008). Holistic paradigms of health and place. In J. Eyles, & A. Williams (Eds.), *Sense of place, health and quality of life* (pp. 45–57). Aldershot, Hampshire, UK: Ashgate.

Tilley, C. (2012). *Interpreting landscapes*. Walnut Creek, CA: Left Coast Press.

Tilley, C., & Cameron-Daum, K. (2017). *An anthropology of landscape*. London: University College London Press.

Tomaney, J. (2012). Parochialism—a defense. *Progress in Human Geography*, *37*(5), 658–672.

Tomaney, J. (2014). Region and place II: Belonging. *Progress in Human Geography*, *39*, 507–516.

Toombs, S. K. (2000). The lived experience of disability. In S. K. Toombs (Ed.), *Handbook of phenomenology and medicine* (pp. 147–161). Dordrecht: Kluwer.

van Eck, D., & Pijpers, R. (2016). Encounters in place ballet: A phenomenological perspective on older people's walking routines in an urban park. *Area*, *49*(2), 166–173.

van Manen, M. (2014). *Phenomenology of practice*. London: Routledge.

Watson, S. (2009). The magic of the marketplace: Sociality in a neglected public space. *Urban Studies*, *46*, 1577–1591.

Williams, D. R. (2014). Making sense of 'place': Reflections on pluralism and positionality in place research. *Landscape and Urban Planning*, *131*, 74–82.

Williams, D. R., & McIntyre, N. (2012). Place affinities, lifestyle mobilities, and quality-of-life. In M. Uysal, R. Perdue, & M. J. Sirgy (Eds.), *Handbook of tourism and quality-of-life research* (pp. 209–231). Cham, Switzerland: Springer.

Whyte, W. (1980). *The social life of small urban spaces*. New York: Project for Public Spaces.

Chapter 3: Parallels between interpersonal and place attachment: An update

Leila Scannell, Elizabeth Williams, Robert Gifford, and Carmen Sarich

INTRODUCTION

Place attachment, the cognitive-emotional bonds between individuals or groups and their important places (e.g., Low & Altman, 1992; Mihaylov & Perkins, 2014), continues to attract widespread interest across disciplines (Turton, 2016). Recent work has identified new processes (e.g., Bailey, Devine-Wright & Batel, 2016), types (Lewicka, 2013), antecedents (Dwyer, Chen & Lee, 2019), mediators and moderators (Ramkissoon & Mavondo, 2015), and outcomes of place attachment (e.g., Sullivan & Young, 2018). The understanding of place attachment might be furthered by considering more established theories of human bonding, to determine which elements apply to person-place bonds.

Specifically, interpersonal attachment theory (i.e., Ainsworth, 1967; Bowlby, 1969/1982) has contributed to, and may continue to inspire, place attachment research. In short, Bowlby (1969/1982) reasoned that an innate psychological system regulates proximity to an "attachment figure," a specific person who provides an individual with security and comfort in the face of threats. Ainsworth (1967) further delineated individual differences in attachment, called "attachment styles." Since these seminal works appeared, attachment theory has remained prominent across various sub-disciplines of psychology and has made contributions to counseling, social work, and other areas of practice (Holmes, 2014).

Some commonalities between the two theories have been identified (Fried, 2000; Giuliani, 2003; Little & Derr, 2018; Morgan, 2010). Our 2014 chapter on this subject (Scannell & Gifford, 2014) asserted that although they are distinct constructs, place attachment shares a number of key parallels with interpersonal attachment. The present chapter revisits this comparison; updates it in light of recent research findings, trends, and applications; and offers a new agenda for future place attachment research that is informed by interpersonal attachment theory.

ATTACHMENT PROCESSES

Interpersonal attachment processes

A starting point to compare interpersonal and place attachment is to evaluate the similarities in key psychological processes. Bowlby (1969/1982) delineated four psychological processes that characterize interpersonal attachment relationships: proximity-maintenance, safe haven, secure base, and separation distress. Proximity-maintenance involves the regulation of distance between the individual and the "attachment figure," who provides protection and comfort (Bowlby, 1969). This process is thought to have evolved because infants who are able to maintain proximity to their caregivers may be more likely to survive (Bowlby, 1969/1982). When infants perceive threats, their attachment system initiates proximity-maintaining behaviors that serve to adjust distance to their caregiver. The attachment system is deactivated when proximity has been achieved. The child thereby attains a sense of security and comfort and, by serving as the locus for this, the caregiver offers a safe haven for the child.

This safe haven is transformable into a secure base where the child's exploration and affiliation systems can function while the connection to the caregiver is reestablished repeatedly (Feeney & Thrush, 2010; Grossmann & Grossmann, 2019). Security allows the child to venture out and interact with the surrounding environment while remaining within range, allowing them to achieve protection as needed.

Attachment relationships can suffer from prolonged periods of separation. Infants who are unable to attain proximity to their attachment figure experience separation distress, manifested through protest, then despair, and, eventually, detachment, when the child resists forming close bonds with others (Bowlby, 1969).

More recent models describe how attachment-related behaviors, affects, and cognitions unfold in a sequential process (Mikulincer & Shaver, 2018). First, individuals (children as well as adults) monitor their environments for threats, and if one is detected, the attachment system is activated. Second, individuals monitor the availability of their attachment figure. If attachment figures are available and responsive, proximity is sought and security is achieved. Third, if the attachment figure is unavailable, individuals must resort to a secondary strategy: hyperactivation, in which individuals demand attention from the attachment figure by exaggerating threats, or deactivation, in which individuals deny the need for proximity and instead become overly self-reliant. The chronic use of these strategies leads to individual differences called attachment styles.

Place attachment processes

Place attachment appears to present comparable psychological processes to those of interpersonal attachment but that differs somewhat in how they are expressed. Proximity-seeking is a hallmark of interpersonal attachment processes that is also exhibited toward places, such as when individuals elect to live in a place or spend time there. Vacationers may revisit certain travel destinations (Dwyer et al., 2019; Vada, Prentice, & Hsiao, 2019). Some religious groups incorporate pilgrimages as a way of maintaining proximity to sacred spaces (Mazumdar & Mazumdar, 2004; Ruback, Pandey, & Kohli, 2008). Even when a place is not physically proximal, the benefits of proximity can be achieved through visualization. Drawing on experimental methods from interpersonal attachment research (e.g., Mikulincer,

Hirschberger, Nachmias, & Gillath, 2001), participants who visualized a place of attachment (as compared to a neutral place) reported greater current levels of self-esteem, belongingness, and meaningfulness following the visualization (Scannell & Gifford, 2017a).

Although most research highlights the benefits of proximity-seeking to place, researchers also recognize that person-place bonds are not always positively valenced, can be negative or ambivalent (Manzo, 2014; Roster, Ferrari, & Jurkat, 2016), and can sometimes pose danger. A systematic review focusing on place attachment in relation to natural environmental risks and hazards revealed that individuals who are strongly attached are less willing to evacuate or relocate in the face of risks, and are more likely to return following disasters, even when risks remain (Bonaiuto, Alves, De Dominicis, & Petruccelli, 2016). Similarly, proximity to an interpersonal attachment figure is not always adaptive, such as when the attachment figure is abusive (e.g., Alexander, 1992), or when attachment anxiety prevents broader exploration of the environment (Ainsworth, Blehar, Waters, & Wall, 1978).

Generally, however, the purpose of proximity-seeking is to access a safe haven. In the case of place attachment, this occurs when using a place to retreat from threats, problem-solve, and gain emotional relief. This has been demonstrated in various samples such as children who retreat to favorite places to regulate their emotions (Korpela, Kyttä, & Hartig, 2002) and adults who recognize safety and security as one of the primary benefits of their important places (Scannell & Gifford, 2017b). Along these lines, place attachment appears to co-vary with increased perceptions of safety; individuals who are more attached to their neighborhoods and homes tend to perceive them as safer than do others who are less attached (e.g., Brown, Perkins, & Brown, 2003).

The safe-haven function of place attachment may be especially important for marginalized groups and individuals who face numerous stressors in their everyday lives (Fried, 2000). However, the structures that create and maintain comfortable places for dominant groups can limit the ability of those who are less powerful to access safe havens (Anguelovski, 2013). For example, safety may be more elusive for some groups, given housing instability, lack of control of resources, and greater exposure to stressful living conditions in low-income settings, such as noise, pollution, violence, and stigma (Kleit & Manzo, 2013). On the other hand, marginalized groups can also seek, create, and re-appropriate spaces wherein they can achieve a sense of safety and freedom (Anguelovski, 2013).

A third process relevant to both interpersonal and place attachment occurs when the attachment figure serves as a secure base that promotes exploration. Places of attachment can provide a reference point and anchor for wider expeditions (Fried, 2000), or they can serve as the object of the exploration itself, such as when individuals form attachments to interesting travel destinations (Dwyer et al., 2019) or utilize a place to escape from daily routines (Wildish, Kearns, & Collins, 2016). Place attachment-supported exploration can occur at a group level, such as when a strong sense of nationalism contributes to quests to explore terrestrial environments and beyond, as is seen in the history of space exploration (e.g., Siddiqi, 2010). Unlike an interpersonal attachment figure, however, places of attachment should not be assumed to be stable or fixed entities from which exploration can be launched; rather, place attachment can also include both fixed (i.e., stasis, and rootedness) and fluid (i.e., changing, moving, and relational) aspects that can be configured in various ways (Di Masso et al., 2019).

Finally, as with interpersonal attachment, separation distress can occur when person-place bonds are disrupted, such as through threatening changes (Bailey et al., 2016), anticipated involuntary separation (Billig, 2006), and actual separation (Scannell, Cox, Fletcher, & Heykoop, 2016). For example, the loss of place following forest fires (Cox & Perry, 2011; Felix et al., 2015), tornados (Silver & Grek-Martin, 2015), floods (Scannell, Cox, & Fletcher, 2017), and other natural and human-caused disasters can produce disorientation, grief, and disruptions in identity and functioning among residents (Scannell et al., 2016, 2017).

THE DEVELOPMENT OF ATTACHMENT BONDS

The development of interpersonal attachment

Given that interpersonal and place attachment share some defining features, bonds may develop in similar ways. The attachment system is present at birth, but its organization changes over the lifespan (Bowlby, 1969/1982). To engage caregivers, newborns are equipped with innate attachment behaviors such as crying and clinging. Around 6–9 months, infants enter a sensitive period when the attachment bond becomes more concrete and may begin to experience separation anxiety when the caregiver is absent. Independence slowly widens as children spend more time away from their caregivers (Marvin & Britner, 1999). Eventually, a greater need for autonomy arises in adolescence, but attachment persists, and adolescents usually continue to use their parents as a secure base and source of support. Romantic and other attachments formed in adolescence and adulthood can contribute to, or alter, the structure of individuals' mental models of relationships. Thus, although parental attachments can continue to exert a strong influence, they do not preclude the development of new bonds.

The development of place attachment

Comparably less is known about the development of place attachment, but a number of routes through which person-place bonds are initiated and consolidated have been proposed. Place attachment in childhood may develop through a widening of children's secure base from the caregiver to their home and outward to the neighborhood, and eventually to the larger community (Hay, 1998). Another model depicts the development of place attachment and interpersonal attachment as part of a synchronous, mutually reinforcing process (Morgan, 2010). When the physical environment is rich with fascinating stimuli, it can activate the exploratory system. Children then move from their caregivers to play in the environment. Should they become threatened or distant from a caregiver, proximity is sought.

From this secure base, the exploration-proximity cycle continues and, over time, two internal working models develop: one of the child-caregiver dyad, and one of the child-place dyad.

Recently, more research has considered the formation of place attachment in adulthood. Some scholars have posited that individual memories, milestones, or other experiences support the development of place attachment (Scannell & Gifford, 2017b). Indirect experiences with a place through stories, media, and music can also contribute to the development of place attachment by transferring symbolic meaning, developing a sense of "vicarious insideness," and evoking positive emotional associations with a place or places (Bolderman & Reijnders, 2019; Hosany, Buzova & Sanz-Blas, 2019). Indeed, like interpersonal attachments, place attachment can develop toward multiple places. Given the rise in transnational mobility, the development of multiple (and simultaneously held) place attachments is an increasingly important phenomenon (Di Masso et al., 2019; Gustafson, 2014; Rishbeth, 2014).

The development of place attachment appears to vary with certain sociodemographic characteristics. For example, compared to urban and semi-rural residents, place attachment among rural residents may develop more quickly and stem from the physical characteristics of the environment, such as green space (Turton, 2016). Other factors thought to influence the development of place attachment include length of residence, social ties, and awareness of an area's heritage (Lewicka, 2011; Turton, 2016). Furthermore, while interpersonal attachment is understood to be an innate developmental mechanism, "place attachments are not inherently stable psychological constructs, but rather are informed across time and space by an array of mobility conditions and the relational configurations which underpin them" (Di Masso et al., 2019, p. 131).

In contrast to interpersonal attachment research, place attachment is more often considered within a socioecological framework, which has informed the understanding of its development. That is, place attachment researchers more actively explore community, physical, cultural, and political influences in the development of the person-place bond. Some have begun to detail how place attachment is constructed through cultural processes (Najafi & Shariff, 2014; Ruback, Pandey, & Kohli, 2008; Youngs, 2017). A more complex perspective acknowledges that bonds to places strengthen and weaken over time through combinations of individual, group, and cultural processes. Cross (2015) proposed seven dynamic and co-occurring processes for the formation of place attachment, including sensory, narrative, historical, spiritual, ideological, commodifying, and dependence processes. Another view is that place attachment is continually constructed through dialogue among many individuals who determine the meanings of places, which are frequently contested by actors with various degrees of power (Di Masso et al., 2014, p. 75).

Despite growing research on the development of place attachment, further work is needed to synthesize and substantiate the proposals about how place attachment develops across the lifespan, and a socioecological framing of this would be informative. Research might also clarify when and how place attachment develops among young children. Interpersonal attachment research, which has successfully linked attachment formation to cognitive development such as operational thought (e.g., Ainsworth, 1967; Jacobsen, Edelstein, & Hofmann, 1994), could usefully guide research on place attachment development in early childhood.

INDIVIDUAL DIFFERENCES IN ATTACHMENT

Interpersonal attachment styles

Attachment-related affect, cognition, and behavior differ across individuals. Indeed, many studies have explored individual differences called attachment styles (Ainsworth, 1967; Ainsworth et al., 1978). For infants, three categories of attachment were initially proposed: secure, anxious-ambivalent, and avoidant. Ainsworth found that in secure infant-caregiver dyads, infants are more likely to seek proximity to their caregiver when distressed and are more successfully comforted by them. In anxious-ambivalent dyads, infants displayed protest and distress when separated from their caregiver, and an angry response upon reunion (Ainsworth et al., 1978). In avoidant dyads, infants showed little reaction when separated from their caregiver and ignored them upon their return (Ainsworth et al., 1978). Later, a fourth category called disorganized attachment was proposed (Main & Solomon, 1990), characterized by inconsistent, responses from the infant, oscillating between avoidance and anxiety. Most research on adult interpersonal attachment discusses similar styles but maintains that they range along two continuous dimensions: anxiety and avoidance (Brennan, Clark, & Shaver, 1998), and securely attached individuals score low on both dimensions.

Place attachment styles

Some researchers have attempted to investigate stable individual differences in place attachment, through various lines of inquiry. One is whether interpersonal attachment styles moderate the strength of attachment to place. In support of this, having an insecure interpersonal attachment style is linked to lower levels of place attachment, place-related need fulfillment, and neighborhood social bonds (Tartaglia, 2006). Also, children with an anxious attachment style are more likely to experience homesickness than their secure counterparts, who are more independent and willing to explore while away from home (Thurber & Sigman, 1998). Furthermore, individuals with a secure interpersonal attachment style are more likely to report stronger attachment to their workplace (Scrima, Rioux, & Di Stefano, 2017). Together, these studies suggest that person-place bonding may be influenced by interpersonal attachment style.

Another line of inquiry focuses on whether different stable place attachment styles exist and, if so, whether they are comparable to interpersonal attachment styles. In one such attempt, place attachment styles positively correlated with their interpersonal attachment style counterparts (McBain, 2010). However, the construct validity and reliability of this measure remains unestablished. Others have suggested that workplace attachment styles may exist (Scrima et al., 2017). Therefore, evidence as to whether interpersonal attachment styles translate to place attachment styles remains inconclusive.

A different approach has been to establish individual differences in place attachment that do not parallel interpersonal attachment styles but that appear to vary by distinct sociodemographic and psychological profiles. Lewicka (2013) identified two main dimensions, along which five types of residential attachment vary: (1) localism, characterized as anchoring in one's own neighborhood, including long time residency and an interest in local history; and (2) activity, broadly defined by physical, cultural, and social activity, shorter residency, and openness to change. Localism separates the attached (traditional and active) and non-attached (alienated, place relative, and placeless), and activity differentiates between the traditionally attached, alienated, and place relative and the actively attached and placeless participants. A sixth type of place attachment is a traditional/active type experienced by individuals who grew up in a place, moved away for a short period of time, had a negative experience in the new place, and returned to their home community to settle (Bailey et al., 2016). It is characterized by low involvement with local activities, but an interest in local history. According to Lewicka, demographic and psychological characteristics underlie the strength and adaptability of these attachment types. An interesting extension of this work would be to determine whether residential attachment types apply at the group level.

STABILITY OF ATTACHMENT

How stable are attachment patterns throughout the lifespan?

An important question about attachment styles is the extent to which they are stable, and whether early attachment representations persist later in life. Fraley (2002) argued that a prototype of attachment is generated from infants' early experiences with their caregivers, and that this early representation remains somewhat stable over the lifespan. Although people may construct additional representations for new relationships, the default is that the prototype will retain its influence through a self-fulfilling prophecy (Fraley, 2002). In support of this, empirical data generally reveal moderate stability over time; however, some researchers have taken these medium-sized correlations as evidence that attachment styles also have the capacity to fluctuate over time (Pinquart, Feußner, & Ahnert, 2013).

Place attachment stability

As compared to interpersonal attachment, fewer studies have investigated the stability of place attachment over time. In one study, participants selected their favorite place type and rated their level of attachment to a specific favorite place (Korpela, Ylén, Tyrväinen, & Silvennoinen, 2009). Ten months later, participants typically reported the same favorite type of place and specific favorite places.

Some work has investigated the stability of place attachment in the context of physical place change. In a longitudinal study assessing feelings of place attachment to a park before, during, and after renovations, individuals who were more strongly attached to the park before it closed were more likely to return when it reopened, but they also experienced a decrease in bonding both during renovations and two months afterward (Cheng & Chou, 2015). Conversely, those who were initially less attached to the park experienced an increase in attachment during and after the renovation. Wherein place disruption was relatively temporary (3–5 months) and attachment was measured shortly after park reopening, additional longitudinal studies should consider longer place disruptions and whether initial place bonds are reestablished over a longer period of time.

Another study revealed that attachment to a particular place can be less stable among adolescents and young adults who are navigating life transitions that involve a change in location (Elder, King, & Conger, 1996). Similarly, Bailey et al. (2016) further argue that ongoing life events and place changes, or "life-place trajectories," combine to influence place attachment type (i.e., as specified in Lewicka's, 2013 typology) to a current place. Specifically, a place attachment type emerges from a confluence of factors including one's mobility patterns throughout their life, life events (e.g., change in employment), the degree of continuity of their habitation, social networks in the town since childhood, and the similarity of the region to other settlement places from which they have relocated. Acknowledging these influences, the extent to which these types of attachment remain stable (or not) remains unclear. Therefore, a longitudinal study exploring the stability of place attachment types over time would address the question about place attachment stability and could examine the relative contributions of varying influences over time.

In sum, the stability of interpersonal and place attachment has been investigated in different ways. Interpersonal attachment researchers have focused on the stability of attachment styles while place attachment researchers have focused on the stability of place attachment types or strength. The existence of a place attachment style or schema exerting an influence over time remains to be seen. Some scholars have asserted that place attachment bonds are continually changing across time and space (Di Masso et al., 2019), which suggests that studies of individual differences should be mindful of context, change, and other more fluid place attachment processes.

RESPONDING TO DISRUPTED BONDS

Interpersonal attachment

A vast body of literature on grief and bereavement has illuminated various ways that people respond to the loss of interpersonal attachment figures. The dual process model of grieving (Stroebe & Schut, 2010) posits that bereaved individuals experience an oscillation between (1) a loss orientation, in which they process the loss and may respond by relinquishing, continuing, or relocating bonds; and (2) a restoration orientation, in which they attend to life changes that have resulted from the loss, such as changes to identity, activities, and so on. Much of this work considers the potential adaptive nature of continuing bonds, the "ongoing inner relationship with the deceased individual by the bereaved individual" (Stroebe & Schut, 2005, p. 477). This may include reminiscing about the deceased, keeping their possessions, looking at photographs, internalizing their values and beliefs, or more interactive connections such as writing, praying, or attempting to communicate with them. Results are mixed as to whether these behaviors are adaptive, when, and for whom (Stroebe & Schut, 2005), and expectations about continuing or relinquishing bonds vary by culture (Rothaupt & Becker, 2007).

The grief process for attachment relationships can be particularly dysregulating, not only from losing a loved one, but also from losing the source of emotion regulation and support that the attachment figure would have previously provided (Sbarra & Hazan, 2008). Adaptive responses thus require individuals to find alternate ways to self-soothe and gain a sense of security. Some individuals benefit from the support of friends, family, or new romantic partners. Therefore, turning to alternate attachment figures or forming new attachments can sometimes reestablish a sense of security. Cognitive processes, such as making sense of the loss, reorganizing thoughts about the attachment figure, reappraising the loss as less threatening, and other attempts to support self-regulation have also been identified as strategies that can assist with the loss of an attachment figure (Sbarra & Hazan, 2008).

Responses to disrupted place bonds

As mentioned, disrupted place bonds can produce separation distress, including grief and anxiety (e.g., Brown & Perkins, 1992; Fried, 1963/2000). Less research has been devoted to understanding the adaptive (and maladaptive) cognitive-behavioral responses that follow. However, several responses have been identified. As occurs with disrupted interpersonal attachment bonds, individuals who experience disrupted place ties may similarly make efforts to continue the bonds. When physical proximity is not possible, representations or thoughts about a place allow individuals to feel close to it. People sometimes bring objects or photographs of the previous place to the new place (Ryan & Ogilvie, 2001; Scharp, Paxman, & Thomas, 2016) or reminisce about feelings of comfort experienced there (Scharp et al., 2016).

Related responses are "interchangeability," and "place-congruent continuity," when individuals seek features in the new place that resemble, or fulfill the same functions as the previous place (Marcus, 1992; Ryan & Ogilvie, 2001; Twigger-Ross & Uzzell, 1996). For example, one might visit a local beach because it resembles one from back home and offers a similar capacity for psychological restoration. For migrants, this phenomenon offers a way to support the simultaneous existence of, and reflect on differences among, multiple place attachments (Rishbeth, 2014, this volume). Efforts to recreate a previous place bond are sometimes reflected in communities' urban planning (Smith & White, 2004). This can occur following a disaster, when community members draw upon previous place meanings to determine what and how to rebuild (Cox & Perry, 2011).

Although maintaining connections to previous places of attachment can be used to navigate place disruption, it can be maladaptive when it prevents adjustment or bonding to a new place. Students living away from home who have more social ties in their hometowns and lack of affective attachment to their new community are more likely to be homesick (Scopelliti & Tiberio, 2010). In contrast, the formation of a new place bond can assist with adjustment, well-being, and health (Hornsey & Gallois, 1998). One recommendation to alleviate homesickness, therefore, is to establish everyday social and behavioral routines and activities that encourage bonding to the new place (Scharp et al., 2016). These new routines can be reinforced by priming feelings of comfort, safety, and social support characteristic of "home": displaying photos of loved ones; reminiscing about feelings of safety; as well as initiating social contact and support, especially amongst family and friends from home.

In the longer term, residents sometimes adapt to place changes as they use the new environment and have new experiences there. Among residents living near a large hydroelectric dam, those from four cohorts all felt connected to the present dam landscape, even if they had lived in the area prior to its construction (Keilty, 2015). Their connection was based on various recreational, aesthetic, and other lifestyle benefits they accrued from the landscape. Thus, although the initial disruption from the dam construction may have changed the meanings of the original place bond, residents were able to adapt and reconnect to the modified place.

These findings about place disruption appear congruent with the dual process model of grief. Coping with homesickness includes processes that oscillate between experiencing the loss and maintaining connections to the previous place and establishing routines and bonds with the new place (Fried, 2000; Stroebe, Schut, & Nauta, 2016). The dual process model of grief offers a useful framework to better understand place-related grief and coping, and further supports our claim that interpersonal and place relationships share some commonalities. Future work should generate empirical evidence to evaluate the relevance of this model across various types of place disruptions, both self-initiated or involuntary, such as those that result from disaster loss. It should also consider how grief operates at a group level, specifying how families, communities, and cultural groups prepare for and navigate place loss.

Another interesting response to place disruption occurs when individuals draw upon the benefits and capital generated by the previous place bond to assist with the transition. Even when the physical place is lost, benefits of the bond can help with recovery, such as the social capital that was rooted in place which allows individuals to come together after a disaster and offers instrumental and social support (Norris, Stevens, Pfefferbaum, Wyche, & Pfefferbaum, 2008). In contrast, the residual benefits of disrupted interpersonal bonds may be less evident, especially given the dysregulation that occurs when attachment figures are no longer available to provide support (Sbarra & Hazan, 2008).

CONCLUSION

A growing body of research supports the view that some elements of interpersonal attachment are relevant to place attachment. Both types of attachment can be maintained through proximity-seeking, and if positively valenced, can provide individuals with a sense of safety and comfort. When the bonds are disrupted, individuals can experience grief and may respond by attending to the loss and continuing old bonds, and to new life changes and establishing new bonds.

The developmental course of place attachment is less well understood than that of interpersonal attachment. One difference is that place attachment researchers have more frequently considered influences across socioecological systems, such as culture, political, economic, and other influences. Despite this, the role of finances, education, social mobility, and access to safe and comfortable places deserves more attention in studies on place attachment development and stability.

Although numerous studies have detailed interpersonal attachment styles and their implications, place attachment researchers have yet to clarify whether stable, place attachment styles exist. However, six place attachment types have been identified (Bailey et al., 2016; Lewicka, 2013), which should fuel research investigating their stability and influence on other person-environment relations such as pro-environmental behavior or disaster resilience.

One caution in comparing interpersonal and place attachment is that leaning on interpersonal attachment theories as a basis of inquiry may lead to an overemphasis on the individual level of analysis and may limit the understanding of social, cultural, and political influences on the expression of place attachments. Another concern is that comparing interpersonal and place attachments could perpetuate sedentarist assumptions of place attachment that are already overemphasized in the place attachment literature, thus overlooking other possibilities of how place attachment can include both static and fluid elements (e.g., see Di Masso et al., 2019).

Places may not be responsive, communicating, and caring attachment figures in the same way that human caregivers may be. Despite the differences in place and person attachment, the parallels between them are still noteworthy and suggest some commonalities in bonding across various attachment figures at least at the individual level. Perhaps most importantly, the comparisons should guide the development of future place attachment methodology and theory development, toward a better understanding of causal place attachment principles and their variations across contexts.

REFERENCES

Ainsworth, M. D. S. (1967). *Infancy in Uganda: Infant care and the growth of love*. Baltimore: Johns Hopkins University Press.

Ainsworth, M. D. S., Blehar, M., Waters, E., & Wall, S. (1978). *Patterns of attachment: A psychological study of the strange situation*. Hillsdale, NJ: Erlbaum.

Alexander, P. C. (1992). Application of attachment theory to the study of sexual abuse. *Journal of Consulting and Clinical Psychology*, *60*(2), 185–195.

Anguelovski, I. (2013). New directions in urban environmental justice: Rebuilding community, addressing trauma, and remaking place. *Journal of Planning Education and Research*, *33*(2), 160–175.

Bailey, E., Devine-Wright, P., & Batel, S. (2016). Using a narrative approach to understand place attachments and responses to power line proposals: The importance of life-place trajectories. *Journal of Environmental Psychology*, *48*, 200–211.

Billig, M. (2006). Is my home my castle? Place attachment, risk perception, and religious faith. *Environment and Behavior*, *38*, 248–265.

Bolderman, L., & Reijnders, S. (2019). Sharing songs on Hirakata Square: On playlists and place attachment in contemporary music listening. *European Journal of Cultural Studies*, 1–17.

Bonaiuto, M., Alves, S., De Dominicis, S., & Petruccelli, I. (2016). Place attachment and natural hazard risk: Research review and agenda. *Journal of Environmental Psychology*, *48*, 33–53.

Bowlby, J. (1969). *Attachment and loss: Vol. 1. Attachment*. New York: Basic Books.

Bowlby, J. (1982). *Attachment and loss: Vol. 1. Attachment* (2nd ed.). New York: Basic Books.

Brennan, K. A., Clark, C. L., & Shaver, P. R. (1998). Self-report measurement of adult attachment: An integrative overview. In J. A. Simpson, & W. S. Rholes (Eds.), *Attachment theory and close relationships* (pp. 46–76). New York: Guilford.

Brown, B. B., & Perkins, D. D. (1992). Disruptions in place attachment. In I. Altman, & S. M. Low (Eds.), *Place attachment* (pp. 79–304). New York: Plenum.

Brown, B., Perkins, D. D., & Brown, G. (2003). Place attachment in a revitalizing neighbourhood: Individual and block levels of analysis. *Journal of Environmental Psychology*, *23*, 259–271.

Cheng, C. K., & Chou, S. F. (2015). The influence of place change on place bonding: A longitudinal panel study of renovated park users. *Leisure Sciences*, *37*(5), 391–414.

Cox, R. S., & Perry, K. M. E. (2011). Like a fish out of water: Reconsidering disaster recovery and the role of place and social capital in community disaster resilience. *American Journal of Community Psychology*, *48*(3–4), 395–411.

Cross, J. E. (2015). Processes of place attachment: An interactional framework. *Symbolic Interaction*, *38*(4), 493–520.

Di Masso, A., Dixon, J., & Durrheim, K. (2014) Place attachment as discursive practice. In L. Manzo & Devine-Wright, P. (Eds.), *Place attachment: Advances in theory, methods and research*. (pp. 75–86). New York: Routledge.

Di Masso, A., Williams, D. R., Raymond, C. M., Buchecker, M., Degenhardt, B., Devine-Wright, P., … & von Wirth, T. (2019). Between fixities and flows: Navigating place attachments in an increasingly mobile world. *Journal of Environmental Psychology*, *61*, 125–133.

Dwyer, L., Chen, N., & Lee, J. (2019). The role of place attachment in tourism research. *Journal of Travel & Tourism Marketing*, *36*(5), 645–652.

Elder, G. H., King, V., & Conger, R. D. (1996). Attachment to place and migration prospects: A developmental perspective. *Journal of Research on Adolescence*, *6*, 397–425.

Feeney, B. C., & Thrush, R. L. (2010). Relationship influences in exploration in adulthood: The characteristics and functions of a secure base. *Journal of Personality and Social Psychology*, *98*, 57–76.

Felix, E., Afifi, T., Kia-Keating, M., Brown, L., Afifi, W., & Reyes, G. (2015). Family functioning and posttraumatic growth among parents and youth following wildfire disasters. *American Journal of Orthopsychiatry*, *85*, 191–200.

Fraley, R. C. (2002). Attachment stability from infancy to adulthood: Meta-analysis and dynamic modeling of developmental mechanisms. *Personality and Social Psychology Review, 6*, 123–151.

Fried, M. (1963). Grieving for a lost home. In L. J. Duhl (Ed.), *The urban condition: People and policy in the metropolis* (pp. 124–152). New York: Simon & Schuster.

Fried, M. (2000). Continuities and discontinuities of place. *Journal of Environmental Psychology, 20*, 193–205.

Giuliani, M. V. (2003). Theory of attachment and place attachment. In M. Bonnes, T. Lee, & M. Bonaiuto (Eds.), *Psychological theories for environmental issues* (pp. 137–170). Aldershot: Ashgate.

Grossmann, K., & Grossmann, K. E. (2019). Essentials when studying child-father attachment: A fundamental view on safe haven and secure base phenomena. *Attachment & Human Development*, 1–6.

Gustafson, P. (2014). Place attachment in an age of mobility. In L. C. Manzo, & P. Devine-Wright (Eds.), *Place attachment: Advances in theory, methods, and applications* (pp. 37–48). New York, NY.

Hay, R. (1998). Sense of place in developmental context. *Journal of Environmental Psychology, 18*, 5–29.

Holmes, J. (2014). *John Bowlby and attachment theory*. Routledge.

Hornsey, M., & Gallois, C. (1998). The impact of interpersonal and intergroup communication accommodation on perceptions of Chinese students in Australia. *Journal of Language and Social Psychology, 17*, 323–347.

Hosany, S., Buzova, D., & Sanz-Blas, S. (2019). The influence of place attachment, ad-evoked positive affect, and motivation on intention to visit: Imagination proclivity as a moderator. *Journal of Travel Research*.

Jacobsen, T., Edelstein, W., & Hofmann, V. (1994). A longitudinal study of the relation between representations of attachment in childhood and cognitive functioning in childhood and adolescence. *Developmental Psychology, 30*(1), 112.

Keilty, K. (2015). *Understanding landscape values and baselines of acceptability on the Mactaquac Dam and headpond, New Brunswick*. Unpublished Doctoral Dissertation, Dalhousie University, Nova Scotia, CA.

Kleit, R. G., & Manzo, L. C. (2013). Refugees and public housing redevelopment. *Geography Research Forum, 33*, 7–37.

Korpela, K. M., Kyttä, M., & Hartig, T. (2002). Children's favorite places: Restorative experience, self-regulation and children's place preferences. *Journal of Environmental Psychology, 22*, 387–398.

Korpela, K. M., Ylén, M., Tyrväinen, L., & Silvennoinen, H. (2009). Stability of self-reported favourite places and place attachment over a 10-month period. *Journal of Environmental Psychology, 29*, 95–100.

Lewicka, M. (2011). Place attachment: How far have we come in the last 40 years? *Journal of Environmental Psychology, 31*, 207–230.

Lewicka, M. (2013). Localism and Activity as two dimensions of people–place bonding: The role of cultural capital. *Journal of Environmental Psychology, 36*, 43–53.

Little, S., & Derr, V. (2018) The influence of nature on a child's development: Connecting the outcomes of human attachment and place attachment. In A. Cutter-Mackenzie, K. Malone K., & E. Barratt Hacking (Eds.), *Research handbook on childhoodnature* (pp. 1–28). Cham: Springer.

Low, S. M., & Altman, I. (1992). Place attachment: A conceptual inquiry. In I. Altman, & S. M. Low (Eds.), *Place attachment* (pp. 1–12). New York: Plenum.

Main, M., & Solomon, J. (1990). Procedures for identifying infants as disorganized/disoriented during the Ainsworth Strange Situation. In Greenberg, M. T., Cicchetti, D., & Cummings, M. (Eds.), *Attachment in the preschool years: Theory, research, and intervention* (pp. 121–160). Chicago: The University of Chicago Press.

Manzo, L. C. (2014). Exploring the shadow side: Place attachment in the context of stigma, displacement, and social housing. In L. C. Manzo, & P. Devine-Wright (Eds.), *Place attachment: Advances in theory, methods, and applications* (pp. 178–190). New York, NY: Routledge.

Marcus, C. C. (1992). Environmental memories. In I. Altman, & S. M. Low (Eds.), *Place attachment* (pp. 87–112). New York: Plenum.

Marvin, R. S., & Britner, P. A. (1999). Normative development: The ontogeny of attachment. In J. Cassidy, & P. R. Shaver (Eds.), *Handbook of attachment: Theory, research, and clinical applications* (pp. 44–67). New York: Guilford.

Mazumdar, S., & Mazumdar, S. (2004). Religion and place attachment: A study of sacred places. *Journal of Environmental Psychology*, *24*, 385–397.

McBain, K. A. (2010). *Adult Attachment theory and attachment to place: exploring relationships between people and places* (Doctoral dissertation, James Cook University).

Mihaylov, N., & Perkins, D. D. (2014). Community place attachment and its role in social capital development. In L. C. Manzo, & P. Devine-Wright (Eds.), *Place attachment: Advances in theory, methods, and applications* (pp. 61–74). New York, NY: Routledge.

Mikulincer, M., Hirschberger, G., Nachmias, O., & Gillath, O. (2001). The affective component of the secure base schema: Affective priming with representations of attachment security. *Journal of Personality and Social Psychology*, *81*(2), 305.

Mikulincer, M., & Shaver, P. R. (2018). Attachment theory as a framework for studying relationship dynamics and functioning. In A. L. Vangelisti, & D. Perlman (Eds.), *The Cambridge handbook of personal relationships* (2nd ed.) (pp. 175–185). New York, NY: Cambridge University Press.

Morgan, P. (2010). Towards a developmental theory of place attachment. *Journal of Environmental Psychology*, *30*, 11–22.

Najafi, M., & Shariff, M. K. B. M. (2014). Public attachment to religious places: A study of place attachment to mosques in Malaysia. *International Science Index*, *18*(1), 284–295.

Norris, F. H., Stevens, S. P., Pfefferbaum, B., Wyche, K. F., & Pfefferbaum, R. L. (2008). Community resilience as a metaphor, theory, set of capacities, and strategy for disaster readiness. *American Journal of Community Psychology*, *41*(1–2), 127–150.

Pinquart, M., Feußner, C., & Ahnert, L. (2013). Meta-analytic evidence for stability in attachments from infancy to early adulthood. *Attachment & Human Development*, *15*(2), 189–218.

Ramkissoon, H., & Mavondo, F. T. (2015). The satisfaction–place attachment relationship: Potential mediators and moderators. *Journal of Business Research*, *68*(12), 2593–2602.

Rishbeth, C. (2014). In L. C. Manzo, & P. Devine-Wright (Eds.), *Place attachment: Advances in theory, methods, and applications* (pp. 100–111). New York, NY: Routledge.

Roster, C. A., Ferrari, J. R., & Jurkat, M. P. (2016). The dark side of home: Assessing possession 'clutter' on subjective well-being. *Journal of Environmental Psychology*, *46*, 32–41.

Rothaupt, J. W., & Becker, K. (2007). A literature review of Western bereavement theory: From decathecting to continuing bonds. *The Family Journal*, *15*(1), 6–15.

Ruback, R. B., Pandey, J., & Kohli, N. (2008). Evaluations of a sacred place: Role and religious belief at the Magh Mela. *Journal of Environmental Psychology*, *28*(2), 174–184.

Ryan, M. M., & Ogilvie, M. (2001). Examining the effects of environmental interchangeability with overseas students: A cross cultural comparison. *Journal of Marketing and Logistics, 13,* 63–74.

Sbarra, D. A., & Hazan, C. (2008). Coregulation, dysregulation, self-regulation: An integrative analysis and empirical agenda for understanding adult attachment, separation, loss, and recovery. *Personality and Social Psychology Review, 12*(2), 141–167.

Scannell, L., Cox, R. S., & Fletcher, S. (2017). Place-based loss and resilience among disaster-affected youth. *Journal of Community Psychology, 45*(7), 859–876.

Scannell, L., Cox, R. S., Fletcher, S., & Heykoop, C. (2016). "That was the last time I saw my house": The importance of place attachment among children and youth in disaster contexts. *American Journal of Community Psychology, 58*(1–2), 158–173.

Scannell, L., & Gifford, R. (2014). Comparing the theories of interpersonal and place attachment. In L. C. Manzo, & P. Devine-Wright (Eds.), *Place attachment: Advances in theory, methods, and applications* (pp. 23–36). New York, NY: Routledge.

Scannell, L., & Gifford, R. (2017a). Place attachment enhances psychological need satisfaction. *Environment and Behavior, 49*(4), 359–389.

Scannell, L., & Gifford, R. (2017b). The experienced psychological benefits of place attachment. *Journal of Environmental Psychology, 51,* 256–269.

Scharp, K. M., Paxman, C. G., & Thomas, L. J. (2016). "I want to go home" homesickness experiences and social-support-seeking practices. *Environment and Behavior, 48*(9), 1175–1197.

Scopelliti, M., & Tiberio, L. (2010). Homesickness in university students: The role of multiple place attachment. *Environment and Behavior, 42,* 335–350.

Scrima, F., Rioux, L., & Di Stefano, G. (2017). I hate my workplace but I am very attached to it: Workplace attachment style: An exploratory approach. *Personnel Review, 46*(5), 936–949.

Siddiqi, A. A. (2010). Competing technologies, national(ist) narratives, and universal claims: Toward a global history of space exploration. *Technology and Culture, 51*(2), 425–443.

Silver, A., & Grek-Martin, J. (2015). "Now we understand what community really means": Reconceptualizing the role of sense of place in the disaster recovery process. *Journal of Environmental Psychology, 42,* 32–41.

Smith, J. S., & White, B. N. (2004). Detached from their homeland: The Latter-day Saints of Chihuahua, Mexico. *Journal of Cultural Geography, 21,* 57–76.

Stroebe, M., & Schut, H. (2005). To continue or relinquish bonds: A review of consequences for the bereaved. *Death Studies, 29*(6), 477–494.

Stroebe, M., & Schut, H. (2010). The dual process model of coping with bereavement: A decade on. *OMEGA-Journal of Death and Dying, 61*(4), 273–289.

Stroebe, M., Schut, H., & Nauta, M. H. (2016). Is homesickness a mini-grief? Development of a dual process model. *Clinical Psychological Science, 4*(2), 344–358.

Sullivan, D., & Young, I. F. (2018). Place attachment style as a predictor of responses to the environmental threat of water contamination. *Environment and Behavior, 52*(1), 3–32.

Tartaglia, S. (2006). A preliminary study for a new model of sense of community. *Journal of Community Psychology, 34,* 25–36.

Thurber, C. A., & Sigman, M. D. (1998). Preliminary models of risk and protective factors for childhood homesickness: Review and empirical synthesis. *Child Development, 69,* 903–934.

Turton, C. J. (2016). *Defining residential place attachment and exploring its contribution to community and personal environmental actions.* Unpublished Doctoral Dissertation, University of Surrey, Guildford, UK.

Twigger-Ross, C. L., & Uzzell, D. L. (1996). Place and identity processes. *Journal of Environmental Psychology*, *16*(3), 205–220.

Vada, S., Prentice, C., & Hsiao, A. (2019). The influence of tourism experience and well-being on place attachment. *Journal of Retailing and Consumer Services*, *47*, 322–330.

Wildish, B., Kearns, R., & Collins, D. (2016). At home away from home: Visitor accommodation and place attachment. *Annals of Leisure Research*, *19*(1), 117–133.

Youngs, Y. (2017). Constructing place attachment in Grand Teton National Park. In J. S. Smith (Ed.), *Explorations in Place Attachment* (pp. 117–131). London, UK: Routledge.

Chapter 4: In search of roots: Restoring continuity in a mobile world

Maria Lewicka

THE WORLD ON THE MOVE

Human beings have always been moving although some periods in the history of humankind were marked by greater mobility while others were more stable. About 40,000 years ago our ancestors left the African savannah and spread in different directions populating successive continents. Ever since that time, people moved, driven by both push and pull forces. Overpopulation, climatic changes, wars and political conflicts on one hand, and the promise of better living conditions and new territories, on the other, made people leave their homelands and take the challenge of exploring the unknown.

Movement and migrations characterize both ancient and modern societies. Few residents of contemporary western cities or towns can trace their origin in their present residence to more than three or four generations back and this concerns both the mobile American society and the relatively immobile countries in Central-Eastern Europe (Cohn & Morin, 2008; Lewicka, 2012). Given that mobility has been accompanying humankind since its early origin, it is intriguing that only in the last couple of decades social scientists took active interest in its various forms and psychological consequences. This has been termed the "mobility shift" and contrasts with the "sedentary" paradigm that until recently dominated social sciences, particularly sociology, human geography, and environmental psychology (Cresswell, 2006, 2010, 2012; Hannam, Sheller, & Urry, 2006; Sheller & Urry, 2006). Focus on fixity was best expressed through the concept of place attachment and the emphasis on the value of rootedness (Hay, 1998; Low & Altman, 1992). It has been assumed—and there was rich empirical support for this claim—that people value stable relations with their places of residence, and that disruption of this relation is a cause of psychological disturbances, equally severe as disruption of the relationship with a loved one (Brown & Perkins, 1992; Fried, 1963; Fullilove, 2005). These findings were difficult to reconcile with the new paradigm that assumed that mobility is a norm rather than exception in human life. As Cresswell (2006, p. 1) put it, "mobility is central to what it is to be human."

In this chapter, I will address the issue of the relationship between residential mobility and place attachment. First, I will posit that the way mobility may affect our emotional bonds with places depends on many factors, of which perhaps the most important is the extent to which it is forced or voluntary. Second, based on existing research findings, I will argue that although residential mobility indeed is increasingly present in our everyday life, we should not close our eyes to the even more frequent cases of immobility. Third, I will present evidence that place attachment is not a uniform concept and that dependent on its type it may stand in different relations, positive or negative, to the duration of residency, and thus mobility. Finally, I will present arguments that people feel an emotional bond with a place based on the perceived continuity of oneself-in-that-place. Since mobility, particularly residential mobility, means a disruption of this continuity, the chapter will conclude with some speculations, supported by empirical evidence, on what measures people can take in order to restore the broken continuity and thus "replant" or "reattach" to a new place. The chapter is largely based on findings collected in the countries of the Global North (the US and Europe) although some reference to the Global South is also made. Nevertheless, as the evidence from cultural psychology demonstrates (e.g., Nisbett, 2004), neither the psychological phenomena nor their underlying processes are universal and therefore should not be generalized from one to another cultural context.

MOBILITY: THE PUSH AND THE PULL DRIVES

Although most of our motives are mixed, people's motivation to move may be roughly divided into the "push" and the "pull" drives.[1] In other words, one may move because one has been pushed out of the present place by unfavorable circumstances or some external (e.g., political) decision or because one has been pulled by the attraction of a new place. It seems that whereas the early studies carried out within the "sedentary" paradigm focused mostly on the (negative) consequences of the push moves, the "mobility paradigm" nowadays tends first and foremost to look for (positive) examples of the pull ones. Hence, dependent on the paradigm, the emphasis is placed either on the value of stability or of movement (for more detail on the implications of these two strands, see Cresswell, 2006).

The consequences of the push moves are hardly positive. The first-known scientific observation of the deleterious consequences that an unwanted break with the home place can have on people's well-being was made in 1688 by the Swiss medical student, Johannes Hofer. In his doctoral dissertation, Hofer described symptoms of a malady observed among Swiss soldiers and mercenaries who had to leave their Alpine homes to wage war. The symptoms included constant thinking about home, insomnia, heart problems, and fever (McCann, 1941). The author concludes that the only cure for this malady for which he coined the word "nostalgia" (from *nostos*—return to the native land and *algos*—pain) was to return home. Much later, in the early 1960s of the twentieth century, a sociologist Marc

Fried (1963) investigated reactions of Boston inhabitants to the forced relocation to seemingly better housing conditions during the so-called urban renewal project in the West End, observing similar psychological and physiological reactions as the ones described 300 years ago by Hofer. The need for stable relations with homes was so strong that it led Fried (2000) to question the value of place attachment since it inhibits mobility and thwarts chances for individual development.

Forced relocation is almost always a traumatic life event. It means giving up control over one's life, breaking ties with the community, and replacing the familiar with the unknown. The consequences may be particularly detrimental in the case of those who do not have sufficient psychological resources to face new challenges, such was the case of the majority of those forcefully relocated during the urban renewal projects (Fullilove, 2005; Manzo, Kleit, & Couch, 2008). Similar findings have been reported in other social and political contexts. For example, Boğaç (2009) described weak emotional bonds with new places of residence and a sense of temporariness among forcefully relocated Cyprus Turks even thirty years after relocation. Similar reactions were observed in Israel among the forcefully relocated Israeli citizens (Possick, 2004; Schnell & Mishal, 2008), and the forcefully relocated Poles and Ukrainians after WWII (Wylęgała, 2014). Scanlon and Devine (2001) reviewed literature concerning the influence of frequent moves on school achievements of children from low-income families, another vulnerable group, pointing to their negative consequences both for school grades and for the development of social ties with peers. Exhaustive reviews of the (negative) consequences of unwanted and unplanned moves have been presented by Heller (1982) and Brown and Perkins (1992). Now, in the twenty-first century, the world witnesses waves of political and economic migrations from war and the poverty-stricken countries, such as Syria, Sudan, and Afghanistan. With the global temperature rising with the present speed we can soon expect massive migrations of people from desert areas of Africa and Asia to the more benevolent territories (Bates, 2002; Epule, Peng, & Lepage, 2015). Our present emphasis on the pull motives should not make us close our eyes to the tragedy of those whose motivation to move is driven by external forces.

Nevertheless, along with the processes of globalization, technological development, and the growing affluence of western societies, both in the works of scholars and in the actual behavior of citizens, particularly those residing in the Global North, the negative "push" drives have given way to the positive "pull" motivation. People—at least in western societies—at present move not only to escape unbearable life conditions but also to maximize profits and personal experiences. Mobility has become a part of a lifestyle and of a professional career for people with options and resources. People find jobs in new locations, spend holidays in hitherto unknown parts of the world, marry partners of different ethnicities, and consequently change their country of residency. Students and academics participate in conferences and study programs abroad. With the growing affluence of western societies, people can afford to have more than one home, sometimes located in two different countries (Gustafson, 2009; Williams & van Patten, 2006). Opening of borders and abolition of visas for the majority of European and American citizens, together with cheap flights and fast transportation systems, have intensified regular travels within the continents and across the ocean.

This latter type of mobility differs from forced relocations. First, it is often self-initiated and therefore accompanied by the sense of control on the part of the moving agent. Second, a great number of moves are temporary like when people oscillate between two different residencies, commute to work, take holidays abroad, or participate in conferences. These moves are accompanied by a sense of thrill and exploration rather than nostalgia after the irreversibly lost place. Third, and perhaps the most importantly, these new forms of mobility become increasingly common due to the rising affluence of societies where some citizens can afford to lead the often costly life in multiple places and who have enough resources, both material and social, to cope with new situations. This also includes the scholars themselves who undoubtedly belong to the most mobile fractions of their societies (Zencey, 1996). One can even speculate that it is the mobile life of contemporary academics that initiated the mobility paradigm in science and the unconditionally positive evaluation given to the mobility-related terms (Cresswell, 2006).

At the same time, the researchers began to wonder how can the new paradigm be reconciled with the abundant evidence that points to the value of stable relations with place and to psychological profits drawn from place attachment, collected so far (Di Masso et al., 2019; Gustafson, 2002). Two possible answers are offered here and they will be developed in the consecutive sections: the first one questions the claim that (residential) mobility is an omnipresent phenomenon. This leaves room for studies of the rootedness-based traditional forms of place attachment. The second argument questions the homogeneous nature of place attachment and assumes that some people may get attached to places even if they have not resided there long.

SPACES OF PLACES OR SPACES OF FLOW?

Paradigms sensitize scholars to selectively look for the paradigm-confirming evidence. Hence, along with the "mobility paradigm" shift, there is a tendency to ignore the fact that the residential "spaces of flow" are a share of a smaller portion of the society than are "spaces of places" (Castells, 2000), and hence that the majority of the populations tend to be relatively immobile. If, as the statistics show (The UN Migration Agency, 2018), international migration in 2017 amounted to 3.3 percent of the global population (the figure is relatively stable over longer time periods), then it means that every year almost 97 percent of people stay in their own country of birth. According to the same source, the within country migration in 2017 was 10 percent of the world population, which means that 90 percent did not move home. Residential (im)mobility is present both in the Global North and in the Global South. Data concerning American residential mobility based on systematic Census data show a declining trend, reaching 10.1 percent in year 2017, the lowest number since 1948, and the same seems to apply to residential mobility in the UK (Frequent Movers, 2019). European countries differ in how mobile their citizens are (Eurostat, 2017), with people in the Nordic countries much more mobile than those in the south and the east. Nevertheless even in the most mobile Sweden, about 60 percent did not move home in the five-year period prior to the survey. As people become richer, the residential mobility declines: home owners move home significantly less often than renters. Most of the moves are before the age of 30, after that people tend to settle down (Eurostat, 2017). People move homes on average four times in their life (Frequent Movers, 2019). However, most of the moves are in the close vicinity of their previous home, within the same city or region and this is true both for the Global North (Cohn & Morin, 2008; Eurostat, 2017; Laczko, 2005) and the Global South (Awad & Natarajn, 2018). This has consequences for place attachment: the smaller the distance from the previous residence is, the easier the adjustment to a new place (Heller, 1982; Tognoli, 2003).

The above does not preclude that people nowadays are influenced by a great variety of forms and consequences of mobility (Cresswell, 2006; Hannam, Sheller, & Urry, 2006) which can affect their place attachment. For example, people may change their views of their residence place and hence decrease or increase attachment when comparing it with other places during their tourist or professional visits (Case, 1996), when facing the growing ethnic diversity of their neighborhoods, due to the inflow of immigrants (Dinesen, Schaeffer, & Sønderskov, 2020), or when a highway or other globalization product is built close to their living place (Devine-Wright, 2009). Internet connection and virtual mobility may insert a paradoxical effect on people's residential mobility, as it may decrease the propensity for physical movements. Easy access to internet-based communication over long distances, increased popularity of telework, distance learning instead of physical school attendance, or video conferences that replace physical presence—all this may make radical changes of the residence place unnecessary (Breines, Raghuram, & Gunter, 2019; Cooke & Shuttleworth, 2017). All of this taken into account, it seems that the future of the studies that relate place attachment to mobility should perhaps focus also on the effects of the exposure to other products of the globalized and mobile world and not only on the effects of moving homes.

PLACE ATTACHMENT: ITS MEASUREMENT AND TYPES

Place attachment is traditionally defined as an affective bond that connects people to places (Low & Altman, 1992), usually residential ones but also places of recreation, second homes, places of work or sport activities (for a review, see Farnum, Hall, & Kruger, 2005; Lewicka, 2011; Manzo, 2003). The term "affective bond" implies a special emotional relationship. Like other forms of attachment (e.g., interpersonal attachment, Ainsworth, 1989; Scannell & Gifford, 2014), place attachment implies "anchoring" emotions in the object of attachment, feelings of belonging, willingness to stay close, and a wish to return when away.

There is a significant body of evidence, collected with existent measurement instruments, to suggest that the majority of people worldwide feel attached to their places of residence. A glance at a summary of results drawn from quantitative surveys in countries, such as the US (Nielsen-Pincus, Hall, Force, & Wulfhorst, 2010; White, Virden, & Riper, 2008), Germany (Lalli,1992), Italy (Bonaiuto, Fornara, & Bonnes, 2006), Spain (Hernandez, Hidalgo, Salazar-Laplace, & Hess, 2007), France (Fleury-Bahi, Félonneau, & Marchand, 2008), Great Britain (Devine-Wright, 2013), or Poland and Ukraine (Lewicka, 2012), show that in all studies the average score of declared place attachment is above the midpoint of the scale, somewhere between 3 and 4 on a 5-point scale, between 4 and 5 on a 7-point scale, and above 2.5 on a 4-point scale.

Most studies show that duration of residency, the opposite of residential mobility, along with strong neighborhood ties, is one of the most consistent predictors of place attachment (Lewicka, 2011; Smaldone, 2006). This finding, however, at least partly may be an artifact of the employed methodology. Since it has been assumed that attached people stay longer in the place than those who are unattached (Riger & Lavrakas, 1981), the most popular scales of place attachment usually include items that directly address this assumption (e.g., "I would regret having to move to another neighbourhood/house/city," Hernandez et al., 2007; "It would be very hard for me to leave the neighborhood", Bonaiuto et al., 2006). No wonder then that duration of residency has been found to be one of the most consistent predictors of place attachment.

However, is rootedness produced by length of residency the only form of place attachment? Almost thirty years ago, in the book which is a predecessor of this one, David Hummon (1992) presented a five-fold typology of different ways in which people can relate to their places of residence. This typology went beyond the habitual concept of place attachment as a homogenous phenomenon by distinguishing its two qualitatively different types (everyday and ideological rootedness) and three different types of unattachment (alienation, place relativity, and placelessness). The psychological reality of these five types of relatedness, originally identified on the basis of qualitative interviews performed in an American town, was later confirmed in two country-wide quantitative surveys, one carried out in Poland and the other in Ukraine (Lewicka, 2013). Similar types have also been identified in Britain as a result of qualitative research (Bailey, Devine-Wright, & Batel, 2016).

One of the measures used by Lewicka (2013) to create this typology was a scale of attachment to one's own city/town that distinguished between traditional attachment (agreement with statements such as "Even if there are better places, I am not going to move out of this city") and active attachment (items such as "I like to wander around my city and discover new places"). Both scales correlated with the "standard" place attachment scale (Lewicka, 2013).

The two forms of place attachment, differentiated by Hummon, turned out to represent cores of two qualitatively different personality types (Lewicka, 2013).

The traditionally attached people were less educated and older, their social relations were mostly restricted to the closest social circles, they were generally less active and held more conservative values than did the actively attached participants. In comparison, the actively attached were better educated, had more extensive networks of social ties, including both close and more distant social relations, and scored higher on a number of measures of cultural capital, such as reading and musical preferences (Lewicka, 2013). In short, while the traditionally attached were mostly" localized," the actively attached were able to combine local engagement with more "cosmopolitan" interests (Lewicka, 2013).

Given the psychological differences between these two types of attachment, we expect that they might also differ in the nature of processes through which they develop emotional bonds with residence places. The traditionally attached represents the "everyday" type of attachment; it is therefore plausible to expect that their emotional ties are mostly due to their autobiographical rootedness in the place—as a function of residence length. In contrast, attachment of individuals who represent the self-initiated active type of attachment should be less related to the length of residency in the place. Several studies by the author of this chapter on the nationwide samples and in several individual cities in Poland, Ukraine, and Lithuania between 2009 and 2014 confirmed these predictions: while both "standard" place attachment and the traditional attachment correlated significantly with the length of residency, active attachment either was uncorrelated or even correlated negatively (Lewicka, 2018).

Active attachment may help people adapt to a new culture. Niewczas (2017) in an internet study of Polish new immigrants to Ireland found that the best positive predictor of acculturation into an Irish society was active attachment to the new city of residence, while traditional attachment and attachment to the place of origin left in Poland were negative predictors. These findings demonstrate that mobility does not preclude place attachment and that some people are capable of developing emotional bonds with places in which they have not resided long.

Similar conclusions have been drawn by other scholars. For example, Gustafson (2009) showed that Swedish international business travelers, that is, a highly mobile professional group with a strong cosmopolitan orientation, displayed a stronger attachment to their closest neighborhood and were even more involved in local affairs than were the more "localized" Swedish citizens (Gustafson, 2009). Also having two residences, one in the country of origin, another in a more benevolent climate, does not undermine place attachment to the home in the country of origin (Gustafson, 2009; McHugh & Mings, 1996). In survey studies, carried out in Britain, Savage, Bagnall, and Longhurst (2005) distinguished between "elective belonging" that depicted newly settled residents who actively chose their place of living and "dwelling" descriptive of the long-term residents of the same area. Both groups showed attachment to their present places of residency despite the differences in residence duration. A subsequent survey of a representative sample of British citizens (Bennett et al., 2009; Savage, 2010) revealed psychological differences between elective belongers and dwellers that were similar to the differences between actively and traditionally attached in Lewicka's (2013) study. One of the differences consisted in the elective belongers having higher cultural capital, a more positive attitude towards reading books and displaying higher cultural activity in the form of museum attendance and interest in historical heritage than dwellers (Savage, 2010). As I will show in the last section of the chapter, these are resources that help to grow roots in a new place.

The above does not mean that all people are attached to their places of residency. Among the five types of people-place bonds distinguished by Hummon (1992), and confirmed by Lewicka (2013) and Bailey et al. (2016), three types, place relativity (conditional place attachment), alienation (dislike of place), and placelessness (place indifference), were less attached than others. Of these, the most interesting is the placeless type that includes people who do not need place for self-definition and life satisfaction. In Lewicka's (2012) studies, education, that is, upward mobility, was positively associated with two of the five types: the actively attached and the placeless (Lewicka, 2012, 2013). This means that as a society moves up the educational ladder, its members will direct their activity either at their local environment, increasing the number of grassroots activists, or at targets outside their locality, such as family, friends, or an individual's professional career. Certain combinations of both are probable, too.

RESTORING CONTINUITY IN A MOBILE WORLD

There is abundant evidence that sense of continuity, both on the individual and collective level, is an important motive of personal and group identity (Sani, Herrera, and Bowe, 2009; Smeekes & Verkuyten, 2014). Research demonstrates that children with whom parents talk about their family history are better adjusted and have stronger identities and self-esteem than those who only live in the present (Fivush, Bohanek, & Duke, 2008). In support of this, Apfelbaum (2000) cited findings collected among immigrant families in France showing that their children were more successful in a new place when "they have heard stories at home of what life was before their parents migrated and when they therefore have a sense of continuity between past and present" (p. 1011). As Dunkel (2005) argued, most existing measures of identity share a significant amount of variance with continuity; thus, the two are conceptually related.

Perceived continuity of oneself in a place contributes to place identification and place attachment. Of the two major identity motives, distinctiveness and continuity (Twigger-Ross & Uzzell, 1996; Vignoles, 2011), the place-related continuity seems even more important for development of emotional bonds with a place than place-related distinctiveness. In my own studies (Lewicka, 2017), carried out in seven big Polish cities, including the country capital, sense of place-continuity ("I feel that my life is a part of my city's history") was a better predictor of attachment to the city than place-distinctiveness ("That I am from this city makes me distinct from residents of other cities").

Place-related continuity is disrupted when people leave the place. If the move is temporary, the distance from home may reinforce people's ties with their residence places in line with the known proverb that "absence makes the heart grow fonder" (Case, 1996). When, however, the move is permanent or long term, the continuity with the place of origin is broken, and new bonds will have to be developed that will restore continuity (Brown & Perkins, 1992). In the last section of this chapter, I focus on the measures that mobile people can take in order to restore their sense of place-related continuity and develop attachments to a new place.

Places can serve as sources of personal continuity and they can do it in at least three different ways. Two of them have been described by Twigger-Ross and Uzzell (1996), and called, respectively, place-congruency and place-reference. **Place-congruent continuity** refers to the sense of personal continuity, which is based on a match between the self-concept and the place's features, and the **place-referent continuity** refers to a situation when the place serves as a trigger for autobiographical or group memories. The third way is through the **perceived continuity of place**, that is, it refers to a situation where place is perceived through its history and thus when the focus is on the continuity not of the person but of the place (Lewicka, 2012; Wheeler, 2017).

Restoring place-congruent continuity

If one has control over one's moves, it is possible to satisfy the place-congruent continuity by choosing a new location that is consistent with one's self-concept and life style. Feldman (1990) used the term "settlement identity" for a similar phenomenon, describing people's identification not with specific places but with categories of places (e.g., myself as an urban vs. countryside person). Choosing a place which matches one's self-concept and which has familiar features reinforces the sense of personal continuity and thus helps to grow roots in a new place. Oishi, Miao, Koo, Kiesling, and Ratliff (2012) empirically demonstrated that residential mobility fosters familiarity seeking and familiarity liking. This preference for familiarity is, according to the authors, the reason why the US, which is one of the most individualistic nations in the world, at the same time has the most uniform landscape (housing, shopping malls, food chains, etc.). In five consecutive studies, including experimental ones, Oishi et al. (2012) demonstrated the causal link between propensity to move and preference for the familiar elements of an urban landscape.

Restoring place-referent continuity

Place-referent continuity is more difficult to restore in a short time. Place-related memories, particularly those that concern childhood places, are an important source of personal identity (Cooper Marcus, 1992; Knez, 2006) and they constitute what Rowles (1990) has termed "autobiographical insideness." The place-referent continuity is based on both conscious and implicit memories of places.

Seamon (1980) introduced the concept of "time-space routines" (also termed "place-ballet") to describe automatic, daily routines performed in specific places, which he viewed as the basis for the existential relationship between people and places. Implicit memories are acquired through "living" a place and therefore need time to develop. Relocation means disruption of habits and it can lead to estrangement and feelings of alienation.

However, autobiographical memories associated with previous places of residence can be used as a means of adapting to new places and thus can help mobile individuals to develop attachment to new places. Recent research on the psychological functions of nostalgia offers some ideas on how this can happen. As the huge research program concerned with psychological functions of nostalgia shows (for a review, see Routledge, 2016), nostalgia should not be understood as a sentimental longing for what is no longer present but rather as a powerful psychological resource which people spontaneously use in order to restore self-continuity disrupted by major life turns and traumatic life events (McAdams, 2008; Sedikides, Wildschut, Gaertner, Routledge, & Arndt, 2008). Nostalgia is adaptive: it helps to put together broken parts, builds a bridge between past and present, increases self-esteem and life satisfaction, and reinforces social ties. One may expect that it will also strengthen bonds with the present residence place as well.

Nostalgia-triggering major life events might affect life through different means, not all of them involving relocation. However, there are good grounds to assume that nostalgic autobiographical memories may also help to overcome spatial discontinuities. Although the term "nostalgia" has not been used by Rishbeth and Powell (2013), their qualitative research carried out among immigrants to Britain confirms the role of autobiographical memories associated with the places of origin in shaping attachments to new places. According to the authors (p. 175) "(the memories) shape a sense of belonging, which allows individuals who are comparatively new to the area to develop feelings of rootedness."

Another example of the constructive role of nostalgia is the history of Eva Hoffman, a Polish Jew born in Cracow, Poland, whose family survived WWII, and who emigrated to Canada with her parents and younger sister when she was a teenager. For many years, she fought with a profound sense of un-rootedness in the new place. This resulted in an autobiographical book "Lost in translation" that records her struggle "to throw a bridge between the present and the past" and thus "make the time move" in the new place (Hoffman, 1989, pp. 116–117). Torn between nostalgia and alienation, she succeeded in overcoming her sense of un-rootedness through investigations of her personal past. Interestingly, as her reminiscences show, she obtained a fast foothold in her new country only after having paid a real visit to her old home in Cracow in the mid-1970s.

Restoring continuity through exploring local history
The third way in which place can be used to restore the disrupted continuity is through the **perception of continuity of the new place**, that is, through taking active interest in the history of this place. Places, like people, have history. Some

places have a longer history than others, and obviously a long history is a source of pride for its residents (Lowenthal, 1985). History is an asset of a place. Cities or city districts with long histories are tourist attractions, those without history usually are not. There are numerous psychological benefits of studying the past. Historicity distinguishes meaningful locations from standardized non-places (Beatley, 2004; Norberg-Schultz, 1980), and historical places are objects of stronger emotional attachments than places deprived of history (Devine-Wright & Lyons, 1997; Lewicka, 2012).

Perceived continuity of a place contributes to the sense of personal continuity of its residents and thus to place attachment. I will therefore posit that active interest taken in the history of one's new place (e.g., one's city, street or house) is a means through which a newcomer may feel a part of the place's history. "The more we understand about the beginnings and evolution of a place, the greater importance that place will assume in our lives. These are connections we need for our sense of groundedness and are requisite elements in building commitments to place" (Beatley, 2004, p. 53).

There is growing empirical evidence, drawn from both quantitative and qualitative research, which supports this claim. Rebecca Wheeler (2017), based on the qualitative studies carried out among inhabitants of a small rural English village, including members of local history groups, demonstrated the role of the "creative nostalgia," as she called it, in providing a sense of continuity among the village residents. Moreover, much against the popular claim that focus on the past promotes a wish to preserve the status quo, this sense of history-based continuity not only facilitated place attachment but also made people more willing to accept modernization changes to their rural landscape.

In my own studies that included interviews with country- and city-wide representative samples carried out in three different countries, Poland, Ukraine, and Lithuania, the declared interest in local history consistently predicted attachment to places of residency (Lewicka, 2008, 2012). Interest in local history was also found to facilitate place attachment among fresh immigrants to a new country. Niewczas (2017) in an internet study of the Polish immigrants to Ireland (between one and five years of stay) showed that it was interest in the local history that was the most significant predictor of attachment to the new place of residency; it was more important than time of residency, acculturation to the Irish culture, or command of the (English) language.

CONCLUSIONS

Evidence shows that mobility does not preclude attachment. There is also evidence for the opposite claim: mobility, particularly forced mobility, may undermine attachment and lead to root shock. If one looks at these two types of evidence not as a manifestation of universal rules, proof for either the sedentary or nomadic concept of human nature, but as related to different types of mobility and different forms of attachment, then the contradiction disappears. People whose attachment is mostly due to the place-dependent daily routines and habits may respond nega-tively to relocation, while those whose attachment is a function of active coping may be able to adapt to a new environment with relative ease. In this chapter, I have also shown that people may resort to different measures in order to restore the broken continuity: they may choose places that match their self-concept, they may use nostalgic memories to build a bridge between their past and present, or they may focus on the place history and thus increase their sense of sharing personal continuity with that of the new place. As Michael Mayerfield Bell (1997) says, we inherit places, whether it is our new office or neighborhood, together with the "ghosts" of those who lived there before us. These ghosts give meanings to the place and help us feel one with it but, as time goes on, we replace them with our own ghost—a sign that we have appropriated the place and made it our own.

ACKNOWLEDGEMENT

Preparation of this chapter was supported by the National Science Center, the Opus grant Nr 2017/25/B/HS6/00137.

NOTE

1 The pull-push is a continuum rather than distinct categories. Mobility for entertainment such as tourism and mobility as an escape from war or persecution are in reality two poles of a large spectrum of the pull-push mobility drives, of which the majority is a mixture of the two. According to Awad and Natarajn (2018), the push-pull distinction is political: many state laws treat better the "push" than the "pull" migrants.

REFERENCES

Ainsworth, M. D. S. (1989). Attachment beyond infancy. *American Psychologist, 44*, 709–716.

Apfelbaum, E. R. (2000). And now what, after such tribulations? Memory and dislocation in the era of uprooting. *American Psychologist, 55*, 1008–1013.

Awad, I., & Natarajn, U. (2018). Migration myths and the global south. *Cairo Review, 30*, 46–54.

Bailey, E., Devine-Wright, P., & Batel, S. (2016). Using a narrative approach to understand place attachments and responses to power line proposals: The importance of life-place trajectories. *Journal of Environmental Psychology, 48*, 200–211. DOI:10.1016/j.jenvp.2016.10.006

Bates, D. C. (2002). Environmental refugees? Classifying human migrations caused by envir-onmental change. *Population and Environment, 23*(5), 465–477.

Beatley, T. (2004). *Native to nowhere: Sustaining home and community in a global age.* Washington: Island Press.

Bennett, T., Savage, M., Silva, E., Warde, A., Gayo-Cal, M., & Wright, D. (2009). *Culture, class, distinction.* London: Routledge.

Boğaç, C. (2009). Place attachment in a foreign settlement. *Journal of Environmental Psychology, 29*, 267–278.

Bonaiuto, M., Fornara, F., & Bonnes, M. (2006). Perceived residential environment quality in middle- and low-extension Italian cities. *European Review of Applied Psychology, 56*, 23–34.

Breines, M. R., Raghuram, P., & Gunter, A. (2019). Infrastructures of immobility: Enabling international distance education students in Africa to *not* move. *Mobilities*, *14*(4), 484–499. DOI:10.1080/17450101.2019.1618565

Brown, B. B., & Perkins, D. D. (1992). Disruptions in place attachment. In I. Altman, & S. M. Low, (Eds.). *Place attachment* (pp. 279–304). New York: Plenum Press.

Case, D. (1996). Contributions of journeys away to the definition of home: An empirical study of a dialectical process. *Journal of Environmental Psychology*, *16*, 1–15.

Castells, M. (2000). *The rise of the network society: The information age: Economy, society, and culture*. Oxford: Blackwell Publishers Ltd.

Cohn, D., & Morin, R. (2008). Who moves? Who stays put? Where's home? Pew demographic trends. Washington DC: Pew Research Center. <http://pewsocialtrends.org/assets/pdf/Movers-and-Stayers.pdf> (accessed 15 March 2012).

Cooke, T. J., & Shuttleworth, I. (2017). The effects of information and communication technologies on residential mobility and migration. *Population, Space and Place*, *24*, e2111. https://doi.org/10.1002/psp.2111

Cooper Marcus, C. (1992). Environmental memories. In I. Altman, & S. M. Low (Eds.), *Place attachment* (pp. 87–112). New York and London: Plenum Press.

Cresswell, T. (2006). *On the move: Mobility in the modern western world*. New York, London: Routledge.

Cresswell, T. (2010). Mobilities I: Catching up. *Progress in Human Geography*, *35*, 550–558.

Cresswell, T. (2012). Mobilities II: Still. *Progress in Human Geography*, *36*, 645–653.

Devine-Wright, P. (2009). Rethinking NIMBYism: The role of place attachment and place identity in explaining place-protective action. *Journal of Community and Applied Social Psychology*, *19*, 426–441. https://doi.org/10.1002/casp.1004

Devine-Wright, P. (2013). Explaining 'NIMBY' objections to a power line: The role of personal, place attachment and project-related factors. *Environment & Behavior*, *45*, 761–781.

Devine-Wright, P., & Lyons, E. (1997). Remembering pasts and representing places: The construction of national identities in Ireland. *Journal of Environmental Psychology*, *17*, 33–45.

Di Masso, A., Williams, D. R., Raymond, C., Buchecker, M., Degenhardt, B., Devine-Wright, P., … & von Wirth, T. (2019). Between fixities and flows: Navigating place attachments in an increasingly mobile world. *Journal of Environmental Psychology*, *61*, 125–133. https://doi.org/10.1016/j.jenvp.2019.01.006

Dinesen, P. T., Schaeffer, M., & Sønderskov, K. M. (2020). Ethnic diversity and social trust: A narrative and meta-analytical review. *Annual Review of Political Science*, *23*, 441–465.

Dunkel, C. S. (2005). The relation between self-continuity and measures of identity. *Identity: An International Journal of Theory and Research*, *5*, 21–34. DOI:10.1207/s1532706xid0501_2

Epule, T. E., Peng, C., & Lepage, L. (2015). Environmental refugees in sub-Saharan Africa: A review of perspectives on the trends, causes, challenges and way forward. *GeoJournal*, *80*, 79–92. https://doi.org/10.1007/s10708-014-9528-z

Farnum, J., Hall, T., & Kruger, L. E. (2005). *Sense of place in natural resource recreation and tourism: An evaluation and assessment of research findings*. General Technical Report, PNW-GTR-660, United States Department of Agriculture, Pacific Northwestern Research Station.

Eurostat. (2017). People in the EU—Statistics on geographic mobility. https://ec.europa.eu/eurostat/statistics-explained/index.php/People_in_the_EU_-_statistics_on_geographic_mobility

Feldman, R. (1990). Settlement identity: Psychological bonds with home places in a mobile society. *Environment and Behavior*, *22*, 183–229.

Fivush, R., Bohanek, J. G., & Duke, M. (2008). The intergenerational self: Subjective perspective and family history. In F. Sani (Ed.), *Self continuity* (pp. 131–143). New York: Psychology Press.

Fleury-Bahi, G., Félonneau, M-L., & Marchand, D. (2008). Processes of place identification and residential satisfaction. *Environment and Behavior, 40*, 669–682.

Frequent Movers. (2019). https://masterremovers.co.uk/2019/01/17/how-frequently-do-people-move-house-in-the-uk-compared-to-europe/

Fried, M. (1963). Grieving for a lost home. In L. J. Duhl (Ed.), *The urban condition* (pp. 151–171). New York: Basic Books.

Fried, M. (2000). Continuities and discontinuities of place. *Journal of Environmental Psychology, 20*, 193–205.

Fullilove, M. T. (2005). *Root shock. How tearing up city neighborhoods hurts America, and what we can do about it*. New York: One World, Balantine Books.

Gustafson, P. (2002). *Place, place attachment and mobility: Three sociological studies*. Goteborg Studies in Sociology No 6. Department of Sociology, Gotenburg University.

Gustafson, P. (2009). More cosmopolitan, no less local. *European Societies, 11*, 25–47.

Hannam, K., Sheller, M., & Urry, J. (2006). Editorial: Mobilities, immobilities and moorings. *Mobilities, 1*, 1–22.

Hay, R. (1998). Sense of place in developmental context. *Journal of Environmental Psychology, 18*, 5–29.

Heller, T. (1982). The effects of involuntary residential relocation: A review. *American Journal of Community Psychology, 10*, 471–492.

Hernandez, B., Hidalgo, M. C., Salazar-Laplace, M. E., & Hess, S. (2007). Place attachment and place identity in natives and non-natives. *Journal of Environmental Psychology, 27*, 310–319.

Hoffman, E. (1989). *Lost in translation*. London: Vintage Books.

Hummon, D. M. (1992). Community attachment. Local sentiment and sense of place. In I. Altman, & S. M. Low (Eds.), *Place attachment* (pp. 253–277). New York and London: Plenum Press ISSP.

Knez, I. (2006). Autobiographical memories for places. *Memory, 14*, 359–377.

Laczko, L. S. (2005). National and local attachments in a changing world system: Evidence from an international survey. *International Review of Sociology, 15*, 517–528.

Lalli, M. (1992). Urban-related identity: Theory, measurement, and empirical findings. *Journal of Environmental Psychology, 12*, 285–303.

Lewicka, M. (2008). Place attachment, place identity and place memory: Restoring the forgotten city past. *Journal of Environmental Psychology, 28*, 209–231.

Lewicka, M. (2011). Place attachment: How far have we come in the last 40 years? *Journal of Environmental Psychology, 31*, 207–230.

Lewicka, M. (2012). *Psychologia miejsca (Psychology of place)*. Warsaw: Wydawnictwo Naukowe "Scholar".

Lewicka, M. (2013). Localism and activity as two dimensions of people-place bonding: The role of cultural capital. *Journal of Environmental Psychology, 36*, 43–53. http://dx.doi.org/10.1016/j.jenvp.2013.07.002

Lewicka, M. (2017). *Place identity: Between ethocentrism and openness. Role of the perceived continuity of place*. Paper presented at the annual meeting of the Polish Association of Social Psychology, September, Toruń, Poland.

Lewicka, M. (2018). *Mobility does not prevent place attachment: On active and everyday attachments in a mobile world*. Paper presented at the IAPS conference, July, Rome, Italy.

Lowenthal, D. (1985). *The past is a foreign country*. Cambridge: Cambridge University Press.

Low, S. M., & Altman, I. (1992). Place attachment: A conceptual inquiry. In I. Altman, & S. M. Low (Eds.), *Place attachment* (pp. 1–12). New York: Plenum Press.

Manzo, L. (2003). Beyond house and haven: Toward revisioning of emotional relationship with places. *Journal of Environmental Psychology*, *23*, 47–61.

Manzo, L. C., Kleit, R. G., & Couch, D. (2008). "Moving once is like having your house on fire three times": The experience of place and displacement among residents of a public housing site. *Urban Studies*, *45*(9), 1855–1878.

Mayerfield Bell, M. (1997). The ghosts of place. *Theory & Society*, *26*, 813–836.

McAdams, D. P. (2008). Personal narratives and the life story. In J. Robins, & L. Pervin (Eds.), *Handbook of personality: Theory and research* (pp. 242–262). New York: Guilford Press.

McCann, W. H. (1941). Nostalgia: A review of the literature. *Psychological Bulletin*, *38*, 165–182. DOI:10.1037/h0057354

McHugh, K. E., & Mings, R. C. (1996). The circle of migration: Attachment to place and aging. *Annals of the Association of American Geographers*, *86*, 530–550.

Nielsen-Pincus, M., Hall, T., Force, J. E., & Wulfhorst, J. D. (2010). Sociodemographic effects on place bonding. *Journal of Environmental Psychology*, *30*, 443–454.

Niewczas, K. (2017). *Polscy migranci w Irlandii. Przywiązanie do miejsca zamieszkania a strategie akulturacyjne (Polish immigrants in Ireland: Place attachment and accultiuration strategies)*. Unpublished MA Dissertation, University of Warsaw, Warsaw.

Nisbett, R. E. (2004). *The geography of thought. How Asians and Westerners think differently … and why*. New York: Free Press.

Norberg-Schultz, C. (1980). *Genius loci. Towards a phenomenology of architecture*. New York: Rizzoli.

Oishi, S., Miao, F. F., Koo, M., Kiesling, J., & Ratliff, K. A. (2012). Residential mobility breeds familiarity seeking. *Journal of Personality and Social Psychology*, *102*, 149–162.

Possick, C. (2004). Locating and relocating oneself as a Jewish Settler on the West Bank: Ideological squatting and eviction. *Journal of Environmental Psychology*, *24*, 53–69.

Riger, S., & Lavrakas, P. J. (1981). Community ties: Patterns of attachment and social interaction in urban neighborhoods. *American Journal of Community Psychology*, *9*, 55–66.

Rishbeth, C., & Powell, M. (2013). Place attachment and memory: Landscapes of belonging as experienced post-migration. *Landscape Research*, *38*, 160–178.

Routledge, C. (2016). *Nostalgia. A psychological resource*. New York and London: Routledge, Taylor & Francis Group.

Rowles, G. D. (1990). Place attachment among the small town elderly. *Journal of Rural Community Psychology*, *11*, 103–120.

Sani, F., Herrera, M., & Bowe, M. (2009). Perceived collective continuity and ingroup identification as defence against death awareness. *Journal of Experimental Social Psychology*, *45*, 242–245.

Savage, M. (2010). The politics of elective belonging. *Housing, Theory and Society*, *27*, 115–161.

Savage, M., Bagnall, G., & Longhurst, B. (2005). *Globalization and belonging*. London: Sage Publications.

Scanlon, E., & Devine, K. (2001). Residential mobility and youth well-being: Research, policy and practice issues. *Journal of Sociology and Social Welfare*, *XXVIII*, 119–138.

Scannell, L., & Gifford, R. (2014). Comparing the theories of interpersonal and place attachment. In: L. Manzo, & P. Devine-Wright (Eds.), *Place attachment: Advances in theory, methods and research* (pp. 23–36). New York: Routledge/Francis & Taylor.

Schnell, I., & Mishal, S. (2008). Place as a source of identity in colonizing societies: Israeli settlements in Gaza. *Geographical Review*, *98*, 242–259.

Seamon, D. (1980). Body-subject, time-space routines, and place-ballets. In A. Buttimer, & D. Seamon (Eds.), *The human experience of space and place* (pp. 148–165). New York: St. Martin's Press.

Sedikides, C., Wildschut, T., Gaertner, L., Routledge, C., & Arndt, J. (2008). Nostalgia as enabler of self continuity. In F. Sani (Ed.). *Self continuity* (pp. 227–239). New York: Psychology Press.

Sheller, M., & Urry, J. (2006). The new mobilities paradigm. *Environment and Planning A*, *38*, 207–226.

Smaldone, D. (2006). *The role of time in place attachment*. Proceedings of the 2006, Northeastern Recreation Research Symposium.

Smeekes, A., & Verkuyten, M. (2014). Perceived group continuity, collective self-continuity, and in-group identification. *Self and Identity*, *13*, 663–680.

The UN Migration Agency. (2018). *World migration report 2018*. Geneva: International Organization for Migration.

Tognoli, J. (2003). Leaving home: Homesickness, place attachment and transition among residential college students. *Journal of College Student Psychotherapy*, *18*, 35–48.

Twigger-Ross, C., & Uzzell, D. L. (1996). Place and identity processes. *Journal of Environmental Psychology*, *16*, 139–169.

Vignoles, V. (2011). Identity motives. In S. J. Schwartz, K. Luyckx, & V. Vignoles (Eds.), *Handbook of identity theory and research* (pp. 403–432). London: Springer.

Wheeler, R. (2017). Local history and productive nostalgia? Change, continuity, and sense of place in rural England. *Social & Cultural Geography*, *18*, 466–486.

White, D. D., Virden, R. J., & Riper, C.J. (2008). Effects of place identity, place dependence, and experience-use history on perceptions of recreation impacts in a natural setting. *Environmental Management*, *42*, 647–657.

Williams, D. R., & van Patten, S. (2006). Home and away? Creating identities and sustaining places in a multi-centered world. In N. McIntyre, & K. E. McHugh (Eds.), *Multiple dwelling and tourism: Negotiating place, home and identity* (pp. 32–50). Cambridge, MA: CAB International.

Wylęgała, A. (2014). *Przesiedlenia a pamięć: Studium (nie) pamięci społecznej na przykładzie ukraińskiej Galicji i polskich "Ziem Odzyskanych" Relocations and memory: Study of the social (non)memory In Ukrainian Galicia and Polish, Recovered Lands*. Toruń: Wydawnictwo UMK.

Zencey, E. (1996). The rootless professors. In W. Viteki, & W. Jackson (Eds.), *Rooted in the land: Essays on community and place* (pp. 15–19). New Haven and London: Yale University Press.

Chapter 5: Place attachment as discursive practice: The role of language, affect, space, power, and materiality in person-place bonds

Andrés Di Masso, John Dixon, and Kevin Durrheim

INTRODUCTION

In this chapter, we outline a discursive perspective on human-environment relations, focusing on the process of place attachment. We begin by introducing some conceptual and methodological principles of discursive psychology, discussing some recent environmental psychological research that has been influenced by the so-called discursive turn. We then detail the more specific implications of discursive psychology for understanding place attachment dynamics. The central argument is that rather than treating attachment as a deep-seated, internalized, emotional affinity that individuals experience toward particular places, discursive research treats it as a phenomenon that is linguistically constructed as individuals, together, formulate the everyday meanings of person-in-place relationships. Finally, seeking to transcend some potential limitations of the discursive approach, we discuss how discursive practices of place attachment are inevitably intertwined with affective, spatial, material, embodied, and political practices. We conclude by highlighting how future research on place attachment should investigate complex "assemblages" (Di Masso & Dixon, 2015) of linguistic and other kinds of practices, thereby providing a more comprehensive and dynamic perspective on the politics of people-place bonds.

DISCURSIVE PSYCHOLOGY: SOME ASSUMPTIONS, CONCEPTS, AND METHODOLOGICAL PRINCIPLES

As its epistemological and ontological starting point, the discursive approach assumes the study of everyday language use is fundamental to understanding social and psychological reality. In so doing, it reflects a broader trend in the social sciences and humanities often referred to as "the discursive turn" (e.g., Harré, 2001). A distinctive feature of this "turn" is the now familiar yet still controversial shift from a representational to a constructionist philosophy of language. Most research conducted under the aegis of "environmental psychology," for example, has treated language either as (1) an expression of already-formed inner cognitions or emotions, (2) a transparent medium through which external realities are represented, or (3) a complex amalgam of the two. By contrast, constructionist research treats language as constitutive of both mind and reality. It holds that both our lived experiences (e.g., our thoughts, feelings, motivations) and the meanings we attribute to the world "out there" are actively created through day-to-day linguistic practices and that this process is, in turn, delimited by the shared language that culture makes available to us.

Out of this broader constructionist philosophy of language, discursive psychology has emerged as a specific tradition of research over the past few decades, albeit a tradition that exploits parallel developments in the sociology of scientific knowledge, conversation analysis, ethnomethodology, philosophy of language and semiology. Potter and Wetherell's (1987) "Discourse and Social Psychology" provided the field's seminal text. Other developments are indebted to Billig (1987), Edwards and Potter (1992), Edwards (1997), Potter (1996), and Wetherell (1998), amongst others, whose work inspired a burgeoning research enterprise (for reviews, see Edwards, 2005; Potter, 2007). A special issue of the *British Journal of Social Psychology* published in 2012 celebrated the 25th anniversary of Discursive Psychology, providing an overview of its development (Augoustinos & Tileaga, 2012). Stokoe and Tileaga (2015) similarly offer a useful perspective on the field's emergence, key contributions, and potential future directions.

The kinds of questions that have preoccupied those working in this field make for an instructive introduction to its conceptual and methodological priorities. Discursive psychologists focus on how people create versions of social and psychological reality in and through their everyday language use (the question of construction), and on how such constructions of social and psychological reality are designed to appear objective and "real-seeming," that is, to simply "mirror" entities, processes, relationships, or events that exist independent of the speakers' perspectives (the question of epistemological orientation). Another key question is how interacting speakers orientate to the moral dimension of what is "going on" between them, treating as an interactional concern issues such as interest, agency, responsibility, etc. (the question of accountability). Relatedly, the discursive approach examines what kinds of social actions are performed by everyday accounts of social and psychological realities, that is, how such accounts work in interaction as forms of blaming, justifying, excusing, excluding, threatening, etc. (the question of action orientation). Since versions of reality change depending on the shifting social functions accomplished across different contexts and interaction sequences, discursive researchers also explore the instability of meaning (the question of variability). Finally, there is an interest in pinpointing how everyday accounts are designed to promote particular versions of social and psychological reality whilst undermining alternative versions (the question of rhetorical organization), and how local patterns of argumentation reflect, appropriate, and transform wider historical and political systems of meaning (the question of the relationship between local arguments and ideological traditions) (see Edwards & Potter, 1992; Potter, 1996, for details).

As this series of questions and associated concepts begin to illustrate, to adopt a discursive psychological viewpoint is to move "the *analytic* and *explanatory* focus from cognitive processes and entities to discursive practices and the resources they draw on" (Potter, 1998, pp. 235–236, italics in the original). Clearly, this shift has methodological as well as conceptual implications.

Discursive research generally uses a qualitative method known as discourse analysis, which has developed as a way of analyzing linguistic data of widely varying kinds (e.g., telephone conversations, interviews, media reports, letters, transcripts of legal proceedings, recordings of counseling sessions, social media postings/tweets). The practicalities of doing discourse analysis are complicated by a number of factors. First, the method is not reducible to a fixed recipe of steps; instead, it involves the flexible, imaginative, and context-specific application of general principles. It thus relies heavily on the analyst's interpretative skill and insight, even if numerous "how to" textbooks have appeared over the years (e.g., Lyons & Coyle, 2007). Second, different varieties of discourse analysis tend to treat linguistic practices, devices, and features quite differently. Researchers employing approaches derived from conversation analysis (e.g., Antaki & Widdicombe, 1998), for instance, typically focus on the unfolding minutiae of ordinary interactions, such as turn-taking, intonation, pausing, or word-choice, and they prioritize the meticulous collection (and transcription) of naturally occurring conversations gathered "in the field." Researchers employing rhetorical analyses, by contrast, typically focus on broader patterns of argumentation, often with a view to exploring their sociopolitical origins, content, contexts, and consequences (e.g., Billig, 1991).

Notwithstanding this methodological variety, several broad principles unite different styles of discursive research in psychology. First and foremost, most analysts acknowledge that textual data are important in their own right. They are not merely a conduit to mental processes or reflections of already existing external realities; they are the very stuff of our social and psychological lives. Second, most analysts acknowledge the interactional, moral and political consequences of varying ways of constructing reality, including the psychological reality of how people think, feel, and act in particular situations. That is, they treat language as performative and functional and not simply as descriptive (indeed, in much discursive work descriptions are themselves analyzed in terms of their strategic consequences in performing social actions such as blaming, justifying, and attributing causality; e.g., see Edwards & Potter, 1992). Third, most analysts recognize that constructions of reality are typically variable and contested and that, by implication, they are often designed to warrant particular versions of reality (defensive rhetoric) whilst challenging alternatives (offensive rhetoric) (Potter, 1996). Finally, most analysts accept some common criteria for evaluating the validity of discourse analytic research. They generally accept, for example, that they should make publicly available the textual data on which particular interpretations are based (e.g., in the form of transcribed extracts of conversations or interviews) and thus open up their interpretations to future challenge, qualification or refinement. As in any developing field, of course, there are some shared guidelines (Goodman, 2017) as well as healthy debates about the most effective ways of gathering, representing, and analyzing data (e.g., see Speer, 2002; Potter & Hepburn, 2005).

THE DISCURSIVE APPROACH IN PEOPLE-ENVIRONMENT RESEARCH

The significance of language in the formation of person-environment relations has been periodically highlighted by researchers working across a range of disciplinary traditions. Tuan (1980, p. 6) once observed, for example, that "City people are constantly 'making' and 'unmaking' places by talking about them." Reflecting on how place identities are narratively informed, Sarbin (1983) emphasized how by telling stories in which we "locate" ourselves in material and symbolic environments, we are able to form a coherent sense of self. Along related lines, Low (1992) proposed a typology of place attachment in which the twin practices of storytelling and place-naming bind us to places, while Riley (1992) stressed how people set in the landscapes personal stories related to fantasy as an internal narrative. In each of these examples, the role of language in shaping the nature, meaning and lived experience of human-environment relations has been treated as central, although without the explicit aim of doing a discourse analysis. As Tuan (1991) has observed, however, that role has historically been under-specified in people-environment research. Indeed, until comparatively recently, for instance, it has been barely featured in environmental psychology (see Aiello & Bonaiuto, 2003; Dixon & Durrheim, 2000; Di Masso, Dixon, & Pol, 2011, for exceptions).

Discursive researchers began in the 2000s to systematically address this gap in ways that are relevant to studying place attachment dynamics. For example, Wallwork and Dixon (2004) explored varying rhetorical constructions of the "countryside" in newspaper accounts produced by the Countryside Alliance, a rural lobby group based in the UK. They argued that such constructions were designed, among other things, to justify controversial practices such as fox hunting and hare-coursing. By portraying rural environments as the romantic landscape of Britishness (e.g., as an emotionally "living" and "breathing" place) and hunting as an atavistic feature of that landscape, they sought to cast it as an organic expression of national identity. In discursive terms, Wallwork and Dixon demonstrated how producing a particular version of the countryside (i.e., construction) provided a group-related justification (i.e., action-orientation) that built on and reproduced the nationalistic imaginary (i.e., ideological effects).

Investigating relations located at a more intimate socio-spatial scale, Stokoe and Wallwork (2003) conducted a conversation-analytic study of everyday disputes between neighbors in community mediation sessions and televised documentaries. They found that accounts of spatial behavior often played a central role in such disputes, with transgressions of spatial boundaries being cast as transgressions of the moral boundaries of "good" neighborly relations. At the same time, the line between "private" and "public" space seemed to be subtle, contingent, and constantly shifting—something (re)negotiated in context rather than a fixed or immutable boundary. As the authors argued, in order to protect entitlements related to the private space, such space must be discursively defined and delimited. Consequently, "participants" accounts were littered with symbols of bounded private space (e.g., "doors," "walls," "fences," and "gates") (Stokoe & Wallwork, 2003, p. 563).

In a related series of studies, Dixon, Levine, and McAuley (2006); Di Masso et al. (2011); Di Masso (2012, 2015); and Gray and Manning (2014) all illustrate the rhetorical organization of spatial discourse, by showing how constructions of "public space" such as a town square, a local park or a street corner may serve, among other functions, to legitimize the exclusion of socially unwanted people and activities, thereby promoting an exclusive definition of the "proper" citizen. Yet, they also demonstrated how such constructions typically navigate an "ideological dilemma" (Billig et al., 1988) about the very nature of public space, a dilemma that involves competing ideas about what is a public space for and what are the legitimate boundaries of the "public" social category.

In their research on desegregation in post-apartheid South Africa, Dixon and Durrheim explored the role of place discourse in warranting and resisting social change (Dixon, Foster, Durrheim, & Wilbraham, 1994; Dixon & Durrheim, 2000, 2004; Durrheim & Dixon, 2005). Their study of changing relations within a coastal village in the Western Cape, for instance, demonstrated how white residents' opposition to desegregation was framed in the shared language of environmental despoliation and deep nostalgia for the loss of the place's character, as expressed via a sustained campaign of protest letters to local newspapers (Dixon et al., 1994. By constructing an emerging community of black residents as a threat to the "fragile" local ecology and natural aesthetic beauty of the village, such residents not only sought to justify their exclusion, but also to cast their presence there in the (racial) symbolism of filth, pollution, danger, and place defilement.

As these initial examples show, discursive research addresses two relatively neglected features of person-place bonds. The first feature concerns the social dimension of place meanings. As Auburn and Barnes (2006) point out, environmental psychology has typically emphasized individual cognitions about place. It has thus under-specified the interactional processes through which place meanings become collectively shared, disseminated and deployed. Discursive researchers would insist that such processes occur primarily within our day-to-day language use. The second feature concerns what discursive researchers have termed the "action-orientation" of everyday discourse (Edwards & Potter, 1992)—a concept that sensitizes us to the strategic and political consequences of everyday constructions of the material environment. By depicting certain kinds of people or behaviors (e.g., black "squatters") as incongruent with a normative conception of place (e.g., a bio-regime of ecological importance and fragility), for instance, the language of place may justify particular kinds of sectional interests. This is closely related to the argument that "good" and "bad" behavior, "(im)proper" practices and "(in)admissible" social groups are often defined in spatial terms (Cresswell, 1996), thereby shaping and reinforcing normative geographies of exclusion (Sibley, 1995).

Of more specific relevance to the present chapter is discursive research that has directly explored the psychological dimension of the relationship between people and places. Dixon and Durrheim's (2000) critique of the traditional concept of place-identity in environmental psychology addressed this topic in some detail and anticipated several later studies. Whilst commending environmental psychologists for recognizing how questions of "who we are" are always intimately related to questions of "where we are," Dixon and Durrheim argued that research on place-identity focuses heavily on individualistic cognitions and feelings such as a personal sense of belonging, "insideness," pride and self-expression (though for exceptions see, e.g., Bonauito et al., 1996; Devine-Wright & Lyons, 1997), often overlooking the social, cultural and discursive dimensions of person-place bonds. In order to address this gap, they recommended an approach that treats place-identity as (1) something that people create together as they routinely talk about self-in-place relationships, (2) something that people use as an interactional resource to perform varying kinds of social and rhetorical work, and (3) something that is embedded within broader ideological traditions for defining and regulating person-place relations so as, for example, to maintain certain kinds of socio-spatial entitlements.

Drawing broadly on the discursive approach, later studies have shown how constructions of place-identity feature within discourse about intra-national migration (McKinlay & McVittie, 2007), environmental threat (Hugh-Jones & Madill, 2009), and tourism (McCabe & Stokoe, 2004), to mention but a few examples. Interestingly, such work has also shown how ostensibly private and personal constructions of place-identity are themselves constantly shaped by wider cultural meanings through which individuals actively fashion a sense of identity. Taylor (2004, 2005), for instance, conducted a discursive-narrative analysis of constructions of place belonging and identity in a sample of women most of whom had moved home once or on several occasions in their lives. She found that women's accounts were often designed to resist a broader "counter-narrative" that stressed their lack of authentic rootedness to place—a so-called born-and-bred construction founded on characteristics such as being a native, having a local accent or living long term in a given town or city. This narrative of authenticity, Taylor argued, had to be reflexively navigated in the course of the interviews as women sought to reconstruct a sense of belonging, inclusion, and attachment in their new places of residence. Taken together, what these discursive studies tell us is that, just as place meanings and people-place relations are dynamically and strategically constructed in talk and interaction, so too are place attachments.

IMPLICATIONS OF THE DISCURSIVE APPROACH FOR UNDERSTANDING PLACE ATTACHMENT

In the emerging tradition of discursive work on place-identity, one can also glimpse the beginnings of a productive reformulation of the concept of place attachment. As the contributors to this volume have elaborated, this concept has traditionally been used to designate the bonds that individuals develop with places over time—a sense of connection built up gradually as individuals occupy, use, and experience a given environment (e.g., Low & Altman, 1992). Psychologists have typically defined this sense of attachment as a deep-seated, internalized, emotional affinity toward place. Research on this "affinity" has sought to elucidate not only the nature of person-place bonds, but also their complex interrelations with a range of social and environmental behaviors (e.g., willingness to support conservation initiatives). More broadly, the concept of place attachment has featured in a rich tradition of work within human geography. Whether framing attachment as a fleeting or superficial connection to place or as an authentic, even existential, sense of "root-edness," such work has pointed to its phenomenological significance. After all, to echo Relph's classic dictum, to be human "is to live in a world that is filled with significant places: to be human is to have and know your place" (Relph, 1976, p. 1; original emphasis, although we would note the political and normative ramifications of the latter expression).

As with the broader concept of place-identity, however, the majority of research has treated place attachment as an intra-psychic process—something that reflects thoughts and feelings going on inside the mind of the individual as a result of his/her personal experiences within particular physical environments. Exceptions can be cited of course. Scannell and Gifford (2010, p. 6) have asked, for example, "…does attachment to place support goals at a *group level*?" (our emphasis). Relatedly, Lewicka (2011, p. 226) has urged researchers to locate place attachment studies "within a larger sociopolitical context than has been done so far," and to clarify the social "processes through which people form their meaningful relations with places."

The kind of approach that we are proposing develops these general calls for a more social perspective on place attachment in a specific direction. The discursive perspective treats place attachment as a linguistic practice that cannot be understood outside of the interactional, cultural, and institutional contexts in which it emerges. As should be evident by now, it entails a re-conceptualization of place attachment as a discursive resource that individuals deploy within their everyday interactions and that carries consequences for reproducing or challenging the socio-spatial order. After all, in publicly expressing bonds of attachment to a place, we may be doing far more than expressing internal feelings that would otherwise remain within the private recesses of our minds. Regardless of any private sense of emotional bonding, we may be performing social actions whose situated effects, quite literally, can move mountains (see Macnaghten, 1993). Sometimes those effects may occur at a micro-interactional level, as individuals seek, for example, to legitimate the "authenticity" of particular forms of identity (e.g., membership as a "local" resident) or account for particular environmental behaviors (e.g., picking up litter). Sometimes they may have consequences at broader socio-political level; for instance, constructions of place attachment may justify relations of spatial inclusion-exclusion or warrant or resist environmental change. In short, while accepting the obvious point that people forge subjective

Table 5.1
Contrast between a traditional and a discursive approach to place attachment

Parameters	Cognitive/representationist approach to place attachment	Discursive/constructionist approach to place attachment
Location	Internal, psychological experience	External, publicly available discursive resource
Ontological nature	Cognition	Social practice
Explanatory level	Individual in a social context	Socio-cultural construction of the person-in-interaction
Pragmatic function	Accomplishes individual functions (e.g., survival, self-regulation, self-continuity)	Accomplishes social actions and realizes interaction work (e.g., blames, excludes, warrants, builds credible identities)
Epistemological function	Mediates people-place relations	Constructs people-place relations
Context-(in)dependency	Individual/Group property	Context-occasioned, dialogic construction
Temporality	Main focus on stability of meaning	Main focus on variability of meaning
Political focus	Little rhetorical/ideological relevance	Significant rhetorical/ideological relevance

ties to places that are emotionally significant in their lives, discursive researchers open up new ways of looking at the nature and functions of place attachment.

Table 5.1 highlights some basic points of comparison between the discursive and mainstream psychological conceptions of place attachment. Most of these points should be clear from our earlier discussion. However, one is worth addressing a little further, if only to distinguish discursive work from related work in other traditions. The discursive perspective does not simply acknowledge that place meanings are collectively shared, culturally embedded and implicated when we form a sense of attachment to place (e.g., see Devine-Wright & Lyons, 1997; Stokols & Shumaker, 1981). Nor does it simply echo the well-established point that attachment to place occurs through the mediation of place meanings rather than through individuals' direct or "unmediated" experiences of physical environments (e.g., Canter, 1977; Stedman, 2003). Instead, the main contribution of the discursive approach is to shift analytic and conceptual focus onto a new object of inquiry: the everyday linguistic practices through which place meanings and associated person-place relations are created, reproduced, and contested.

This re-conceptualization of place attachment as discursive practice (see Di Masso, Dixon, & Durrheim, 2014) has been applied in recent years to study people-place emotional bonds in a range of contexts and topics, such as urban displacement (Manzo, 2014), rural conservation (Masterson, Spierenburg, & Tengö, 2019), public health (Aceros, 2018), migration (Hall, 2018), objection to the siting of electricity power lines in the countryside (Batel et al., 2015, related to Wallwork & Dixon's (2004) study on the rhetorical construction of the British countryside), or residential satisfaction (Di Masso, Dixon, & Hernández, 2017).

Hence, exploring the rhetoric of the HOPE VI (Housing Opportunities for People Everywhere) urban restructuring program in the US, Manzo (2014) showed how institutional and media discourses were created to justify relocation of impoverished populations in public housing by rhetorically depicting such populations as isolated, severely distressed and desperately willing to leave the area. This construction was in sharp contrast with the local inhabitants' reported desire not to leave the area on the grounds of their attachment to the place. Manzo thus argues that the constructions of place attachment mobilized in urban regeneration programs can ideologically support or resist normative views of the social order (i.e., dispossessing or empowering impoverished and stigmatized population).

Along similar lines, Masterson et al. (2019) examined the rhetorical construction of place-meanings and people-place bonds involved in a project for fencing a protected area for conservation on the Wild Coast in South Africa. They concluded that a dominant "win-win" narrative, based on economic benefits for the local population, was successfully undermined by a community counter-narrative of place bonding, which proposed a relationship to the land based on local ownership and small-holder agricultural development for food security.

Relatedly, Hall (2018) applied the discursive approach to examine place attachments to the UK and to the homeland by UK residents from Zimbabwe. Foregrounding the shifting and ambivalent bonds toward both places, she concluded that "the invocation of the root metaphor and the born-and-bred narrative in the interviewees' talk about their place attachments embedded it in a wider social process in which the relationship between particular people and places is naturalised, and a distinction is set up between those who authentically belong and those who are newcomers or outsiders" (p. 16) (see Taylor, 2004, 2005).

A further example is provided by Aceros's (2018) study of attachment to home in Catalunya, which used focus groups with telecare elderly users, relatives, professionals, and volunteers. Aceros argues that place attachment discourses warrant the virtues of telecare services and connect the everyday politics of care with neoliberal ideology, fostering an individualized, demand-focused, and family-centered model of care giving.

The bulk of this emerging work illustrates the potential value of the discursive approach, which has been framed by some authors as a paradigmatic example of qualitative research in environmental psychology (Seamon & Gill, 2016; Manzo & Pinto de Carvalho, Chapter 7, this volume; see also Cross, 2015, on the discursive-narrative approach to place attachment).

DISCOURSE AND BEYOND: PLACE ATTACHMENT AS "ASSEMBLAGE"

The discursive approach to place attachment provides a lens through which to view the dynamic, socially constructed, action-oriented, historically situated, and politically consequential nature of people-place emotional affinities. However, the problem of understanding human-environment relations, in turn, brings into sharper focus a critical potential limitation of the discursive approach, which we deem particularly relevant for future research on the topic of place attachment. Specifically, by focusing on linguistic accounts, researchers may underplay the material practices through which place attachments are created and experienced.

Such attachments may be enacted as people physically appropriate places or intervene within their material and symbolic design. Protective territorial feelings, for example, may be formulated not only through everyday language use, but also through the active shaping of the physical environment, for example, through the installation of fences, walls, signs, and myriad other boundary markers. Likewise, identification with place may be formulated not only by "locating" the self in everyday talk (Dixon & Durrheim, 2000), but also by engaging in material practices that create environments designed to promote certain versions of self and other, encouraging some of us to feel "at home," and others to feel estranged. In short, discursive research needs to grapple with the problem of interrelating linguistic practices with the other embodied and material practices through which place attachment is constructed.

At the same time, even if place attachment researchers accept that this emerging tradition of work offers important insights, we suspect that many might question the wholesale shift of explanatory focus toward language in the study of emotional experiences of place. They would not be alone. Across the social sciences, the social constructionist perspective on emotion has been increasingly challenged by a new "affective turn" that, though acknowledging the importance of studying linguistic practices, has called for a renewed emphasis on the embodied nature of emotions. For some scholars, this turn needs to challenge the primacy of linguistic practices of meaning-making and indeed focus attention on experiences that are ultimately irreducible to language (e.g., Clough & Halley, 2007). We believe, instead, that place attachment research needs to develop new ways of integrating the study of linguistic construction with the study of other processes implicated in our emotional lives, including processes that emerge from the fact that we are embodied as well as articulate beings (Harré, 1999; see also Lewicka's (2011) recommendation that place attachment research needs to focus on "embodied" cognition).

From this perspective, place attachment might be reconceived as the emergent product of a complex interplay between words, bodily practices, material architecture and artifacts, that, working in conjunction, constantly serve to (re)create individuals' affective "experiences" of place. This approach challenges conventional psychological assumptions by locating emotion and cognition not in the internal workings of the individual mind but throughout "…the range and entire patterning of affective assemblages operating in important scenes in everyday life, along with their social consequences and entailments" (Wetherell, 2012, p. 52). In this frame, discursive dynamics of meaning-making are examined in their articulation with seemingly extra- or pre-discursive practices and "realities" (e.g., the body, emotions, or space). Yet, it is argued that what makes affective patterns meaningful and powerful is precisely their discursive embeddedness, which "…provides the means for affect to travel" (Wetherell, 2012, p. 19), that is, for affect to become socially, psychologically and politically intelligible and to flow through society.

This theoretical approach demands a re-conceptualization of discursive practices of place attachment in terms of their broader entanglement with other processes and materialities that both shape, and are shaped by, those same discursive practices. Affect and thought are connected through discourse, yet the affective patterns shaping people's emotional connections to places are traced beyond the discursive domain of linguistic practice as analysts seek to recover their interrelations with the material, ideological, and embodied realm.

Durrheim, Rautenbach, Nicholson, and Dixon's (2013) study of nightclubs in South Africa offers a clear example of this kind of approach. Their ethnography showed that cocktail bars were discursively constructed as sites of male-centered heterosexual opportunity, thereby depicting women's identity as sexualized objects of desire. This process of meaning-making demanded many other material structures and embodied practices, such as the aesthetic design of the place, its visual imagery, the dress codes and the conduct of staff and patrons, which ranged from mundane activities such as sitting, walking, and talking to overtly sexualized practices of flirting, watching, and dancing. According to Durrheim et al., this "affective assemblage" of (discursive, bodily, spatialized) practices together constituted the cocktail bar as a space of heterosexual and heteronormative desire, which privileged certain ways of saying, being, feeling and acting, certain bodies, and certain gendered and sexualized identities. Moreover, successful participation in this form of social life and personal experience of place demanded a proper "affective tuning" with the club's "vibe" or atmosphere, shaping the "feeling of place" as something that was actively recreated by the participants through discourse.

The core idea in Durrheim et al.'s (2013) notion of "affective patterns" draws on Wetherell's (2012, pp. 15–19) concept of "assemblage," "something, in other words, that comes into shape and continues to change and refigure as it flows on," as part of "an organic complex in which all the parts relationally constitute each other." Extending this line of argument, Di Masso and Dixon (2015) proposed the notion of "place-assemblages," understood as "fleeting crystallizations that emerge through the indissoluble composition of properties and practices, and not from the interaction between ontologically bounded spaces or bodies or discourses" (p. 49). Their study focused on an urban conflict over the redevelopment, design, and management of an empty urban space in the old town of Barcelona during a controversial urban regeneration program. Di Masso and Dixon argued that the efficacy of the political strategy of the protesters who occupied the area, as well as of the institutional redevelopment plans, could be understood only if their (de) legitimizing place-discourses were analyzed in their articulation with the specific emplacement and movements of objects (e.g., trees, benches), textual signs (e.g., "Police forces out"), territorial markers (e.g., concrete walls impeding access), and located bodies (e.g., human chains protecting the area from eviction). Affect toward the place was produced and channeled there through the entwined action of meaningful discourses and material practices that were mutually motivated, signified, and reinforced. This entwined action, for example, was conveyed via the geo-indexical meaning of words embedded in the walls of the area (e.g., "1, 2, 3, boom" written on the fence, discursively announcing its imminent physical destruction by the occupants protesting against the official plans).

These studies clearly problematize a "purely" discursive conceptualization of place attachment as involving "solely" linguistic practices. However, they also extend the potential of the discursive approach by locating its analytic focus in the entanglement of discourse with other material and embodied practices that, quite literally, require linguistic constructions of place attachment for affect to become subjectively meaningful and socially consequential. Most importantly, we argue that the analytic concept of assemblage is particularly useful in understanding the micropolitics of place attachment, that is, the extent to which structural power relations are partially conveyed through everyday enactments of people-place affective bonds (Di Masso et al., 2017). Discursive practices can shape and contest place attachments in ways that connect affect with gender inequalities (Durrheim et al., 2013), or with exclusionary urban strategies against the socio-economically disadvantaged (Di Masso & Dixon, 2015; Manzo, 2014). These gender-based and class-based place attachment constructions are often entwined with broader territorial (e.g., housing conditions, urban segregation), socio-economic (e.g., lower income) and embodied (e.g., sexualized bodies) conditions, that delineate the performative limits of discourse, as much as they provide the basis for constructing new place-discourses as materially and geographically situated language in use.

Recent research along these lines has supported the need to articulate methods for studying materiality together with language (Aagaard & Matthiesen, 2016). Other authors have referred to the "subpolitics" of place-making as a way of conceptualizing how text, talk and things congregate to produce resistance to urban and industrial development (Buizer & Turnhout, 2011). At an empirical level, the place-assemblage approach has also proved to be a useful framework to study people-place bonds and place attachment in gentrified urban areas (Sánchez & Vivas, 2018) and in urban zones affected by socio-natural disasters with subsequent attempts of relocation (Berroeta, Pinto de Carvalho, Di Masso, & Ossul, 2017).

CONCLUSION

From a discursive perspective, place attachment can be construed as an important entry in the rich "psychological thesaurus" (Edwards, 2005) that we use to construct the meaning of human-environment relations. By shifting analytic attention away from the internal experiences of the socially isolated individual and toward to the practices through which individuals jointly warrant, contest and transform human-environment relationships, we believe that discursive research has the potential to enrich the field. The discursive approach extends, questions, and contests the fundamental assumptions of the traditional cognitive approach to place attachment. While it does not deny the cognitive significance of place attachment for the individual, it certainly challenges its cognitivist reduction to a mentally enclosed experience.

We have advocated a discursive approach to place attachment, but have also underlined a central limitation of this approach, namely, its tendency to neglect both material practices and embodiment in favor of an exclusive focus on linguistic practices. Addressing this limitation, we have argued that place attachment can be better conceived of as a dynamic entanglement or "assemblage" between language-in-use and other material, embodied and spatial practices that work together to co-construct the affective bonding of people to places. Future research on place attachment can benefit from this theoretical framework, which we would argue is particularly useful to explore the politics of people-place bonds.

REFERENCES

Aagaard, J., & Matthiesen, M. (2016). Methods of materiality: Participant observation and qualitative research in psychology. *Qualitative Research in Psychology*, *13*(1), 33–46.

Aceros, J. (2018). En casa mientras puedas. Construcción discursiva del apego al hogar en personas mayores. *Athenea Digital*, *18*(3), 1–27.

Aiello, A., & Bonaiuto, M. (2003). Rhetorical approach and discursive psychology: Study of environmental discourse. In M. Bonnes, T. Lee, & M. Bonaiuto (Eds.), *Psychological theories for environmental issues* (pp. 235–270). Aldershot: Ashgate.

Antaki, C., & Widdicombe, S. (Eds.). (1998). *Identities in talk*. London: Sage.

Auburn, T., & Barnes, R. (2006). Producing place: A neo-Schutzian perspective on the 'psychology of place'. *Journal of Environmental Psychology*, *26*(1), 38–50.

Augoustinos, M., & Tileaga, C. (2012). Twenty-five years of discursive psychology. *British Journal of Social Psychology*, *51*(3), 405–412.

Batel, S., Devine-Wright, P., Wold, L., Egeland, H., Jacobsen, G., & Aas, O. (2015). The role of (de-)essentialisation within siting conflicts: An interdisciplinary approach. *Journal of Environmental Psychology*, *44*, 149–159.

Berroeta, H., Pinto de Carvalho, L., Di Masso, A., & Ossul, I. (2017). Place attachment: A psycho-environmental approach to affective attachment to the environment in residential habitat reconstruction processes. *Revista INVI*, *32*(91), 113–139.

Billig, M. (1987). *Arguing and thinking: A rhetorical approach to social psychology*. Cambridge: Cambridge University Press.

Billig, M., Condor, S., Edwards, D., Gane, M., Middleton, D., & Radley, A. (1988). *Ideological dilemmas: A social psychology of everyday thinking*. London: Sage.

Billig, M. (1991). *Ideology and opinions*. London: Sage.

Bonaiuto, M., Breakwell, G. M., & Cano, I. (1996) Identity Processes and Environmental Threat: the Effects of Nationalism and Local Identity upon Perception of Beach Pollution. *Journal of Community & Applied Social Psychology*, 6(3), 157–175.

Buizer, M., & Turnhout, E. (2011). Text, talk, things, and the subpolitics of performing place. *Geoforum*, *42*(5), 530–538.

Canter, D. (1977). *The psychology of place*. New York, NY: Architectural Press.

Clough, P., & Halley, J. (Eds.). (2007). *The affective turn: Theorizing the social*. Durham, NC: Duke University Press.

Cresswell, T. (1996). *In place/out of place: Geography, ideology, and transgression*. Minneapolis, MN: University of Minnesota Press.

Cross, J. (2015). Processes of place attachment: An interactional framework. *Symbolic Interaction*, *38*(4), 493–520.

Devine-Wright, P., & Lyons, E. (1997). Remembering pasts and representing places: The construction of national identities in Ireland. *Journal of Environmental Psychology*, *17*(1), 33–45.

Di Masso, A. (2015). Micropolitics of public space: On the contested limits of citizenship as a locational practice. *Journal of Social and Political Psychology*, 3(2), 63–83.

Di Masso, A., Dixon, J., & Pol, E. (2011). On the contested nature of place: 'Figuera's Well,' 'The Hole of Shame,' and the ideological struggle over public space in Barcelona. *Journal of Environmental Psychology*, *31*(3), 231–244.

Di Masso, A. (2012). Grounding citizenship: Toward a political psychology of public space. *Political Psychology*, *33*(1), 123–143.

Di Masso, A., Dixon, J., & Durrheim, K. (2014). Place attachment as discursive practice. In L. Manzo, & P. Devine-Wright (Eds.), *Place attachment: Advances in theories, methods and applications* (1st ed.) (pp. 75–86). London: Routledge.

Di Masso, A., & Dixon, J. (2015). More than words: Place, discourse and the struggle over public space in Barcelona. *Qualitative Research in Psychology*, *12*(1), 45–60.

Di Masso, A., Dixon, J., & Hernández, B. (2017). Place attachment, sense of belonging and the micro-politics of place satisfaction. In G. Fleury-Bahi, E. Pol, & Ó. Navarro (Eds.), *Handbook of environmental psychology and quality of life research* (pp. 85–104). London: Springer.

Dixon, J., & Durrheim, K. (2000). Displacing place-identity: A discursive approach to locating self and other. *British Journal of Social Psychology*, *39*(1), 27–44.

Dixon, J., & Durrheim, K. (2004). Dislocating identity: Desegregation and the transformation of place. *Journal of Environmental Psychology*, *24*(4), 455–473.

Dixon, J., Foster, D., Durrheim, K., & Wilbraham, L. (1994). Discourse and the politics of space in South Africa: The 'squatter crisis'. *Discourse & Society*, *5*(3), 277–296.

Dixon, J., Levine, M., & McAuley, R. (2006). Locating impropriety: Street drinking, moral order, and the ideological dilemma of public space. *Political Psychology*, *27*(2), 187–206.

Durrheim, K., & Dixon, J. (2005). Studying talk and embodied practices: Toward a psychology of materiality of 'race relations'. *Journal of Community & Applied Social Psychology*, *15*(6), 446–460.

Durrheim, K., Rautenbach, C., Nicholson, T., & Dixon, J. (2013). Displacing place-identity: Introducing an analytics of participation. In B. Gardener, & F. Winddance-Twine (Eds.), *Geographies of privilege* (pp. 43–70). Cambridge: Cambridge University Press.

Edwards, D. (2005). Discursive psychology. In K. L. Fitch, & R. E. Sanders (Eds.), *Handbook of language and social interaction* (pp. 257–273). Hillsdale, NJ: Lawrence Erlbaum Associates.

Edwards, D. (1997). *Discourse and cognition*. London: Sage.

Edwards, D., & Potter, J. (1992). *Discursive psychology*. London: Sage.

Goodman, S. (2017). How to conduct a psychological discourse analysis. *Critical Approaches to Discourse Analysis across Disciplines*, 9, 142–153.

Gray, D., & Manning, R. (2014). 'Oh my god, we are not doing nothing': Young people's experiences of spatial regulation'. *British Journal of Social Psychology*, *53*(4), 640–655.

Hall, L. (2018). The discursive approach to place attachment explored through talk about places of residence produced by UK residents from Zimbabwe. *Qualitative Research in Psychology*. DOI:10.1080/14780887.2018.1545067.

Harré, R. (1999). Discourse and the embodied person. In D. Nightingale, & J. Cromby (Eds.), *Social constructionist psychology: A critical analysis of theory and practice* (pp. 97–112). London: Open University Press.

Harré, R. (2001). The discursive turn in social psychology. In D. Shiffrin, D. Tannen, & H. Hamilton (Eds.), *The handbook of discourse analysis* (pp. 688–706). Minneapolis: Blackwell.

Hugh-Jones, S., & Madill, A. (2009). 'The air's got to be far cleaner here': A discursive analysis of place-identity threat. *British Journal of Social Psychology*, *48*(4), 601–624.

Lewicka, M. (2011). Place attachment: How far have we come in the last 40 years?. *Journal of Environmental Psychology*, *31*(3), 207–230.

Low, S. (1992). Symbolic ties that bind. In I. Altman, & S. Low (Eds.), *Place attachment* (pp. 165–185). New York: Plenum Press.

Low, S., & Altman, I. (1992). Place attachment: A conceptual inquiry. In I. Altman, & S. Low (Eds.), *Place attachment* (pp. 1–12). New York: Plenum Press.

Lyons, E., & Coyle, A. (Eds.). (2007). *Analysing qualitative data in psychology*. London: Sage.

Macnaghten, P. (1993). Discourses of nature: Argumentation and power. In E. Burman, & I. Parker (Eds.), *Discourse analytic research: Repertoires and readings of texts in action* (pp. 52–71). London: Routledge.

Manzo, L. (2014). Exploring the shadow side: Place attachment in the context of stigma, displacement and social housing. In L. Manzo, & P. Devine-Wright (Eds.), *Place attachment: Advances in theories, methods and applications* (1st ed.) (pp. 178–190). London: Routledge.

Masterson, V., Spierenburg, M., & Tengö, M. (2019). The trade-offs of win-win conservation rhetoric: Exploring place meanings in community conservation on the Wild Coast. *South Africa. Sustainability Science*, *14*(3), 639–654.

McCabe, S., & Stokoe, E. (2004). Place and identity in tourists' accounts. *Annals of Tourism Research*, *31*(3), 601–622.

McKinlay, A., & McVittie, C. (2007). Locals, incomers and intra-national migration: Place-identities and a Scottish island. *British Journal of Social Psychology*, *46*(1), 171–190.

Potter, J. (1996). *Representing reality: Discourse, rhetoric and social construction*. London: Sage.

Potter, J. (1998). Discursive social psychology: From attitudes to evaluative practices. *European Review of Social Psychology*, *9*(1), 233–266.

Potter, J. (2007). *Discourse and psychology* (3 Vols.). London: Sage.

Potter, J., & Hepburn, A. (2005). Qualitative interviews in psychology: Problems and possibilities. *Qualitative Research in Psychology*, *2*(4), 38–55.

Potter, J., & Wetherell, M. (1987). *Discourse and social psychology. Beyond attitudes and behaviour*. London: Sage.

Relph, E. (1976). *Place and placelessness*. London: Pion.

Riley, R. (1992). Attachment to the ordinary landscape. In I. Altman, & S. Low (Eds.), *Place attachment* (pp. 13–35). New York: Plenum Press.

Sánchez, J., & Vivas, P. (2018). La ciudad creativa y cultural como espacio de exclusión y segregación. Analizando la Placica Vintage de Zaragoza: Materialidades, prácticas, narrativas y virtualidades. *Eure*, *44*(133), 211–232.

Sarbin, T. (1983). Place-identity as a component of self: An addendum. *Journal of Environmental Psychology*, *3*(4), 337–342.

Scannell, L., & Gifford, R. (2010). Defining place attachment: A tripartite organizing framework. *Journal of Environmental Psychology*, *30*(1), 1–10.

Seamon, D., & Gill, H. (2016). Qualitative approaches to environment-behavior research: Understanding environmental and place experiences, meanings, and actions. In R. Gifford (Ed.), *Research methods for environmental psychology* (pp. 115–135). Chichester: Wiley-Blackwell.

Sibley, D. (1995). *Geographies of exclusion: Society and difference in the West*.London: Routledge.

Speer, S. (2002). 'Natural' and 'contrived' data: A sustainable distinction? *Discourse Studies*, *4*(4), 511–525.

Stedman, R. (2003). Is it really just a social construction? The contribution of the physical environment to sense of place. *Society and Natural Resources*, *16*(8), 671–685.

Stokoe, L., & Tileaga, C. (2015). *Discursive psychology: Classic and contemporary issues.* London: Taylor Francis.

Stokoe, E., & Wallwork, J. (2003). Space invaders: The moral-spatial order in neighbour dispute discourse. *British Journal of Social Psychology*, *42*(4), 551–569.

Stokols, D., & Shumaker, S. (1981). People in places: A transactional view of settings. In J. H. Harvey (Ed.), *Cognition, social behavior and the environment* (pp. 441–488). Hillsdale, NJ: Lawrence Erlbaum Associates.

Taylor, S. (2004). Identity trouble and place of residence in women's life narratives. In N. Kelly, C. Horrocks, K. Milnes, B. Roberts, & D. Robinson (Eds.), *Narrative, memory and everyday life* (pp. 97–105). Huddersfield: University of Huddersfield.

Taylor, S. (2005). Identity trouble and opportunity in women's narratives of residence. *Auto/Biography*, *13*(3), 249–265.

Tuan, Y. (1980). Rootedness versus sense of place. *Landscape*, *24*(1), 3–8.

Tuan, Y. (1991). Language and the making of place: A narrative-descriptive approach. *Annals of the Association of American Geographers*, *81*(4), 684–696.

Wallwork, J., & Dixon, J. (2004). Foxes, green fields and Britishness: On the rhetorical construction of place and national identity. *British Journal of Social Psychology*, *43*(1), 21–39.

Wetherell, M. (1998). Positioning and interpretative repertoires: Conversation analysis and post-structuralism in dialogue. *Discourse & Society*, *9*(3), 387–412.

Wetherell, M. (2012). *Affect and emotion: A new social science understanding.* London: Sage.

PART II

Methods

Chapter 6: Theoretical and methodological aspects of research on place attachment

Bernardo Hernández, M. Carmen Hidalgo, and Cristina Ruiz

CONCEPTUALIZATION OF PLACE ATTACHMENT

Slow, *unclear*, *stuck*, *lack of theory*, *little empirical progress* … these terms were used to describe research on place attachment in the thorough review by Lewicka (2011a) and these concerns were shared by other authors (Giuliani, 2003; Hernández, Hidalgo, Salazar-Laplace, & Hess, 2007; Jorgensen & Stedman, 2006; Scannell & Gifford, 2010). Unfortunately, the substantial increase in the scientific production related to the study of the bonds between humans and places has not been accompanied enough by advances in the theoretical and empirical aspects.

Most researchers agree that the main reason behind this lack of progress is the proliferation of concepts and measurements proposed for characterizing emotional bonds between humans and places. *Topophilia*, *rootedness*, *place dependence*, *place identity*, *urban identity*, *place attachment*, *sense of place*, *sense of community*, or *community attachment* are examples of the wide array of existing terms. The problem is not new. Twenty years ago, this terminological and conceptual chaos led Giuliani and Feldman (1993) to state that "the most important challenge for researchers in this area of inquiry is to integrate different viewpoints and approaches" (p. 271). Regrettably, still today many authors highlight that challenge, thus confirming the insufficient progress achieved in this aspect.

Since the first works in the field, the number of different conceptual frameworks proposed is indeed colossal. Incorporating more recent research into the PA review for this new edition of the book, we continue to find that diversity regarding the conceptualization of place attachment and related phenomena is maintained (cf. Devine-Wright, 2011; Droseltis & Vignoles, 2010; Fornara, Bonaiuto, & Bonnes, 2010; Hesari et al., 2018; Huang, Hung, & Chen, 2018; Lewicka, 2011b; Magalhães & Calheiros, 2015; Morgan, 2010; Rollero & De Piccoli, 2010a; Raymond, Brown, & Weber, 2010; Scannell & Gifford, 2010; Scopelliti & Tiberio, 2010). This variety illustrates the plurality of concepts that researchers in the field must manage. We review below a selection of the main proposals in the

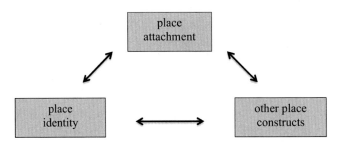

Figure 6.1
Place attachment as a one-dimensional concept.

literature. As shown in Figure 6.1, there are almost as many approaches as combinations of the different elements.

1   Several researchers consider place attachment as a one-dimensional concept related, at the same level, with concepts such as place identity or place dependence (Figure 6.1, e.g., Devine-Wright, 2011; Fornara et al., 2010; Giuliani, 2003; Hernández et al., 2007; Rollero & De Piccoli, 2010a).

2   Other proposals consider it a multidimensional construct that incorporates a number of different factors: 2, 3, or 5 (see Figure 6.2). For example, based on the approach of Stokols and Shumaker (1981), Williams and Vaske (2003) define place attachment as a superordinate concept with two dimensions: place dependence and place identity. Kyle, Graefe, and Manning (2005) add a third factor, namely, social bonds. Lewicka (2011b) suggests five types of place attachment: place inherited, place discovered, place relativity, place alienation, and placelessness. Likewise, Raymond et al. (2010) propose a five-dimensional model of

Figure 6.2
Place attachment as a dimension of a supraordered concept.

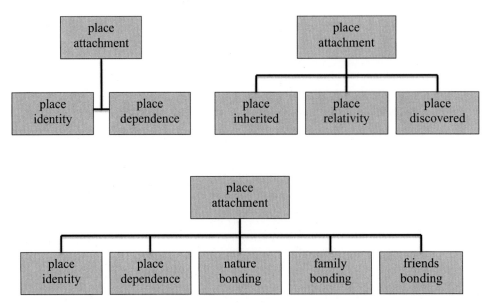

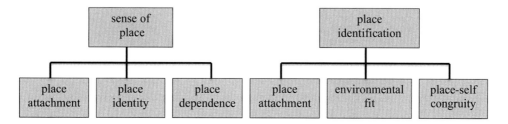

Figure 6.3
Place attachment as a
multidimensional concept.

place attachment comprising place identity, place dependence, nature bonding, family bonding, and friend bonding. Chen, Dwyer, and Firth (2014) propose a model with six dimensions, maintaining place identity and place dependence, unifying the social dimension (place social bonding) and adding place memory, place expectation, and place affect, and verifying that the six dimensions function better as first-order factors than together as a second-order factor.

3   Finally, other authors consider place attachment as a subordinate concept or a dimension of a more general concept (Figure 6.3). For example, for Lalli (1992), place attachment is a component of urban-related identity. Jorgensen and Stedman (2001, 2006) propose place attachment, place dependence, and place identity as dimensions of sense of place. Likewise, Droseltis and Vignoles (2010), using confirmatory factor analysis, distinguished three dimensions (attachment/self-extension, environmental fit, and place-self-congruity) of another concept: place identification. Hesari et al. (2018) carried out a confirmatory factor analysis to test if place attachment is a second-order factor with place dependence, place identity, place affect, and place social bonding, finding indicators with adequate fit. For their part, Magalhães and Calheiros (2015) confirmed the suitability of PA as a second-order factor with five dimensions (place dependence, place identity, place affect, place social bonding, and natural bonding), but this conceptualization was particularly adapted to youth in residential institutions and would need further testing for suitability with other populations.

This conceptual diversity implies an associated heterogeneity in evaluation and measurement procedures, both qualitative and quantitative. Undoubtedly, the previous list confirms the need for a qualitative leap forward in the conceptualization of place attachment and other related concepts. Regarding the phases described by Low and Altman (1992), we believe that the scholarly discourse is now in a position to pass from the second phase "in which scholars described the phenomenon with greater rigor, developed taxonomies of sub-types" (p. 3), to the third one in which "there is a development of systematic theoretical positions" (ibidem).

In this line, Scannell and Gifford (2010) proposed a three-dimensional framework of place attachment intended to integrate and structure the variety of definitions in the literature. The framework treats place attachment as a multidimensional concept with *person*, *psychological process*, and *place* dimensions (PPP). According to the person dimension, place attachment occurs both at the individual and group levels. They define three psychological processes for place attachment: affect (emotion), cognition (identity), and behavior (action). Finally, the place dimension is divided into two levels: social and physical place attachment. In this model place attachment is defined as "a bond between an individual or group and a place that can vary in terms of spatial level, degree of specificity, and social or physical features of the place, and is manifested through affective, cognitive, and behavioral psychological processes" (Scannell and Gifford, 2010, p. 5).

This definition is linked to those by other authors (e.g., Brown & Perkins, 1992; Devine-Wright, 2011; Fornara et al., 2010; Giuliani, 2003; Jorgensen & Stedman, 2006; Low & Altman, 1992; Manzo & Perkins, 2006). Nevertheless, the authors of the PPP model consider that previous models are limited, representing only parts of the whole (see Scannell & Gifford, 2010 for a critique of previous models) and that the PPP framework provides a more inclusive view of place attachment. Along these lines we find other recent studies that have, in addition to the processes, looked at the characteristics of place and the personal and group variables involved (Clark, Duque-Calvache, & Palomares-Linares, 2017; Mandal, 2016; Taima & Asami, 2018; Xu, de Bakker, Strijker, & Wu, 2015).

In summary, the conceptualization of place attachment is plural and diverse and has generated a multiplicity of theoretical structures and relationships with other concepts. The coexistence of different theoretical and empirical approaches in this field is a defining characteristic that can be considered a problem or seen as an advantage, as it reveals the usefulness of this psycho-environmental process.

QUANTITATIVE METHODS FOR EVALUATING PLACE ATTACHMENT

The wide variety of conceptual models discussed in the previous section leads naturally to a lack of uniformity in the operationalization of the concepts and the evaluation procedures. This has resulted in some scholars promoting quantitative approaches; others callings for qualitative approaches, and still others endorsing a mixed method approach. In this chapter, we focus on quantitative approaches, the qualitative contributions being examined by Manzo and Pinto de Carvalho in this book.

Although laboratory measures or observational techniques have proliferated lately, most quantitative procedures for measuring attachment to place involve the use of questionnaires. Some authors use one or two items (e.g., Dallago et et al., 2009; Korpela, Ylén, Tyrväinene, & Silvennoinen, 2009, see ahead) but the majority use Likert-type scales, composed of a varied number of items. Instruments have proliferated in the last decade, but their heterogeneity in scope, size, and range has prevented the unification of results. In the following sections, some of the scales are presented that have received significant theoretical or empirical support, classified following the scheme of Figure 6.1, and we describe problems related to their reliability and validity.

Scales for place attachment

Among the one-dimensional scales (Figure 6.1) is the scale by Bonaiuto, Aiello, Perugini, Bonnes, and Ercolani (1999) of attachment to the neighborhood. A validation study by Fornara et al. (2010) in small and medium urban contexts retained four out of the original eight items: "This neighborhood is part of me," "I don't feel integrated in the neighbourhood," "This is the ideal neighborhood for me," and "It would be very hard for me to leave this neighborhood." Optimal levels of reliability (over 0.7 alpha) were reported for this scale when applied to studies in a large city (Rollero & De Piccoli, 2010a, 2010b).

Lewicka (2005, 2010) also proposed a scale with a single-factor structure, originally with 24 items (later reduced to nine items) mostly focusing on feelings and emotions toward places ("I miss the place when I am not here," "I feel safe here"), but it also containing items related to identity (e.g., "this place is a part of myself"). Lewicka (2011b) confirmed that this scale measures a single factor but also introduced a new scale to evaluate differences in the ways people relate to their place of residence. From an exploratory factorial analysis, five factors were identified: a traditional form of attachment (place inherited: "Even if there are better places, I am not going to move out of this city"), an active form of attachment (place discovered: "I like to wander around my city and discover new places"), and no or conditional attachment (place relativity: "I could equally well live here as in any other city"; place alienation: "dislike for the place and estrangement from it"; and placelessness: "indifference and no need to create emotional bonds with places").

The scale published in Hernández et al. (2007) and later confirmed by Ruiz, Hernández, and Hidalgo (2011) also considers place attachment as a one-dimensional concept. The authors developed an instrument to measure place attachment (an emotion: "I like living in this neighbourhood") and place identity (a form of self-concept: "I feel I belong to this neighbourhood") as two separate related variables, but not as dimensions of the same concept. The differences between both variables were confirmed in a confirmatory analysis using the simultaneous group comparison procedure. In an independent confirmatory analysis, Vidal, Valera, and Peró (2010) obtained similar results. Two relevant studies using this scale in a UK context found optimal reliability, thus confirming the consistency of the scale (Devine-Wright, 2011; Devine-Wright & Howes, 2010).

A second category includes scales that evaluate place attachment as a multidimensional construct with different numbers of factors (Figure 6.2). Among the most adopted ones, the scale by Williams and Roggenbuck (1989) identified potential items related to two main factors: place identity ("I feel X is a part of me," "I identify strongly with X") and place dependence ("X is the best place for what I like to do," "No other place can compare to X"). Several studies focused on the validation of this scale. Williams and Vaske (2003) performed a confirmatory factorial analysis to ratify the existence of the abovementioned factors and to test the validity of the proposed 12 items. Additionally, the authors substantiated the convergent validity of the scales using three independent variables that they deemed related to attachment: frequency of visits to the place, perceived familiarity, and degree to which the place is considered special. An interesting result of this work is that attachment measurements are found not to be generalizable across dimensions (i.e., scores on the one dimension cannot be generalized to another), suggesting that identity and dependence are phenomena related to place attachment, but not necessarily dimensions of it.

In turn, Kyle et al. (2005) use eight items from the scale by Williams and Roggenbuck (1989), adding four new items to measure a third factor: social bonds ("I have a lot of fond memories about X," "I have a special connection to X and the people who hike along it"). Structural equation modeling is used to compare the relationship among the three potential relation models between the factors. These models are based on three hypotheses: (1) the set of 12 items measures a single factor of place attachment, (2) there are three first-order factors that conform a multidimensional measure for place attachment, and (3) a second-order factor exists that can unify the three first-order factors. Although both models 2 and 3 have the same levels of statistical adjustment, the authors chose model 2 because they consider it more coherent with the findings of previous works (i.e., that the three factors behave independently against other variables). Therefore, their scale measures three *different* factors: place identity, place dependence, and social bonds.

The work of Raymond et al. (2010) is also based on the scale by Williams and Roggenbuck (1989), adding items focused on social bonds and nature bonds. After performing a factorial analysis, they select nineteen items, grouped in five dimensions: place identity ("I identify strongly with X"), place dependence ("No other place can compare to X"), nature bonding ("When I spend time in the natural environment in X, I feel a deep feeling of oneness with the natural environment"), family bonding ("I live in X because my family is here"), and friend bonding ("Belonging to volunteer groups in X is very important to me") (see Figure 6.2). Some of these items are related to restoration, others are related to memories and others to the bonding to the place inhabitants. Again, the question is whether these five factors are indicators of place attachment or independent interrelated variables.

Finally, there are scales in which place attachment is a component of a supraordinate concept. Jorgensen and Stedman (2001, 2006) consider place attachment as one of the three dimensions (the other two being place identity and place dependence) of a second-order factor that they call sense of place (Figure 6.3). To measure place attachment, they use four items related to the emotions produced by staying in a place (happiness, relaxation, e.g., "I feel relaxed when I'm at my lake property") or by having to leave (anxiety, nostalgia, e.g., "I really miss my lake property when I'm away from it for too long"). Hesari et al. (2018) use an adapted version of this scale along with other items from Kyle et al. (2005). In the same line, Droseltis and Vignoles (2010) include seven items in their scale of place identification (Figure 6.3): emotional attachment/self-extension (three items, e.g., "I feel this place is part of who I am"), environmental fit (two items, e.g., "I feel this is the place where I fit"), and place-self-congruity (two items, e.g., "This place reflects the type of person I am").

Problems related to validity

The methodological problems posed by the evaluation of place attachment are not only caused by the diversity of proposed scales for measuring the same concept, but by different foci on behaviors, attitudes, and beliefs even while using the same definition of place attachment. This also introduces problems of validity of the measurement. Place attachment is sometimes defined as an emotional bond, but the proposed scales include items related to other aspects such as identity, preference, or restorativeness. Korpela et al. (2009) for instance propose two items to measure place attachment: "I would miss this place if I moved somewhere else" consistent with their interpretation of place attachment as an emotional bond, and "Even if I visit this place frequently I don't get tired of it," which is normally used to evaluate perceived restorativeness. In the same line, Dallago et al. (2009) conceive place attachment as an emotional bond related to the perception of safety but use two items that are related to the quality of life ("Do you think that the area in which you live is a good place to live?"). The fact that a place can offer a good quality of life does not necessarily mean that people have attachment bonds to it.

Another frequent problem is that even the same authors use different scales in different studies. Hidalgo and Hernández (2001) used a scale to evaluate attachment to home, neighborhood, and city, with a distinction between three components: general ("I would be sorry to move out of my x, without the people who live there"), physical ("I would be sorry if I and the people who I appreciated in the x moved out"), and social ("I would be sorry if the people who I appreciated in the x moved out"). They later proposed an improved scale (Hernández et al., 2007) focusing on generic emotions associated to the place ("I like living in this neighbourhood," "When I'm away, I'm happy to come back"). Likewise, Brown, Brown, and Perkins (2004) measured place attachment based on unhappiness associated with moving, but Brown, Perkins, and Brown (2004) based the measurement on how proud people are of their homes. Scopelliti and Tiberio (2010) established a differentiation between attachment and identity, but they used a "multiple place attachment" scale to measure neighborhood attachment, in which they included items related to identification, lack of opportunities and social relations, and a different scale to measure city attachment based on two factors: emotional bonds and personal development. Similarly, Jorgensen and Stedman (2001, 2006) proposed a three-factor scale for sense of place, considering place attachment as an emotional bond, but in another study, Stedman (2003) used a different scale including items related to identity and dependence, which he considered separate factors.

Another aspect worth noting is that place attachment has been operationalized differently in different topical contexts. For instance, the scale by Williams and Roggenbuck (1989) has been applied especially for rural environments, while other scales (Bonaiuto et al., 1999; Hidalgo & Hernández, 2001; Lewicka, 2005, 2008) have been mostly adopted for urban environments. In an attempt to test the validity of the scale in Williams and Vaske (2003), Wynveen et al. (2017) analyzed the stability of the structure of the scale; comparing the responses of persons from distinct cultures, they found small differences in the functioning of the items. They concluded that it would be recommendable to adapt the scale to the specific contexts in which it is going to be applied.

It is therefore necessary, together with a greater conceptual precision, to also advance the validation of the scales used. There are very few works focused on this objective. It would be desirable to develop methodological works that help us select those items that are more suitable in order to evaluate each concept.

Combined methods

Combined quantitative measurements with qualitative procedures have been proposed in an attempt to evaluate more precisely the manifestations of place attachment (Blaikie, 2000; Boğaç, 2009; Devine-Wright and Howes, 2010; Ryan, 2009). For example, Boğaç (2009) analyses the degree to which people feel physically and socially attached to the place where they have been forced to move, compared with children who have always lived in the same place. Questionnaires, semi-structured interviews, and exercises of mental cartography (i.e., drawing tasks) are used. It is not clear, though, how the analysis of the data gathered and the interpretation of the results have been performed. No inter-rater reliability system or predetermined categorization is used to ensure the objectivity of the analysis.

Using a combined methodology, Ryan (2009) analyzed the impact of place attachment on shopping behavior in a rural town in Australia. Similarly to Beckley et al. (2007) in a qualitative phase they use photographs provided by the participants and interviews. The results of this phase are then used in a quantitative phase to develop a questionnaire to gather the necessary data to validate a model of relations between variables expressed as structural equations. However, the publication does not describe the type of questions used in the questionnaire, nor does it provide statistics of the obtained model, apart from the percentage of explained variance.

The combination of qualitative and quantitative methods can improve the understanding of psycho-environmental process when structured systems for data collection and appropriate strategies for exploiting the data gathered are combined, as in the study of Devine-Wright and Howes (2010). This study combines interviews, discussion groups, and questionnaires for measuring the disruption in place attachment in an area where a project for installing a wind energy park has been presented. Discussions were recorded to ensure adequate transcription and to enable further analysis based on a category system. The responses were analyzed using inter-rater reliability and reached a 97 percent of agreement, allowing the authors to obtain frequencies for each category and a ranked list of the most frequent topics. Quantitative data, however, show only correlations or

ANOVA for each variable, although a theoretical model of relationships between variables is proposed. Path analysis could have been used.

METHODOLOGICAL DESIGNS IN PLACE ATTACHMENT RESEARCH

This section analyzes the statistical analyses most frequently used in place attachment studies, as well as some more recent research designs.

Statistical analysis

From the perspective of the research design, we highlight the correlational character of many of the studies. In general, the data analysis performed in these works uses non-inferential statistical techniques and has a univariate character. The objectives of those statistical analyses can be structured in four categories.

First, there are analyses aimed at revealing the psychometric properties of the instruments used to measure place attachment. Studies of this type usually report the global scoring of the participants in the scale, and the obtained reliability, mainly based on the internal consistency calculated through Cronbach's alpha coefficient. For example, Ruiz and Hernández (2014) used a unifactorial place attachment scale, verifying that the reliability was greater than .80 and calculating the average of each participant to relate it to the rest of the variables. Likewise, Toruńczyk-Ruiz (2013), from a scale of seven items with Cronbach's alpha coefficient of .83, calculated the averages to compare natives and non-natives.

A second category includes statistical analyses aimed at establishing relations between place attachment and other bonds with place (e.g., rootedness, place dependence, place identity) and to identify correlates (including both predictors and consequences) of place attachment. In the analyses of the antecedents of place attachment, the goal is to identify variables that influence the magnitude of the established bonds. The most frequently analyzed predictors are socio-demographic (time length of residence, age, socioeconomic level) and socio-environmental (noise, overcrowding, type of housing, etc.) variables. With regard to consequent variables, the impact of place attachment on attitudes such as public acceptance of policy measures or behaviors such as mobility, pro-environmental behavior, and community participation has been studied. The most frequently used statistical analyses are simple linear correlation and multiple regression, in which place attachment can take the role of predictor or the role of consequent variable, as well as path analysis and structural equations (Bonaiuto et al., 1999; Droseltis & Vignoles, 2010; Jorgensen & Stedman, 2006; Rollero & De Piccoli, 2010a; Sullivan & Young, 2018; Taima & Asami, 2018). In some cases, logistical models have also been used to predict behavior based on attachment (Clark et al., 2017).

The third group of analyses is formed by those that compare the degree of place attachment between different groups, normally defined by socio-demographic variables like place of origin, sex, or place of residence. This type of analysis is also used to compare the degree of place attachment of the participants toward different places, for instance, comparing attachment between residential and wilderness areas (Williams, Patterson, & Roggenbuck, 1992) or between neighborhood, city, region, and country (Hidalgo & Hernández, 2001; Mandal, 2016; Shamai & Ilatov, 2005). Variance analysis and average contrast, normally of a univariate nature, are the most usual statistical methods in this type of analysis. However, it is important to highlight that analysis of mediators and moderators and multivariate analysis are increasingly being used (Anton & Lawrence, 2016; Gosling & Williams, 2010; Hernández et al., 2007; Vaske & Kobrin, 2001).

The last category comprises the studies intended to evaluate the structural dimension of the construct with an emphasis on the validation of the theory and of the instruments used (Droseltis & Vignoles, 2010; Hernandez, Hidalgo, Salazar-Laplace, & Hess, 2007; Kyle et al., 2005; Lewicka, 2011b; Raymond et al., 2010; Vaske & Kobrin, 2001). In this sense, we are witnessing an increase in the use of more robust statistical methods, with the goal of validating the accuracy of theoretical models. Confirmatory factorial analysis and structural equation models are among the most widely adopted analyses in this category. The increasing use of these procedures reveals a certain advance in this area of research because they require the existence of a previous theoretical conception that is not necessary in descriptive or exploratory studies (Hesari et al., 2018; Huang et al., 2018; Wynveen et al., 2017; Xu et al., 2015).

Recent designs

The incorporation of experimental or quasi-experimental designs has gradually increased, with the aim of testing the effect of attachment on psychological variables, such as well-being or other processual or behavioral variables, as well as to verify the efficacy of interventions. Thus, for example, Scannell and Gifford (2017) used an experimental design, in which 133 participants were induced into different emotions by a manipulated game on a computer and then invited to mentally visualize a place of attachment (one group) or a neutral place (a second group) and complete a survey with a place attachment scale, the Positive and Negative Affect Schedule, and a Need-Threat Scale to examine changes in psychological need satisfaction. They found that place attachment visualizations increased participant's level of self-esteem, meaning, and the sense of belonging to the group. Chang, Hou, Pan, Sung, and Chang (2015) used a quasi-experimental design with 87 university students to evaluate whether augmented reality guidance promote more sense of place (place attachment, place dependence, and place identity) and learning performance than audio-guidance and no-guidance. Augmented reality is a technological application used to assist historical or museums visits. This adds digital information on real objects or places for the purpose of enhancing the user experience. The results show how the use of digital technology to provide information on heritage sites contributes to increasing learning and sense of place.

Geographical information systems (GIS) have had a growing presence in research in this field and are a tool with great potential. Their use typically generates a mapping of places using diverse computer systems and permits researchers to relate characteristics of a place with other variables.

However, it is also possible to generate such maps using strategies for gathering data based on the responses of residents or on census data. Thus, for example, Brown, Raymond, and Corcoran (2015) analyzed place attachment in an area of Australia through spatial mapping using participatory GIS. Participants were asked to identify one place attachment area in the map, which they most strongly identified with and/or depend on for their lifestyle and livelihood. The authors found differences in the function of socio-demographic variables and household location, with economic values being representative of place dependence and social values of place identity, which were treated as dimensions of place attachment. Taima and Asami (2018), using census maps, tested differences based on personal characteristics (gender, age, income, etc.) and related to place (population, resources, etc.) and developed a map based on level of attachment in each zone of Kanto, a Japanese region, that includes both urban areas and rural locations. They used the Raymond et al. (2010) scale that adds to place identity and place dependence, two other dimensions: nature bonding and friends bonding.

CONCLUSIONS

The analytic review of the literature presented in this chapter highlights the need for place attachment studies to be founded on a precise definition of the concept and a consistent correspondence between the theory and the measurement procedures adopted. Research in this field should progress from analyzing *what* and *how much* to analyzing other questions such as *how*, *where*, *when*, and *why*. Lewicka (2011a) and Droseltis and Vignoles (2010) suggest that the Person dimension of the PPP model has received more attention than Place and Process, and that the emphasis put on the differences among individuals has probably inhibited the development of a theory of place attachment. We share their view and consider that although place characteristics, such as type and size (Casakin, Hernández, & Ruiz, 2015; Mandal, 2016), or others related to persons, such as gender, age, or self-efficacy (Brown et al., 2015; Xu et al., 2015), have received a certain amount of attention, it would be interesting to know more about the psychological process dimension (what are the properties of this bond, how it contributes to the identity, and what are the related behaviors) and about the place dimension (what types of places generate more attachment, what are the characteristics of those places, etc.).

With respect to measurement procedures, it would be desirable to use scales with adequate psychometric properties. When proposing new scales, their need must be justified, detailing why existing scales were not used, the theoretical model that underpins the new scale, and demonstrating adequate psychometric reliability and validity properties. In particular, the validity property is a weak aspect in the operationalization of place attachment. We consider that the investigations carried out so far do not allow us to classify the scales according to their greater or lesser validity. It would be advisable that part of the research effort be devoted to comparing the validity of the different scales proposed to measure place attachment.

Likewise, the use of combined methods (qualitative and quantitative) would facilitate the transfer of information between different disciplines, provided that standard methods for obtaining and interpreting the data are used. The use of experimental procedures allows a greater control over the antecedent and/or consequent variables of place attachment, as well as to identify causal relations between these variables. Additionally, the use of GIS allows the relation of geographic characteristics of the place with the psychological processes implied in the attachment to the place, which would lend more attention to Place and Process as has been pointed out above.

Regarding the statistical analyses, our recommendation is twofold. On the one hand, they must ensure consistency between the theory and the measurement procedures adopted. On the other hand, we recommend the use of multivariate analysis and statistical procedures to validate the accuracy of the theoretical model proposed. Additionally, path analysis and structural equation modeling allow researchers to test complex relationships between variables and confirm indirect relationships between them.

Finally, a dynamic conception of the relation between people and places in the line proposed by Manzo (2003) and Devine-Wright (2014) could be useful. In this sense, the use of longitudinal studies could contribute to a better understanding of place attachment. Correlational and qualitative studies, characteristic of research in place attachment, are in most cases based on information obtained in a single point in time. The limited number of longitudinal studies is surprising, especially if we consider that the developmental aspects of the bonds between people and places were highlighted in seminal studies of the area (Hay, 1998). Some recent works have tried to capture changes in place attachment bonds (Anton & Lawrence, 2016; Chow & Healy, 2008; Korpela et al., 2009; Ruiz et al., 2011; Tabernero, Briones, & Cuadrado, 2010). Despite their limitations (comparing samples with different length of residence, carrying out short follow-ups, or collecting data at only two specific times), these results confirm that research on the development of place attachment is hopeful.

REFERENCES

Anton, C. E., & Lawrence, C. (2016). The relationship between place attachment, the theory of planned behaviour and residents' response to place change. *Journal of Environmental Psychology, 47*, 145–154.

Beckley, T. M., Stedman, R. I., Wallace, S. M., & Ambard, M. (2007). Snapshots of what matters most: Using resident-employed photography to articulate attachment to place. *Society and Natural Resources, 20*, 913–929.

Blaikie, N. (2000). *Designing social research: The logic of anticipation*. Cambridge: Polity Press.

Boğaç, C. (2009). Place attachment in a foreign settlement. *Journal of Environmental Psychology, 29*, 267–278.

Bonaiuto, M., Aiello, A., Perugini, M., Bonnes, M., & Ercolani, A. P. (1999). Multidimensional perception of residential environment quality and neighbourhood attachment in the urban environment. *Journal of Environmental Psychology*, *19*, 331–352.

Brown, B. B., & Perkins, D. D. (1992). Disruption in place attachment. In I. Altman, & S. W. Low (Eds.), *Place attachment* (pp. 279–304). New York: Plenum.

Brown, B. B., Brown, G., & Perkins, D. D. (2004). New housing as neighborhood revitalization place attachment and confidence among residents. *Environment and Behavior*, *36*, 749–775.

Brown, B. B., Perkins, D. D., & Brown, G. (2004). Incivilities, place attachment and crime: Block and individual effects. *Journal of Environmental Psychology*, *24*, 359–371.

Brown, G., Raymond, C. M., & Corcoran, J. (2015). Mapping and measuring place attachment. *Applied Geography*, *57*, 42–53.

Casakin, H., Hernández, B., & Ruiz, C. (2015). Place attachment and place identity in Israeli cities: The influence of city size. *Cities*, *42*, 224–230.

Chang, Y. L., Hou, H. T., Pan, C. Y., Sung, Y. T., & Chang, K. E. (2015). Apply an augmented reality in a mobile guidance to increase sense of place for heritage places. *Journal of Educational Technology & Society*, *18*, 166–178.

Chen, N. C., Dwyer, L., & Firth, T. (2014). Conceptualization and measurement of dimensionality of place attachment. *Tourism Analysis*, *19*, 323–338. doi.org/10.372 7/108354214X14029467968529

Chow, K., & Healy, M. (2008). Place attachment and place identity: First year undergraduates making the transition from home to university. *Journal of Environmental Psychology*, *28*, 362–372.

Clark, W. A., Duque-Calvache, R., & Palomares-Linares, I. (2017). Place attachment and the decision to stay in the neighbourhood. *Population, Space and Place*, *23*(2), e2001. DOI:10.1002/psp.2001

Dallago, L., Perkins, D. D., Santinello, M., Boyce, W., Molcho, M., & Morgan, A. (2009). Adolescent place attachment, social capital, and perceived safety: A comparison of 13 countries. *American Journal of Community Psychology*, *44*, 148–160.

Devine-Wright, P. (2014). Dynamics of place attachment in a climate changed world. In L. Manzo, & P. Devine-Wright (Eds.), *Place attachment: Advances in theory, method and applications* (pp. 165–177). Abingdon, Oxford: Routledge.

Devine-Wright, P. (2011). Place attachment and public acceptance of renewable energy: A tidal energy case study. *Journal of Environmental Psychology*, *31*, 336–343.

Devine-Wright, P., & Howes, Y. (2010). Disruption to place attachment and the protection of restorative environments: A wind energy case study. *Journal of Environmental Psychology*, *30*, 271–280.

Droseltis, O., & Vignoles, V. L. (2010). Towards an integrative model of place identification: Dimensionality and predictors of intrapersonal-level place preferences. *Journal of Environmental Psychology*, *30*, 23–34.

Fornara, F., Bonaiuto, M., & Bonnes, M. (2010). Cross-validation of abbreviated perceived residential environment quality (PREQ) and neighborhood attachment (NA) indicators. *Environment and Behavior*, *42*, 171–196.

Giuliani, M. V. (2003). Theory of attachment and place attachment. In M. Bonnes, T. Lee, & M. Bonaiuto (Eds.), *Psychological theories for environmental issues* (pp. 137–170). Aldershot: Ashgate.

Giuliani, M. V., & Feldman, R. (1993). Place attachment in a developmental and cultural context. *Journal of Environmental Psychology*, *13*, 267–274.

Gosling, E., & Williams, K. J. H. (2010). Connectedness to nature, place attachment and conservation behavior: Testing connectedness theory among farmers. *Journal of Environmental PsyEchology*, *30*, 295–304.

Hay, R. (1998). Sense of place in developmental context. *Journal of Environmental Psychology*, *18*, 5–29.

Hernandez, B., Hidalgo, M. C., Salazar-Laplace, M. E., & Hess, S. (2007). Place attachment and place identity in natives and non-natives. *Journal of Environmental Psychology*, *27*, 310–319.

Hesari, E., Peysokhan, M., Havashemi, A., Gheibi, D., Ghafourian, M., & Bayat, F. (2018). Analyzing the dimensionality of place attachment and its relationship with residential satisfaction in new cities: The case of Sadra, Iran. *Social Indicators Research*, *142*, 1–23.

Hidalgo, M. C., & Hernandez, B. (2001). Place attachment: Conceptual and empirical questions. *Journal of Environmental Psychology*, *21*, 273–281.

Huang, W. J., Hung, K., & Chen, C. C. (2018). Attachment to the home country or hometown? Examining diaspora tourism across migrant generations. *Tourism Management*, *68*, 52–65.

Jorgensen, B. S., & Stedman, R. C. (2001). Sense of place as an attitude: Lakeshore owners attitudes toward their properties. *Journal of Environmental Psychology*, *21*, 233–248.

Jorgensen, B. S., & Stedman, R. C. (2006). A comparative analysis of predictors of sense of place dimensions: Attachment to, dependence on, and identification with lakeshore properties. *Journal of Environmental Management*, *79*, 316–327.

Korpela, K. M., Ylen, M., Tyrväinen, L., & Silvennoinen, H. (2009). Stability of selfreported favorite places and place attachment over a 10-month period. *Journal of Environmental Psychology*, *29*, 95–100.

Kyle, G., Graefe, A., & Manning, R. (2005). Testing the dimensionality of place attachment in recreational settings. *Environment and Behavior*, *37*, 153–177.

Lalli, M. (1992). Urban-related identity: Theory, measurement, and empirical findings. *Journal of Environmental Psychology*, *12*, 285–303.

Lewicka, M. (2005). Ways to make people active: Role of place attachment, cultural capital and neighborhood ties. *Journal of Environmental Psychology*, *4*, 381–395.

Lewicka, M. (2010). What makes neighborhood different from home and city? Effects of place scale on place attachment. *Journal of Environmental Psychology*, *30*, 35–51.

Lewicka, M. (2011a). Place attachment: How far have we come in the last 40 years?. *Journal of Environmental Psychology*, *31*, 207–230.

Lewicka, M. (2011b). On the varieties of people's relationships with places: Hummon's typology revisited. *Environment and Behavior*, *43*, 676–709.

Lewicka, M. (2008). Place attachment, place identity, and place memory: Restoring the forgotten city past. *Journal of Environmental Psychology*, *28*, 209–231.

Low, S. M., & Altman, I. (1992). Place attachment: A conceptual inquiry. In I. Altman, & S. W. Low (Eds.), *Place attachment* (pp. 1–12). New York: Plenum.

Magalhães, E., & Calheiros, M. M. (2015). Psychometric properties of the Portuguese version of place attachment scale for youth in residential care. *Psicothema*, *27*(1), 65–73.

Mandal, A. (2016). Size and type of places, geographical region, satisfaction with life, age, sex and place attachment. *Polish Psychological Bulletin*, *47*(1), 159–169. DOI:10.1515/ppb-2016-0018

Manzo, L. C. (2003). Relationships to non-residential places: Towards a reconceptualization of attachment to place. *Journal of Environmental Psychology*, *23*(1), 47–61.

Manzo, L. C. (2005). For better or worse: Exploring the multiple dimensions of place meaning. *Journal of Environmental Psychology*, *25*, 67–86.

Manzo, L. C., & Perkins, D. D. (2006). Finding common ground: The importance of place attachment to community participation and planning. *Journal of Planning Literature*, *20*, 335–350.

Morgan, P. (2010). Towards a developmental theory of place attachment. *Journal of Environmental Psychology*, *30*, 11–22.

Raymond, C. M., Brown, G., & Weber, D. (2010). The measurement of place attachment: Personal, community, and environmental connections. *Journal of Environmental Psychology*, *30*, 422–434.

Rollero, C., & De Piccoli, N. (2010a). Place attachment, identification and environment perception: An empirical study. *Journal of Environmental Psychology*, *30*, 198–205.

Rollero, C., & De Piccoli, N. (2010b). Does place attachment affect social well-being? *Revue Européenne de Psychologie Appliqué*, *60*, 233–238.

Ruiz, C., Hernández, B., & Hidalgo, M. C. (2011). Confirmation of the factorial structure of neighbourhood attachment and neighbourhood identity scale. *PsyEcology*, *2*(2), 207–215.

Ruiz, C., & Hernández, B. (2014). Emotions and coping strategies during an episode of volcanic activity and their relations to place attachment. *Journal of Environmental Psychology*, *38*, 279–287.

Ryan, M. (2009). Mixed methodology approach to place attachment and consumption behaviour: A rural town perspective. *The Electronic Journal of Business Research Methods*, *7*, 107–116.

Scannell, L., & Gifford, R. (2010). Defining place attachment: A tripartite organizing framework. *Journal of Environmental Psychology*, *30*, 1–10.

Scannell, L., & Gifford, R. (2017). Place attachment enhances psychological need satisfaction. *Environment and Behavior*, *49*, 359–389.

Scopelliti, M., & Tiberio, L. (2010). Homesickness in university students: The role of multiple place attachment. *Environment and Behavior*, *42*(3), 335–350.

Shamai, S., & Ilatov, Z. (2005). Measuring sense of place: Methodological aspects. *Tijdschrift voor Economische en Sociale Geografie*, *96*, 467–476.

Stedman, R. C. (2003). Is it really just a social construction?: The contribution of the physical environment to sense of place. *Society and Natural Resources*, *16*, 671–685.

Stokols, D., & Shumaker, S. A. (1981). People in places. A transactional view of settings. In J. Harvey (Ed.), *Cognition, social behavior and the environment* (pp. 441–488). Hillsdale, NJ: Lawrence Erlbaum Associates.

Sullivan, D., & Young, I. F. (2018). Place attachment style as a predictor of responses to the environmental threat of water contamination. *Environment and Behavior*, *52*(1), 3–32.

Tabernero, C., Briones, E., & Cuadrado, E. (2010). Changes in residential satisfaction and place attachment over time. *PsyEcology*, *1*(3), 403–412.

Toruńczyk-Ruiz, S. (2013). Neighbourhood attachment and city identity in ethnically mixed areas: Comparison of natives and migrants in four European cities. *Estudios de Psicología*, *34*(3), 339–343.

Taima, M., & Asami, Y. (2018). Estimation of average place attachment level in a region of Japan. *GeoJournal*, *84*(5), 1365–1381.

Vaske, J. J., & Kobrin, K. C. (2001). Place attachment and environmentally responsible heavier. *The Journal of Environmental Education*, *32*, 16–21.

Vidal, T., Valera, S., & Peró, M. (2010). Place attachment, place identity and residential mobility in undergraduate students. *PsyEchology*, *1*(3), 353–369.

Williams, D. R., & Roggenbuck, J. W. (1989). *Measuring place attachment: Some preliminary results*. Paper presented at the session on outdoor planning and management, NRPS Symposium on Leisure Research, San Antonio, Texas.

Williams, D. R., & Vaske, J. J. (2003). The measurement of place attachment: Validity and generalizability of a psychometric approach. *Forest Science*, *49*(6), 830–840.

Williams, D. R., Patterson, M. E., & Roggenbuck, J. W. (1992). Beyond the commodity metaphor: Examining emotional and symbolic attachment to place. *Leisure Sciences*, *14*, 29–46.

Wynveen, C., Schneider, I. E., Cottrell, S., Arnberger, A., Schlueter, A. C., & Von Ruschkowski, E. (2017). Comparing the validity and reliability of place attachment across cultures. *Society & Natural Resources*, *30*(11), 1389–1403. DOI:10.1080/08941920.2017.1 295499

Xu, M., de Bakker, M., Strijker, D., & Wu, H. (2015). Effects of distance from home to campus on undergraduate place attachment and university experience in China. *Journal of Environmental Psychology*, *43*, 95–104.

Chapter 7: The role of qualitative approaches to place attachment research

Lynne C. Manzo and Laís Pinto de Carvalho

Much has been written about place attachment as a construct over the years. Yet, less attention has been paid to the broad methodological aspects of place attachment, the epistemological underpinnings, and the political implications of researchers' choice of paradigms.[1] In particular, the place attachment literature is lacking an examination of the role and value of qualitative or more subjectivist and critical reflexive[2] approaches as well as considerations of what such approaches can afford in terms of our understanding of the phenomenon.

To address this gap, this chapter aims (1) to present different onto-epistemological approaches to researching and understanding place attachment, and (2) to examine the specific role and value of qualitative/subjectivist/critically reflexive approaches in terms of *what they make room for* in our understanding of place attachment—that is, how such approaches can broaden our way of studying and understanding place attachment. We contend that qualitative/subjectivist/critically reflexive approaches are essential to exploring the less well-understood and emergent aspects of place attachment. These aspects include place experiences that are not captured in existing measurement tools—for example, how place attachments are complicated by power relations, and how attachments play a role in people's response to place change and increasing socio-spatial precarity (e.g., vulnerability due to displacement via disasters, gentrification). We therefore aim to shed light on the unique strengths of a qualitative/subjectivist/reflexive approach to research on place attachments.

ONTO-EPISTEMOLOGICAL APPROACHES TO RESEARCH

In order to achieve the goals of this chapter, it is necessary to consider the researcher's fundamental beliefs about reality and knowledge that undergird their methodological choices when conducting research. This is important because different views of reality (ontology) and what constitutes valid knowledge (epistemology) ultimately drive how researchers study the phenomena that they seek to understand, such as place attachment. Historically, researchers have made a distinction between two broad onto-epistemological paradigms: the quantitative and qualitative. The quantitative paradigm is predicated on positivism, a premise that there is a single external reality that is objectively knowable and that can be interpreted through reason and logic. In this paradigm, researchers strive to be detached from what they study with the belief that findings will thereby depend on the nature of what is being studied rather than on the beliefs, values, and choices of the researcher. Such objectivity, it has been argued, ensures that the researchers have "constrained their personal prejudices" (Payne & Payne, 2004, p. 153) leading to more reliable findings. In this paradigm, rigor is achieved through the establishment of a standardized set of protocols and procedures that can be applied to any context, as the aim is to establish generalizable knowledge. Toward that end, researchers tend to prefer experimental designs and random sampling techniques with large samples so that findings might be generalized to the larger population whom that sample is meant to represent. Data collected in this paradigm tend to be numeric in nature and analyzed through statistical tests.

In contrast, the qualitative paradigm emerged as social scientists sought to apply the philosophical concept of "*verstehen*" (translated from German loosely as "to understand" or "to interpret") to study human experience and to develop a method to capture the processes through which humans come to know the world (Lapan, Quartaroli, & Riemer, 2011). On this foundation, the qualitative paradigm gathers data in the form of natural language and expressions of experiences, including visual expressions (Levitt et al., 2018). Scholars from this epistemological position challenge the notion that an independent reality exists outside of any investigation or observation.[3] They further question the feasibility and value of objectivity, which feminist scholar Donna Haraway (1988) has famously called the "god trick" because objectivist knowledge is presented as a disembodied and transcendent "gaze from nowhere" (p. 581). Some scholars have argued that positivist objectivity is not just unnecessary, but undesirable. Consequently, a qualitative approach not only accepts subjectivity but also encourages researchers to examine closely their own positionality by being reflexive in the research process (Guba & Lincoln, 1994). This reflexivity is a methodological principle that calls for self-awareness and careful reflection throughout all phases of the research process regarding the relationships among the researcher(s), research participants, and the subject matter under study.

The onto-epistemological framework guiding qualitative work also calls for reconsideration of traditional interpretations of validity and reliability. By implementing verification strategies and self-adjusting during the process of research, qualitative researchers move the responsibility for incorporating and maintaining reliability and validity from external reviewers' judgments to the investigators themselves (Morse, Barrett, Mayan, Olson, & Spires, 2002). As a result, the hallmarks of rigor in the qualitative paradigm focus on prioritizing context sensitivity, being transparent in the research process, involving research participants in data analysis to "truth test" the work, and centering relationality as a way to be accountable to the broader community to which the research participants belong. This measure of rigor also stems from a critique of extraction methodologies (De Sousa Santos, 2016), or modes of research where the information generated does not offer benefits to the people and communities whom the researchers engage. However, there is a tendency to evaluate qualitative research against conventional scientific (i.e., quantitative) criteria of rigor (Sandelowski, 1986), thus marginalizing such research endeavors.

Debates about the utility of perpetuating a quantitative and qualitative binary have grown, and there is an important movement away from this divide (see, e.g., Bassi, 2014; Di Masso, Dixon, and Durrheim, 2014; Seamon & Gill, 2016). According to Mazumdar (2005), a more appropriate nomenclature for different research paradigms would be in epistemological terms, for example, positivist approaches and nonpositivistics. Bassi (2014) goes further advocating for replacing the quantitative-qualitative binary with a continuum of critical reflexivity. This framework focuses more on the ethical implications of using certain methods, including asking for what and for whom the research is being conducted, what the research sustains, and what it overcomes.

The quantitative-qualitative binary is also problematic because within each of these paradigms, there is a diversity of perspectives and epistemologies. For example, the qualitative approach is not singular but composed of a theoretical and procedural multiplicity, including pragmatism, grounded theory, symbolic interactionism, narrative research, discourse analysis, phenomenology, ethnomethodology, intuitive inquiry, performative research, non-representational research, affect-based research, ethnography and auto-ethnography, social constructionism, critical theory (Marxist, feminist, cultural, critical race, queer, postcolonial, disability theories), action research, and advocacy/participation studies (Seamon & Gill, 2016). Further, a researcher might employ qualitative data collection techniques typical of that paradigm but approach their research with a positivistic framework. For example, a researcher might conduct in-depth interviews but still seek to approximate objectivity in the classic positivist sense in their analysis by seeking to quantify the textual data or make generalizable claims (see, e.g., the debate between Williams & Patterson, 2007, and Beckley, Stedman, Wallace, & Ambard, 2007 on this matter).

Similarly, although the quantitative methodology is usually carried out under a positivist or postpositivist[4] understanding of reality, this is not the case *a priori*. For example, Kwan (2002) argues that researchers can approach GIS as a positivist technological tool, which would limit our understanding and use of it, or we can seek more critical applications, including its use to gather qualitative data. In one study, Kwan (2008) uses GIS along with oral histories and diary data to understand the "emotional geographies" of Muslim women in the US after 9/11. She created visual narratives that document Muslim women's emotional responses to place over time. These narratives ran counter to the then-dominant anti-Muslim sentiment. Hence, quantitative tools and research can also have a reflexive and critical character (Parker, 2007, 2014; Pinto do Carvalho & Cornejo, 2018) particularly when the data are non-numeric (e.g., visual, textual).

This suggests that neither quantitative nor qualitative approaches have an exclusive claim on challenging normative orders. Thus, relying on a quantitative-qualitative binary can be counterproductive as particular onto-epistemological assumptions are not naturally given by the data production strategies chosen by the researcher. We therefore posit that conceptual and methodological heterogeneity is critical to a full appreciation of the dynamic aspects of place attachments and their various manifestations. To contribute to that heterogeneity, our particular focus in this chapter is on what Denzin (2017) calls the "multiple interpretive community" typically comprised of "qualitative researchers ... united by the avowed humanistic and social justice commitment to study the social world from the perspective of the interacting individual" (p. 10).

ONTO-EPISTEMOLOGICAL PARADIGMS IN PLACE ATTACHMENT RESEARCH

To address the onto-epistemological paradigms framing place attachment research, it is useful to consider first the paradigmatic underpinnings of research on place. This area of research gained momentum in the mid-twentieth century with the emergence of environmental psychology (Altman & Rogoff, 1987; Saegert & Winkel, 1990) and the humanistic critique in geography, including phenomenology (Buttimer, 1976; Seamon, 1979; Tuan, 1977). Place research advanced through multiple concurrent trends including: (1) "critiques of cognitive information processing theories [in psychology] ... in which the environment was reduced to stimulus," (2) the articulation of a transactional approach for studying people in their physical context, and (3) "anti-positivistic reactions to mainstream geography's emphasis on place as ... container of action" (Williams, 2014, p. 90).

As Williams and Patterson (2005) note, research on place was initially slow to spread outside of humanistic geography and phenomenology because of the dominance of the positivistic paradigm and quantitative approaches in environment and behavior research (see also Low & Altman, 1992). Much early research in environmental psychology inherited the dominant socio-cognitivist approach in psychology that brought with it positivist assumptions about people-place relationships. As Stokols (1990) noted, this work was based in an instrumental perspective that measured different qualities and features of the environment and how these influenced human thought and behavior (Williams, 2014). Still, alongside this trend emerged qualitative and phenomenological work as an important endeavor against this "over-scientification" of people-place relationships (Di Masso, personal communication; see Canter, 1977; Relph, 1978 for the early debate).

Just as place research is not grounded in a single research tradition, neither are studies of place attachment. Williams (2014) posits that the legacy of place attachment research includes two conceptions of place as a locus of attachments or as a center of meaning, with the former approach considering place attachment "narrowly as an affective bond," while the latter examines the ways that people construct and express meaning. He further posits that the place as locus of attachment approach has been "quite amenable to psychometric methods of measuring individual differences" across various contexts (p. 93), while research taking the latter approach which is typically captured through discourse and narrative, lends itself to a more qualitative approach (Williams, 2014). However, the distinction between these approaches to place attachment may not always lend themselves to the adoption of a particular paradigm, as we see in studies that take a mixed methods approach (e.g., Devine-Wright, 2011; Devine-Wright & Howes, 2010).

Using their own framework for organizing the body of place attachment research, Di Masso et al. (2014) make a distinction between what they call a "cognitive/representationalist" approach and a "discursive/constructionist" approach. The cognitive/representationalist approach tends to focus on the internal, psychological experience of individuals, and the way that attachments accomplish individual functions, for example, survival, self-regulation, and self-continuity (Di Masso et al., 2014, p. 81). In contrast, a discursive/constructionist approach sees people-place relations as a context-specific, dialogic, social construction with a focus on variability of meanings that have "significant rhetorical/ideological relevance" (p. 81). This approach to place attachment, they argue, releases us from seeing attachment as a deep-seated internalized affinity to places that individuals experience, to seeing attachments as linguistically and socially constructed. Still, as we shall illustrate, there are other approaches beyond these that warrant consideration.

Despite articulations of divergent approaches to researching place attachment (See Table 7.1), a dominant thread within place attachment research has arguably been situated within the positivist and postpositivist paradigm—that is, the place as locus of attachment thread according to Williams (2014), or the cognitive-representationalist approach as articulated by Di Masso et al. (2014). Working from the post/positivist paradigm, scholars have focused on how best to measure place attachment with the use of scales to determine the intensity of attachments to certain locations, and to establish the reliability and validity of the survey instrument (see, especially, Kyle et al., 2005; Raymond et al, 2010; Williams & Vaske, 2003). As a result, much place attachment research has sought to standardize measures and procedures, to generalize knowledge about place attachments and to look for causal relationships. The dominance of this trend is verified in Lewicka's (2011) review of forty years of place attachment research. Some have speculated this trend toward positivism and measurement may be due, in part, to a legacy of social science research approaches to phenomena as placed outside of situated processes (Di Masso & Castrechini, 2012). This decontextualization has had important consequences for research on people-place relations and place attachment in particular—for example, the de-politicization of these relations, the predominance of individualistic approaches to understanding attachments, and the overlooking of experiences not captured in behavioral or cognitive approaches structured into popular place attachment survey instruments. A critical goal of this chapter, therefore, is to shed light on the nature and value of a more qualitative/subjectivist/critically reflexive approach to studying place attachment. In the following sections, we

Table 7.1

Comparison of paradigmatic approaches to research, especially as related to place attachment

	Positivist Approaches	Subjectivist/Critically Reflexive Approaches
Research interest	Explanation: prediction and control	Understanding, criticism, and transformation/restitution and emancipation
Ontology	Realism, typically singular reality but possible multiple subjectivities (biases) Apprehensible reality	Historical realism (critical paradigm): reality shaped by social, political, cultural, economic, ethnic, and gender values; crystallized over time; and relativism (constructivist paradigm): local and specific co-constructed realities
Epistemology	Objectivist	Transactional subjectivist
Methodology	Experimental/Manipulation of variables	Dialogical/Hermeneutical/Dialectic
Values	Excludes/Denies values; seeks to avoid researcher subjectivity (bias)	Includes values, recognizes importance of positionality/reflexivity
Methods	Predominance of quantitative (e.g., large-scale surveys)	Predominance of the qualitative (e.g., narrative and graphic approaches)
Approaches to place attachment	Place attachment as universal and apprehensible phenomenon Search for generalization and causality through standardized measures Emphasis on explaining individual processes Place attachment usually not studied as a political phenomenon	Place attachment as context-occasioned and socially constructed phenomenon Search for experience, meanings and their variability, situated in singular contexts Emphasis on exploring individual and collective processes and lived experiences Place attachments usually studied as a political phenomenon, affected by power relations
Liberative/Change potential	Liberative potential through innovative/critical use of traditional tools (e.g., GIS)	Liberative potential through the critical data production strategies, analysis, and dissemination of results. Positivistic analysis of qualitative data can perpetuate status quo/hegemonic approaches

Source: Di Masso et al. (2014) and Guba and Lincoln (1994) modified by the authors of this chapter. Our intention here is to highlight substantial differences between these distinct approaches. We recognize that they are but two of many approaches, and that they might be, in some aspects, more like anchors on a continuum with more nuanced or hybrid approaches between them. For example, postpositivist critical research could acknowledge the researcher's influence/positionality and might include mixed methods. However, it is also true that while some aspects of research paradigms might fit on a continuum, others, like ontology, are incommensurable.

therefore focus on how qualitative/subjectivist/critically reflexive approaches can expose new possibilities in the study of place attachments.

CONTRIBUTIONS OF THE QUALITATIVE/SUBJECTIVIST/CRITICALLY REFLEXIVE APPROACH TO PLACE ATTACHMENT

In this section, we posit that a qualitative/subjectivist/critically reflexive approach is particularly helpful in revealing aspects of place attachment that are less evident in dominant approaches. This includes how (1) place attachments are influenced by their situatedness in particular geopolitical contexts and power relations; and how (2) place attachments are experienced in non-normative ways, as nonpositivistic/qualitative approaches are less likely to reify and reproduce hegemonic understandings of how people relate to place. We wish to highlight these aspects of place attachment because we believe that more dominant approaches risk overlooking and further marginalizing already marginalized experiences and people, which does not serve to advance our understanding of this important phenomenon. We present some empirical examples to demonstrate a diversity of contexts and insights provided by this approach to place attachment research.

Place attachments are influenced by their situatedness in particular geopolitical contexts and power relations

As Haraway (1988) argued years ago, we need situated and embodied knowledge (i.e., knowledge tied to the specifics of embodied political identities) as an argument against unlocatable knowledge claims. Place attachment research conducted from a more qualitative, subjectivist, critically reflexive approach helps demonstrate the situatedness of place attachment in its larger geopolitical context because it makes room for people's own narratives and contextualized knowledge. It is less interested in the strength of place attachment than in the nature of the experience as lived and described by research participants themselves. As such, it also calls out the situatedness of researchers themselves (Breuer & Roth, 2003). This is critical to acknowledge since most studies of place attachment are about, and produced from, the global north, especially Anglo-Saxon contexts. It stands to reason, then, that if we accept knowledge as situated per Haraway (1988), then we need to hear from a much wider array of voices. Currently, much of what we know about place attachments is geared toward dominant experiences of the global north and from other dominant groups (i.e., people from western, educated, industrialized, rich, and democratic societies long considered "standard subjects" that are actually outliers) (Henrich, Heine, & Norenzayan, 2010).

Qualitative research has been particularly useful in revealing the political component of place attachment, challenging notions such as social conflict, power struggles, and social change. For example, using discourse analysis, Dixon and Durrheim (2000) studied racial exclusion on the beaches of South Africa when apartheid was progressively dismantled. By closely analyzing newspaper articles in the period from 1982 to 1995, they were able to identify the racist rhetoric through which ideological constructions of the place were made. Further research by the authors based on in-depth interviews of holiday-goers on a desegregated beach revealed not only the emotional and symbolic significance of place, but also how the beach served as a site for the expression of white South African identity for white respondents (Dixon & Durrheim, 2004). The open-ended approach employed in this research enabled these politicized and spatialized articulations of identity to emerge via a nuanced examination of respondents' accounts of desegregation.

Di Masso, Dixon, and Pol's (2011) study of place meaning and attachment to a public space in Barcelona reveals how practices of attributing meaning and value to places are often more conflict-ridden, action-oriented, and politically charged than is implied by much research around place attachment. In this study, the authors conducted a discourse analysis with 186 media reports from newspapers across a ten-year span, and conducted in-depth interviews with different actors representing citizen and government organizations, to understand their positions in relation to the development of the contested public space. For each site studied, they found rhetorically opposed constructions of place meanings among citizens and protesters on the one hand, and developers and local administrators on the other. They argue that a rhetorical analysis enabled these meanings and dimension of place meaning and attachments to emerge.

In another example, Pinto de Carvalho (2018) studied a small urban community's response to, and recovery from, a volcanic eruption in Chile. In this study, the researchers employed participatory photographic techniques and walking interviews that focused on people's life stories around place to understand the recovery process and the impacts of the volcanic eruption on local residents' place attachments. These methods enabled researchers to see how place attachment intersected with the politics of place, revealing tensions between the official discourse around a neoliberal way of recovery and reoccupation of affected areas, and residents' experiences of place and of disruption. The research revealed that the state declared only the poor areas on the periphery of the city as unfit for residential use due to the volcanic risk, fragmenting the community by requiring people to relocate in different cities. Further, discourse analysis uncovered how the official designation of places as uninhabitable territory and as places of vulnerability that were illegal to enter contrasted with residents' views of the territory as a lived place of attachments and community. Indeed, poor residents with little political power disobeyed the state and chose to return to their precarious homes even without basic services such as running water. The approach taken in this research demonstrates the power of place attachments, the impact of its political dimensions, and the need for reconstruction strategies to prioritize the care, dignity, and livelihoods of community members.

Another qualitative study of place attachments and post-disaster recovery in Christchurch, New Zealand, revealed several critical dimensions of place attachments that might not otherwise be revealed through quantitative techniques (Durgerian, 2019). Here, the researcher examined what she called the "emotional infrastructure" of the citizens of Christchurch, observing how attachments to place helped support the recovery process. In particular, Durgerian notes that the open-ended nature of the interviews she conducted, and the intentional effort to hear people talk about their experience in their own terms, revealed dimensions of place attachment that might not otherwise be evident. For example, people got attached to temporary places for meeting basic survival needs—like locations of a bank of temporary latrines and places to get fuel for cooking because they also became critical social meeting spaces where people could share experiences, maintain social ties, and rebuild community.

Durgerian (2019) also notes how critical an awareness of her positionality was during this research. For example, she made a concerted effort to reach out to members of the indigenous Maori community to learn about their experiences of the earthquake recovery process. Although she was mainly an "outsider" as a US citizen conducting this research, there were a few critical ways that she approached the research that altered the trajectory of her work. She notes that intentionally approaching people with a curiosity about their stories, and enabling participants to begin and end these stories as participants saw fit was critical. In addition, she made a point of engaging Maori leaders with a purposeful approach of "deep listening" and "authenticity" which helped establish relationships of mutual trust.

Durgerian further explains that a major influence on building relationships was clarifying her "place to stand" or what in Maori is known as *tūrangawaewae*, and her place in time through her genealogy or *whakapapa*. To do this, she provided each participant with a personalized greeting card of photos of the canoe she made as a young girl with her father, explaining how those photos connected her to family and place. This expression of her own situatedness opened doors to relationships that helped her to understand far more about place attachments in Christchurch than she might otherwise have understood. Together, the studies described in this section demonstrate just some of the ways that qualitative/subjectivist/reflexive methods can be used to reveal the role of power, politics, and conflict in place attachment.

Place attachments are experienced in non-normative ways

In this section, we posit that a qualitative/subjectivist/reflexive approach to studying place attachments is also particularly well suited for enabling non-hegemonic perspectives of place to be heard. This is because such an approach allows for people to describe their diverse experiences of place in their own terms/images, and because a reflexive approach requires a particular sensitivity to the very power relations that impact marginalized groups. Here, we consider place attachments in a context of non-normative place experiences—for example, how place attachments are connected to identity and identity politics as revealed by the stories of marginalized people, and how attachments to domestic space/home can be complicated by mixed emotions and experiences.

Research has demonstrated that for marginalized groups, attachments to place are formed through complicated relationships often forged by exclusion. For example, using in-depth, semi-structured interviews, Manzo (2005) found that for LGBQT+ participants, the places to which they were attached were places of belonging secured for them in dynamic relation to places of exclusion and alienation (see also Chamlee-Wright & Storr, 2009; Gorman-Murray, 2007). For some, their place of residence was one such place of alienation and rejection and their place attachments were carved from relationships with other places where they could safely be themselves and be accepted. Their stories were related to places instrumental to their experience of "coming out," which included gay neighborhoods, community and drop-in centers, bars, book stores, and friend's homes where they were accepted and safe. These interviews also illustrated how negative and ambivalent feelings and experiences were a critical part of people's attachments to place. Measuring place attachment through established scales would not have revealed the nuances and dynamism of place attachments that this study demonstrated, for example, the aforementioned dynamic relation between exclusion and belonging, and tensions around the notion of home.

The nuanced complexities of place attachments are also well illustrated through qualitative research in contexts of ethnic-racial relations. For example, Fullilove (2014, this volume, Chapter 11) describes how African-Americans formed attachments to "beloved communities" that were culturally rich centers of belonging created through a history of racism and exclusion, from slavery to "redlining" (discriminatory practices of demarcating urban areas where banks would avoid investing) and gentrification/displacement today. Her critically reflexive, qualitative approach with particular attention to race and power revealed rich layers of complex place attachments that were continually navigated and negotiated through history, borne from a tension between serial displacement and the constant moving and rebuilding of Black communities. Similarly, Durgerian's (2019) critically reflexive approach and use of in-depth interviews in the previously mentioned study in post-earthquake Christchurch revealed that for indigenous Maori participants, the earthquake was, in its own way, a "welcome disruption to a damaging normal." The rich narratives that were gathered demonstrated an important distinction between indigenous and settler ways of relating to the land and how Maori cultural history was erased by colonization. Because of that history, Maori participants saw the earthquake as a way to disrupt the colonial identity of the city and enable a more inclusive vision that accommodated Maori history, identity, and presence to be acknowledged and created (Durgerian, 2019). These perspectives, often marginalized in society and in research, were revealed through the flexible, open-ended, and narrative approaches taken in these studies.

A qualitative approach to place attachments also enables consideration of the complexities of emotional responses to place, revealing how one's residence can sometimes be characterized by negative and ambivalent feelings. This is an extension of earlier feminist literature that challenged the then-prevailing view of domestic space as a place of peace and refuge, noting instead its role as a site of women's reproductive and care work, where experiences of loneliness, isolation, seclusion, invasion of privacy, and violation of rights can occur (Ahrentzen, 1992; Massey, 1994/2001; McDowell, 1997). Along the same lines, Moore (2000) links the study of place attachment to critical studies of the home, making visible the diversity and tensions in attachments to the residence that incorporate understandings of the material, political, and cultural production in which these experiences are developed. Similarly, for González (2005), home involves aspects of both topophilia (love of place) and topophobia (fear of place). Through the use of in-depth interviews with rural women from southwestern Spain with little formal education who are not employed outside the home, this study demonstrates how the same space can be lived differently by women and men, and how relationships to home can reproduce ideologies, stereotypes, alienation, and gender violence. Overall, this study reminds us of how place attachments can be saturated with sometimes contradictory emotions.

Explorations of place attachments in public/social housing demonstrate that people's attachments to place can run counter to dominant discourses about that housing. For example, studies of forced relocation through urban restructuring programs in the US (Manzo, 2014) and Europe (Kleinhans & Kearns, 2013) reveal that people's relationship with their housing was quite complex, and that it was complicated, in part, by the contrast between residents' lived experience of place and the rhetoric of "severe distress" that was deployed to justify the demolition of their housing. For example, Manzo, Kleit, and Couch (2008) found that public housing residents had strong bonds to their housing and enjoyed thriving mutual support systems among neighbors despite the housing being labeled as distressed by local housing authorities and slated for demolition. This created a great deal of ambivalent emotions among residents revolving around four competing themes; feelings that community was a good and supportive place to live, discomfort over the stigma of living in public housing, anger and fear about being forced to move, and struggling to exonerate the housing authority's requirement to relocate because of their power and because residents were told it was in their best interest to move. The use of in-depth interviews with residents revealed the active process of meaning making as residents struggled with the externally imposed label of distress in contrast to their own experiences of place and the necessity to move. The qualitative approach enabled us to gain an understanding of the agency of residents—particularly poor people who are often stripped of their agency—in a way that could not have been revealed by surveys alone.

SUMMARY

To truly understand any phenomenon through research, we "need multiple paradigms and critical reflexive approaches to have a better account of the world" (Haraway, 1988, p. 579), what Patterson and Williams (2005) have called "critical pluralism." Conceptual and methodological heterogeneity is essential for a full appreciation of place attachment and its various manifestations and dynamics. In this chapter, we sought to highlight the role and value of qualitative/subjectivist/critical reflexive approaches to place attachment as a means to understand those aspects of the phenomenon that are less well understood by research thus far, including place attachments that fall outside of normative expectations and experiences. In particular, we have argued that research from a qualitative/subjectivist/critical reflexive perspective allows for a range of marginalized place experiences to be explored and offers unique insights into place attachments that are distinct from the kind of data obtained from established quantitative measures.

In their critical analysis of Latin American environmental psychology in the first decade of the millennium, Wiesenfeld and Zara (2012) observed that the ethical-political dimensions of place research have been neglected. This includes questioning the neutrality of researchers, the emphasis on the study of individual processes isolated from the particular and political contexts in which people are immersed, and the use of research knowledge in service of relations of inequality, oppression, and exploitation—for example, normalizing white middle class educated experience as "standard" (Henrich et al., 2010). We maintain that the same challenges hold true for much place attachment research today. Qualitative, subjectivist, and critically reflexive approaches can help scholarship on place attachments break away from these trends by its vigilance to power relations in the research process, and by including voices from the margins through the use of narrative and image-based approaches that enable people to tell stories of place in their own terms.

Denzin (2017) recently noted that "critical qualitative research is under assault" as "scholars around the world … struggle against the regulatory practices of neoliberalism" (p. 15). In light of this context, we have sought to highlight some of the unique dimensions of qualitative, subjectivist, and critically reflexive approaches to studying place attachments. Going forward, it would be helpful to keep in mind that research on place attachments that is conducted in a politically aware manner also makes room for research to initiate social change. That is, reflecting on "who owns the research issues, who initiates them, in whose interests the research is carried out … what counts as knowledge and who is transformed by it" can enable place attachment work to not only capture a fuller range of the human experiences of place, it can enable people to partake of their own liberation (Edwards & Brannelly, 2017, p. 272).

We close this chapter by inviting an opening—of a renewed discussion regarding the epistemological and methodological implications of place attachment research. It is essential for researchers to ask: What is the contribution of our epistemological and methodological decisions to our understanding of place attachments? Does the design of our research reproduce existing power dynamics or reveal and challenge them? Do we design research that involves people as active agents of their attachment experience? These are critical questions we must ask ourselves if we are to truly understand the full multitude of ways that people form place attachments. We must understand place attachments and what they represent in people's own terms in their lives in a way that can be more understanding and sensitive to people's unique experiences and not merely reproduce what we already know or assume.

NOTES

1 While Hernández et al. (2014; this volume, Chapter 6) provide a fine overview of theoretical and methodological aspects of place attachment research, the focus is more heavily on quantitative approaches, and while Seamon and Gill (2016) offer an excellent overview of qualitative methods, it is more broadly about methods for environmental psychology as a discipline rather than place attachment research specifically.

2 It is our contention that a qualitative approach to research is commensurate with subjectivist and critically reflexive approaches in that they all consider knowledge as positional and subjective, and they do not see this as a methodological shortcoming. Further, critical reflexivity calls for explicit consideration of the process of knowledge construction including acknowledging how a researcher's background and position affect

the research. Rather than considering this a reliability problem, it is viewed as providing a richer understanding of the phenomenon under study (Cohen & Crabtree, 2006).

3   While most qualitative researchers disagree with the objectivity espoused by positivism, others maintain that qualitative work can still be conducted within a positivistic framework. An extension of this is evident in "mixed methods" research that combines qualitative and quantitative data collection and/or analysis. However, as Williams and Patterson (2007) point out, this is really a mixing of distinct research paradigms and it remains an open debate whether these can be integrated in a single research design and how such work should be evaluated.

4   Like positivists, post-positivists believe there is a reality independent of our thinking about it, but they recognize that all observation is fallible and all theory revisable. Consequently, they emphasize the importance of multiple measures and use of triangulation to better understand the subject at hand (Trochim, 2020).

REFERENCES

Ahrentzen, S. (1992). Home as a workplace in the lives of women. In I. Alman, & S. Low (Eds.), *Place attachment* (pp. 113–138). London: Plenum Press.

Altman, I., & Rogoff, B. (1987). World views in psychology: Trait, interactional, organismic, and transactional perspectives. In D. Stokols, & I. Altman (Eds.), *Handbook of environmental psychology* (Vol. 1, pp. 1–40). New York: Wiley.

Bassi, J. (2014). Quantitative/qualitative: The Paleozoic debate. *Forum: Qualitative Social Research*, *15*(2), Art. 7. http://dx.doi.org/10.17169/fqs-15.2.1993

Beckley, T., Stedman, R., Wallace, S., & Ambard, M. (2007). Snapshots of what matters most: Using resident-employed photography to articulate attachment to places. *Society & Natural Resources*, *20*(10), 913–929.

Breuer, F., & Roth, W. (2003). Subjectivity and reflexivity in the social sciences: Epistemic windows and methodical consequences. *Forum: Qualitative Sozialforschung*, *4*(2), Art. 25. http://dx.doi.org/10.17169/fqs-4.2.698

Buttimer, A. (1976). Grasping the dynamism of lifeworld. *Annals of the Association of American Geographers*, *66*(2), 277–292.

Canter, D. (1977). *The psychology of place*. London: Architectural Press.

Chamlee-Wright, E., & Storr, V. (2009). "There's no place like New Orleans": Sense of place and community recovery in the ninth ward after hurricane Katrina. *Journal of Urban Affairs*, *31*(5), 615–634. https://doi.org/10.1111/j.1467-9906.2009.00479.x

Cohen, D., & Crabtree, B. (2006). *Reflexivity in qualitative research guidelines project*. http://qualres.org/HomeRefl-3703.html. Retrieved online February 14, 2020.

De Sousa Santos, B. (2016). Epistemologies of the South and the future. *From the European South*, *1*, 17–29.

Denzin, N. (2017). Critical qualitative inquiry. *Qualitative Inquiry*, *23*(1), 8–16. https://doi.org/10.1177/1077800416681864

Devine-Wright, P. (2011). Place attachment and public acceptance of renewable energy: A tidal energy case study. *Journal of Environmental Psychology*, *31*, 336–343.

Devine-Wright, P., & Howes, Y. (2010). Disruption to place attachment and the protection of restorative environments: A wind energy case study. *Journal of Environmental Psychology*, *30*, 271–280. https://doi.org/10.1016/j.jenvp.2010.01.008

Di Masso, A., & Castrechini, A. (2012). Imaginative critique of the contemporary city. *Athenea Digital: Revista de Pensamiento e Investigación Social*, *12*(1), 3–13. https://doi.org/10.5565/rev/athenead/v12n1.1002

Di Masso, A., Dixon, J., & Durrheim, K. (2014). Place attachment as discursive practice. In L. Manzo, & P. Devine-Wright (Eds.), *Place attachment: Advances in theory, methods and applications* (pp. 75–86). New York: Routledge.

Di Masso, A., Dixon, J., & Pol, E. (2011). On the contested nature of place: 'Figuera's Well,' 'The Hole of Shame' and the ideological struggle over public space in Barcelona. *Journal of Environmental Psychology*, *31*, 231–244. https://doi.org/10.1016/j.jenvp.2011.05.002

Dixon, J., & Durrheim, K. (2000). Displacing place-identity: A discursive approach to locating self and other. *British Journal of Social Psychology*, *39*, 27–44. https://doi.org/10.1348/014466600164318

Dixon, J., & Durrheim, K. (2004). Dislocating identity: Desegregation and the transformation of place. *Journal of Environmental Psychology*, *24*, 455–473. http://dx.doi.org/10.1016/j.jenvp.2004.09.004

Durgerian, L. (2019). *Emotional infrastructure through time, place and disruption: Fostering a culture of care in post-earthquake Christchurch, New Zealand*. Unpublished Master's Thesis, University of Washington.

Edwards, R., & Brannelly, T. (2017). Approaches to democratizing qualitative research methods. *Qualitative Research*, *17*(3), 271–277. https://doi.org/10.1177/1468794117706869

Fullilove, M. (2014). "The frayed knot": What happens to place attachment in the context of serial forced displacement. In L. Manzo & P. Devine-Wright (Eds.),*Place attachment: Advances in theory, methods and applications*. New York: Routledge.

Gorman-Murray, A. (2007). Reconfiguring domestic values: Meanings of home for gay men and lesbians. *Housing, Theory and Society*, *24*(3), 229–246. https://doi.org/10.1080/14036090701374506

González, B. (2005). Topophilia and topophobia: The home as an evocative place of contradictory emotions. *Space and Culture*, *8*(2), 193–213. https://doi.org/10.1177/1206331204273984

Guba, E., & Lincoln, Y. (1994). Competing paradigms in qualitative research. In N. Denzin, & Y. Lincoln (Eds.), *Handbook of qualitative research* (pp. 105–117). Thousand Oaks, CA: Sage.

Haraway, D. (1988). Situated knowledges: The science question in feminism and the privilege of partial perspective. *Feminist Studies*, *14*(3), 575–599. https://doi.org/10.2307/3178066

Henrich, J., Heine, S., & Norenzayan, A. (2010). The weirdest people in the world? *Behavioral and Brain Sciences*, *33*, 61–135.

Hernandez, B., Hidalgo, M. C., & Ruiz, C. (2014). Theoretical and methodological aspects of research on place attachment. In L. Manzo, & P. Devine-Wright (Eds.). *Place attachment: Advances in theory, methods and applications* (pp. 125–138). London: Routledge.

Kleinhans, R., & Kearns, A. (2013). Neighborhood restructuring and residential relocation: Towards a balanced perspective on relocation processes and outcomes. *Housing Studies*, *28*(2), 163–176. https://doi.org/10.1080/02673037.2013.768001

Kwan, M. (2002). Is GIS for women? Reflections on the critical discourse in the 1990s. *Gender, Place and Culture: A Journal of Feminist Geography*, *9*(3), 271–279. https://doi.org/10.1080/0966369022000003888

Kwan, M. (2008). From oral histories to visual narrative: Representing the post-September 11 experiences of Muslim women in the USA. *Social & Cultural Geography*, *9*(6), 653–669. https://doi.org/10.1080/14649360802292462

Kyle, G., Graefe, A., & Manning, R. (2005). Testing the dimensionality of place attachment in recreational settings. *Environment and Behavior*, *37*(2), 153–177. https://doi.org/10.1177/0013916504269654

Lapan, S. D., Quartaroli, M. T., & Riemer, F. J. (Eds.). (2011). *Qualitative research: An introduction to methods and designs*. Hoboken, NJ: John Wiley & Sons.

Levitt, H. M., Bamberg, M., Creswell, J. W., Frost, D. M., Josselson, R., & Suárez-Orozco, C. (2018). Journal article reporting standards for qualitative primary, qualitative meta-analytic, and mixed methods research in psychology: The APA Publications and Communications Board task force report. *American Psychologist*, *73*(1), 26–46. http://dx.doi.org/10.1037/amp0000151

Lewicka, M. (2011). Place attachment: How far we come in the last 40 years? *Journal of Environmental Psychology*, *31*, 207–230. https://doi.org/10.1016/j.jenvp.2010.10.001

Low, S., & Altman, I. (1992). Place attachment: A conceptual inquiry. In I. Alman, & S. Low (Eds.), *Place attachment* (pp. 1–12). New York/London: Plenum Press.

Manzo, L. (2014). Exploring the shadow side: Place attachment in the context of stigma, displacement, and social housing. In L. Manzo, & P. Devine-Wright (Eds.). *Place attachment: Advances in theory, methods and applications* (pp. 178–190). London: Routledge.

Manzo, L. C. (2005). For better or worse: Exploring multiple dimensions of place meaning. *Journal of Environmental Psychology*, *25*(1), 67–86. https://doi.org/10.1016/j.jenvp.2005.01.002

Manzo, L. C., Kleit, R. G., & Couch, D. (2008). "Moving three times is like having your house on fire once": The experience of place and impending displacement among public housing residents. *Urban Studies*, *45*(9), 1855–1878. https://doi.org/10.1177/0042098008093381

Massey, D. (1994/2001). *Space, place, and gender*. Minneapolis: University of Minnesota Press.

Mazumdar, S. (2005). Religious place attachment, squatting, and "qualitative" research: A commentary. *Journal of Environmental Psychology*, *25*, 87–95. https://doi.org/10.1016/j.jenvp.2004.09.003

McDowell, L. (1997). *Undoing place? A geographical reader*. London/New York: Arnold.

Moore, J. (2000). Placing home in context. *Journal of Environmental Psychology*, *20*, 207–217. https://doi.org/10.1006/jevp.2000.0178

Morse, J., Barrett, M., Mayan, M., Olson, K., & Spires, J. (2002). Verification strategies for establishing reliability and validity in qualitative research. *International Journal of Qualitative Methods*, *1*(2), 13–22. https://doi.org/10.1177/160940690200100202

Parker, I. (2014). Critical reflexive humanism and critical constructionist psychology. *Psychology after deconstruction* (pp. 29–38). London: Routledge.

Parker, I. (2007). Critical psychology: What it is and what it is not. *Social and Personality Psychology Compass*, *1*(1), 1–15. https://doi.org/10.1111/j.1751-9004.2007.00008.x

Patterson, M. E., & Williams, D. R. (2005). Maintaining research traditions on place: Diversity of thought and scientific progress. *Journal of Environmental Psychology*, *25*(4), 361–380.

Payne, G., & Payne, J. (2004). Objectivity. *Sage key concepts: Key concepts in social research* (pp. 153–157). London: SAGE Publications, Ltd. https://doi.org/10.4135/9781849209397

Pinto de Carvalho, L. (2018). Lo político del apego al lugar: subjetividades espacializadas en Chaitén Sur, un territorio inhabitable. [Unpublished doctoral thesis]. Pontificia Universidad Católica de Chile.

Pinto de Carvalho, L., & Cornejo, M. (2018). Towards a critical approach to place attachment: A review in contexts of infringement of the right to adequate housing. *Athenea Digital*, *18*(3), e2004. https://doi.org/10.5565/rev/athenea.2004

Raymond, C. M., Brown, G., & Weber, D. (2010). The measurement of place attachment: Personal, community, and environmental connections. *Journal of Environmental Psychology*, *30*(4), 422–434. https://doi.org/10.1016/j.jenvp.2010.08.002

Relph, T. (1978). The psychology of place review. *Environment and Planning A*, *10*, 237–238.

Saegert, S., & Winkel, G. H. (1990). Environmental psychology. *Annual Review of Psychology*, *41*, 441–477. https://doi.org/10.1146/annurev.ps.41.020190.002301

Sandelowski, M. (1986). The problem of rigor in qualitative research. *Advances in Nursing Science*, *8*(3), 27–37. https://doi.org/10.1097/00012272-198604000-00005

Seamon, D. (1979). *A geography of the lifeworld*. New York: St. Martin's.

Seamon, D., & Gill, H. (2016). Qualitative approaches to environment-behavior research: Understanding environmental and place experiences, meanings and actions. In R. Gifford (Ed.). *Research methods in environment-behavior research* (pp. 115–136). New York: Wiley/Blackwell.

Stokols, D. (1990). Instrumental and spiritual views of people-environment relations. *American Psychologist*, 45, 641–646.

Trochim, W. M. (2020). Historical roots of qualitative research. In S. D. Lapan, M. Quartaroli, & F. Riemer (Eds.). *Qualitative research: An introduction to methods and designs*. San Francisco, CA: Jossey-Bass.

Tuan, Y. F. (1977). *Space and place: The perspective of experience*. Minneapolis: University of Minnesota Press.

Wiesenfeld, E., & Zara, H. (2012). Latin-American environmental psychology in the first decade of the millennium: A critical analysis. *Athenea Digital*, *12*(1), 129–155. https://doi.org/10.5565/rev/athenead/v12n1.985

Williams, D. R. (2014). "Beyond the commodity metaphor" revisited: Some methodological reflections on place attachment research. In. L. C. Manzo, & P. Devine-Wright (Eds.). *Place attachment: Advances in theory, methods and applications* (pp. 89–99). London: Routledge.

Williams, D. R., & Patterson, M. (2007). Snapshots of what exactly? A comment on methodological experimentation and conceptual foundations in place research. *Society & Natural Resources*, *20*(10), 931–937. https://doi.org/10.1080/08941920701537015

Williams, D. R., & Patterson, M. (2005). Maintaining research traditions on place: Diversity of thought and scientific progress. *Journal of Environmental Psychology*, *25*, 361–380. https://doi.org/10.1016/j.jenvp.2005.10.001

Williams, D. R., & Vaske, J. J. (2003). The measurement of place attachment: Validity and generalizability of a psychometric approach. *Forest Science*, *49*(6), 830–840. https://doi.org/10.1093/forestscience/49.6.83

Chapter 8: Articulating transnational attachments through on-site narratives and collaborative creative processes

Clare Rishbeth

At the heart of any attachment is a story. It may be the story of a moment, a day, a year. Or, more commonly, the stories are ones that emerge gradually, take shape, backtrack, repeat in parts, tail away, reappear. People bring their own stories to places they love and places they hate. And then they tell their own stories about these self-same places; each story of an intersection of site, time, and human experience.

Within a tradition of qualitative enquiry, researchers venture into other people's territory and ask to hear their stories. Asking questions, listening, recording, interpreting, representing, disseminating; these actions are the authoritative foundations of research activity. And through these, we aim to pay appropriate attention to everyday life, to represent both the telling detail and the broader patterns of their attachments to place.

Though the majority of place attachment research looks at quantifying dimensions of attachment (Lewicka, 2011), there has also been a significant strand of qualitative work which recognizes the role of the story, and indeed, the multiplicity of stories that represent the complexity of understanding shared spaces (Manzo & Pinto de Carvalho, Chapter 7, this volume; Sandercock, 2003). A skillful interviewer draws out the contexts behind the anecdotes and helps the interviewee shape meaning from their own experience. This research work has developed our understanding of place attachment from a positive/negative dichotomy to one where individual narratives bridge multiple feelings and experiences from both the past and the present; the psychological process dimension of place attachment in the framework developed by Scannell and Gifford (2010).

This chapter discusses how it is possible to keep a focus on prompting narratives, as with a traditional method such as the in-depth interview, but design a richer and more responsive research environment specifically appropriate to researching place attachment. Qualitative research methods explicitly informing theories of "place attachment" have tended to focus on focus groups and interviews, with some limited exploration of visual techniques (Lewicka, 2011). The central significance of the field of environmental psychology has inevitably informed the common methods used. Patterson and Williams, in their discussion of place research (2005), urge "critical pluralism," the need to learn from the integrity of different research traditions and expertise. I suggest that inspiration from a wider range of disciplines concerned with people-place relationships, such as geography, anthropology, ethnography, documentary filmmaking and landscape architecture, can provide fruitful avenues for methodological development, as well as broadening our understanding of how place impacts a range of people.

In this chapter, I explore the inter-relationship between these two forms of diversity: the potential of more innovative qualitative methods, and supporting articulation of place attachments with "harder to reach" participant groups—people who are difficult to include within more traditional research projects due to practical, cultural, or linguistic barriers. I describe two methodological approaches which may offer greater richness to explorations of place attachment and can complement existing research practice in representing commonly marginalized viewpoints. The first is located storytelling to explore experiential qualities of attachment; "the 'experience-in-place' that creates meaning" (Manzo, 2005, p. 74). The second is use of audio and visual methods that support unexpected responses and diverse voices. I explore the potential of integrating these two approaches through two research projects and give some indication of how the methods informed research findings relating to place attachments in mundane urban settings.

TWO METHODOLOGICAL APPROACHES TO EXTEND OR DEEPEN QUALITATIVE RESEARCH ON PLACE ATTACHMENT

Located storytelling to explore experiential qualities of attachment

The standard in-depth interview has rich data to offer the qualitative researcher exploring place meaning and attachments. However, by focusing purely on a recounted narrative in a somewhat artificial circumstance, we may miss much else that is important about being a person in a place. Amin (2008) suggests that space is "collectively experienced as a form of tacit, neurological and sensory knowing" (p. 11). Ethnographic approaches aim to include research participants in a more active relationship with both the researcher and the topic of research, which can increase focus on sensory qualities of being (Pink, 2009). This goes beyond a simple categorization of place with regard to touch, smell, or sound—though this is already a step beyond what is usually discussed in an interview setting. Such an approach moves toward articulating a sensory connection between people and place: a "zone of entanglement" (Ingold, 2008, p. 1797) or "throwntogetherness" (Massey, 2005, p. 140).

Interrogating the body-place relationship implies the importance of on-site research. If we are to consider the lived experience of neighborhoods and the full range of places in one's daily rounds, then it is necessary to develop methods which bridge notional boundaries where the characteristics of not only "destination locations" but journeys and in-between spaces are explored. And to develop narratives which can represent the relevance of "every touching experience of architecture [as] multi-sensory: qualities of space, matter and scale are measured equally by the eye, ear, nose, skin, tongue, skeleton and muscle" (Pallasmaa, 2005, p. 41).

A general interest in sensory qualities of space has shaped a research strand in anthropology and geography that looks at outdoor walking practices (Adams & Guy, 2007; Bates & Rhys-Taylor, 2017; Ingold & Lee, 2008). This often takes the form of the "go-along" interview, essentially an interview conducted while the interviewee and participant walk together (Carpiano, 2009; Kusenbach, 2003), which has evolved into techniques loosely termed "sensewalking" or "sensory urbanism" (Adams & Guy, 2007; Low, 2013), and into participatory community processes (e.g., experiential group walks with older adults, Fang et al, 2016). Participatory on-site methods have also informed community planning processes with diverse community groups (e.g., Kretzman & McKnight, 1993). A few studies have compared findings on people's experience of outdoor places between on-site- and indoor-located interviews and strongly support the additional richness generated by the outdoor-based methods (Evans & Jones, 2011; Hart, 1979). Though this dynamic has been discussed with regard to research on outdoor places, the critical distinction is whether research is conducted *in situ* to the place that is the focus of the research or in a different location.

This chapter makes the case for research that pays careful attention to individual responses to particular places, proposing that bodily experiences, temporal factors, social dynamics, and cultural expectations can be more clearly understood through the particular than through broad generalizations. This is not to negate or minimize the significance and interplay of multiple place attachments. Affect, cognition, and behavior are engaged as the process dimension of attachment, as outlined by Scannell and Gifford (2010), and experiences of one place are strongly informed by memories of that place and by comparisons with other places. In particular, this chapter will emphasize temporal change and embodied movement.

Collaborative and creative methods surface unexpected findings and diverse voices

On-site research methods aim to counterbalance the "distancing" between experience and story that can be an outcome of standard interviews. In a similar way, collaborative and participatory approaches aim to reduce the "distancing" between researcher and participant by addressing the power relations inherent in the dynamic of the researcher and the researched (Kindon et al, 2008). These approaches often utilize creative processes to facilitate the participant as generator of guiding questions and primary data. Israel et al (1998) argue the importance of researchers and participants working together in order to refine methods relevant to a specific cultural context. Some humility and flexibility is required of the researcher to do this; a recognition that the participant may have the best questions as well as the best answers, and may perceive a different, more relevant scope, to the area of inquiry. These methods cannot be standardized between participants as easily as more traditional methods, and indeed this is rarely the aim

(Patterson & Williams, 2005). The strength of this approach lies in "obliqueness": the ability to discover deeper truths and ambiguities, to tread gently, to connect between a place and an emotional response (Rishbeth, 2020). Engagement with creative methods can be especially useful when the participant group may be less able or willing to articulate their experiences in a more formal interview situation: children, people communicating in a language different from the researcher's, or those who may be wary or less inclined to answer questions set by a person in a privileged position.

In this chapter, I outline two research projects which took collaborative approaches and utilized creative processes to explore place experiences and attachments. The first, Walking Voices (2006), used self-recorded audio while walking around a residential neighborhood in Sheffield. In the second, The Bench Project, academics collaborated with a filmmaker and two third-sector (non-profit) organizations, attending to the everyday practices of people using a park and a square in two outer London boroughs.

WALKING VOICES

The Walking Voices project was an eighteen-month research project which focused on Burngreave, a neighborhood with high ethnic diversity in Sheffield, a city in the north of England.[1] The research addressed how everyday places within this area were perceived and valued by residents from different migrant backgrounds. Creative and collaborative processes steered the design of the research methods, the primary focus of which was self-recorded audio recordings made on site by participants. The participants were all first-generation migrants, living in Burngreave.

Research questions focused largely on intangible, ambiguous qualities: the role of memory in shaping place attachment, the importance of temporal aspects of place experience, and the complexity of transnational attachments. These were researched with a population where the majority do not speak English as a first language, who often live in conditions of disadvantage, have conflicting pressures on their time, and are sometimes cautious about the role of research and people in authority. We aimed to recruit participants across age, gender, religion, and countries of birth. Atypical of most migration focused research, and because we were exploring notions of a shared neighborhood, we recruited across ethnic groups, encompassing diverse life circumstances rather than essentializing bounded national or ethnic identities (Glick, Schiller & Çağlar, 2009). We were however restricted to working with participants who had a reasonable level of spoken English,[2] the primary language used within the project.

Using locational storytelling and participatory audio methods helped address these challenges within a rigorous research framework. Privileging storytelling, rather than answering questions in a typical interview method, cast participants as experts in the field and helped engage participants in actively shaping the focus of their contributions. Working with high status partners (in this case the regional

BBC radio station) gave value to participants' work and improved dissemination with wider community. To support reliable findings that could capture the immediacy and specificity of place experience, it was important for the methods to respond flexibly to participants' own interpretations of multiple places, enabling them to direct their own focus of interest and level of engagement. This focus on place enabled the voicing of self through a gathering of responses, opening up rather than presupposing different axes of personal and community identity. Though working with a small sample size, we increased the validity of findings through ongoing contact with participants over a period of three months, generating multiple recordings with each individual. This built trust between researchers and participants, gradually helping them gain confidence in articulating sometimes complex experiences and emotions.

Familiarization and recruitment

The initial months of the project were an immersive experience in the neighborhood. We were aware of the problems of over-researching users of local cultural and religious centers, so though we did contact some key neighborhood organizations, we also used highly informal approaches for meeting potential participants: chatting to people in parks and on the street, and taking part in recreational community activities. We gradually selected our participants, six men and five women, ages spanning 20–60, with different employment status, family networks, physical abilities, and access to transportation. All had migrated to the UK, some recently and some decades ago. Their countries of origin were Jamaica, the Yemen, Kurdistan, Pakistan, and Somalia.

Key fieldwork process: Self-recorded, on-site audio

The participants were loaned mini-disk recorders for a three-month period spanning late summer to early winter 2006. Their brief was to regularly record live commentaries during walks or times outside, describing the location, their movements, and thoughts prompted by the changing experience of their neighborhood. The participants were trained by BBC Radio Sheffield in the use of mini-disk recorders for this purpose, and it was clearly stated that the recordings (anonymized when appropriate) would be used both for the research project and for possible broadcast on local radio. We asked participants to aim to make recordings independently, about once a week over a period of a few months. In reality, only a few made this many (four participants completed seven or more), and most made significantly less (the average number of recordings was 4.5). However, the recordings made were much longer than anticipated, the average length was approximately thirty minutes, and sometimes up to one hour. Fifty recordings were made in total.

Working with locational storytelling and participant-led audio methods

Our approach facilitated complex narratives through which participants expressed their engagement with outdoor places in their neighborhood and elsewhere, and their changing ideas of their sense of self in relation to these places. It is true that awareness of the recording's end uses will have shaped accounts to differing degrees, though the overall impression listening to the recordings is of people talking to close friends rather than presenting themselves to a broader audience. By recounting a multiplicity of stories, reactions, and distractions, participants align the temporal qualities of moving through both physical and mental space in the process of talking about the meaning of place and their attachments to them, as demonstrated in this recording made by Ahmed, who grew up in The Yemen:

> Some day we were driving down here, it was night time, and the moon was full. Just right at the top there. And it was beautiful. I stopped there and took a picture of it. [...] It was such a beautiful day and clear sky and a full moon. It was beautiful. That's what we are planning, if we going to move, one day from this house ... it has to have a view. Either sea, or like this view, because I love it, I love it.

The methodology was designed to minimize the power dynamics between participants and researcher, by "absenting" the researcher from the recordings and establishing the participant's role as experts in their own localities. The majority of recordings were entirely self-directed, giving participants control of places selected for commentary, and the depth and range of their discussions. However, for some, the act of walking and simultaneously making recordings seemed too strange or embarrassing in practice, and other participants simply forgot to do it. The use of paired walking (researcher with participant) was the most common modification. We did this with about half the participants for some or all of their recordings. During the paired walks, the researcher tried to maintain a position of "active listening" rather than questioning. Though reducing the level of self-direction, these recordings tended to be longer than those made independently, and the presence of the researcher often stimulated a deeper level of reflection.

Analysis and dissemination

The analysis was based on transcripts of all the walks, and data were coded using NVivo software. To provide a broader context and a more collaborative interpretative lens to the emerging findings, we then undertook ten "standard" interviews (indoors, semi-structured): four with participants and six with contacts in environmental and community organizations. In these interviews, we shared reflections on the data, checking our initial analysis, and considered potential implications for neighborhood regeneration.

Working with BBC Radio Sheffield shaped the rationale of using on-site audio recordings and had status and appeal within the group of participants and their wider communities. At the end of the project, the station broadcasted audio clips from the on-site recordings (with participants' permission), and a radio journalist interviewed some participants and the researcher about the project and their reflections on living in Burngreave. Through this process, the attachments of first-generation migrants to their neighborhood were made public, an important sharing of stories in an authoritative and accessible form.

The project findings expanded ideas of transnational place attachments in a number of ways (see Rishbeth & Powell, 2013 for fuller discussion). The methods used meant that participants focused on the importance of what they happened upon on their daily routes, the moments and materiality of everyday life. Glimpses of familiarity in landscapes—visually, through activities or social patterns—allow individuals who are new to an area to recognize starting points of belonging and place attachment, or at least an environment which is not completely alien (Rishbeth & Powell, 2013). Recognizing differences between past and present places can highlight values previously taken for granted, the experience of migration inevitably leading to questioning links between cultural heritage, personal identity, and attachments with specific places. Our findings certainly supported notions of multiple, simultaneous place attachments for participants (Giuliani et al, 2003; Manzo, 2003; Scopelliti & Tiberio, 2010). Engagements with new-to-them places, and the overlaying of memories, can provide tangible markers of establishment, of moving on from a newcomer or outsider status to someone who belongs. The role of memory in place attachment appears not simply as nostalgia, but one form of creative process that aids engagement between the local and geographically distant locations. Attachments to specific locations do appear to have a role in a process of settling, recognizing how one might authentically belong in a different cultural environment and take part in this new community (Amsden et al, 2010).

THE BENCH PROJECT

The Bench Project took place in London in 2015 and was initially informed by a more practical question: What is the value and social role of benches in the urban environment? Through this micro focus, we aimed to explore wider themes—what it means for a person or group to "take up space" in an urban outdoor environment, and some of the controls integral to public space design and management that support or curtail this activity.

In common with Walking Voices, we were interested in mundane experiences of local places and representing narratives of belonging or isolation by local residents. This time, the funding and organization of the project enabled different means of participant engagement and an approach that used filmmaking, combining visual and audio storytelling. The research was a year-long collaboration between a cross-sector, cross-disciplinary team of five, all named as investigators in the grant and with shared responsibility for the delivery of the project.[3] We drew on the differing expertise and skills of academics (from Landscape Architecture and Geography), third-sector colleagues (The Young Foundation, London and Greenwich Inclusion Project—a local anti-hate crime organization), and the academic, artist, and documentary filmmaker Esther Johnson. The two London-based organizations had responsibility for employing two local fieldworkers who spent time on the chosen sites, engaging with the various people sitting on benches, identifying possible film participants and supporting relationships between these and the filmmaker.

In developing the methodological approach to the project, and through this a nuanced understanding of place attachment, we extended Richardson's (2015) work on schizocartography. This is an approach that aims to integrate the complexity of individual narratives and personal agency into the dominant "top-down" stories of place history (Rishbeth & Rogaly, 2018, pp. 287–288). Richardson (2015) affirms "the presence of the body in space, subjective reactions to place, or a search for something that may reveal 'the other' of a place." She discusses the importance of historical and temporal dynamics in order to "reclaim the subjectivity of individuals" in "spaces that have been co-opted by various capitalist oriented operations" and recognizes that "the individual's response to a space will not necessarily be the same at a different moment in time or upon another visit" (Richardson, 2015, pp. 182, 186, 188–189).

Johnson's (2018) approach to filmmaking exemplifies this framing, moving from "a didactic approach, in which an authoritarian voiceover would tell the viewer about the design and use of the spaces" to an approach in which "the viewer would gain a heightened perceptual sense of place, becoming a stranger who joins one of the contributors on their bench" (Johnson, 2018, p. 208).

The reflexivity of this method seemed useful to us in responding to the social contexts of the two locations: an extensive grassed open space in St. Helier, Sutton, and a recently redeveloped urban square in the center of Woolwich, east London. Both sites were in areas of London characterized by low incomes, with many residents adversely impacted by ten years of government instigated "austerity politics" with the withdrawal or reduction of many public services. Woolwich is the more ethnically diverse, with just 37 percent of residents identifying as white British (2011 census), including recent rises in number of people with Nepali, Ghanaian, Nigerian, or eastern European heritage (Bates, 2017, p. 58). It is also in the process of becoming better connected to central London, with a new high-speed rail link due to open soon. Four years prior to our research, this site, Gordon Square, was redeveloped by Gustafson Porter, a renowned landscape architecture firm. Though this greatly enhanced the facilities and safety of the square, and was largely welcomed by users, it was also emblematic of high-income development leading to gentrification of this part of London.

Integration of filmmaking and research methods

As co-produced research, the methods and intended outcomes of the project reflected the various interests and agendas of the research team and led to a range of outputs, most notably an eighteen minute film (Johnson, 2015), a report (Bynon & Rishbeth, 2015), and an academic paper (Rishbeth & Rogaly, 2018). Of these, the film most strongly reflected aspects of place attachment, using juxtapositions of spoken word and visual framing to reflect some of the place values held by people spending time in the two different spaces. Johnson's commitment to respectful and non-extractive approaches to the participants included multiple meetings before

Figure 8.1
Michael in Gordon Square.
Source: Esther Johnson
(used with permission).

the filming days (interviews, recorded interviews, still photographs, See Figure 8.1), and opportunities for each to respond to her initial storyline and choice of shots by means of mid-edit private screening, access to the film online or in hardcopy form.

While the practice of film or video making is often primarily considered a visual medium, the approach that Johnson takes to working with participants reflected something of the audio methods of Walking Voices. Recognizing the artificiality and awkwardness of "straight to camera" dialogue, she instead audio records all her interviews first, on site, including background noises and incidental distractions. Her rapport with participants allows a free-form storytelling to emerge

Figure 8.2
Sitting up on bench backs,
Gordon Square.
Source: Esther Johnson
(used with permission).

around the themes of the research—sociability and solitude, the individual in relation to others, temporality, and the site itself. The inclusion of Johnson as filmmaker in the core research team, including developing the initial bid and full involvement in all team workshops, was an important part of the process, ensuring the film was not an attractive "add on" but integral to the process of inquiry.

The film captures many insights regarding the social value of these two places: The potential for varied connections (with friends and strangers), and the ability simply to be outside of a (sometimes constraining) home environment.

Joe (eighteen years old) talks about Gordon Square a social hub for friends living in disparate areas of the Borough.

> If you spent longer than a week in Woolwich, yeah. you would see so much stuff, you'd just see everything. Obviously, I'm not from round here, I live somewhere else. But I come here with all my friends. This is a meeting point init. To meet up init. Like he's from somewhere else, I'm from somewhere else, She lives somewhere else, Everyone's from somewhere else, init. But when we tell someone to come to Woolwich, like. We is here, init like.

Margaret explains how the natural qualities of St. Helier Open Space bring some calmness to her young daughter:

> We just live nearby. So whenever we pass by here she goes on here. Actually it's good for her because she's got autism, so for us it's really beneficial. She loves, because of the sense issue, she takes off her shoes, she likes to be on the grass, yeh and then the circle thing [tyre swing] she like to sit there, yes, and she sits sometimes for, on this bench for some time.

Till Sana Rana is one of the Nepalese elders who has fairly recently migrated to the UK after a change in residency rights for ex-servicemen and their families. Most days she spends time with a large group of Nepali friends in Gordon Square, valuing time spent outdoors and being part of the busyness and interest of this place:

> I'm Till Sana Rana. I'm from Nepal. Some people are nice, they say 'Morning' when they pass us. So we say 'Morning' as well. If we knew how to speak English, we could be friends with others. We would have really liked to socialize with others, but can't. We have cried because of the language.

To make the film, Johnson edited the recordings into a montage of monologues, overlaying them with camera views which rested on the participant spending time in the park or the square. While listening, the viewer can see them sitting quietly, looking at others or chatting with friends, with cut-aways both to the broader panorama of urban life and to the telling details of pigeons, pushchairs, scooters, drinks, and bags. Joe sits up on the backs of the benches, (Figure 8.2) drinking pop with his friend Ali and gesturing as they joke. Margaret is laughing as she pushes her daughter on the tyre swing. Till Sana Rana sits in a line of her friends, sitting on newspapers to give some protection and comfort against the cool of the granite bench. The film soundscape carefully includes sounds recorded on site: dogs barking, water, and the sweep of the cleaner's brush. Johnson (2018) explores the potential of this asynchronicity in film editing, "An audience is encouraged to observe a person within a space, and hear intimate stories and thoughts at the same time – the non-synch technique being an attempt to create a gap in which viewers are able to place themselves in the contributor's world. This approach aims to elicit a deeper sensory engagement, to emotionally connect and empathize with contributor's stories" (p. 211).

The film captures the temporality of place experience and is incredibly effective at portraying the vivacity and acute reflection of inner thoughts whilst situated in a shared non-private environment, challenging the viewer to an understanding of place attachment that can be simultaneously deeply personal and "a tacit claiming of belonging within a collective context" (Rishbeth & Rogaly, 2018, p. 295).

Filmmaking collaborations as a means of developing place attachment theory

Unlike Walking Voices, the Bench Project was not specifically designed to explore place attachment or transnational qualities of place. But through responding to the complex social histories and contexts of St. Helier and Woolwich, and as a result of the academic framing we brought to the research, these dimensions were clearly present. As a means of developing theory, the film played a role that was both vital and elusive. To work with a skilled artist was a gift to the research, a generous encounter that allowed an expansion of our vision, enabling different types of noticing and conversation. Within the live research project, the actions of filmmaking rooted us in the tangible, resisting any whimsical abstraction. As time passes, reflection and making connections beyond the specific is important. But even the most detailed research fieldnotes can become distant, less vivid, hard to untangle and remember significance. Thematic coding can un-parcel narrative and dissect experience. But re-watching the film (over fifty times now) pulls one right back into a sensory present, as well as revealing new insights and details. This enables close attention to the individual, linking both their words and the resonances of ease or anxiety within their bodily presence.

In our presentation of this research, both in the written paper and in numerous conference papers, and film screenings, place attachment has been explored through different themes: urban public spaces as sites of care and self-care, and the affordances of benches (often allowing the choice to be still in a space) for supporting a longer timeframe of connection with the place and people around, leading to a greater sense of inclusion. In both sites, residents made references to change, to places being protected—*I'm so glad that they've never built on this, cos I thought they would*, or place-change—*a few years ago it was just a dingy little square*. Transnational themes were explored through the involvement of the Nepali community living in Woolwich (supported largely due to working with a

Nepali speaking fieldworker, Samprada Mukhia).[4] The participants talked about the unfamiliarity of a "park" typology in their previous, predominantly rural life in Nepal—*we used to go to the forest to get wood and grass, then we would come home and sit together. So our home was the park*. They appreciated the resource of Gordon Square as a gathering place where both men and women could gather and chat in larger numbers. This extended into more of a collective experience than the findings of the Walking Voices project suggested, the human creativity of adapting to different place typologies whilst often valuing continuity in patterns of socializing (Rishbeth & Powell, 2013). Some of these transnational connections became especially pertinent in April 2015 when a devastating earthquake hit Nepal. Gordon Square became important in multiple ways, in part because of the presence of a large public television. Scenes and information about the damage played on loop against the everyday busyness of the square, a source of emotional connection and information for the Nepali local community, and a site where personal consolation and practical fundraising was located (Rishbeth & Rogaly, 2018, p. 293).

The challenge in a project like the Bench Project is communicating theory beyond the research setting. The academic sphere is predominantly one developed through verbal and written means. The use of still photography can be incorporated but often grudgingly, often in small grayscale images. In our academic writing describing locations and participants, we struggled to do justice to the film's elegance and visual shortcuts. It is not only a challenge of format. Due to film festival premiere entry requirements, only an evocative but short edit of the film is open access (Nowness, 2016). The film has, however, been shown in many places, from a leisure center in St. Helier to an architecture film festival in Rotterdam. It was of immediate value (and also status) to our third-sector collaborators, and gift copies of the DVD with photo-record booklet were given to all participants. Films can go places where academic papers struggle to go, and this too is one way of advancing engagement with academic theory.

THE POTENTIAL OF COLLABORATIVE AND LOCATED METHODS TO CONTRIBUTE PLACE ATTACHMENT RESEARCH

Both Walking Voices and The Bench Project developed novel methods in order to address the challenges of working with a particular group of participants, and focusing on connected and multiple scales of outdoor place experience. The methodological approaches evolved with regard to research practice and ethics, one which may be broadly applicable to many qualitative research projects on place attachment.

Specific methods used will depend on the resources and partnerships available, and the relevance to potential participants. As with all methods, it is important to acknowledge challenges and limitations. The high level of researcher involvement needed to support ongoing participation will often not be feasible. Research questions related to multiple pre-selected sites will not be addressed with methods that give autonomy of place selection to participants, and exploration of temporality limited to the times available for filming or photography. These methodological approaches will never offer reliable generalizations, for example, comparing responses with regard to gender or ethnic background, which are more appropriately addressed with quantitative methods.

Openness to more collaborative and flexible modes of research practice is a timely challenge for researchers of place attachment. As noted by Robson (2002, p. 216), "If notions of collaboration and participation are taken seriously, then some power of decision about aspects of the design and data collection are lost to the researcher. This may well be a price worth paying." The findings aim to shed light on the nuances and interactions between people and place, to provoke insights, relevance, and representation that may be missed by larger scale studies, which, by necessity, apply a "coarser grain" of response. Working through these challenges in a reflective and transparent way, with careful, slow interpretation, is important in establishing the integrity of the research (Finney & Rishbeth, 2006). In the Walking Voices project repeated contact with participants for over half a year, in comparison to the standard single contact interview, was useful in establishing trust and adapting methods to individuals. In the Bench Project, with a dispersed research team, giving relative autonomy to local fieldworkers ensured an informed response to context. In both projects, we aimed as far as possible to understand the recordings and interviews alongside broad insight into participants' circumstances, values, and life choices.

The findings of this research make a clear contribution to understandings of transnational place attachments. The ingenuity of these projects articulated the voices of diverse groups of people who would not have considered involvement in more traditional research, and who are less often heard in public discourses. The use of participatory methods did support unexpected findings, with a wide range of visual, social, political, ecological, and historic issues alluded to or specifically discussed by participants, a diversity that we would have not been able to predict in planning a traditional structured interview. A method based on locational storytelling and capturing spontaneous emotional responses proved to be especially appropriate when looking at the sensory and experiential qualities of memory and connection, of social activity and cultural identities.

Arguably, research on place attachment has not wrestled enough with broader debates on representing often disenfranchised populations and the ethics of research processes. Located and collaborative methodological approaches can be especially useful for research in cross-cultural situations, offering a more inclusive way of engaging with research topics for many people. Addressing power relations in research settings and giving a greater role to participants in framing their own understanding of research questions can have a dual benefit. Participants are situated as experts, credited with different types of knowledge and experience, and become involved in a process that they view as meaningful, with scope to develop their own skills. Researchers gather material for analysis that simply wouldn't be accessible through more traditional methods, entering into a more open dialogue which acknowledges the inherent complexity of people's identities and experiences of place. As such, findings arising from these forms of research practice can come closer to an insider view of a neighborhood (Nicotera, 2007). Connections between how outdoor places are designed—their physicality and affordances—and how they are interpreted by users have particular relevance for developing appropriate social policy, planning, and design practice (e.g., Bynon & Rishbeth, 2015).

These multiple challenges—to develop theory, to engage participants meaningfully, and to inform practice—can and should be a broad ambition of research into people and place. Ultimately, utilizing a broader range of methods can only lead to a richer and more relevant understanding of the complexity of real places, and people's attachment to them.

NOTES

1 The research was conducted from 2006 to 2007 by myself (Lead Investigator) and Dr. Mark Powell (Research Associate). It was funded by the Economic and Social Research Council of the UK. Burngreave is a 20-minute walk from Sheffield city centre and is one of the city's most ethnically diverse neighborhoods (44% residents were from non-White-British ethnic groups, 22% were born overseas). Forty-eight percent of homes are categorized as experiencing multiple aspects of disadvantage. All 2001 census data.

2 We acknowledge the limitations of this practical requirement. In particular, the elder Pakistani community was largely excluded. We addressed this in part by conducting one individual interview (female) and two group interviews (male) with this resident group.

3 The project was funded by the UK Arts and Humanities Research Council, reference AH/M006107/1. The research team was led by Clare Rishbeth, with co-investigators Ben Rogaly, Esther Johnson, Radhika Bynon (The Young Foundation), Jasber Singh (Greenwich Inclusion Project). The two local fieldworkers were Samprada Mukhia and Diana Coman.

4 Johnson subsequently made a 4-minute edit of the eighteen minute film specifically representing the experience of the Nepali elders in Gordon Square: https://www.now-ness.com/story/alone-together-the-social-life-of-park-benches-esther-johnson

REFERENCES

Adams, M., & Guy, S. (2007). Editorial: Senses and the city. *The Senses and Society, 2,* 133–136.

Amin, A. (2008). Collective culture and urban public space. *City, 12*(1), 5–24.

Amsden, B., Stedman, R., & Kruger, L. (2010). The creation and maintenance of sense of place in a tourism-dependent community. *Leisure Sciences, 33*(1), 32–51.

Bates, C. (2017). Desire lines: Walking in Woolwich. In C. Bates, &A. Rhys-Taylor (Eds.), *Walking through social research* (pp. 54–69). London: Routledge.

Bates, C. & Rhys-Taylor, A. (Eds.). (2017). *Walking through social research*. London: Routledge.

Bynon, R., & Rishbeth, C. (2015). *Benches for everyone: Solitude in public, sociability for free*. London: The Young Foundation.

Carpiano, R. M. (2009). Come take a walk with me: The "go-along" interview as a novel method for studying the implications of place for health and well-being. *Health & Place, 15,* 263–272.

Evans, J., & Jones, P. (2011). The walking interview: Methodology, mobility and place. *Applied Geography*, *31*(2), 849–858.

Fang, M. L., Woolrych, R., Sixsmith, J., Canham, S., Battersby, L., & Sixsmith, A. (2016). Place-making with older persons: Establishing sense-of-place through participatory community mapping workshops. *Social Science & Medicine*, *168*, 223–229.

Finney, N., & Rishbeth, C. (2006). Engaging with marginalised groups in public open space research: The potential of collaboration and combined methods. *Planning Theory & Practice*, *7*(1), 27–46.

Giuliani, M. V., Ferrara, F., & Barabotti, S. (2003). One attachment or more? In G. Moser, E. Pol, Y. Bernard, M. Bonnes, J. A. Corraliza, & M. V. Giuliani (Eds.), *People, places and sustainability: 21st century metropolis* (pp. 111–122). Göttingen: Hogrefe & Huber.

Glick Schiller, N., & Çağlar, A. (2009). Towards a comparative theory of locality in migration studies: Migrant incorporation and city scale. *Journal of Ethnic and Migration Studies*, *35*(2), 177–202.

Hart, R. (1979). *Children's experiences of place*. New York: Irvington Publishers.

Ingold, T. (2008). Bindings against boundaries: Entanglements of life in an open world. *Environment and Planning A*, *40*, 1796–1810.

Ingold, T., & Lee, J. (2008). *Ways of walking: Ethnography and practice on foot*. London: Ashgate.

Johnson, E. (Director). (2015). *Alone together, the social life of benches* [Film]. Blanche Pictures.

Kindon, S., Pain, R., & Kesby, M. (2008). *Participatory action research approaches and methods: Connecting people, participation and place*. London: Routledge.

Kretzman, J., & McKnight, J. (1993). *Building communities from the inside out: A path toward finding and mobilizing a community's assets*. Chicago, IL: ACTA Publications.

Kusenbach, M. (2003). Street phenomenology: The go-along as ethnographic research tool. *Ethnography*, *4*, 455–485.

Israel, B., Schulz, A., Parker, E., & Becker, A. (1998). Review of community-based research: Assessing partnership approaches to improve public health. *Annual Review of Public Health*, *19*, 173–202.

Johnson, E. (2018). Alone together—Documentary filmmaking and stories of well-being in outdoor spaces. In R. Coles, S. Costa, & S. Watson (Eds.), *Pathways to well-being in design: Examples from the arts, humanities and the built environment* (pp. 203–222). Oxon: Routledge.

Lewicka, M. (2011). Place attachment: How far have we come in the last 40 years? *Journal of Environmental Psychology*, *31*, 207–230.

Low, K. E. Y. (2013). Sensing cities: The politics of migrant sensescapes. *Social Identities*, *19*(2), 221–237.

Manzo, L. (2003). Beyond house and haven: Toward a revisioning of emotional relationships with places. *Journal of Environmental Psychology*, *23*, 47–61.

Manzo, L. (2005). For better or worse: Exploring multiple dimensions of place meaning. *Journal of Environmental Psychology*, *23*, 67–86.

Massey, D. (2005). *For space*. London: Sage.

Nicotera, N. (2007). Measuring neighborhood: A conundrum for human services researchers and practitioners. *American Journal of Community Psychology*, *40*, 26–51.

Pallasmaa, J. (2005). *The eyes of the skin*. Chichester: Wiley.

Patterson, M., & Williams, D. (2005). Maintaining research traditions on place: Diversity of thought and scientific progress. *Journal of Environmental Psychology*, *25*, 361–380.

Pink, S. (2009). *Doing sensory ethnography*. London: Sage.

Richardson, T. (2015). Developing schizocartography: Formulating a theoretical methodology for a walking practice. In T. Richardson (Ed.), *Walking inside out: Contemporary British psychogeography* (pp. 181–194). London: Rowman and Littlefield.

Rishbeth, C., & Powell, M. (2013). Place Attachment and memory: Landscapes of belonging as experienced post-migration. *Landscape Research*, *38*(2), 165–183.

Rishbeth, C., & Rogaly, B. (2018). Sitting outside: Conviviality, self-care and the design of benches in urban public space. *Transactions of the Institute of British Geographers*, *43*(2), 284–298.

Rishbeth, C. (2020). The collective outdoors: Memories, desires and becoming local in an era of mobility. In V. Mehta, &D. Palazzo (Eds.), *Companion to public space* (pp. 27–34). London: Routledge.

Robson, C. (2002). *Real world research* (2nd ed.). Oxford: Blackwell.

Sandercock, L. (2003). Out of the closet: The importance of stories and storytelling in planning practice. *Planning, Theory and Practice*, *4*(1), 11–28.

Scannell, L., & Gifford, R. (2010). Defining place attachment: A tripartite organizing framework. *Journal of Environmental Psychology*, *30*, 1–10.

Scopelliti, M., & Tiberio, L. (2010). Homesickness in university students: The role of multiple place attachments. *Environment and Behavior*, *42*, 335–350.

Chapter 9: Beyond the "local": Methods for examining place attachment across geographic scales

Christopher Raymond and Sarah Gottwald

INTRODUCTION

Places to which people can become attached can vary in scale from very small objects to a building, neighborhood, district, city, country, state, parts of or the whole continent or planet Earth (e.g., Altman & Low, 1992; Canter, 1997; Lewicka, 2010; Tuan, 1977). However, over forty years of place attachment research has typically investigated the quality or intensity of place attachment at the neighborhood scale (Giuliani, 2003), followed by home and city (Lewicka, 2011), which we collectively refer to as the "local." Some research suggests that people form attachments to places outside of their local neighborhood or city (Manzo, 2003), or indeed at the scales of region, country or continent (e.g., Brown, Raymond, & Corcoran, 2015; Devine-Wright, Price, & Leviston, 2015).

In the first edition of this book, Manzo and Devine-Wright (2014) highlight the plurality in which place attachment is used and defined. This chapter includes two further related key concepts: **place meanings** (or meaningful places) and **place values** in order to embrace the multiplicity of spatial methods for assessing people-place relations beyond the local. Place attachment is defined here as the emotional connection between people and place (Low & Altman, 1992). Place meaning is the descriptive, symbolic meaning that people ascribe to a place (Smaldone, Harris, & Sanyal, 2008; Stedman, 2016). Place values reflect an operational bridge between held and assigned values (Brown, 2005). Held values are enduring beliefs about the importance of a specific mode of conduct or an end state of existence (Rokeach, 1973), whereas assigned values express the importance of an object relative to other objects (Brown, 1984).

Here we consider four different classes of methods for comparing place attachment and related concepts of place meanings and place values beyond the local (i.e., across multiple levels of geographic scale). **Interviews and focus groups** involve the exploration of place attachment or place meanings to different spatial scales through exploratory discussions about which places (at participant or researcher-defined scales) are important to the respondents, and what these places mean to them (Gustafson, 2001). **Survey methods** involve the use of in-person, online or mail-based surveys that ask individuals to rate the extent to which they feel an attachment to areas of geographic scale pre-defined by the researcher (e.g., home, city, state, country) (Devine-Wright et al., 2015; Gustafson, 2009a). **Participatory mapping methods** combine survey-based methods with an online or hard copy mapping component (e.g., Brown, 2005, 2012). Unlike in interview or survey-based methods, the geographic scale is not necessarily pre-defined. Participants are asked to assign place values, meanings, or attachments to areas on a map. **Spatial navigation methods** employ dominantly qualitative methods like walking interviews, photo elicitation, geonarratives (qualitative GIS approaches integrating narrative analysis) or mental mapping, sometimes enhanced by quantitative information (e.g., GIS data), in order to create information on how humans perceive environments with respect to meaning and spatial cognition (Bell, Phoenix, Lovell, & Wheeler, 2015; Holton, 2015; McCunn & Gifford, 2018; Ryan, 2009; Stedman, Beckley, Wallace, & Ambard, 2004; White & Green, 2012). Unlike participatory mapping methods, emphasis is placed on a more liberal elaboration/ exploration of place imageability, that is, "that quality in a physical object which gives it a high probability of evoking a strong image in any given observer" (Lynch, 1960, p. 9).

We are not aware of any research that has critically reflected on the different methods for assessing the variation in place attachment (and related constructs) across spatial scales beyond the local. In response, we first introduce each method and then compare their strengths and limitations with reference to empirical examples (see Table 9.1 for a summary). In recognition that methodologies for comparing place attachment beyond the local are still in their infancy, we offer future directions for methods development in areas such as understanding the interplay between place attachment, temporal scale, and geographic scale.

Interviews and focus groups. For interviews and focus groups aimed at studying place attachment, the objective is to shed light on variations in place meanings or place attachment across geographic scales under investigation (Jorgensen & Stedman, 2011), rather than statistical representation, generalization, and explanation. In interviews, participants are asked to reflect on the importance of special places over the course of the interview. Building upon Canter's (1997) hypothesis that different spatial scales may be attributed with different meanings, Gustafson (2001) used interviews to develop a three-pole framework of place meanings. He finds that smaller scaled places (residences and neighborhood) are consistently more associated with the self, and larger scaled places (nations and continent—mostly Europe) associated with others or the environment. Li and McKercher (2016) used in-depth, semi-structured interviews to identify four home return travel patterns (North America-China) of Chinese migrants, each influenced by the individual's migration history, personal and national identity, and strength of place attachment to ancestral hometowns. They conclude that migrants' place attachment evolves over time and space—sometimes the scale of place attachment expands as a result of many years of living outside of one's place of origin, reinforcing the view that mobile persons are more likely to develop attachments to larger places than their homes or local communities (Gustafson, 2009a, 2009b).

Table 9.1
Summary of the strength and limitations of existing methods for assessing place attachment across geographic scales

Method category	Method	Method type and purpose	Strengths	Limitations
1. Interviews and focus groups	Interviews	*Exploring an individual's place meanings across scales and elements of the self, others, or the environment* Alternatively, different scales of place meaning are deduced from one's oral histories	Interviews allow people to talk in their own terms about the places to which they are attached. Multiple places and meanings can emerge, and at different geographic scales. Interviews also allow rich descriptions of peoples lived experience and feelings about places without having to adhere to pre-set questions and language focusing on the aspects of place attachment in which the researcher is interested	Issues of statistical representation and generalization
	Focus groups	*Exploring a group's place meanings across scales.* Small groups share and discuss their place meanings and attachments at different spatial scales and generate a collectively defined map of meanings	Recognizes the importance of deliberative democracy in meaning making. Collective discussion of the subject at hand can generate richer responses than one-on-one interviews and allow the formation of shared meanings. Potential for political representation of place meanings (i.e., representation of different stakeholders of interest	Social desirability bias is a potential greater challenge with focus groups. It is difficult to understand how the place meanings of dominant individuals within the group influence the place meanings of the individual
2. Survey methods	Online or mail-based surveys	*Self-report instruments of place attachment.* Individuals self-report the type and intensity of their place attachment from local to regional or from local to national scales	Identify the differences in the intensity of attachment across scales, and with reference to different socio-demographic or attitudinal profiles Can account for a wider range in geographic scales of attachment (e.g., from the home to the nation) compared with map-based measures of place attachment and interviews and focus groups	Geographic scale is pre-defined by the researcher. Survey results may vary depending on how scale is framed by the researcher Unable to determine the actual area of attachment Difficult to compare place attachment results with spatially referenced data on, e.g., land-use, recreational values
	Online or mail-based surveys, followed by interpolation	*Interpolation of place attachment.* Place attachment is measured with respect to the importance of multiple landscape features Interpolation methods are then used to create composite features representing a single place attachment surface for each participant (see Maguire & Klinkenberg, 2018)	Offers a means to visualize place attachment in three-dimensions as a function of geographic location of feature, importance of feature and distance from memory Assumes that place attachment can be represented as a continuous surface and thus no boundaries exist between place values and place attachment	Internal validity issues—there is disconnect between the theoretically established construct of place attachment, and the conceptualization of place attachment informed by interpolation

(Continued)

145 □

Table 9.1
(Continued)

Method category	Method	Method type and purpose	Strengths	Limitations
3. Participatory mapping	Participatory mapping and psychometric scales	*Map-based proxies of place attachment.* Individuals self-report the type and intensity of their place attachment at one scale. Self-reports of place attachment are then correlated or regressed against the number of special places and place values assigned by the individual	Provide place-specific information that can more accurately guide land-use decisions compared with self-report instruments alone. When regression is used, enables statistical prediction of place attachment based on the assignment of place values and special place points	Statistical relationships between place values, special places, and place attachment are only moderate. Thus, difficult to claim that place values and special places can be used instead of place attachment constructs
	Participatory mapping without psychometric scales	*Map-based measures of place attachment or place meanings.* Individuals are asked to identify the intensity, type, and/or spatial distribution of place attachment or place meanings on maps of a region. These map-based measures are sometimes compared to place values	Provides participants the freedom to define their own areas of place attachment or place meanings. Can spatially overlay biophysical attributes (e.g., administrative boundaries) with place attachment. Thereby enables consideration of cognitive and behavioral elements alongside affective elements (attachments) at multiple geographic scales. Information can be combined with attitude scales to collect information describing the regions' cognitive, affective, and behaviorally based characteristics	Methods currently do not allow differentiation between different dimensions or temporal variations in place attachment, although some variations in place meanings have been identified across geographic scale
4. Spatial navigation methods	Spatial navigation combining focus groups and mapping methods	*Protocol analysis of place imageability.* Individuals are asked to "walk through" a landscape and to remember settings "out loud" from a particular starting point	Offers a means to assess the relationships between the temporal and spatial dimensions of place attachment (i.e., a journey from a particular point in the landscape)	Difficult to assess differences in place attachment across large geographic scales (i.e., beyond the immediately perceived environment). Large commitment required by survey participants to use GPS technologies. Difficulties in interpreting three-dimensional maps

Place meanings have also been explored in focus groups, involving groups collectively identifying and describing their place meanings at different geographic scales, sometimes including drawing shapes on maps (Lowery & Morse, 2013; McIntyre, Moore, & Yuan, 2008). In focus groups, participants are able to share and discuss information about places at different geographic scales. Elicitation of place meanings occurs through communication of social constructions and through social representations (e.g., conservation, development interests) rather than emerging independently as they do in individual interviews (see Kenter, Reed, & Fazey, 2016; Raymond, Kenter, Plieninger, Turner, & Alexander, 2014). McIntyre et al. (2008) conducted focus groups to elicit and spatially define the place values of major user groups and special interest groups in a working forest. Place values were identified at a range of geographic scales, including those at the individual site or special place level, the forest as a whole, and beyond that to regional, national, and global levels. This method is particularly useful when aiming for promoting dialogue, shared understanding, and political representation given the emphasis on group communication, negotiation, and compromise. Unlike survey methods, they also provide detailed insights as to why specific places are important (Lowery & Morse, 2013). However, when employing focus groups alone, it is difficult to separate the values of the individual from those shared by the group. There are also issues associated with social desirability bias in that more dominant voices can influence which place attachments are shared within a group setting. Future research could further develop focus group methods for understanding how place attachments form and change across different geographic scales, and with respect to different types of focus group compositions (e.g., conservation groups compared with development groups and mixed interest groups) and facilitation techniques (e.g., brainstorming vs. structured decision-making techniques).

SURVEY METHODS

In survey methods, participants are typically asked to respond to a set of items on a pre-defined list of measurement scales, but the geographic scale under assessment varies across studies (see Table 9.2 for examples).

Table 9.2
Examples of the different gradients of geographic scales employed when assessing place attachment in survey research

Geographic scale(s) of interest	Reference
House, neighborhood, and city	Hidalgo and Hernandez (2001)
Apartment, house/building, neighborhood, city district, and the city	Lewicka (2010)
"The neighbourhood they live," "The city where they live" (if relevant), "The state or territory they live," or "Australia"	Devine-Wright et al. (2015)
The natural resource management region	Brown and Raymond (2007)
Urban area and eco-region	Ardoin, Gould, Lukacs, Sponarski, and Schuh (2019)

The benefits of the survey method (in its diversity of forms) are that it enables identification and statistical representation of differences in the intensity of attachment across scales pre-defined by the researcher, and with reference to different socio-demographic or attitudinal profiles. While it is generally accepted that people are more attached to cognitively defined places (Hamilton, Sherman, & Castelli, 2002; Tuan, 1975), empirical findings relating to the scale at which individuals are most attached to are mixed. A U-shaped relationship has been found between scale of place and strength of place attachment, in that participants cite stronger emotional bonds to the extremes of home or city and fewer to the mid-point of the scale of neighborhood (Hidalgo & Hernandez, 2001; Lewicka, 2010; Vidal, Valera, & Peró, 2010). Other studies have found that individuals form relationships to much larger scales beyond one's place of residence. Laczko (2005) included country, continent, and more local scales and found that participants reported the strongest attachment to their country and the least attachment to their continent. In Australia, global place attachment was found to be significantly higher than attachment to the neighborhood, city/town, or state/territory, but national level place attachment was highest of all (Devine-Wright et al., 2015). A follow-up study using a similar method in the UK also found that national scale attachment was stronger than global or local (Devine-Wright & Batel, 2017).

It is possible that the framing of scale complicates the relationship between geographic scale and place attachment in survey research. A study of residents in Portugal found that when the place context is framed as an area of residence, participants are more likely to refer to the city or neighborhood; when framed in the city context they refer more to the city and region; and in the European and USA context they refer more to the country (discussed in Bernardo & Palma-Oliveira, 2012). Also, framings may vary across interest groups. Farmers in South Australia tended to frame scale in the context of the agricultural area around their home, natural resource managers tended to frame the scale of place as the whole region, and other residents defined their scale of place attachment in the context of their own home or property (Brown, Raymond, & Corcoran, 2015).

To further complicate the relationships between place attachment and scale in survey research, a final set of survey methods do not distinguish between place attachment and specific spatial scales. Instead, the interplay between distance and place attachment is presented as a continuous or smooth surface. Emphasis is on "interpolating" place attachment from survey data whereby points with known values are used to estimate values at other unknown points. In the first known interpolation study of place attachment, Maguire and Klinkenberg (2018) used surveys to ask park visitors to identify the type and intensity of emotion associated with multiple park features. They were then asked to rate importance of the feature and the distance at which they were no longer aware of the feature. For each feature, a surface was created using indicators of importance and distance, which were then combined to create a composite feature. All composite features were then combined using an interpolation function to create a place attachment surface for the participant. Scale was represented as a function of distance from memory, which is a different understanding of geographic scale compared with asking individuals to self-report place attachment at specific geographic scales in survey research. Using this method, it is possible that small, detailed features within the immediate area of purview are prioritized over larger, more abstract features.

Together, these studies demonstrate that survey methods can be applied in a variety of ways to understand the variability in place attachment across geographic scale, resulting in potentially paradoxical results. Some studies reveal strong connections to home and neighborhood, whereas other studies reveal stronger connections to country. In interpolation, the distinctions between home, neighborhood, and much larger scales are "smoothed" using complex modeling techniques to avoid large distinctions. Hence, the way that scale is framed in survey research has a strong influence on the results that are obtained. Surveys on place attachment and geographic scale may benefit from a second stage of interviewing involving exploration of how participants categorize geographic scale and the relationship of scale to place attachment.

PARTICIPATORY MAPPING

Participatory mapping methods have drawn on the place attachment concept with the goal of identifying ways that this concept can inform land-use planning, design, and decision-making. Unlike self-report instruments, the mapping of special places provides more fine-scaled and detailed information to guide land-use planning and enables the identification of spatially explicit and commensurable risk indices to inform the management of land-use conflicts.

Participatory mapping techniques can be used to assess *map-based proxies of place attachment* enabling participants to map place values and special places, as well as respond to place attachment survey items in a survey. Responses to place attachment scales in surveys are correlated with place values or special places to identify spatial location and type of landscape attributes that are reliable proxies of place attachment. Using the results of the statistical analysis, researchers make inferences about the spatial variability in place attachment. Brown and Raymond (2007) showed that mapped values and "special places" provide a reasonable proxy for psychometric measures of place attachment. Aesthetic, spiritual, therapeutic, and wilderness values spatially co-locate with the mapping of "special places" and overall place attachment. The mapping of spiritual value was a particularly strong predictor of the psychological state of place attachment. This finding is consistent with lessons from community design studies showing that sacred places have predictable origins and commonly express our growth and identity (Hester, 2014). From a wider perspective, it demonstrates the importance of considering the concept of place spirituality as a paradigm for understanding the relationship between place experiences and place attachment (building on Counted & Zock, 2019).

Participatory mapping methods can also be used for assessing *map-based measures of place attachment*. In the south east of South Australia, survey participants were requested to identify the outer boundaries of an area in the study region that they strongly identified with and depended on for the lifestyle and livelihood using points, lines, or polygons (i.e., straight line segments connected to form a closed shape) (Brown et al., 2015). This method is analogous to cognitive mapping methodologies in the broader geography literature which enable the subjective measurement of definitions of neighborhood scale (Hays & Kogl, 2007; Lee, 1968) or areas beyond the residential neighborhood (Brunckhorst & Reeve, 2006). However, unlike cognitive mapping, spatial information can be combined with attitude scales to collect information describing the regions' cognitive, affective, and behaviorally based characteristics (Jorgensen & Stedman, 2011).

Studies drawing on map-based measures of place attachment have shown that the place attachment areas mapped by respondents are highly variable. In the south east of South Australia, farmers assigned place attachment at much finer scales (average area of 518 square kilometers) compared to natural resource management practitioners (average area of 2287 square kilometers). The values home range area (i.e., minimum convex polygon of mapped place values for each participant) was significantly and positively correlated with the area of place attachment. About 57% of participants identified their values home range as being larger than the place area (Brown et al., 2015).

It is also possible to examine how place meanings are associated with landscape features of varying scale and shape. In the Lahn river basin, Germany, researchers examined the associations among residents' place meanings and landscape features, in addition to their personal characteristics and place values and behavior (Gottwald & Albert, 2018)). Additional analysis by Gottwald for this chapter highlights that 30% of respondents assigned their place meanings to a rather elongated course, 19% defined a specific point, and 19% to a larger spatial area (with the remaining 32% being non-respondents). Also, there was some variation in place meanings by shape type, particularly between area and point, and line and point.

Together, these studies suggest that residents can assign their place attachment, place values, or place meanings to a variety of geographic scales, as a function of area or shape type. Place values and meaningful places are related to, but not identical to mapped place attachment given the differences in the level of spatial overlap of place values and place attachment and differences in the types of values found across shapes of features on the landscape. The mapping of place values, place meanings, and place attachment represent alternative, but complementary methods for assessing people-place relations across geographic scales. However, using these participatory mapping methods it is difficult to detect how dimensions of place attachment vary across geographic or temporal scales. For example, how aspects of identity, belonging, or dependence vary across different areas and with respect to daily routines, seasons, or other temporal gradients. This is in part because values, meanings, and attachments are abstracted from the moment in which the attachment formed when the individual is asked to assign place attachments and values to static two-dimensional maps. In other words, the dynamic and constituted relationship between people, place, and environment in context is lost (Raymond, Kytta, & Stedman, 2017).

SPATIAL NAVIGATION METHODS

Spatial navigation methods make use of the human brain's capability of "using spatial information to encode and interpret emotional reactions to meaningful places" (McCunn & Gifford, 2018, p. 209). There are different forms to make these cognitive maps, or mental maps, visible. In contrast to the aforementioned methods, spatial navigation methods do not start off using a georeferenced map but are based on the individual's spatial cognition. Egocentric (self-to-object) and allocentric (object-to-object) reference systems are utilized to understand an environment's spatial structure (McCunn & Gifford, 2018), which represent two separate cognitive systems (building on Raymond, Kytta, & Stedman, 2017). In spatial navigation methods, participants can be asked to navigate a place on paper. McCunn and Gifford (2018) asked respondents to draw on paper the representation of the settings they had in mind when responding to items on place attachment, dependence, and identity. The stronger the attachment, the easier it was for respondents to recall and navigate them spatially. White and Green (2012) used mental maps with adolescents to assess the role of social networks and place attachment in shaping attitudes, aspirations, and behaviors. The mental maps were used as a complementary method within focus group discussions as a visual input, allowing comparisons and connection between the different mental maps.

Participants can also physically navigate the place, for example, taking photographs (photo elicitation method), GPS devices (geonarrative), or walking with the researcher during the interview (walking interview) (Amsden et al., 2011). Spatial navigation methods can also be used to assess spatial variability in place attachment, presented through daily routines (Bell et al., 2015). Bell and colleagues invited participants to wear accelerometers (a device worn on the wrist measuring physical activity) and carry GPS units during one week capturing their daily routines. Afterward they interviewed the participants and asked about the place meanings in the map they had created. They found that some participants took detours to include places they feel attached to in their daily routine (Bell et al., 2015). Walking interviews combining GPS and interview have also been developed in order to reduce the time of the data collection process, and to obtain more immediate responses about the relationships between the individual and their environment (Holton, 2015).

The strength of this method is that it enables researchers to understand variability in place attachment or place meanings across geographic and temporal scales, and as a process of navigation though the landscape. Spatial navigational methods are based on the individual's cognitive ability to reproduce space either by drawing, guiding a researcher or in everyday life. The different scales of place attachment are accounted for as participants reproduce their perceived boundaries of the places they are attached to by, for example, taking a photo or drawing them. Further, these methods can also highlight the temporal variability, for example, by using GPS devices over a longer time period, inviting people to include old/historical photographs or doing interview walks with undergraduate students.

However, spatial navigation methods have some weaknesses. Walking emphasizing physical form could result in symbolic meanings of places being overlooked or under-represented. It also seems difficult to apply this method at scales beyond the neighborhood or city. The use of GPS devices provides the advantages of producing a georeferenced map over a longer time period; however, post hoc interviews are required to understand the content of these places. Collaboration of the participants is crucial as the technology is not "fool-proof" and the different steps (wearing GPS devices, interviews) require further commitment on the behalf of the participant (Bell et al., 2015). The mental maps drawn by the participants are able to capture large and small scales, including different time periods, but there are technical difficulties associated with translating these three dimensional landscapes into data that can be systematically compared and analyzed (Gillespie, 2010).

SUMMARY AND FUTURE DIRECTIONS

Despite the inextricable link between the physical and subjective elements of place attachment, methods development relating to place attachment (and associated constructs) across geographic scales is still in its infancy. Currently, four main types of methods exist that can address place attachment across geographic scales: interviews and focus groups involving the open exploration of place and scale; survey techniques involving researcher-derived interpretations of scale; participatory mapping methods for identifying map-based proxies of place attachment (e.g., special places), and map-based measures; and spatial navigational measures enabling assessment of place attachment along navigation routes from a particular point. These methods can be presented on a spectrum from those which represent scale through self-report instruments (e.g., pre-defined scale items) or open-ended questions, those that ask individuals to represent scale on a geographic map, and those that represent scale as a process of navigation (Figure 9.1). We have also represented the common concepts for understanding place with respect to each method. Interviews, focus groups, and survey methods have each been used to understand the variation in place attachment across local, regional, national, and global scales. Participatory mapping studies on the relationships between place attachment and place values have been largely restricted to local and regional assessments, and spatial navigation methods generally relate to one's immediate perceived environment (the local scale).

Another way to distinguish methods relates to the extent to which the technique predefines the geographic scale. Survey methods offer the strictest boundaries of scale to the participants as they relate the place attachment scales directly

Figure 9.1
Summary of the spectrum
of existing methods
for understanding the
relationships between
place attachment and
geographic scale.

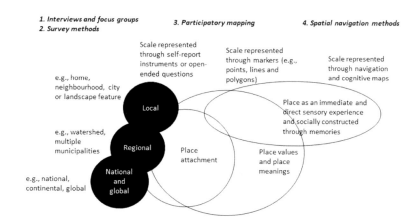

to pre-defined loci of attachment (e.g., home, country, and world). Participatory mapping methods also set a strict boundary of scale (e.g., a natural resource management region), but within that boundary they can freely locate areas of value, meaning, or attachment (e.g., home, town, stream, sub-region). Spatial navigation methods like GPS tracking, photo elicitation, and especially mental mapping methods also provide a boundary of scale and allow participants to choose areas within that boundary to focus on; a key exception being walking interviews where the scale is restricted due to physical limitations. Most freedom of scale exists for interview and focus groups, where a certain boundary is given by the researcher, but respondents are able to mention any scale.

Despite these differences in scale of application, we have identified mixed results concerning the relationships between place attachment and place scale. Some studies emphasize the importance of the local whereas other studies emphasize the importance of the regional, national, or global. These inconclusive results can partly be attributed to the different ways in which individuals frame or assess the scale of place attachment. Deeper exploration of the ontology of scale and place attachment is needed to clarify these framing effects, particularly with reference to mobility aspects. Research could compare different framings of scale and place attachment with respect to highly mobile and relatively fixed individuals (building on Di Masso et al., 2019). Importantly, what are the psychological differences in the scale of place attachments of new residents (including new migrants) with more fluid mobility configurations compared with longer term residents with more fixed place configurations?

The chapter also offered insights concerning the interplay between place values and place attachment across geographic scales. Participatory mapping studies reveal that place values occur over a larger mean area than place attachment, but there are important areas of overlap. In other terms, place attachment is a component of one's values home range, and these results have been confirmed at local and regional scales of management. However, place values remain a moderate predictor of place attachment (Brown & Raymond, 2007). One may question what spatial qualities of place, beyond those represented by place values, help define map-based place attachment. To this end, assessing the causal relationships between place meanings, place values, and place attachment may be a fruitful line of enquiry. We encourage further research combining participatory mapping, interviews, and focus groups to better understand the ontological relationships between place values, place meanings, and place attachment.

The interplay between spatial and temporal variability remain implicit in most place attachment research. Here we showed that spatial navigation methods deal with direct perception-action processes, in addition to processes of social construction, because they are grounded in sensory dynamics and cognitive maps. In contrast, participatory mapping and other forms of interviews and surveys focus on place values and attachments grounded in more stable forms of meaning-making. Raymond et al. (2017) argue that an interplay exists between place attachment that is immediately perceived and place attachment that is socially constructed over longer term processes of meaning-making. It was theorized that fast and slow processes of cognition together contribute to how place attachment forms and changes in a given setting. Direct perception—action processes operate as a subset of Type 1, fast, automatic processes. Socially constructed processes are a subset of Type 2, slow processes grounded in reasoning—thinking is slow, serial, controlled, effortful, and rule-governed (building on: Herschbach, 2015; Kahneman, 2012). Equally, processes of social construction may stem from the "steady accretion of sentiment over the years" (Tuan, 1977, p. 32). Such relationships require empirical grounding. Combining spatial navigation methods with participatory mapping as well as interviews, focus groups and survey methods may help how place values and place attachment as an immediate, direct experience relates to longer term forms of meaning making engrained in memory of experiences or events. Future research could consider the relationships between place attachment, geographic and temporal scale across these types of cognition, and with reference to different forms of rapid changes to social and ecological contexts (i.e., place changes).

The three-dimensional qualities of place are absent in current discussions on place attachment and scale. All studies on the relationships between place attachment and scale have been undertaken in two-dimensional environments, but the interplay between height, width, and depth of place is rarely considered. In the architecture literature, general descriptions have been made relating to place attachment and typologies of building designs (e.g., location, open space, function) (Saymanlier, Kurt, & Ayiran, 2018). Three dimensional visualizations, including 3D participatory mapping methodologies, will have an important role in relating the physical qualities of places-to-place attachment. Also, the rapid rise in virtual reality technology provides an important and now feasible pathway for running experiments that assess the relationships between place attachment and geographic scale in natural and built environments.

REFERENCES

Amsden, B. L., Stedman, R. C., & Kruger, L. E. (2011). The creation and maintenance of sense of place in a tourism-dependent community. *Leisure Sciences*, *33*(1), 32–51. https://doi.org/10.1080/01490400.2011.533105

Ardoin, N. M., Gould, R. K., Lukacs, H., Sponarski, C. C., & Schuh, J. S. (2019). Scale and sense of place among urban dwellers. *Ecosphere*, *10*(9), 1–14. https://doi.org/10.1002/ecs2.2871

Bell, S. L., Phoenix, C., Lovell, R., & Wheeler, B. W. (2015). Using GPS and geo-narratives: A methodological approach for understanding and situating everyday green space encounters. *Area*, *47*(1), 88–96. https://doi.org/10.1111/area.12152

Bernardo, F., & Palma-Oliveira, J. (2012). Place Identity: A central concept in understanding intergroup relationships in the urban context. *The role of place identity in the perception, understanding, and design of built environments* (pp. 35–46). https://doi.org/10.2174/97816080541381120101

Brown, T. C. (1984). The concept of value in resource allocation. *Land Economics*, *60*(3), 231–246.

Brown, G. (2012). Public participation GIS (PPGIS) for regional and environmental planning: Reflections on a decade of empirical research. *URISA Journal*, *25*(2), 7–18.

Brown, G., Raymond, C. M., & Corcoran, J. (2015). Mapping and measuring place attachment. *Applied Geography*, *57*, 42–53. https://doi.org/10.1016/j.apgeog.2014.12.011

Brown, G. (2005). Mapping spatial attributes in survey research for natural resource management: Methods and applications. *Society & Natural Resources*, *18*(1), 17–39. https://doi.org/10.1080/08941920590881853

Brown, G., & Raymond, C. M. (2007). The relationship between place attachment and landscape values: Toward mapping place attachment. *Applied Geography*, *27*(2), 89–111. https://doi.org/10.1016/j.apgeog.2006.11.002

Brunckhorst, D., & Reeve, I. (2006). A geography of place: Principles and application for defining 'eco-civic' resource governance regions. *Australian Geographer*, *37*(2), 147–166. https://doi.org/10.1080/00049180600672334

Canter, D. (1997). The facets of place. *Toward the integration of theory, methods, research, and utilization* (pp. 109–147). Boston, MA: Springer US. https://doi.org/10.1007/978-1-4757-4425-5_4

Counted, V., & Zock, H. (2019). Place spirituality. *Archive for the Psychology of Religion*, *41*(1), 12–25. https://doi.org/10.1177/0084672419833448

Devine-Wright, P., & Batel, S. (2017). My neighbourhood, my country or my planet? The influence of multiple place attachments and climate change concern on social acceptance of energy infrastructure. *Global Environmental Change*, *47*, 110–120. https://doi.org/10.1016/J.GLOENVCHA.2017.08.003

Devine-Wright, P., Price, J., & Leviston, Z. (2015). My country or my planet? Exploring the influence of multiple place attachments and ideological beliefs upon climate change attitudes and opinions. *Global Environmental Change*, *30*, 68–79. https://doi.org/10.1016/j.gloenvcha.2014.10.012

Di Masso, A., Williams, D. R., Raymond, C. M., Buchecker, M., Degenhardt, B., Devine-Wright, P., … von Wirth, T. (2019). Between fixities and flows: Navigating place attachments in an increasingly mobile world. *Journal of Environmental Psychology*, *61*, 125–133. https://doi.org/10.1016/J.JENVP.2019.01.006

Gillespie, C. A. (2010). How culture constructs our sense of neighborhood: Mental maps and children's perceptions of place. *Journal of Geography*, *109*(1), 18–29. https://doi.org/10.1080/00221340903459447

Giuliani, M. (2003). Theory of attachment and place attachment. In M. Bonnes, T. Lee, & M. Bonaiuto (Eds.), *Psychological theories for environmental issues* (pp. 137–170). Aldershot: Ashgate.

Gottwald, S., & Albert, C. (2018). Assessing sense of place to support river landscape planning. In Y. Huisman, K. D. Berends, I. Niesten, & E. Mosselman (Eds.), *The future river: NCR DAYS 2018 Proceedings* (pp. 60–61). Netherland Centre for River Studies Publication 42-2018. https://doi.org/10.3182/20060705-3-fr-2907.00123

Gustafson, P. (2001). Meanings of place: Everyday experience and theoretical conceptualizations. *Journal of Environmental Psychology*, *21*(1), 5–16. https://doi.org/10.1006/jevp.2000.0185

Gustafson, P. (2009a). Mobility and territorial belonging. *Environment and Behavior*, *41*(4), 490–508. https://doi.org/10.1177/0013916508314478

Gustafson, P. (2009b). More cosmopolitan, no less local. *European Societies*, *11*(1), 25–47. https://doi.org/10.1080/14616690802209689

Hamilton, D. L., Sherman, S. J., & Castelli, L. (2002). A group by any other name—The role of entitativity in group perception. *European Review of Social Psychology*, *12*(1), 139–166. https://doi.org/10.1080/14792772143000049

Hays, R. A., & Kogl, A. M. (2007). Neighborhood attachment, social capital building, and political participation: a case study of low- and moderate-income residents of Waterloo, Iowa. *Journal of Urban Affairs*, *29*(2), 181–205. https://doi.org/10.1111/j.1467-9906.2007.00333.x

Herschbach, M. (2015). Direct social perception and dual process theories of mindreading. *Consciousness and Cognition*, *36*, 483–497. https://doi.org/10.1016/j.concog.2015.04.001

Hester, R. (2014). Do not detach! Instructions from and for community design. *Place attachment: Advances in theory, methods and applications* (pp. 191–206). Oxon: Routledge.

Hidalgo, M. & Hernandez, B. (2001). Place attachment: Conceptual and empirical questions. *Journal of Environmental Psychology*, *21*(3), 273–281. https://doi.org/10.1006/jevp.2001.0221

Holton, M. (2015). Adapting relationships with place: Investigating the evolving place attachment and 'sense of place' of UK higher education students during a period of intense transition. *Geoforum*, *59*, 21–29. https://doi.org/10.1016/J.GEOFORUM.2014.11.017

Jorgensen, B. S., & Stedman, R. C. (2011). Measuring the spatial component of sense of place: A methodology for research on the spatial dynamics of psychological experiences of places. *Environment and Planning B: Planning and Design*, *38*(5), 795–813. https://doi.org/10.1068/b37054

Kahneman, D. (2012). *Thinking, fast and slow*. New York: Farrar, Strauss and Giroux.

Kenter, J. O., Reed, M. S., & Fazey, I. (2016). The deliberative value formation model. *Ecosystem Services*, *21*, 194–207. https://doi.org/10.1016/j.ecoser.2016.09.015

Laczko, L. S. (2005). National and local attachments in a changing world system: Evidence from an international survey. *International Review of Sociology*, *15*(3), 517–528. https://doi.org/10.1080/03906700500272525

Lee, T. (1968). Urban neighbourhood as a socio-spatial schema. *Human Relations*, *21*(3), 241–267. https://doi.org/10.1177/001872676802100303

Lewicka, M. (2010). What makes neighborhood different from home and city? Effects of place scale on place attachment. *Journal of Environmental Psychology*, *30*(1), 35–51. https://doi.org/10.1016/j.jenvp.2009.05.004

Lewicka, M. (2011). Place attachment: How far have we come in the last 40 years? *Journal of Environmental Psychology*, *31*(3), 207–230. https://doi.org/10.1016/j.jenvp.2010.10.001

Li, T. E., & McKercher, B. (2016). Effects of place attachment on home return travel: A spatial perspective. *Tourism Geographies*, *18*(4), 359–376. https://doi.org/10.1080/14616688.2016.1196238

Low, S. M., & Altman, I. (1992). *Place attachment*. Boston, MA: Springer US. https://doi.org/10.1007/978-1-4684-8753-4_1

Lowery, D. R., & Morse, W. C. (2013). A qualitative method for collecting spatial data on important places for recreation, livelihoods, and ecological meanings: Integrating focus groups with public participation geographic information systems. *Society & Natural Resources*, *26*(12), 1422–1437. https://doi.org/10.1080/08941920.2013.819954

Lynch, K. (1960). Kevin Lynch: The image of the city 1. *The image of the city*, 1–14. https://doi.org/10.1525/sp.1960.8.3.03a00190

Maguire, B., & Klinkenberg, B. (2018). Visualization of place attachment. *Applied Geography*, *99*(August 2017), 77–88. https://doi.org/10.1016/j.apgeog.2018.07.007

Manzo, L. C. (2003). Beyond house and haven: Toward a revisioning of emotional relationships with places. *Journal of Environmental Psychology*, *23*(1), 47–61.

Manzo, L. C., & Devine-Wright, P. (Eds.). (2014). *Place attachment advances, advances in theory, methods and applications*. New York: Routledge.

McCunn, L. J., & Gifford, R. (2018). Spatial navigation and place imageability in sense of place. *Cities*, *74*, 208–218. https://doi.org/10.1016/J.CITIES.2017.12.006

McIntyre, N., Moore, J., & Yuan, M. (2008). A place-based, values-centered approach to managing recreation on Canadian crown lands. *Society and Natural Resources*, *21*(8), 657–670. https://doi.org/10.1080/08941920802022297

Raymond, C. M., Kenter, J. O., Plieninger, T., Turner, N. J., & Alexander, K. A. (2014). Comparing instrumental and deliberative paradigms underpinning the assessment of social values for cultural ecosystem services. *Ecological Economics*, *107*, 145–156. https://doi.org/10.1016/j.ecolecon.2014.07.033

Raymond, C. M., Kyttä, M., & Stedman, R. (2017). Sense of place, fast and slow: The potential contributions of affordance theory to sense of place. *Frontiers in Psychology*, *8*(September). https://doi.org/10.3389/fpsyg.2017.01674

Rokeach, M. (1973). *The nature of human values*. New York: Free Press. https://psycnet.apa.org/record/2011-15663-000

Ryan, M. (2009). Mixed methodology approach to place attachment and consumption behaviour: A rural town perspective. *Electronic Journal of Business Research Methods*, *7*(1), 107–116.

Saymanlier, A. M., Kurt, S., & Ayiran, N. (2018). The place attachment experience regarding the disabled people: The typology of coffee shops. *Quality & Quantity*, *52*(6), 2577–2596. https://doi.org/10.1007/s11135-017-0678-1

Smaldone, D., Harris, C., & Sanyal, N. (2008). The role of time in developing place meanings. *Journal of Leisure Research*, *40*(4), 479–504.

Stedman, R. C. (2016). Subjectivity and social-ecological systems: A rigidity trap (and sense of place as a way out). *Sustainability Science*, *11*(6), 891–901. https://doi.org/10.1007/s11625-016-0388-y

Stedman, R., Beckley, T., Wallace, S., & Ambard, M. (2004). A picture and 1000 words: Using resident-employed photography to understand attachment to high amenity places. *Journal of Leisure Research*, *36*(4), 580–606.

Tuan, Y.-F. (1975). Place: An experiential perspective. *Geographical Review*, *65*(2), 151. https://doi.org/10.2307/213970

Tuan, Y. (1977). *Space and place: The perspective of experience*. London: Edward Arnold.

Vidal, T., Valera, S., & Peró, M. (2010). Place attachment, place identity and residential mobility in undergraduate students | Apego al lugar, identidad de lugar y movilidad residencial en estudiantes de grado. *Psyecology*, *1*(3). https://doi.org/10.1174/217119710792774834

White, R. J., & Green, A. E. (2012). The use of mental maps in youth research: Some evidence from research exploring young people's awareness of and attachment to place. *Innovations in youth research* (pp. 58–76). London: Palgrave Macmillan UK. https://doi.org/10.1057/9780230355880_4

PART III

Applications

Chapter 10: Community responses to environmental threat: Place cognition, attachment, and social action

Nikolay L. Mihaylov, Douglas D. Perkins,
and Richard C. Stedman

Place attachment is a multi-faceted, multi-disciplinary concept. People's emotional bonding with meaningful spaces fulfills fundamental human needs (Relph, 1976). Community attachment is an important motivation to spend time in one's neighborhood, talking to neighbors sociably or about local problems and ideas for solutions, and rather than flee, to stay and fight—that is, to create social capital and participate in collective efforts to preserve, protect, or improve the community (Manzo & Perkins, 2006; Mihaylov & Perkins, 2014). Those efforts are often in response to some perceived threat to residents' health, safety, property, and/or quality of life, which may also disrupt the very place attachments that led to residents' community commitment and engagement (Brown & Perkins, 1992).

This chapter reviews, analyzes, and builds upon theory and research across multiple disciplines on residential community place attachment and its relationship to both psychological and collective responses to environmental threats, such as disasters or land development, with particular attention to energy exploration and extraction. We will explore the ways in which place attachment is shaped, nurtured, and experienced within the context of community, and what other community-focused cognitions and behaviors place attachment influences. In doing so we ask, how does community place attachment differ from other forms, focuses, and levels of place attachment? To what extent is community place attachment shared (i.e., it is community-focused, but is it also a *communal* phenomenon?) and in what ways does *community-level* place attachment manifest itself? How does community place attachment differ from related concepts such as community place identity and sense of community? How does community place attachment relate to social and place development or disruption? The first half of this chapter is organized around the theoretical model of community place attachment and other responses to environmental threats proposed in the prior edition of this chapter (Mihaylov & Perkins, 2014). This chapter expands on emphasizing applications of community place attachment via two brief case studies of the role of place attachment, place cognition, and social action in response to hydraulic fracturing ("fracking") for oil and gas in Bulgaria and the US.

COMMUNITY PLACE ATTACHMENT

We accept others' definitions of place attachment as consisting of person, place, and psychological or process dimensions (Scannell & Gifford, 2010) and address all three dimensions, but regarding the person dimension, we are more concerned with *collective/group* than individual aspects of place attachment. In terms of the process dimension, we see *emotional* bonds to home/community and *cognitive* aspects of place memory, knowledge, understanding, and meaning as important but emphasize collective *behaviors* to protect, preserve, and defend one's community. Our focus on the place dimension includes attachment to *residential community environments* as well as the *proximal natural environment*, which is often overlooked by community researchers, but may strongly influence community place attachment.

Researchers identify different scales of place attachment, including home, neighborhood, and city levels (Kasarda & Janowitz, 1974), but suggest one's residence and city tend to elicit stronger place attachment than does the neighborhood or district level (Lewicka, 2010). We argue that the concept of "community" represents a broader, more flexible scale, however, ranging from one's streetblock (Brown et al., 2003; Perkins et al., 1996) to the neighborhood/village, or city and environs. Greater variance in place attachment exists at mid-level community scales than at the site (e.g., home) or city levels, and greater variance can be explained at the community level (Lewicka, 2010).

We focus particularly on place-based communities. One's locality may be inhabited by multiple social networks or communities of interest or identity, but those can exist apart from place. While place attachment is very relevant to communities of place, social networks determine how much place attachment is a shared, communal rather than individual phenomenon and how agreement among community members regarding place attachment is created.

Community place attachment differs from other forms of place attachment in four main ways: *location*, *level*, *focus*, and *behavioral response*. The *location* of community place attachment is the local area surrounding one's home (including second homes, which can be strong loci of community-based attachment [Stedman, 2006]). *Community-level* place attachment implies some agreement among community members regarding their bonds to place. Consensus is greater in some communities than in others, and in most places, residents vary greatly in their attachment to the same community. The *focus* of community place attachment is more holistic than a particular favorite object, building, or natural space; it relates to one's residential and public environs and surrounding landscape as a whole place. What makes community place attachment truly unique, however, are the complex place and social cognitions, emotions, and behaviors, in response to environmental disruptions or threats, that inform an interpretive process at both the individual and community level and that lead to *collective, community-level actions, adaptations*, or *acceptance* of the disruption (Stedman, 2016).

PLACE ATTACHMENT AND COMMUNITY-FOCUSED SOCIAL COGNITIONS AND BEHAVIORS

Place attachment is closely tied to various other community perceptions, emotions, and behaviors. A study of adolescents found that place attachment is significantly related to social capital and feelings of safety in all 13 European countries studied (Dallago et al., 2009). Another study measured community-level place attachment differently than individual place attachment in two ways: by asking about pride and attachment to streetblock and neighborhood separately from home interior, exterior, and yard; and by aggregating to the block/community level and using multilevel analysis (Brown et al., 2003, 2004). Community place attachment was associated with fewer perceived incivilities (e.g., gang activity), criminal victimization and fear, and more physical revitalization on one's block. Place attachment is generally assumed to develop slowly over time, but studies have found that it can develop quickly in well-designed new communities (Brown et al., 2004) and among second-home owners (Stedman, 2006). Geographic Information System mapping of block-level place attachment over time shows that new developments can actually depress the place attachment of existing nearby residents, however, due to the better condition of new housing and/or the influx of strangers (Perkins et al., 2009).

While those effects confirm the importance of place attachment for residents' quality of life, we are particularly interested in how community place attachment relates to other community-focused cognitions, emotions, and behaviors. We present an ecological model integrating individual and community levels of analysis for understanding the psychological dimensions of people's responses to community environmental threats. We start with Manzo and Perkins's (2006) framework distinguishing physical (place) and social dimensions of community and three psychological dimensions: (1) affective (emotional) bonds to places (place attachment) and/or to people (sense of community); (2) place and community identity, which are related but a separate cognitive dimension; and (3) a behavioral dimension including organized community participation and informal neighboring.

OVERVIEW OF THE FRAMEWORK[1]

We use a disruption-response framework for presenting place attachment and related constructs and articulating their relations to community action. This model is based on studies of local reactions to place disruption, which unfold "in a series of stages involving identification, interpretation, evaluation and forms of coping response" (Devine-Wright & Howes, 2010, p. 277). The model builds on Devine-Wright's stages of psychological response to place change (Devine-Wright, 2009) but focuses on the stages of place disruption, interpretation, and response at both the individual and community levels (see Figure 10.1). A disruption framework highlights place-related individual and community-level psycho-social processes, because disruption triggers and illuminates otherwise latent or taken-for-granted states and attitudes, such as the meanings places hold for inhabitants (Seamon, 2018; Stedman, 2002).

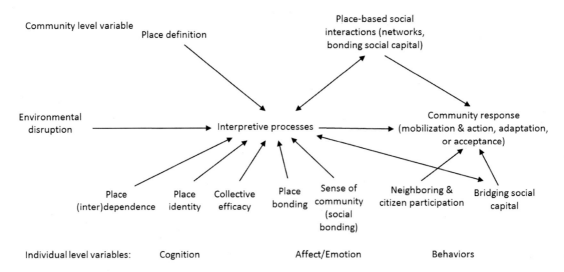

Figure 10.1
A framework of individual
and community place
attachment influences
on interpretations of
environmental disruption
and behavioral outcomes.

ENVIRONMENTAL DISRUPTION

The first component of the disruption model is any disruptive community-level environmental stimulus—a natural or human-made disaster, a planning decision, building or other infrastructure construction or demolition, or just the possibility or threat of some significant environmental change.

INTERPRETIVE PROCESSES

Place attachment scholars study not only the physical aspects of disruption but also the social psychological processes of its interpretation in the community (Devine-Wright, 2009; Jacquet & Stedman, 2014; Scannell & Gifford, 2010). Interpretation of environmental disruption occurs on the individual and community levels by identifying the change, framing it in terms of the physical and symbolic aspects of place, and evaluating it with regard to the centrality of the place and its disrupted features (Devine-Wright, 2009). Community interpretive processes occur in a context of place-based social networks.

Place definition/place meanings. Consistent with Lewicka's (2011a) recommendation, the first component of the model focuses not on the person, but on place definition—the socially constructed and negotiated boundaries of the place and the features and attributes that give it a distinctive meaning and identity in the minds of dwellers (Stedman, 2002): what belongs in the place, what makes it unique. Place boundaries are socially constructed and defined differently by different groups. For example, residents living in a protected area defined the place more narrowly than did people living close to, but outside, the parks (Bonaiuto et al., 2002). The acceptance of change depends on the compatibility of the change with place symbolic, cultural, historic, or functional meanings. In the energy context, attitudes toward construction of a new nuclear reactor depend on perceived contributions of the existing power station to sense of place, a broader concept including both place attachment and place identity (Venables et al., 2012). Communities may respond in opposition to a wind farm (Devine-Wright & Howes, 2010) or in support of a tidal energy converter (Devine-Wright, 2011), depending not only on the different renewable energy sources and disruptions they represent but also the meaning of different places to the local community. Within the interpretive processes of the framework, environmental disruption is translated into the degree of disruption of the defined place: Is the change inside or outside of the place? Is it compatible with the place, historically and currently?

Place dependence. It indicates how well a setting serves an intended use over a range of alternatives (Jorgensen & Stedman, 2001; Raymond et al., 2010). Communities depend on places for desired activities and experiences. In our model, an environmental change is evaluated cognitively according to its disturbance of one's place dependence: Will the change enhance or impede the way the place is used and the types of uses/affordances it facilitates? What alternative places can be accessed for this use? Place dependence is not one-directional. Communities influence place based on residents' sense of community, ownership, and investment, not just in their own properties but in the entire neighborhood or town and environs.

Place identity. It is "a cognitive mechanism, a component of self-concept and/or of personal identity in relation to the place one belongs" (Hernández et al., 2010, p. 281). It is critical to understanding how environmental meanings symbolize or situate, and thus can threaten, individual, and community identity (Bonaiuto et al., 1996). Place identity affects the positive or negative valence of one's attitudes to environmental change after it has been defined in terms of the place and its use. It is threatened when local environmental change is viewed negatively as place disturbance (Devine-Wright & Howes, 2010).

Place bonding. Place bonding, or place attachment, refers to people's emotional ties to a geographic location. We conceptualize place bonding as the affective link to *both* natural and constructed physical environments, rather than frame it as nature bonding only (Raymond et al., 2010). Definitions of place attachment vary. To some, place attachment is a higher order construct comprising place identity, bonding, and dependence; we equate place attachment with place bonding, part of a higher order concept: sense of place (Hernández et al., 2014; Jorgensen & Stedman, 2001). Place bonding usually causes opposition to, and rejection of, place disruption (Devine-Wright & Howes, 2010). Place attachment may lead some communities to accept development, however (Devine-Wright, 2011; Venables et al., 2012). It is worth exploring in those cases whether those attached to a place see development as adding value and reducing other threats while preserving what they like about the place or the unattached may simply be apathetic or oppose development for other, personal reasons (Bailey et al., 2016).

SOCIAL CAPITAL

The right half of the model in Figure 10.1 emphasizes the concept of social cap-ital, and people's behavioral responses, individually and collectively, to the whole disruption-interpretation process. Social capital consists of "the norms, networks, and mutual trust of 'civil society' facilitating cooperative action among citizens and institutions" (Perkins & Long, 2002, p. 291). Perkins and Long (2002) proposed a two-by-two social capital framework: one dimension distinguishes intrapsychic (cognitive/affective) from behavioral responses; the other contrasts informal/spontaneous versus formally organized responses. This yields four components of psycho-behavioral social capital: the informal, affective component is social bonding (or sense of community); the informal behavior is neighboring; the organized, cognitive component is collective efficacy (or empowerment); and the organized behavior is citizen participation in community voluntary organizations.

Sense of community (social bonding). Riger and Lavrakas (1981) identified two dimensions of place attachment that are inherently communal: a feeling of physical *rootedness* in the community, which is related to place identity and inter-dependence, and a sense of social *bondedness* with one's neighborhood. These are core elements of sense of community (Pretty et al., 2003), the informal affective part of social capital, defined as feelings of membership or belongingness to a group, including an emotional connection based on shared history, values, interests, or concerns (Perkins & Long 2002). Sense of community also involves neighbors' trust in each other. It is the affective attachment to the social aspects of community or place and is called positive "social bonding" in Raymond et al.'s (2010) four-pole model of place attachment. This emotional component of both place bonding and social bonding motivates community members to mobilize for collective environ-mental protection (or change) efforts. Sense of community has been linked to place attachment and other positive individual and community outcomes at both the indi-vidual and community scale (Perkins et al., 1996; Perkins & Long, 2002).

Neighboring. It is the help we informally provide, and receive from, neighbors. Unger and Wandersman (1985) identified three components of neighboring behavior: (1) *social* support and network ties (community-level bonding), (2) *cogni-tive* mapping of the physical environment and symbolic communication (captured in our model by place definition, interdependence, and identity), and (3) *affective* attachment to neighbors and to place (sense of community and place bonding). Analysis of neighboring at the individual and community levels finds it closely linked to place attachment (Brown et al., 2003) and citizen participation at both levels (Perkins et al., 1996). Those who participate most in formally organized groups are also more likely to help their neighbors informally—one does not replace the other.

Collective efficacy[2] *(or empowerment).* It can be thought of as people's confidence in the efficacy of organized community action (Perkins & Long, 2002). Empowerment has been defined as a multi-level process by which people gain control over their lives, democratic participation in the life of their community, and a critical understanding of their environment (Perkins et al., 1996) or more simply as "voice and choice." Environmental hazards can be disempowering, as people often have little control over them, unless they collectively mobilize (Rich et al., 1995). Thus, empowerment is critical to both community development and environmental protection (O'Sullivan et al., 1984). Collectively constructed and shared definitions and interpretations of place disruption enable collective action around a common purpose (Benford & Snow, 2000; Hajer, 1995).

Citizen participation. Citizen participation in grassroots voluntary associations (e.g., civic and faith-based organizations, local environmental groups) and other mediating structures is determined by both residents' capacity to respond collectively to environmental hazards and local institutions' capacity for responding to those affected and involving them in making decisions (Rich et al., 1995). Person-environment transactions of place, social bonding, and identity are also important factors in residents' community participation (Perkins et al., 1996).

Place-based social interactions (networks, bonding social capital). Social capital is also defined in terms of strong "bonding" ties and weak "bridging" ties (Granovetter, 1973). Bonding social capital is based on social interactions within the place, including neighboring and networks of trust as a community-level norm. These influence interpretive processes and are relevant to place attachment because social interactions are shaped by settings and spaces. Community attachment is related to social interaction and neighbors watching after each other (Brown et al., 2003). In our model, place-based social interactions have several functions. First, place meanings are mediated through social interaction (Raymond et al., 2010). The community-level interpretation of disruption takes place in the network of interactions between residents (in the top-right, community-behavioral component of the model). Second, social interactions are important routines of a place. Third, networks drive mobilization, as mobilization builds on existing networks (Granovetter, 1973).

Bridging social capital. Bridging ties are the social connections people have that are based, not on emotional bonds, but on utility, with neighbors, merchants, and influential people outside one's community. Bridging capital is important for its literal connections to power and because bonding ties can inhibit dealing with conflict or controversial issues (Granovetter, 1973). Although social capital is usually considered at the community level, we locate bridging ties on the individual level (lower right side of Figure 10.1) because they only apply to certain individuals, usually with more mobility, alternatives, and relationships outside the local community.

COMMUNITY RESPONSE

The response of the community may occur in many forms: mobilization, action, adaptation, and/or acceptance (see far right side of Figure 10.1). Responses to place disruption transpire on both individual and community levels. Individuals may cope with the threat with denial or emotional or physical detachment from the place, or they can engage in individual or collective action in opposition to change or restoration of the disrupted place. On the collective level, communities may adapt to the disruption and redefine the place to accommodate the changes or embark on oppositional or restorative collective action (Devine-Wright, 2009).

We now turn to brief analyses of two cases of community response to environmental disruption, each illustrating different parts of the model.

TWO CASE STUDIES

Case 1: The Threat of Fracking in Bulgaria

Environmental disruption

On June 16, 2011, the Bulgarian government announced that Chevron, a US-based multinational energy company, had been granted a license to explore for shale gas in Bulgaria. Shale gas was to be extracted via hydraulic fracturing (or "fracking"), which involves horizontal drilling of shale formations and high pressure pumping of vast amounts of water mixed with chemicals into the rocks. Fracking is an epitome of an environmental disruption: it carries risks for damaging the air, soil, water, and biodiversity of local communities. There are possible consequences for community cohesion, safety, and traditional way of life due to the individual negotiations of royalties between landowners and companies, the influx of outside workers and the industrial development of a rural area (Colborn et al., 2011; Jacquet, 2014). Between June 2011 and January 2012, local communities in prospective drilling areas in Bulgaria organized protests, petitions, and other forms of non-violent action to compel the National Parliament to impose a ban on fracking. Local organizing efforts grew into a national movement, with over 10,000 people marching in 12 Bulgarian cities on January 14, 2012. Four days later, the Parliament passed a moratorium on fracking by an overwhelming majority (Mihaylov, 2020).

Place definition

The socially defined boundaries of the place under threat expanded quickly via interpretive activities. Opposition against the cabinet's decision started in the town closest to the planned first drilling operation, with a town council vote against it and a protest by local residents. Large-scale opposition developed next in the big cities in the threatened region and the capital, Sofia, which was 300 kilometers away. Activists expanded the boundaries of the protest by asserting that the threat to underground waters affected an aquifer stretching under the whole Bulgarian North-East. Furthermore, this area historically and symbolically is "the Granary of Bulgaria"—feeding the nation and contributing to Bulgaria's fame for agriculture—which gave legitimacy to groups outside the region to join the protests. The place's most emphasized feature was its instrumental value, but it was also framed as a symbol of the natural endowments of Bulgaria.

Place dependence

Activists talked about fracking operations as competing with "agriculture and tourism, and everything nature-related"; activists "wanted clean nature, so [they] could use it as it is, to present it [to tourists] as it is." Such use would be "sustainable" and "planned," whereas fracking was "quick profit, and after us, the deluge." The proponents of fracking, conversely, attempted to underscore other uses of the area, pointing to previous oil extraction there.

The confidence that fracking was a wrong use of natural resources was grounded in the common conviction that clean nature was "the most important asset Bulgaria has," and that "the future of Bulgaria is in agriculture and sustainable tourism because these are the endowments of the climate, nature, all conditions." These natural endowments were seen as "basic values that Bulgaria should protect." The local place became a battleground in the conflict around the independence of the larger space: whereas the pro-fracking claim was that the discovery of gas would secure energy independence for Bulgaria, the activists countered that food and water are more important "because you can do with or without energy independence—many countries are just fine without it; but if you are water- and food-dependent—there is no fixing that."

Place identity and bonding

Place identity and place bonding were also manifested locally and nationally. For example, one of the participants talked about how her land was passed through generations in her family, how she felt the calling to take care of that land, and how important it was for her personal identity. As the place definition was expanded to the national level, so was the identity referent. Many participants outside the threatened area talked about its importance to their national identity. Others, focused on the threat to nature, talked about their self-image and lifestyles as nature-lovers, people for whom nature had intrinsic and not resource value, as a symbol of a simpler, "natural" life "away from it all". Place bonding was amalgamated with patriotism or the love of nature.

The proposed development was incompatible with the place meanings and place attachment as interpreted by activists. Fracking operations were incongruent with people's sense of place; fracking chemicals were incongruent with local life. Gas extraction was incongruent with the regional and national economies and livelihood. Concerned citizens argued that fracking would turn "the Granary of Bulgaria" into a "moon valley" and "industrial site." In sum, it was an "abruptly imposed model from outside, a model that has nothing to do with the endowments of the country."

Within place-related interpretive processes, different local groups started from different perspectives about their place attachment and developed different explanations about the disruption: some used an environmental health discourse, some focused on the value of local nature, some on local use, some saw Bulgaria as the place at stake. However, with interaction in collectives, the different interpretations came into discursive closure (Hajer, 1995) bridging (Benford & Snow, 2000) toward a shared narrative, which enabled a diverse national movement.

Collective efficacy/empowerment

Collective efficacy among activists was reported as a set of cognitions and feelings. For first-time activists, there was an overwhelming sense of freedom to act on a public issue as a member of informal, voluntary, and idealistic groups in contrast to political action as an interest-driven, hierarchical, and controlled structure. Activists also saw themselves as protectors of the common good: nature, Bulgaria, and "the people," in contrast to treasonous and corrupt government; this group identity gave them a sense of historic force. Another very important element of empowerment was local knowledge. Based on their place experiences and interactions, activists were able to understand and highlight issues of application of the technology, for example, local environmental conditions, local geological and landscape peculiarities, local authorities' (in)capacities—all very different from what the proponents described in abstract terms.

Place-based social interactions, sense of community, participation, bridging social capital

The anti-fracking movement demonstrated the greater importance of relationships and networks emerging in mobilization compared to pre-existing sense of community or neighboring relationships. While the protests started in the threatened local community, the mobilization and effective action unfolded in bigger cities where more people and bridging social capital could be mustered. Bonding ties and sense of community were created among first-time activists gradually by staunch preference for informal relationships in local groups. The only pre-existing formal networks of citizen participation were the environmental organizations in Sofia. Bonding and bridging ties within the movement were consistently developed via dedicated Facebook groups. Through intensive personal local interaction and online national connectedness, feelings of trust and respect developed among activists, which facilitated inclusive interpretive processes and the emergence of national leaders and representatives. Key for success were bridging ties with experts, international organizations, and even government officials and politicians.

Case 2: Marcellus Shale Region of the Northeastern US

Environmental disruption

The Marcellus shale region in the northeastern US has seen rapid growth in hydraulic fracturing. The Marcellus deposit underlies multiple states, each with its own trajectory of engagement (Jacquet et al., 2018). Although the Marcellus represents a single gas formation, the overlay of different states, with different governance systems and outcomes, represents a "natural experiment" of sorts. We contrast the experience of two neighboring states—Pennsylvania and New York in response to fracking development (Brasier et al., 2013; Stedman et al., 2012).

The rapid pace and scale of shale gas development in Pennsylvania represents the initial disruption. The environmental, social, and economic impacts extended beyond Pennsylvania to include New York. Beyond direct impacts to the landscape and communities of Pennsylvania, fracking engendered a great deal of public debate, capacity building, research, and reflections about place and the role of energy development in rural environments. We consider these in turn.

Jacquet et al. (2018) label Pennsylvania "the heart of the Marcellus Shale." As of 2018, over 11,000 unconventional gas wells had been drilled in Pennsylvania. Numerous studies have explored impacts on environmental quality, agriculture, and community well-being (Jacquet et al., 2018). These studies frame the effects of development as mostly negative but Bugden and Stedman (2019) present a dissenting view that suggests that development has not been as transformative—positively or negatively—as is commonly considered.

New York had the opportunity to observe the impacts of shale gas drilling in Pennsylvania and passed a moratorium halting development in 2010. A controversial public debate about the future of the industry ensued, protests were held, and public comment solicited. Over 350 municipalities eventually passed ordinances opposing, restricting, or banning development (Dokshin, 2016). In 2014, shale development was banned statewide. The *debate* around shale gas (in part based on experience of place attachment) became a disruption of its own: it is important that "fracking" be examined as a multi-faceted process (Evensen et al., 2014) rather than simply the extraction phase. There were direct effects in New York of gas extraction in Pennsylvania, including regional economic impacts (many of the midsized urban centers where much of the money was spent (Cosgrove et al., 2015).

Place definition and place change

It is important to emphasize our deliberate use of the term "changes" rather than "impacts." While much of the research around Marcellus shale development emphasizes negative outcomes, we assert that some of the changes have more nuance. We emphasize three areas: place dependence; place meanings/identities, or effects on the landscape/local community as symbol; and effects on collective efficacy/empowerment.

The onset of fracking produced impacts (and perhaps more importantly, a lively *discussion* of effects, both positive and negative) to the region, thus bringing place concerns to the fore—concerns that transcended the specifics of shale gas development. Place attachment and related concepts "fly below the radar screen"; often they are made salient by disrupting events that force reflection. There were direct effects both where development happened and spillover effects on regional communities even where there was no development. There were also indirect/anticipatory effects such as discussions about what *might* happen, and potential community response.

Place dependence addresses how gas development affects how the landscape fulfills key functions. The region (both Pennsylvania and the nearby "southern tier" region of New York) is a landscape of rolling hills, small farms, woodlots, tourism/second homes, and small rural communities. Prior to the gas boom, the region was seen as economically stagnant, characterized (like so many rural areas) by the outmigration of young people and general economic decline (Thomas & Smith, 2009).

Rapid gas development in the region—using the "boomtown" frame (Jacquet, 2014) which emphasizes social disruption—has challenged conventional uses of the landscape. Some argue that shale gas development will undercut agriculture in the region: as lessees gain alternative sources of income, they will abandon agriculture. Others assert that leasing revenues may be used to pay off debt, allowing farmers to continue farming into the future. The reality is that each of these scenarios is likely to be true, for different farmers (Paredes et al., 2015). The effects on place dependence for rural communities have been less subtle: the social disruption and in-migration of gas workers has posed a challenge to social relations, employment, and has contributed to increased inequality, homelessness, and strained community services such as schools and health care (Jacquet, 2014).

Place identity and meanings

Engaging more at the level of symbol, people identify with a given landscape/community as embodying certain meanings. The loss of, changes to, or reinforcement of key meanings affects how people identify with place. Rapid energy development has challenged the viability of key symbols such as the region as a "farming place," amenity values and unspoiled nature, and tight knit, egalitarian communities. We should be careful not to overstate this, however, as an extensive history of resource extraction, especially in Pennsylvania, lends some continuity here as well (Bugden et al., 2017): this has been an "energy landscape" for a long time.

Collective efficacy/empowerment

Shale gas development has fostered individual and collective engagement with the community/region as a locus of attachment. Brought to the fore are ideas of place and community, and discussions of visions for the future—both those that embrace shale gas development and those that reject it. In particular, the rapid emergence of shale gas exploration in Pennsylvania afforded New York residents and policy makers this opportunity; divergent community responses speak to the plurality of these visions. Further, the prospects of shale gas development gave New York landowners the opportunity to engage in collective action—as the fate of drilling was being decided, many landowners formed coalitions to engage in collective bargaining. While some negotiations predictably focused on price, others took a broader collective place-based view, engaging terms focused on environmental protection, for example (Jacquet & Stedman, 2011). Finally, although some have asserted (e.g., Mayer et al., 2018) that many rural communities were disadvantaged in their of capacity to engage sophisticated and well-financed energy companies, shale gas development also represented an opportunity for community leaders, residents, and local environmental groups to build leadership.

CONCLUSIONS

This chapter explored the meaning and significance of community-located and community-level place attachment, particularly through two cases of community response to environmental threats. The importance of community-level place attachment is partly psychological, in the same way that other forms of place attachment foster and support individuals' personal sense of identity, stability, power, and development. However, community attachment differs from other forms of place attachment by connecting individuals to their neighbors and places throughout their neighborhood, town, or city, thereby fostering and supporting a collective sense of *community* identity, stability, power, and development. However, what makes community place attachment unique is its integration in a complex and dynamic interpretive process linking both individual and community-level place and social cognitions, emotions, and behaviors, and we see this emerge in response to community-level environmental disruptions or threats which lead to collective actions, adaptations, or acceptance.

Incipient disruption enters an existing community context with community place attachment. The latter shapes the community response but is also shaped by the disruption in an interactive process. As was evident in the two cases, a disruption makes explicit the latent, taken-for-granted place-related meanings, identities, bonds, and relationships. Place attachment shifts from passive to active and self-conscious forms (Lewicka, 2011b) as some aspects of the place and the community become more salient. There is consolidation against the threat but there is also a multitude of new and diverse interpretations, or discourses of the threat as related to place; some discourses even favor the proposed change. In the case of the anti-fracking movement in Bulgaria nature-, community-, health-, and resource-focused discourses were bridged by key concepts like "incongruity" and a common narrative to provide coherence and consolidation on a new level of place meanings. Attachments to place became more salient, and new place identities developed—oppositional, activist, protective, and sometimes solidarity, as in the case of environmental justice organizing. New local knowledge (or new appreciation of it) and a sense of empowerment emerge with regard to the new issue. New interactions—informal and organized—solidify as people discuss and act on the threat. The disruption also redefines the place: in the US case, state and county boundaries were mapped on the space of the Marcellus shale; in Bulgaria, the threatened area was expanded in different ways to regional and national levels, through the framing of the symbolic and material effects of the development. The expansion begot a new scale of community, of interpretive networks and forums, new diversity of interpretations, new levels of coherence, and new bridging connections. The expansion also allowed for a more powerful response—at a national (Bulgaria) or state (US) level, with a new legitimacy and a political sensitivity.

Like spatial awareness in general, place attachments are usually taken for granted. Yet they are powerful motivators for action to preserve and improve our communities for ourselves, our neighbors, and future generations. A disruption, paradoxically, can activate and collectivize in new ways existing place attachments and translate them to social capital and action at the community level so that the full benefits of attachments to cherished places and people are realized.

NOTES

1 See Mihaylov and Perkins (2014) for more details.
2 Not to be confused with sociologists' use of "collective efficacy" as informal social control, neighboring, and sense of community.

REFERENCES

Bailey, E., Devine-Wright, P., & Batel, S. (2016). Using a narrative approach to understand place attachments and responses to power line proposals: The importance of life-place trajectories. *Journal of Environmental Psychology, 48*, 200–211.

Benford, R. D., & Snow, D. A. (2000). Framing processes and social movements: An overview and assessment. *Annual Review of Sociology, 26*, 611–639.

Bonaiuto, M., Breakwell, G. M., & Cano, I. (1996). Identity processes and environmental threat: The effects of nationalism and local identity upon perception of beach pollution. *Journal of Community and Applied Social Psychology, 6*(3), 157–175.

Bonaiuto, M., Carrus, G., Martorella, H., & Bonnes, M. (2002). Local identity processes and environmental attitudes in land use changes: The case of natural protected areas. *Journal of Economic Psychology, 23*(5), 631–653.

Brasier, K. J., McLaughlin, D. K., Rhubart, D., Stedman, R. C., Filteau, M. R., & Jacquet, J. (2013). Risk perceptions of natural gas development in the Marcellus Shale. *Environmental Practice, 15*(2), 108–122.

Brown, B. B., & Perkins, D. D. (1992). Disruptions in place attachment. In I. Altman, & S. Low (Eds.), *Place attachment* (pp. 279–304). New York: Plenum.

Brown, B. B., Perkins, D. D., & Brown, G. (2003). Place attachment in a revitalizing neighborhood: Individual and block levels of analysis. *Journal of Environmental Psychology, 23*, 259–271.

Brown, G., Brown, B. B., & Perkins, D. D. (2004). New housing as neighborhood revitalization: Place attachment and confidence among residents. *Environment and Behavior*, *36*(6), 749–775.

Bugden, D., & Stedman, R. C. (2019). Rural landowners, energy leasing, and inequality in the shale gas industry. *Rural Sociology*, *84*(3), 459–488.

Bugden, D., Evensen, D., & Stedman, R. (2017). A drill by any other name: Social representations, framing, and legacies of natural resource extraction in the fracking industry. *Energy Research & Social Science*, *29*, 62–71.

Colborn, T., Kwiatkowski, C., Schultz, K., & Bachran, M. (2011). Natural gas operations from a public health perspective. *Human and Ecological Risk Assessment: An International Journal*, *17*(5), 1039–1056.

Cosgrove, B. M., LaFave, D. R., Dissanayake, S. T., & Donihue, M. R. (2015). The economic impact of shale gas development: A natural experiment along the New York/Pennsylvania border. *Agricultural and Resource Economics Review*, *44*(2), 20–39.

Dallago, L., Perkins, D. D., Santinello, M., Boyce, W., Molcho, M., & Morgan, A. (2009). Adolescent place attachment, social capital, and perceived safety: A comparison of 13 countries. *American Journal of Community Psychology*, *44*, 148–160.

Devine-Wright, P. (2009). Rethinking NIMBYism. *Journal of Community and Applied Social Psychology*, *19*, 426–441.

Devine-Wright, P. (2011). Place attachment and public acceptance of renewable energy: A tidal energy case study. *Journal of Environmental Psychology*, *31*(4), 336–343.

Devine-Wright, P., & Howes, Y. (2010). Disruption to place attachment and the protection of restorative environments: A wind energy case study. *Journal of Environmental Psychology*, *30*(3), 271–280.

Dokshin, F. A. (2016). Whose backyard and what's at issue? Spatial and ideological dynamics of local opposition to fracking in New York State, 2010 to 2013. *American Sociological Review*, *81*(5), 921–948.

Evensen, D., Jacquet, J. B., Clarke, C. E., & Stedman, R. C. (2014). What's the 'fracking' problem? One word can't say it all. *The Extractive Industries and Society*, *1*(2), 130–136.

Granovetter, M. S. (1973). The strength of weak ties. *American Journal of Sociology*, *78*(6), 1360–1380.

Hajer, M. A. (1995). *The politics of environmental discourse: Ecological modernization and the policy process*. Oxford: Clarendon Press.

Hernández, B., Hidalgo, M. C., & Ruiz, C. (2014). Theoretical and methodological aspects of research on place attachment. In L. C. Manzo, & P. Devine-Wright (Eds.), *Place attachment: Advances in theory, methods and applications* (pp. 125–137). New York: Routledge.

Hernández, B., Martín, A. M., Ruiz, C., & Hidalgo, M. C. (2010). The role of place identity and place attachment in breaking environmental protection laws. *Journal of Environmental Psychology*, *30*(3), 281–288.

Jacquet, J. B. (2014). Review of risks to communities from shale energy development. *Environmental Science & Technology*, *48*(15), 8321–8333.

Jacquet, J. B., Junod, A. N., Bugden, D., Wildermuth, G., Fergen, J. T., Jalbert, K., … & Ladlee, J. (2018). A decade of Marcellus Shale: Impacts to people, policy, and culture from 2008 to 2018 in the Greater Mid-Atlantic region of the United States. *Extractive Industries and Society*, *5*, 596–609.

Jacquet, J., & Stedman, R. C. (2011). Natural gas landowner coalitions in New York state: Emerging benefits of collective natural resource management. *Journal of Rural Social Sciences*, *26*(1), 62–91.

Jacquet, J., & Stedman, R. C. (2014). The risk of social-psychological disruption as an impact of energy development and environmental change. *Journal of Environmental Planning and Management*, *57*(9), 1285–1304.

Jorgensen, B. S., & Stedman, R. C. (2001). Sense of place as an attitude: Lakeshore owners' attitudes toward their properties. *Journal of Environmental Psychology*, *21*, 233–248.

Kasarda, J. D., & Janowitz, M. (1974). Community attachment in mass society. *American Sociological Review*, *39*, 328–339.

Lewicka, M. (2010). What makes neighborhood different from home and city? Effects of place scale on place attachment. *Journal of Environmental Psychology*, *30*(1), 35–51.

Lewicka, M. (2011a). Place attachment: How far have we come in the last 40 years? *Journal of Environmental Psychology*, *31*(3), 207–230.

Lewicka, M. (2011b). On the varieties of people's relationships with places: Hummon's typology revisited. *Environment and Behavior*, *43*(5), 676–709.

Manzo, L. C., & Perkins, D. D. (2006). Finding common ground: The importance of place attachment to community participation and planning. *Journal of Planning Literature*, *20*(4), 335–350.

Mayer, A., Olson-Hazboun, S. K., & Malin, S. (2018). Fracking fortunes: Economic well-being and oil and gas development along the urban-rural continuum. *Rural Sociology*, *83*(3), 532–567.

Mihaylov, N. L. (2020). From victims to citizens: Emerging activist identities in the anti-fracking movement in Bulgaria. *Journal of Community Psychology*, *48*(2), 170–191.

Mihaylov, N., & Perkins, D. D. (2014). Community place attachment and its role in social capital development. In L. C. Manzo, & P. Devine-Wright (Eds.), *Place attachment: Advances in theory, methods and applications* (pp. 61–74). London: Routledge.

O'Sullivan, M. J., Waugh, N., & Espeland, W. (1984). The Fort McDowell Yavapai: From pawns to powerbrokers. *Prevention in Human Services*, *3*(2–3), 73–97.

Paredes, D., Komarek, T., & Loveridge, S. (2015). Income and employment effects of shale gas extraction windfalls: Evidence from the Marcellus region. *Energy Economics*, *47*, 112–120.

Perkins, D. D., Brown, B. B., & Taylor, R. B. (1996). The ecology of empowerment: Predicting participation in community organizations. *Journal of Social Issues*, *52*(1), 85–110.

Perkins, D. D., Larsen, C., & Brown, B. B. (2009). Mapping urban revitalization: Using GIS spatial analysis to evaluate a new housing policy. *Journal of Prevention & Intervention in the Community*, *37*(1), 48–65.

Perkins, D. D., & Long, D. A. (2002). Neighborhood sense of community and social capital: A multi-level analysis. In A. Fisher, C. Sonn, & B. Bishop (Eds.), *Psychological sense of community: Research, applications, and implications* (pp. 291–318). New York: Plenum.

Pretty, G. H., Chipuer, H. M., & Bramston, P. (2003). Sense of place amongst adolescents and adults in two rural Australian towns: The discriminating features of place attachment, sense of community and place dependence in relation to place identity. *Journal of Environmental Psychology*, *23*(3), 273–287.

Raymond, C. M., Brown, G., & Weber, D. (2010). The measurement of place attachment: Personal, community, and environmental connections. *Journal of Environmental Psychology*, *30*(4), 422–434.

Relph, E. (1976). *Place and placelessness*. London: Pion.

Rich, R. C., Edelstein, M., Hallman, W. K., & Wandersman, A. H. (1995). Citizen participation and empowerment: The case of local environmental hazards. *American Journal of Community Psychology*, *23*(5), 657–676.

Riger, S., & Lavrakas, P. J. (1981). Community ties: Patterns of attachment and social interactions in urban neighborhoods. *American Journal of Community Psychology*, *9*, 55–66.

Scannell, L., & Gifford, R. (2010). Defining place attachment: A tripartite organizing framework. *Journal of Environmental Psychology*, *30*(1), 1–10.

Seamon, D. (2018). *Life takes place: Phenomenology, lifeworlds and place making.* New York: Routledge.

Stedman, R. C. (2002). Toward a social psychology of place: Predicting behavior from place-based cognitions, attitude, and identity. *Environment and Behavior*, *34*(5), 405–425.

Stedman, R. C. (2006). Understanding place attachment among second home owners. *The American Behavioral Scientist*, *50*(2), 187–205.

Stedman, R. C. (2016). Subjectivity and social-ecological systems: A rigidity trap (and sense of place as a way out). *Sustainability Science 11*(6), 891–901.

Stedman, R. C., Jacquet, J. B., Filteau, M. R., Willits, F. K., Brasier, K. J., & McLaughlin, D. K. (2012). Marcellus shale gas development and new boomtown research: Views of New York and Pennsylvania residents. *Environmental Practice*, *14*(4), 382–393.

Thomas, A. R., & Smith, P. J. (2009). *Upstate down: Thinking about New York and its discontents.* Lanham, MD: University Press of America.

Unger, D. G., & Wandersman, A. (1985). The importance of neighbors: The social, cognitive, and affective components of neighboring. *American Journal of Community Psychology*, *13*(2), 139–169.

Venables, D., Pidgeon, N. F., Parkhill, K. A., Henwood, K. L., & Simmons, P. (2012). Living with nuclear power: Sense of place, proximity, and risk perceptions in local host communities. *Journal of Environmental Psychology*, *32*(4), 371–383.

Chapter 11: Revisiting "The Frayed Knot": What happens to place attachment in the context of serial forced displacement?

Mindy Thompson Fullilove, MD

A string walks into a bar and asks the bartender for a Singapore Sling. The bartender regards him with a scornful eye and says, "We don't serve strings here!"

Downtrodden but not defeated, the string leaves the bar with a theory of how to get back in. He messes up his hair, ties himself in a loop and walks right back in. The string orders another Singapore Sling. The bartender leers at him and says, "Aren't you that string that was in here just a second ago?"

"Nope," the string says, "I'm a frayed knot."

People pass their lives in specific locations, and, through exchange and inter-relatedness, develop complex and important emotional connections within and to those places. These specific locations are both bounded in a locale and linked to global networks and processes. Place is understood to be at once a geographic site and the social system organized at that location; it operates as a node in the complex global web of economic, social, and physical relationships (Massey, 1995). Dis-*PLACE*-ment, is, by definition, a rupture of the geographic and the social. Disruptions of this kind force people to remake emotional connections, including those we know as "place attachment" (Brown & Perkins, 1992; Chow & Healey, 2008; Fullilove, 1996).

American history is full of stories of displacement that have drawn the attention of scholars (Erikson, 1976; Fried, 1966). The history of the US is also replete with instances in which groups of people have been repeatedly driven from their homes (Fullilove & Wallace, 2011). This chapter will examine what happens to place attachment when people are repeatedly driven from their homes, that is, when they experience serial forced displacement. People who live through such experiences find themselves in a weakened social matrix that undermines the sense of place as a stable and secure object of attachment. Their trust becomes frayed both because of the injuries of disconnection and because of the inadequacy of the place in which they find themselves after relocation. This inadequacy is attrib-utable both to the kinds of destinations selected for forced displacement and the weakened social bonds of those arriving there (Wishart, 1994). Attachment to an insecure and relatively inadequate place is more ambivalent and limited than that to earlier places. Yet observers have noted that, in the face of multiple traumas, deprivations and withering of trust, a connection to the earlier place—a beloved community—may endure (Rúa, 2017; White, 2006; Yatsushiro et al, 1944). Surely among the most famous expressions of this is the toast Jewish people make during the Passover celebration, "Next year in Jerusalem!" Based on these and other observations, I propose what I call the "Frayed Knot Hypothesis." which states:

> Serial forced displacement alters people-place relations, but attachment to a beloved community may be maintained through community practices, invoking the place-that-was in order to restore the beloved community.

I will present the data on which this hypothesis is based by addressing the following questions:

1   What is the beloved community?
2   What is serial forced displacement?
3   How does this process alter people-place relations?
4   How does the connection to the place-that-was endure?
5   How do people get to the place-that-might-be-again?

WHAT IS THE BELOVED COMMUNITY?

The term "beloved community," first proposed by Josiah Royce, is associated with Reverend Dr. Martin Luther King, Jr., who popularized its use during the Civil Rights Movement of the 1950s and 1960s. According to the King Center (2020) website:

> Dr. King's Beloved Community is a global vision, in which all people can share in the wealth of the earth. In the Beloved Community, poverty, hunger and homelessness will not be tolerated because international standards of human decency will not allow it. Racism and all forms of discrimination, bigotry and prejudice will be replaced by an all-inclusive spirit of sisterhood and brotherhood. In the Beloved Community, international disputes will be resolved by peaceful conflict-resolution and reconciliation of adversaries, instead of military power. Love and trust will triumph over fear and hatred. Peace with justice will prevail over war and military conflict.

While no community has attained this vision in full, some communities have been able to develop strong social networks that have supported people in their efforts to solve problems, take care of the vulnerable, and develop rich and fulfilling lives. These communities, because of their solidarity and problem-solving ability, also have the capacity to acquire social, economic, cultural, and political capital. The beloved community might become a threat or an enticement to the powers-that-be because of its growing wealth and power. Such communities have become targets of displacement.

This process of taking land to become rich played an important role in the early phase of capitalism. The point here, however, is that the life of the peasant farmers had rhythms and sensibilities that supported and gave sense to people's lives: what was destroyed was a beloved community. What I have called "root shock"—the traumatic stress reaction to the loss of all or part of one's emotional ecosystem—occurs with such upheavals (Fullilove, 2004). Having lost something so precious, people struggle to rebuild. In the next section, we will examine the special challenges when rebuilding is set back by additional displacement.

WHAT IS SERIAL FORCED DISPLACEMENT?

In contrast to voluntary moves, in which people make the choice to relocate, forced displacement occurs as a result of the imposition of forces greater than the community (Erikson, 1976; Manzo, 2014; Simms, 2008; Wallace, 1957, 1988; Watkins, 2000). Such upheaval undermines the political, social, and economic capital of the displaced; conversely, it enhances the strength and wealth of those who do the displacing. David Harvey (2009) has described this path to wealth and power as "accumulation by dispossession." When the histories of such displacements are bluntly told, for example, as Mann (2011) relates the dispossession of the Powhatans from Jamestown or Wallace and Foner (1993) relate the story of Native American displacement from the Southeastern United States, the stories cast profound aspersion on the powerful forces that carried out such acts. There is, therefore, a strenuous effort to suppress the truth and create a palatable alternative narrative. In spite of the dispersion, disempowerment, impoverishment, and disparagement that characterize serial forced displacement, many people who have lived in a beloved community struggle to maintain a tie to that lived experience.

Colonial and later US governments forced Native people to move repeatedly and, with each upheaval, to places that were smaller, less hospitable, and more profoundly disconnected both from their own land and from the emerging Euro-American society (Jacobs, 1972; Neihardt, 1979; Wishart, 1994). The tribes suffered enormous losses that were aggravated by the decline in the groups' circumstances with each move. There was, in many cases, a complete disconnection of people from their original geographic homeplace. In 1838, the Cherokee people, for example, were forcibly relocated from their tribal lands in the southeast to Indian Territory, what is now Oklahoma, a journey called "The Trail of Tears." Later, as white settlers arrived in the Territory, Native peoples were confined to reservations in marginal parts of the area (Jahoda, 1975).

US federal, state, and local governments have reprised this process of repeated upheaval in their treatment of African Americans, a practice that has been a driving force through much of their history in the Americas up to the present time (Fullilove & Wallace, 2011). African American communities have faced complete disconnection (forced migration from Africa) and incomplete disconnection (story of the Hill District, below) from their places. Because large numbers of people have been involved in this upheaval, which was costly in political, social, economic, and emotional terms, and because these communities have not been enabled by society to make a full recovery from any of the upheavals, serial forced displacement has undermined the matrix of community and its many kinds of wealth (Fullilove & Wallace, 2011). By contrast, the powers that enacted these displacements have profited from accumulation by dispossession (Harvey, 2009).

HOW DOES SERIAL FORCED DISPLACEMENT ALTER PEOPLE-PLACE RELATIONS?

Forced displacement at the level of the family

The displacement of large groups of people shatters existing social and spatial relationships, a process that unfurls in a series of stages (Brown & Perkins, 1992; Chow & Healey, 2008; Devine-Wright, 2009). Families are crucial social support systems for people, and they face enormous strain while going through such transitions. Greene et al (2011) examined the stages of disruption using the resettlement stories of twenty families, representing eighteen countries and six different types of displacement situations. Through the analysis of interviews and fieldnotes, the team identified a four-stage process of antecedent, uprooting, transition, and resettlement, during the course of which people had to let go of their original homeplace and make a new homeplace. Through this process, they renegotiated place attachment.

The antecedent phase was the period during which the families acknowledged the threat that led to the displacement. This was, in some stories, a sudden event, the threat of kidnapping in one instance. In other stories, families grappled with more long-term problems, like discrimination, that inhibited access to opportunity. All families tried to obtain information about the destination, but this was often limited, and they moved with little knowledge of the place to which they were going.

In the uprooting phase, ties with other family members, friends, and communities were broken. This process, "…entailed resigning from jobs and withdrawing from schools and religious affiliations. As a result, individuals were no longer able to engage in their routine daily activities. …families were no longer able to call on others in the community for help with day-to-day activities and emotional support" (Greene et al, 2011, p. 409).

The transition phase encompassed the actual relocation from one place to another. Families had to make a rapid shift, problematic because of all the demands.

> The families had to learn a new language, find employment, become familiar with new surroundings, and obtain basic amenities such as shelter and clothing. In some cases, not knowing the language presented families from mastering their new environment. For example, when a family did not have a command of the language, their employment opportunities were further limited. Some families lacked resources that would have enabled them to learn the language. (Greene et al, 2011, p. 410)

This is an ambivalent period, as mourning the loss of the old place and getting to know the new place are processes unfolding at the same time. One respondent reported, "I used to cry every day. My husband and I felt lost. We sold everything we owned in Argentina to come to America. We had to start everything again. We used to work for 18 hours [a day], seven days a week" (Greene et al, 2011, p. 411).

As they worked their way through the transition, the families entered the resettlement phase, during which they began to make connections to the communities in which they had arrived. Families reported a range of adaptations to the new settings in which they found themselves, some assimilating, others achieving an integrated cultural identity, and a final group maintaining their original cultural identity. For all, some sense of resettlement accompanied the development of significant ties to the new place, for example, through work or school (see also Rishbeth, this volume).

Each of the 20 families Greene and colleagues interviewed had suffered important losses in the displacement process and had worked hard to get through the whole process of resettlement. In looking at such processes at the level of the neighborhood, cases in which whole communities of people are forced to move, the losses are magnified, and the work of re-rooting increased many times. This is because there are collective as well as individual losses. The collective losses, as we will describe in the next section, are very difficult to repair.

Serial forced displacement at the level of the neighborhood

Historians have documented a series of harsh upheavals in Pittsburgh's Hill District, an African American neighborhood located to the north and west of the city's downtown (Glasco,1989; Toker, 1986; Trotter & Day, 2010). The first upheaval was urban renewal carried out in the late 1950s, which demolished the commercial section of the Hill, forcibly displacing 8,000 people, and destroying many businesses, churches, and social organizations. The second was deindustrialization, which deconstructed Pittsburgh's massive industrial base between 1970 and 1990. This had an enormous impact on the Hill District, whose residents were largely employed in the city's unskilled manufacturing sector. The third was the civil insurrection in the 1960s that followed Dr. Martin Luther King Jr.'s assassination, which destroyed an important stretch of commerce in the Middle Hill. The fourth was the incursion of drug dealing, which replaced industry as a source employment and offered solace for the pain of upheaval (Acker, 2009). The fifth was what Hyra (2012) calls "the new urban renewal," so-called revitalization programs, including the HOPE VI program that demolished housing projects and replaced them with mixed-income communities (p. 504). As a result of these processes, the population fell from 38,100 in 1950 to 9,830 in 1990 (Lubove, 1996).

The changes in the Hill were massive. In addition to precipitous population decline, the boundaries of the Hill shifted, the paths linking the Hill to the larger city of Pittsburgh were constricted, the housing stock deteriorated and disappeared, the commercial centers were lost, the many organized centers that provided safe spaces for youth were closed, and the safe outdoors spaces became sites of crime and violence (Fullilove,2004,2013). The Hill was "desertified," meaning that a rich and life-sustaining urban ecosystem was stripped of resources and rendered impotent, just as overworked agricultural lands in the Sahel have dwindled into deserts (Wallace, 1990, p. 811).

In a seminal paper entitled, "Children's lived spaces in the inner city: historical and political aspects of the psychology of place," Eva-Maria Simms (2008) described the lived experience of the Hill during this process of serial displacement. Simms noted:

> I approached the Hill community for this project because I was looking for a coherent, stable neighborhood that had the loyalty of a number of generations of inhabitants who played in the same places. During the interviews with The Hill inhabitants, however, the tragic history of the Hill District became a major player in the constructions of their narratives. Even though the participants did talk about building play-forts in the woods or hiding in the tree in front of the rent-office, the overwhelming story they told about their particular neighborhood was of a childhood embedded in the political and cultural changes in African American culture in the 20th century. (p. 73)

Simms identified three distinct eras in the neighborhood's history. In the first era, from 1930 to 1960, adults and children lived in a highly integrated neighborhood, and children moved fluidly throughout the territory and among the many activities and happenings it offered. They were protected by a net of all adults who felt themselves responsible for a net of all the children. Simms described:

> The relationship between adults and children was clear: Adults cared for the young and had authority. When 19-year-old Dale and his young wife moved to The Hill in 1944, Mrs. Brown, his landlady, he said, "acted like a parent. In fact, she insisted and I still belong to Macedonia Baptist Church" (Dale is now in his 80s). The adults did not play with the children, but because life was so public, the children always had the feeling that some adult, family or neighbor, would watch the[m] from the stoop or porch or through the open kitchen window. When adults were not working, they could be found on their front porches talking to each other across the narrow streets or listening to the radio together. The eyes of the neighborhood rested on its children; "everybody watched everybody," as Faustine said.

The second era, which Simms dated from 1960 to 1980, was a time of transition. Some of the old communal structures survived. For example, the adults of the neighborhood still felt that they could discipline all of the children. But a new anxiety and dissatisfaction were creeping in. Simms writes:

> Like the earlier generation, the children of the 60s and 70s had to obey one rule, which almost all participants in the interviews mentioned: You had to be on your front porch when the streetlights went on at nightfall. But now the coming on

of the streetlights was no longer framed in terms of cozily gathering around the radio to listen to the spooky 1940s *Inner Sanctum* radio show. Mothers made sure that children were in front of the house because they were afraid of the nighttime activity in their neighborhoods. "It saved my life," Lamar observed, because many of the kids he played with at that time, "passed away as kids because they got hung up on heroin."

By the third era, which Simms dated from 1980 to 2004, networks had shrunk from neighborhood-wide connections to connections among a small number of family members and neighbors. Families, which had included large, extended family in the first era, had also become quite small, often consisting of a single mother with her children. Darien, one the interviewees who grew up in that era, coined the phrase "unexpectancy," to describe life in the neighborhood in that era:

> In general, you never know what might happen, you in the hood, just you coming out that door, just to see what's outside, could be "a surprise" everyday. *Unexpectancy*. You know, like I said, you wake up every day and you could think one thing and it could turn out to be another thing, you know, so just with those "situations" at hand as a young'n, as a young kid, that is, it's just different in "My world" considering others. But as I said, depending on where you go and who you be with at those particular times can maybe make you or break you. It's all about survival, when it gets down to it. But life is what you make it, so. Just in general. You know, you never know what lies around what corner, but just gotta be able to be prepared and just hope, you know, you know as they say look both ways before you cross the street, so. That's basically how it is here. Just look both ways (p. 82; emphasis added).

In the context of such massive shifts in the place, what has happened to attachment to place? Simms addresses this point in the following manner:

> Perhaps we can learn a lesson for urban development from the earlier Hill community by understanding that the physical structure of a place is deeply connected to the kind of community practices that exist there. The relationship goes both ways: Places create clearings for communal activities—or foreclose them, as we saw in the housing projects of The Hill. Changes in the community, on the other hand, can redefine what a place means and how it is used.... (p. 87)

The community practices shifted dramatically as the Hill was depleted of resources and became organized in smaller, and less mutually beneficial, social units. The solidarity of the neighborhood in the 1930s was replaced with "unexpectancy," and accompanying behaviors of suspicion and uncertainty. I would like to high-light Simms's term "community practices," which denotes the complex and recip-rocal relationships among people and the economic, social, and physical resources existing in the location.

Table 11.1
Names for the injury to place attachment that follows upheaval

Concept	Definition
Nostalgia	Pain, potentially life-threatening, due to being far from home (Sanchez & Brown,1994)
Root shock	Traumatic stress reaction to the loss of all or part of one's emotional ecosystem (Fullilove, 2004)
Solastalgia	Pain or distress caused by the loss of, or inability to derive, solace connected to the negatively perceived state of one's home environment (Albrecht et al, 2007)
Wounded city	Densely settled locales that have been harmed and structured by particular histories of physical destruction, displacement, and individual and social trauma resulting from state-perpetrated violence (Till, 2012)

Serial forced displacement at the level of the city

Various words and expressions have emerged to convey the hurt that is involved in injuries to place attachment (see Table 11.1). Nostalgia, solastalgia, and root shock point us toward the disorientation and pain that accompany massive changes in place. Karen Till's (2012) concept of the "wounded city" invokes a different perspective. In a seminal paper called, "Wounded cities: memory-work and a place-based ethics of care," she first posits that the city is an "…*oeuvre*, as constituted by its inhabitants through ongoing acts of making place" (p. 7). This closely parallels the concept of the "community practices" that Simms advanced from her work in the Hill.

This lens of the wound to people and their place is, I believe, most helpful for understanding place attachment in the context of serial displacement. On the one hand, the capacity of the collective to carry out placemaking is severely undermined by the depletion of resources, the truncation and dispersal of networks, and the accumulation of sorrow. On the other hand, the living, breathing organism seeks to affirm itself by continuing to be expressive. In this model, place attachment becomes an important, ongoing act of self-affirmation, both of the individual and of the larger, enmeshing communities. But Till also pointed out, "…if individuals and neighborhoods are wounded through displacement, material devastation, and root shock, so too [are] the city and its inhabitants." (p. 7) By forcing our gaze to a higher level of scale—to the city—Till helps us to understand the many levels of scale affected by the rupture of the people-place relationship.

HOW DOES THE CONNECTION TO THE BELOVED PLACE ENDURE?

Life is carried in many objects (O'Brien, 2009). In Pittsburgh's Hill District, I often saw historic photos of the neighborhood on the walls of people's homes, in restaurants and in community centers. Mazumdar and Mazumdar (2016) found that Vietnamese refugees connected to their home country by the design and organization of their interiors, for example, erecting family altars and sheltering the extended family under one roof. Life is carried by individuals. Every group that maintains place attachment has a storyteller who transmits the lived experience of the beloved community. These storytellers may take the history back to origin myths, and they may be the advocates for passing the language of the place to the next generation through language schools and other means (Gross, 2003). Finally, the organizers and leaders are essential to the restoration and maintenance of social bonds, acting to counter the centrifugal force of serial forced displacement.

Alice Mah (2009) captured these processes in a paper describing Walker, a neighborhood in the UK that had lived through deindustrialization and was confronted by a proposal for urban renewal that would demolish much of the area's housing and disperse its remaining population. Mah described:

> Walker is a residential area situated in the East End of Newcastle-upon-Tyne. The East end of Newcastle developed in the late nineteenth century to house industrial workers in shipbuilding, engineering, coal mining, iron, and chemical and glass works. Coal mining had collapsed by the mid-twentieth century, and shipping along the river Tyne (along an area now known as Walker Riverside) began to decline dramatically in the 1960s and 1970s, with the last shipyard, Swan Hunter's, closing in 2006. Population loss during the past thirty-five years has been more severe in Walker than in Newcastle as a whole, dropping from 13,035 in 1971 to 7,725 in 2001. The slow and steady erosion of heavy industries in Walker has been accompanied with neighborhood decline, and the area contains numerous abandoned and derelict residential and industrial buildings. The Walker ward ranked the worst of all twenty-six wards in Newcastle and thirtieth worst of 8,414 wards in England against the 2000 English indices of Deprivation.... (p. 293)

Though it was a poor place, it was filled with tight and functional social networks that dated back generations:

> During a walk around Walker with Tina, a Walker resident, mother of two, and worker in the community and voluntary sector, she illustrated the close community and family networks in Walker: she knew the people, places, politics, and local history of Walker in intimate detail, and she showed me her house and the houses of her mother, grandmother, and brother, all within a couple of blocks.... (p. 285)

Deindustrialization, as I noted above, is an important form of place upheaval (Bluestone & Bennett, 1982; Pappas, 1989). It shifts the organization, rhythm, economic viability, and energy of a place. In Walker, the loss of nearly half of the population was a searing and important injury to the social networks and social functioning of the neighborhood. Places that have been deindustrialized shrink as Walker had, but it has been routinely noted that people who can stay, do. For example, Ginzberg, in a 1930s study of Welsh miners, found that the unemployed men slept more, and the town he was studying went into a kind of stasis, to be reawakened when World War II increased demand for coal and the mines were reopened (Ginzberg, 1991). People, after such a loss, are keenly aware of what-used-to-be and what-is. They try to hold on to what they can.

Newcastle, under the banner of "Going for Growth," proposed a massive reorganization of Walker, with demolition of existing housing and replacement with "modern riverside flats." Mah reported that an "interviewee whose house was under threat of demolition, described how her father's, mother's, and children's homes were all within doors of one another, and thus the impact of demolition and relocation would be 'soul-destroying,' as it would separate the family...." (pp. 295–296)

The community opposed the regeneration plan, forcing the city to enter into protracted and serious negotiations. The key here, in my view, is that the experience of population loss after deindustrialization is what alerted the community to the fact that the new proposals would be "soul-destroying." Alerted to the harm that they faced, residents of Walker opposed the city's plan. The nature of the narrative is fundamental to the action that the residents took.

The lived experience of upheaval alerts leaders to the fact that planners and city officials tend to highlight benefits and understate costs, particularly the costs to the poor people who are actually losing their homes (Manzo et al, 2008; Murphy, 2004). Hence, it shifts the contexts of the conversation in important ways. In the city's narrative, Walker was not worth keeping. In the residents' narrative, it was a supportive and important place. Telling the story of the worth of a place may well be central to maintaining attachment through a series of forced displacements. The story that is being told is the story of the community practices, the ways in which family, friends, and neighborhoods live reciprocally with one another. This is the social process that embeds the individual in the world. The community practices include what is happening and what happened in the past, relating that history is a crucial community practice that supports continuing attachment.

HOW DO PEOPLE GET TO THE PLACE-THAT-WAS-AND-MIGHT-BE-AGAIN?

The "place" that was has been profoundly altered and some fraction of its population is in diaspora. In order to understand what has happened to the place, we have to understand its new geography as

{"the place that was" + "the place that is" + "the dispersion that is"}

Wherever the people are who knew a place, they carry with them the concept of "the place that was." This concept can be passed from one generation to the next, an enduring image of how and where to live (Fullilove, 2004). In spite of trials and tribulations, diseases, and dysfunction, groups retain an image of place.

How, then, does an enduring image get translated into a community practice? Can we see this happen in real time in communities? Can we support and nurture this regeneration of place attachment? Till (2012), in her work on the wounded city, described several settings in which people were engaged in such community practices, lifting up the history of the lost place and using it as a guide to future action.

In the sense of Simms, I propose to consider place attachment as a community practice, deeply intertwined with the economic, physical, and social capacity of the place, that is, the extent to which it is "good enough" to support human life. Equating place with its social, economic, and physical capacities, however, is not quite strong enough to address the perplexing observation that, unlike rats leaving sinking ships, people do not abandon collapsing places.

Jane Jacobs (1991) defined a slum as "a place that people want to leave" (p. 171). Indeed, many people had left the Hill over the years covered in Simms's study. But many people had not left, many who had left wished they could return, and many who had left and did not want to return still clung to memories of happy times they had had in the Hill. In American culture, leaving a place that is falling apart is often proposed as the reasonable solution.[1] That people do not leave, then, raises the question, "Why do they stay?" and outsiders may presume that there is some pathology at work. The Black Phoenix, a young performance artist from the beleaguered city of Newark, NJ, drew cheers from the audience when he recited the following lines at a 2012 poetry lounge:

> We fight here
> We hurt here
> We suffer here
> We die here
> We love here
> *We live here!*[2]

Following his logic, I propose that the factor at play is that place attachment is not only an individual psychological process; it is, at another level of scale, a community practice of love of place. As such it is concerned with affective engagements that defy simple economistic calculations and draw, instead, from people's desire for the sacred (*le désir du sacré*) (Cantal-Dupart,1994).

In my work in the Hill, I saw the community leaders—bearers of the "place that was"—react strongly to a threat to a HOPE VI project, which they saw as a threat to the community's future. Like their counterparts in Walker, the Hill District leaders evinced "place-protective behavior" (Devine-Wright, 2009) which set the neighborhood on a more positive path (Fullilove, 2004; Murphy, 2004).

At the heart of the recovery of people and communities affected by serial displacement are many acts of affirmation. By recognizing and supporting these efforts, we can empower and energize the inherent thrust toward reconnection and re-emergence. The variety and size of such efforts vary, but they can be found wherever disruption—and even serial displacement—has occurred.

In careful examination of the process that followed the successful opposition to HOPE VI demolition, I found that a series of behaviors were initiated that, riffing on Devine-Wright, I will call "place-restorative behavior." My research identified nine "elements of urban restoration," which have been used in the Hill to rebuild the neighborhood. The nine elements are City in mind, Find what you're FOR, Make a mark, Unpuzzle the fractured space, Unslum the neighborhoods, Make meaningful places, Strengthen the region, Show solidarity with all life, and Celebrate your accomplishments (Fullilove, 2013). It is clear, as the process has unfolded to date, that the specifics of what was will never be recreated, but an inclusive, life-sustaining neighborhood, in which children can focus on their art, is certainly possible.

Reverend Dr. Martin Luther King, Jr., was adamant that creating the "beloved community" involved challenging the lies that held the white population in the thrall of hatred and disconnection from humanity. He argued that white people needed the black people's love, which seems incongruous, given that among white people there were those who held great wealth and power (King, 2003). Yet wealth founded on lies, deception, murder, and mayhem has great psychological costs for the wealthy and these costs are passed along to subsequent generations.

I want to return to the Passover ceremony to draw these ideas together. In the spring of 2020, a pandemic caused by a novel coronavirus caused countries to institute physical distancing. The Passover holiday fell in April, as many areas were reaching a peak of infection. Jewish people were not able to gather as they traditionally would. On the other hand, the story of Passover hinges on the ten plagues, which created a deep resonance with current events. What were they to do with this community practice which had been essential to maintaining the image of the beloved community for millenia?

Among some Jewish groups—the ultra-Orthodox Hasidim, for example—the rabbis had the deciding power on such issues as the use of video chats. Among others—especially more secular Jewish people—the families themselves made the decisions. There was some debate, which in itself was affirming of the continuities of culture, as one person noted, "Two Jews, three opinions."

Gahlia Eden, a young filmmaker, shared the story of organizing her observance. She was sheltering in place in Jersey City and planned to join her parents, sisters, and family friends via a video conferencing platform. As she was not with others, she faced the decision of what to do to make the Seder plate and traditional meal. Although people were urged to shop as little as possible, she went to several stores to find what she needed. As the youngest of four sisters, she had not made the meal before or prepared the Seder plate. She made a study guide to clarify all the items, including olives and orange which are items added by her family (Figure 11.1). She made a big pot of Matzoh ball soup, a family tradition, and she was able to deliver portions to two family members living nearby who would be observing from their homes. On the first night of Passover, she joined her

Figure 11.1
Gahlia Eden's study
guide for preparing the
Seder Plate. Photo by
Gahlia Eden, used with
permission.

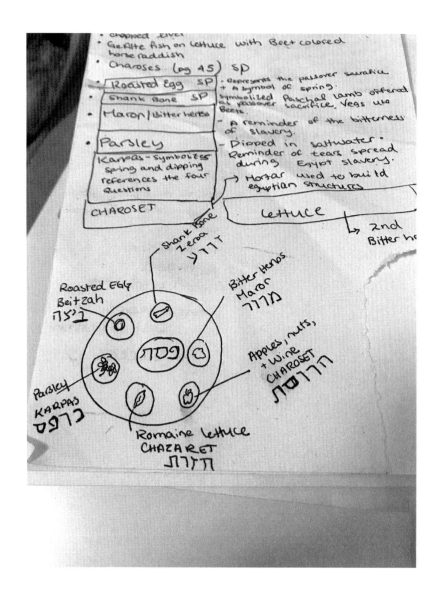

family and friends, as they carried out the Passover ceremony. She used her own Seder plate (Figure 11.2).

Gahlia noted afterward, "It was really, really special. I was bullied for being Jewish for much of my adolescence and to really grow into being proud of my culture through preparing Passover was really empowering."

This story, of a Passover in a time of worldwide forced displacement, illustrates the manner in which a community practice affirms the vision of the beloved community and sustains community members through the latest trial. This test of my Frayed Knot hypothesis offers important affirmation of the possibility of continuity despite serial forced displacement and the role of community practices.

Figure 11.2
The Seder plate created by Gahlia Eden for her Passover, 2020. The items (clockwise, starting from the egg) are roasted egg/ Beitzah, Shankbone/ zeroa (actually a chicken bone and many Jewish vegetarians use beets instead), bitter herbs/ Maror, apples, nuts, and wine:charoset, Riomaine lettuce;chazaret (which is the second bitter herb), parsley/Karpas, and olives and orange which her family adds to the traditional items. Photo by Gahlia Eden, used with permission.

NOTES

1 Consider, as an example, the enthusiasm for the "Move to Opportunity" research pro-ject, which moved low-income families out of their neighborhoods. For a discussion of the project, see Sampson (2008).
2 The Black Phoenix, spoken word about his home, Newark, NJ, at the Poetry Lounge, VAMP 2012.

REFERENCES

Acker, C. J. (2009). How crack found a niche in the American ghetto: The historical epidemi-ology of drug-related harm. *BioSocieties*, *5*, 70–88. DOI:10.1057/biosoc.2009.1
Albrecht, G., Sartore, G.-M., Connor, L., & Higginbotham, N. (2007). Solastalgia: The distress caused by environmental change. *Australasian Psychiatry: Bulletin of*

the Royal Australian and New Zealand College of Psychiatrists, 15(s1), 95–98. DOI:10.1080/10398560701701288

Bluestone, B., & Bennett, H. (1982). The deindustrialization of America: Plant closings, community abandonment, and the dismantling of basic industry. New York: Basic Books.

Brown, B. B., & Perkins, D. D. (1992). Disruptions in place attachment. New York: Plenum Press.

Cantal-Dupart, M. (1994). Merci la Ville! Bordeaux: Investigations Le Castor Astral.

Chow, K., & Healey, M. (2008). Place attachment and place identity: First-year undergraduates making the transition from home to university. Journal of Environmental Psychology, 28(4), 362–372. DOI:10.1016/j.jenvp.2008.02.011

Devine-Wright, P. (2009) Rethinking Nimbyism: the role of place attachment and place identity in explaining place protective action. Journal of Community and Applied Social Psychology. 19(6), 426-441.DOI: 10.1002/casp.1004

Erikson, K. T. (1976). Everything in its path: Destruction of community in the Buffalo Creek Flood. New York: Simon & Schuster.

Fried, M. (1966). Grieving for a lost home: Psychological costs of relocation. In J. Q. Wilson (Ed.), Urban renewal: The record and the controversy (pp. 359–379). Cambridge: The MIT Press.

Fullilove, M. T. (1996). Psychiatric implications of displacement: Contributions from the psychology of place. American Journal of Psychiatry, 153(12), 1516–1523.

Fullilove, M. T. (2004). Root shock: How tearing up city neighborhoods hurts America and what we can do about it. New York: Ballantine Books.

Fullilove, M. T., & Wallace, R. (2011). Serial forced displacement in American cities, 1916–2010. Journal of Urban Health, 88(3), 381–389.

Fullilove, M. T. (2013). Urban alchemy: Restoring joy in America's sorted-out cities. Oakland: New Village Press.

Ginzberg, E. (1991). World without work. New Brunswick: Transaction Publishers.

Glasco, L. (1989). Double burden: The black experience in Pittsburgh. In S. P. Hays (Ed.), City at the point. Pittsburgh: University of Pittsburgh Press.

Greene, D., Tehranifar, P., Hernandez-Cordero, L., & Fullilove, M. (2011). I used to cry every day: A model of the family process of managing displacement. Journal of Urban Health, 88(3), 403–416. DOI:10.1007/s11524-011-9583-4

Gross, L.W. (2003). Cultural sovereignty and Native American hermeneutics in the interpretation of the sacred stories of the Anishinaabe. WicazoSa Review,18(2), 127–134.

King Center. (2020). The beloved community. https://thekingcenter.org/king-philosophy/

King, M. L., Jr. (2003). An experiment in love. In M. L. King, & J. M. Washington (Eds.), A testament of hope: The essential writings and speeches of Martin Luther King, Jr (pp. 16–20). San Francisco, CA: HarperSanFrancisco.

Harvey, D. (2009). The 'new' imperialism: Accumulation by dispossession. Socialist Register, 40(40), 63–87.

Hyra, D. S. (2012). Conceptualizing the new urban renewal: Comparing the past to the present. Urban Affairs Review, 48, 498–527.

Jacobs, J. (1991). The death and life of great American cities. New York: Vintage Books.

Jacobs, W. R. (1972). Dispossessing the American Indian. New York: Charles Scribner's Sons.

Jahoda, G. (1975). The trail of tears: The story of the American Indian removals, 1813–1855. New York: Wings Books.

Lubove, R. (1996). Twentieth century Pittsburgh, volume 2: The post steel era. Pittsburgh: The University of Pittsburgh Press.

Mah, A. (2009). Devastation but also home: Place attachment in areas of industrial decline. Home Cultures, 6(3), 287–309.

Mann, C. C. (2011). 1493: Uncovering the new world Columbus created. New York: Vintage.

Manzo, L. (2014). On uncertain ground: Being at home in the context of public housing redevelopment. *International Journal of Housing Policy*, *14*(4), 389–410.

Manzo, L. C., Kleit, R. G., & Couch, D. (2008). "Moving three times is like having your house on fire once": The experience of place and impending displacement among public housing residents. *Urban Studies*, *45*(9), 1855–1878.

Massey, D. (1995). The conceptualisation of place. In D. Massey, & P. Jess (Eds.), *Aplace in the world? Places, cultures and globalisation* (pp. 87–132). Oxford: Oxford University Press.

Mazumdar, S., & Mazumdar, S. (2016). Interiors and homemaking in displacement: A study of Vietnamese Americans in Southern California. *Journal of Interior Design*, *41*(2), 23–37.

Murphy, P. (November/December 2004). The housing that community built. *Shelterforce Online*. http://www.nhi.org/online/issues/138/bedford.html (Retrieved December 2, 2008).

Neihardt, J. G. (1979). *Black elk speaks: Being the life story of a holy man of the Oglala Sioux*. Lincoln: University of Nebraska Press.

O'Brien, T. (2009). *The things they carried*. New York: Houghton Mifflin Harcourt.

Pappas, G. (1989). *The magic city: Unemployment in a working-class community*. Ithaca: Cornell University Press.

Rúa, M. M. (2017). Aging in displacement: Urban revitalization and Puerto Rican elderhood in Chicago. *Anthropology & Aging*, *38*(1), 44–59.

Sampson, R.J. (2008). Moving to inequality: Neighborhood effects and experiments meet social structure. *American Journal of Sociology*, *114*(1), 189–231.

Sanchez, G. C., & Brown, T. N. (1994). Nostalgia: A Swiss disease. *The American Journal of Psychiatry*, *151*(11), 1715–1716. Retrieved from http://ezproxy.cul.columbia.edu/login?url=http://search.proquest.com/docview/220450056?accountid=10226

Simms, E.-M. (2008). Children's lived spaces in the inner city: Historical and political aspects of the psychology of Place. *The Humanistic Psychologist*, *36*(1), 72–89.

Till, K. E. (2012). Wounded cities: Memory-work and a place-based ethics of care. *Political Geography*, *31*(1), 3–14. DOI:10.1016/j.polgeo.2011.10.008

Toker, F. (1986). *Pittsburgh: An urban portrait*. Pittsburgh: University of Pittsburgh Press.

Trotter, J. W., & Day, J. N. (2010). *Race and renaissance: African Americans in Pittsburgh since World War II*. Pittsburgh: University of Pittsburgh Press.

Wallace, A. (1957). Mazeway disintegration: The individual's perception of socio-cultural disorganization. *Human Organization*, *16*, 23–27.

Wallace, R. (1988). A synergism of plagues: "Planned Shrinkage," contagious housing destruction, and AIDS in the Bronx. *Environmental Research*, *47*, 1–33.

Wallace, R. (1990). Urban desertification, public health and public order: 'Planned shrinkage', violent death, substance abuse and AIDS in the Bronx. *Social Science & Medicine*, *31*(7), 801–813. DOI:10.1016/0277-9536(90)90175-r

Wallace, A., & Foner, E. (1993). *The long, bitter trail: Andrew Jackson and the Indians*. New York: Macmillan.

Watkins, B. X. (2000). *Fantasy, decay, abandonment, defeat, and disease: Community disintegration in central Harlem 1960–1990*. Columbia University, New York.

White, F. (2006). Rethinking Native American language revitalization. *American Indian Quarterly*, *30*(1/2), 91–109.

Wishart, D. J. (1994). *An unspeakable sadness: The dispossession of the Nebraska Indians*. Lincoln: University of Nebraska Press.

Yatsushiro, T., Ishino, I., & Matsumoto, Y. (1944). The Japanese-American looks at resettlement. *Public Opinion Quarterly*, *8*(2), 188–201.

Chapter 12: Place attachment and environment-related behavior

Ferdinando Fornara, Massimiliano Scopelliti, Giuseppe Carrus, Mirilia Bonnes, and Marino Bonaiuto

INTRODUCTION

The present chapter concerns the relationships between place attachment and environment-related behavior, with a specific focus on civic engagement and group identification patterns.

Place attachment represents one of the most debated research themes in environmental psychology, being addressed in many empirical studies and reviews (e.g., Altman & Low, 1992; Di Masso, Dixon, & Hernandez, 2017; Giuliani, 2003; Korpela, 2012; Lewicka, 2011; Morgan, 2010; Scannell & Gifford, 2010a; see also Giuliani & Scopelliti, 2009). Place attachment has been studied mainly as an outcome of humans' transactions with their habitats, and many studies in environment-behavior research tried to answer the question of how the quality of our living environments affects place attachment (e.g., Bonaiuto, Aiello, Perugini, Bonnes, & Ercolani, 1999,; Fornara et al., 2018). Instead, this chapter will review and discuss research focused on the consequences of place attachment over the quality of our environment. In particular, we will review studies suggesting a link between place attachment and environment-related behaviors, and the possible moderators of this relationship, that is, factors that can turn place-attached individuals or groups into either pro- or anti-environmental actors.

Place attachment has been defined in many different ways; nevertheless, most definitions in the literature have underlined the affective (e.g., see Hidalgo & Hernandez, 2001; Riley, 1992) and emotional (e.g., see Hummon, 1992; Lewicka, 2013; Low, 1992) nature of this construct. As claimed by Korpela (2012), the distinctive aspects of place attachment are in fact represented by affect, emotions, and feelings, even though cognitive and behavioral components are very often included in place attachment definitions (e.g., see Jorgensen & Stedman, 2001, 2006; Scannell & Gifford, 2010a). Thus, there is still a general agreement on early definitions, when place attachment was conceived as a set of positive affective bonds between individuals, groups, communities, and their daily life settings (e.g., Shumaker & Taylor, 1983). More recently, it has been pointed out that these bonds can sometimes be ambivalent or even negative (e.g., Manzo, 2005). Moreover, the person-place bond can develop into more or less socially constructive implications, such as when pride of place takes respectively an "authentic" or "hubristic" form (see Bonaiuto, Albers, Ariccio, & Cataldi, 2019): authentic pride is a specific emotion characterized by a proportionate sense of self-esteem and social acceptation, which derives from achievements and goal accomplishments, motivating us to fill our lives with meaning through unstable and controllable attribution processes; instead, hubristic pride is more related to self-views, abilities and character strengths, through stable and uncontrollable attribution processes.

A largely debated issue is about the dimensions of place attachment, and its relations with other constructs involved in people-environment relations. There is general agreement on the importance of including both a social and a physical dimension in the conceptualization of emotional relationship with places (Bonaiuto et al., 1999; Scannell & Gifford, 2010a). Place attachment has also been put in relation with other constructs developed in the environmental and social psychological literature, such as place identity, community identification, or sense of community (e.g., Giuliani, 2003; Lewicka, 2011), and more recently pride of place (Bonaiuto et al., 2019). Other scholars include place identity, place dependence, place affect and social bonding in the place attachment construct, thus conceiving it as a multi-dimensional facet (e.g., see Chen, Dwyer, & Firth, 2018; Han, Kim, Lee, & Kim, 2019; Ramkissoon, Smith, & Weiler, 2013).

For the purposes of this chapter, it is important to underline how studies focusing on these different concepts have often identified common patterns in the consequences that place attachment can have upon individuals' willingness to engage in environment-related or civic activities. Within the broader set of environment-related behaviors[1], two main kinds can be identified: mitigation actions, which refer to behaviors that reduce human impacts on the environment (e.g., lowering energy consumption, increasing recycling, increasing options in favor of biodiversity conservation), and adaption actions, which refer to behaviors that improve human coping in the face of environmental changes (e.g., resilience actions to cope with impending climate change phenomena).

There are different theoretical reasons and consistent empirical evidence to support a connection between place attachment and environment-related behavior.

First, a broad theoretical reason can be drawn from the theory of mother-child attachment in human development (e.g., Bowlby, 1969), which formed the basis for the definition of the concept itself of place attachment and its functions. The theory of attachment assumes that early mother-child positive bonds will drive mutual positive behaviors across the entire lifespan (e.g., Ainsworth & Bowlby, 1965; Bowlby, 1988). Likewise, we should assume that positive affective bonds with one's place should be associated with systematic behavioral tendencies to protect that place (Manzo & Perkins, 2006). This idea was already present in the works of phenomenological place theorists, such as Relph (1976) and Tuan (1977).

Second, a link between place attachment and environment-related behavior is also intrinsically grounded in theoretical models that imply a behavioral component of place attachment. In this regard, Feldman (1996) identified expressions of care and interest for residential settlement typologies, which are likely to be antecedents of positive actions taken toward the same settlement's typologies. More directly, Scannell and Gifford (2010a) suggested that the behavioral component of place attachment can take the form of reconstruction activities after natural disasters, or other "place-protective" behaviors at the specific civic level. Similarly, though within a different perspective, that is, Moscovici's Social Representations Theory, Devine-Wright (2009a) proposed a five-stage model of psychological response to place change, where the behavioral pattern (including "place-protective" collective action of opposition to change) is the last stage, following awareness of change proposals, interpretation of meaning of change for people and places, positive or negative evaluation of change, and coping with it.

A third reason for expecting a link between ties to one's environment and environment-related behavior can be drawn from work on place attachment, civic activism, and community wellbeing. Manzo and Perkins (2006) pointed out that place attachment might motivate efforts to improve one's community, and identified place attachment and participation in neighborhood protection as affective and behavioral place-related community dimensions, respectively. This idea is also central in a work by Keyes (1998) showing that a specific dimension of social wellbeing is social contribution (i.e., the feeling of being a vital member of society, with something of value to contribute). Similarly, Rollero and De Piccoli (2010) found that attachment to the city is a positive predictor of social wellbeing and social contribution. Lewicka (2005) showed how place attachment, together with social capital, is a strong predictor of civic activism by promoting social cohesion (i.e., ties and trust with neighbors), and interest in one's roots (e.g., personal interest for the history of the place of residence and of the family). Scannell and Gifford (2013) found that residents' engagement in climate change issues was higher among those who are more attached to their local areas, probably because they consider that climate change could have local implications, and this would trigger their willingness to act. In a study carried out by Buta, Holland, and Kaplanidou (2014) with residents living in the area of a national park, place attachment emerged as a mediator between community attachment and civic engagement for the park management. A mediation role of place attachment, in this case in the relationship between local civic engagement and personal neighborhood connectedness, emerged also with adolescents (Lenzi, Vieno, Pastore, & Santinello, 2013). More recently, Larson, Cooper, Stedman, Decker, and Gagnon (2018) found that a stronger place attachment promotes both higher community involvement and higher engagement in place-protective behaviors among hunters, birdwatchers, and property owners. Taken together, these studies suggest that more attached individuals are more likely to contribute to the wellbeing of their community through civic activism and the protection of their environment.

A further argument that hypothesizes a path from place attachment to environment-related action can also be drawn from the relations between place attachment and place identity, and in turn, from the relations between place identity and social identity (see Bonaiuto, Breakwell, & Cano, 1996; Twigger-Ross,

Bonaiuto, & Breakwell, 2003 for a more thoroughly discussion of this issue). Social identity theory (SIT) offers a relevant theoretical ground to properly illustrate this argument (e.g., Brown, 2000). SIT was primarily developed to explain social interaction processes like prejudice, inter-group conflict, and in-group favoritism. However, its assumptions can be applied to explain the individual tendency to act in favor of one's own place. According to SIT, individuals who strongly identify with a group tend to act in favor of it, by putting the interests of the group before self-interest (see Hewstone, Rubin, & Willis, 2002).

Likewise, it is possible to assume that individuals who develop a strong place attachment (or strong identification) should put the interests of the place before their self-interest, and therefore behave pro-environmentally (e.g., participating in local pro-environmental initiatives, defending local biodiversity, cleaning up local streets). Developing this theoretical framework for environment-related behaviors, by stressing their collective rather than individualistic nature, Fritsche, Barth, Jugert, Masson, and Reese (2017) proposed a social identity model of pro-environmental action. This model assumes that environmental goals (e.g., coping successfully with climate change-related threats) can be typically reached only if collectively pursued, given that a behavioral change at the collective level is needed. In this regard, people cannot directly observe global complex phenomena like climate change, but only some of its outcomes (e.g., ice melting), and thus such phenomena are socially built within groups and communities through communication processes; in line with SIT assumptions, attitudes, evaluations, and behaviors concerning a given social object are shaped by in-group (e.g., the local community) belongingness.

PLACE ATTACHMENT AND MITIGATION BEHAVIORS

Most research evidence regarding place attachment and environment-related behaviors has focused on specific mitigation behaviors. Various authors assumed that strong ties with one's social-physical environment should lead individuals to adopt more pro-environmental behaviors and lifestyles (see, e.g., Brehm, Eisenhauer, & Krannich, 2004; Halpenny, 2010; Korpela, 2012; Scannel & Gifford, 2010b; Uzzell, Pol, & Badenas, 2002; Vaske & Kobrin, 2001; Vorkinn & Riese, 2001). In their review on factors influencing pro-environmental behavior, Gifford and Nilsson (2014) mention place attachment as one of the determinants among the "personal factors" (e.g., age, gender, childhood experiences, knowledge, education, values and worldviews, personality factors such as openness and agreeableness).

On the whole, various field studies in different contexts provide evidence for a positive link between place attachment and environment-related behaviors (or intentions). This link was found in regard to protected areas or national parks (Buta et al., 2014; Halpenny, 2010; López-Mosquera & Sánchez, 2013; Ramkissoon et al., 2013; Scannell & Gifford, 2010b; Tonge, Ryan, Moore, & Beckley, 2015), recreational settings (Kyle, Absher, & Graefe, 2003; Vaske & Kobrin, 2001; Vorkinn & Riese, 2001; Wilkins & de Urioste-Stone, 2018), rural communities (Brehm, Eisenhauer, & Krannich, 2006; Takahashi & Selfa, 2015), agricultural settings

(Mullendore, Ulrich-Schadb, & Prokopyb, 2015), and coastal areas (Lee & Oh, 2018). A moderating role of place attachment was found between openness (i.e., a personality trait) and liberalism (i.e., a political attitude) on the one hand, and a set of pro-environmental behaviors (such as ecological activism, material, energy, and water consumption, reduction of ecological footprint) on the other (Snider, Luo, & Fusco, 2018). Place attachment emerged as a moderator also between attitudes toward preserving local beaches and willingness to pay for their preservation (Fornara & Caddeo, 2016), and between urban stress and, respectively, household investment in green energy (e.g., installing solar PV panels) and non-littering (Meloni, Fornara, & Carrus, 2019). In all these studies, such relationships were stronger with higher levels of place attachment.

Concerning the relationship between place attachment and mitigation behaviors in the "pride-of-place" perspective (Bonaiuto et al., 2019), a study by Carrus, Bonaiuto, and Bonnes (2005) showed that self-reported feelings of "regional pride" are positively associated with residents' willingness to support the institution of two protected areas in Italy. Although support for national parks might be considered more as a measure of behavioral intentions rather than actual behavior, findings of this study are relevant to the purposes of the present chapter. In fact, the two parks considered in the study were perceived by residents as an effective means to protect the cultural heritage of their region, as well as a way for buffering the poor economic situation of their territories, through the promotion of tourism activities. Therefore, these two parks were seen by local communities as means to maintain (or even to improve) a positive collective self-image and self-esteem, something to be proud of and also useful for local wealth (for a discussion on pride of place and place attachment, see Bonaiuto et al., 2019).

But what if specific environmental policies are not so easily perceived by local communities as in line with the needs, traditions, and cultural heritage of their territory? Should we expect place attachment, or local identity, to be negatively linked to pro-environmental stances, attitudes, and behaviors? The section below on place attachment and anti-environmental behaviors addresses these questions.

PLACE ATTACHMENT AND ADAPTATION BEHAVIORS

Recently, research on adaptation behaviors showed a significant role of place attachment, alongside other environmental psychology processes (for a review, see van Valkengoed & Steg, 2019a, 2019b).

There is mixed evidence of the influence of place attachment on risk coping behaviors at community and/or individual levels. A recent review (Bonaiuto, Alves, De Dominicis, & Petruccelli, 2016) showed that higher levels of place attachment can foster place-protective and pro-environmental behaviors (Zhang, Zhang, Zhang, & Cheng, 2014) and people's resilience toward environmental risks (Boon, 2014; Mishra, Mazumdar, & Damodar, 2010). For example, higher neighborhood attachment positively relates with flood risk perceptions, and predicts relevant concern for it, and related coping behavioral intentions (such as to look for flood risk information or to store useful tools) and to give advice to neighbors (Bonaiuto, De Dominicis, Fornara, Ganucci Cancellieri, & Mosco, 2011). On the other hand, when high-risk perception is associated with high local attachment, the corresponding risk coping intentions (as above) and behavior choices (options to participate in preventive information and training events) are less likely than in the case of association between high-risk perception and low local attachment (De Dominicis, Fornara, Ganucci Cancellieri, Twigger-Ross, & Bonaiuto, 2015).

Under certain circumstances, therefore, strong place attachment may become detrimental for adaptive behaviors: for example, by generally weakening the relation between risk perception and risk coping behaviors; or by hindering resilience actions when they oppose the place attachment default behavioral component (e.g., leaving or detaching from one's own place).

PLACE ATTACHMENT AND TOURISM-RELATED BEHAVIORS

A further research line that has been receiving increasing attention focuses on the selection of tourist and heritage sites as a specific kind of environment-related behavior affected by place attachment. For example, Scarpi, Mason, and Faggiotto (2019) found that the intention to return to a Roman heritage festival was predicted by place attachment, particularly for older visitors and nearby residents. A similar result emerged in a study of two Egyptian oases (Abou-Shouk, Zoair, El-Barbary, & Hewedi, 2018), where the stronger the place attachment, the greater the intention to revisit the site. Another study focusing on the intention to revisit a festival showed the moderating role of place attachment between some features of perceived festival quality (i.e., information provision, place aesthetics, and accessibility) and the outcome dimension: the higher the perceived festival quality, the higher was the intention to visit the festival again, particularly in more attached visitors (Kim, Lee, & Lee, 2017). A study of international tourists who visited Thailand evidenced that place attachment mediates the relationship between emotions (both positive and negative) and place satisfaction (Hosany, Prayag, Van Der Veen, Huang, & Deesilatham, 2017), whilst other studies showed the influence of place attachment components on word-of-mouth behavior to promote the place as a destination (Chen & Dwyer, 2017; Chen et al., 2018). Further, a mediational role of place attachment was found between environmental knowledge and environmentally responsible behavior in tourists who visited the Penghu Islands in Taiwan (Cheng & Wu, 2015).

In sum, this recent research line on the relationship between place attachment and tourism-related choices has evidenced that the more the visitors are attached to the place they are visiting, the higher is the likelihood of positive responses toward such a place.

PLACE ATTACHMENT AND ANTI-ENVIRONMENTAL BEHAVIORS

A key question remains: does place attachment always predict pro-environmental behaviors? Some scholars have argued that the association between place attachment and pro-environmental behavior is still unclear, and that only specific dimensions of place attachment are relevant to pro-environmental behavior. For example, Scannell and Gifford (2010b) showed an effect of attachment to natural environments (i.e., "natural" place attachment), but no effect of attachment to one's city (i.e., "civic" place attachment), on pro-environmental behaviors. Brehm et al. (2006) also showed that distinct forms of place attachment (i.e., socially based attachment vs. attachment to community's natural environment) predicted distinct dimensions of local environmental concern. A study by Gosling and Williams (2010) showed only a modest association of feelings of connectedness to nature in general, and no association at all of attachment to one's own property, respectively, with environment-friendly land use in a group of Australian farmers. Chen et al. (2018) found that the relationship between place satisfaction and the behavior of promoting one's city online is mediated by different place attachment dimensions (i.e., social bonding, place memory and place expectations) in different socio-cultural contexts (i.e., Shangain in China and Sydney in Australia). Anton and Lawrence (2016) found that intention to protest against a local government reform was predicted only by Theory of Planned Behavior (TPB) dimensions—that is, attitude toward the protest, perceived control over the behavior, and subjective norms (a kind of social influence)—and not by place attachment dimensions, but those who considered the reform as negative reported stronger place dependence than those judging the reform as positive. Other studies showed an indirect effect of place attachment on pro-environmental behavior (e.g., mediated by the TPB variables, see Han et al., 2019).

Can place attachment be negatively related to pro-environmental behavior, and under what circumstances? Two field studies on local residents' willingness to oppose the institution of natural protected areas shed light on this, demonstrating that economic interest in the exploitation of natural resources may link place attachment and place identity to local opposition to natural protected areas (Bonaiuto et al., 2002). In fact, protected areas can be perceived (particularly by local residents) as limiting or threatening the traditional economic activities of local rural populations. Indeed, rural residents are usually less ecologically oriented than urban inhabitants, since they are more likely to see natural resources as a source for their daily sustenance (Bogner & Wiseman, 1997). Similarly, both supporters and opponents of a planned biosphere reserve showed a higher level of place identity and place dependence (considered as two place attachment dimensions) than waverers who were less sure about the proposal (Huber & Arnberger, 2016). Here, supporters perceive the protected area as an opportunity, whereas opponents felt worried about the possible negative economic consequences, since the establishment of a biosphere reserve in their living area was perceived as a threat to their local traditions.

Furthermore, natural protected areas are often perceived by local communities as an imposed decision, or as an unfair interference of authorities into local affairs (e.g., Stoll-Kleemann, 2001). Bonaiuto et al. (2002) showed that the institution of a protected natural area was perceived by a local group as a potential threat to their autonomy and identity. Bonaiuto et al. (2002) also suggested that if local authorities underestimate the importance of participatory processes and inclusive governance, it is easy to create a vicious circle. The perception of an imposed decision can lead some residents to reinforce their local ties and place attachment, and to reinforce their opposition toward that protected area. Although, on a general political level, one might argue that the imposition of a protected area by the government should not be presumed to be pro-environmental action, it is generally assumed that accepting the institution of protected areas is a way to contribute to biodiversity conservation (West & Brechin, 1991), and therefore any protest against it is necessarily "anti-environmental" or at least less pro-environmental.

A series of subsequent works on the role of place attachment in shaping local acceptance of wind turbines in the UK provided similar findings, and offered an even more complex point of view on the relations between place attachment and environmentalism (e.g., Devine-Wright, 2005, 2009a, 2009b; Devine-Wright & Howes, 2010; see also Haggett, 2011). In particular, place attachment was predictive of local negative reactions to offshore wind turbines, particularly among communities having more interests in keeping the visual appearance of their coastal landscape unaltered because of well-developed tourism activity. In this case, two opposite interpretations of the same finding hold, so that it is difficult to establish an association of place attachment with either pro- or anti-environmental stances. In fact, if seen from a global perspective, opposing renewable energy generation through wind turbines can be judged as anti-environmental. However, if seen from a local perspective, keeping unaltered a beautiful coastal landscape can be judged as pro-environmental. In other words, both those who support and those who oppose the wind turbines can be considered as pro-environmental, as they simply refer to different environmental scales (global vs. local, respectively).

Interestingly, a common aspect emerged in studies where a clear, local economic interest collided with specific environmental policy measures (i.e., land use for farming and agriculture vs. protected area designation: Bonaiuto et al., 2002; Carrus et al., 2005; and tourism activity in beautiful coastal locations vs. offshore wind energy generation: Devine-Wright, 2009b). In these cases, place attachment formed the basis for anti-environmental attitudes and behaviors, such as protest or refusal to comply with environmental regulations. Conversely, when the same environmental policies are perceived as potentially beneficial (or neutral) to local economic activities, then local attachment is positively related to pro-environmental attitudes and behaviors, and it supports compliance to environmental regulations (Carrus et al., 2005). In other words, as Devine-Wright (2009a) suggested, whether place attachment will lead to negative or positive evaluations of environmental policies depends on the interpretation of these policies; place attachment may positively correlate with support for pro-environmental projects, when these are interpreted as place enhancing. However, it must be acknowledged that it is difficult to disentangle the different issues emerging in these cases: clashes between local economic and environmental values and clashes between environmental benefits at different local versus global spatial scales.

CONCLUSION

In this chapter, we discussed the relationship between place attachment and environment-related attitudes, intentions, and behaviors. In particular, we addressed the distinction between mitigation scenarios, related to those behaviors that preserve the environment, and adaptation scenarios, related to those behaviors for coping successfully with negative environmental events.

Regarding mitigation scenarios, the literature provides various theoretical arguments and empirical evidence for a positive link between local attachment and pro-environmental behavior. Place-attached individuals tend to be more keen to protect their place, to engage in civic activities that are beneficial to the local environment, and to appreciate and protect the local natural resources. Yet, other studies reviewed in this chapter provided evidence suggesting a negative link between place attachment and pro-environmental efforts such as nature preserves when they are seen as threatening local identity or economic interests. In sum, it seems that if an environmental policy brings some sort of advantage to a local territory, then place attachment (or local identity) is predictive of pro-environmental stances. Conversely, when environmental policies are perceived (or represented through social construction processes by mass media and local groups) as incompatible with local economic wealth, then attachment drives local opposition and resistance to change.

Regarding adaptation scenarios, place attachment may form a barrier to risk coping when the requested action overtly contradicts the place attachment behavioral component (i.e., leaving vs. staying). But also, under a strong risk exposure, place attachment may subtly weaken the risk perception-risk coping link, therefore buffering the alertness-reactivity link, similarly to what happens in interpersonal attachment dynamics (Bonaiuto et al., 2016). Ongoing research shows, however, that these tricky mechanisms—supposedly behind some paradoxical effects that residential place attachment can exert on adaptation actions—can turn into the usual pattern of results where place attachment positively predicts environmentally adapting behaviors, by simply considering the degree of place attachment to the place the person should go to (i.e., the safety area) rather than to the place the person should evacuate from (i.e., home): a stronger (vs. weaker) place attachment to the target safety area drives more adaptive behavioral choices within a simulated environmental risk scenario (e.g., see Ariccio et al., 2020).

About the role of place attachment in attitudes, intentions, and behaviors related to visiting tourist and heritage sites, research findings have shown that a stronger attachment to the visited place is related to positive patterns toward such a place, in terms of intention to return, place satisfaction, place promotion, and place preservation. Thus, the development of the attachment pattern toward tourist and heritage places should be considered as pivotal for increasing both tourism-related outcomes (in terms of number of visitors, promotion, etc.) and environmentally responsible behaviors in those places.

From a practical point of view, the findings reviewed in this chapter offer a better understanding of factors and conditions that drive an individual, group, or community to more or less sustainable or adaptive behaviors, and how place attachment can play a crucial role in such actions. These factors should be taken into account when proposing policies, environmental transformations, or community interventions aimed at promoting more sustainable or adaptive environmental management and human lifestyles. Inclusive governance and participatory processes are crucial to secure the social, cultural, and economic sustainability and adaptability of environmental policies (e.g., Churchman & Sadan, 2004). Socially shared and accepted policy decisions are also more likely to drive everyday behaviors and decisions (Uzzell, 2003). Resident-based environmental policies are then more likely to get higher consensus and public support, and thus to be more efficacious in the long run, also because of place attachment issues. In fact, when environmental policies (and related environmental transformations) are perceived as compatible to an individual's self-concept (either in terms of place attachment, or personal, social, and place identity), people may be more willing to comply with them. Conversely, environmental policies or transformations clashing with the local feelings of attachment and identity of individuals, groups, and communities might run the risk of being misunderstood, perceived as threatening, and even rejected, thus being less sustainable and adaptive in the long run.

NOTE

1   We use across the text the term "environment-related behavior" for referring to an overarching category that includes all those behaviors related to the environment, but not necessarily positive for it (thus including, beside pro-environmental behaviors, also adaptation behaviors, tourism-related behaviors, and anti-environmental behaviors). Nevertheless, we use the more common term "pro-environmental behavior" in those sentences where there is specific reference to behaviors, which are positive for the environment.

REFERENCES

Abou-Shouk, M. A., Zoair, N., El-Barbary, M. N., & Hewedi, M. M. (2018). Sense of place relationship with tourist satisfaction and intentional revisit: Evidence from Egypt. *International Journal of Tourism Research, 20*, 172–181.

Ainsworth, M., & Bowlby, J. (1965). *Child care and the growth of love.* London: Penguin Books.

Altman, I., & Low, S. M. (Eds.) (1992). *Place attachment.* New York: Plenum.

Anton, C. E., and Lawrence, C. (2016) 'The relationship between place attachment, the theory of planned behaviour and residents' response to place change', *Journal of Environmental Psychology* 47: 145-154.

Ariccio, S., Petruccelli, I., Ganucci Cancellieri, U., Quintana, C., Villagra, P., & Bonaiuto, M. (2020). Loving, leaving, living: Evacuation site place attachment predicts natural hazard coping behavior. *Journal of Environmental Psychology, 70*, 101431.

Bonaiuto, M., Aiello, A., Perugini, M., Bonnes, M., & Ercolani, A. P. (1999). Multidimensional perception of residential environment quality and neighbourhood attachment in the urban environment. *Journal of Environmental Psychology*, *19*, 331–352.

Bonaiuto, M., Albers, T., Ariccio, S., & Cataldi, S. (2019). Pride of place in a religious context: An environmental psychology and sociology perspective. In V. Counted & F. Watts (Eds.), *Religion and place: Psychological perspectives* (in press). New York: Palgrave Macmillan.

Bonaiuto, M., Alves, S., De Dominicis, S., & Petruccelli, I. (2016). Place attachment and natural hazard risk: Research review and agenda. *Journal of Environmental Psychology*, *48*, 33–53.

Bonaiuto, M., Breakwell, G. M., & Cano, L. (1996). Identity processes and environmental threat: The effects of nationalism and local identity upon perception of Beach Pollution. *Journal of Community and Applied Social Psychology*, *6*, 157–175.

Bonaiuto, M., Carrus G., Martorella, H., & Bonnes, M., (2002). Local identity processes and environmental attitudes in land use changes: The case of natural protected areas. *Journal of Economic Psychology*, *23*, 631–653.

Bonaiuto, M., De Dominicis, S., Fornara, F., Ganucci Cancellieri, U., and Mosco, B. (2011) 'Flood risk: the role of neighbourhood attachment. In G. Zenz, R. Hornich (Eds.), in *Proceedings of the International Symposium UFRIM. Urban Flood Risk Management - Approaches to Enhance Resilience of Communities*, Graz: Verlag der Technischen Universität Graz.

Bogner, F. X., & Wiseman, M. (1997). Environmental perception of rural and urban pupils. *Journal of Environmental Psychology*, *17*, 111–122.

Boon, H. J. (2014). Disaster resilience in a flood-impacted rural Australian town. *Persistent Link*, *71*, 683e701.

Bowlby, J. (1969). *Attachment and loss (volume 1) attachment*. London: Hogarth.

Bowlby, J. (1988). *A secure base*. London: Routledge.

Brehm, J. M., Eisenhauer, B. W., & Krannich, R. S. (2004). Dimensions of community attachment and their relationship to well-being in the amenity-rich rural west. *Rural Sociology*, *69*, 405–429.

Brehm, J. M., Eisenhauer, B. W., & Krannich, R. S. (2006). Community attachments as predictors of local environmental concern. The case for multiple dimensions of attachment. *American Behavioral Scientist*, *50*, 142–165.

Brown, R. (2000). Social identity theory: Past achievements, current problems and future challenges. *European Journal of Social Psychology*, *30*, 745–778.

Buta, N., Holland, S. M., & Kaplanidou, K. (2014). Local communities and protected areas: The mediating role of place attachment for pro-environmental civic engagement. *Journal of Outdoor Recreation and Tourism, 5–6*, 1–10.

Carrus, G., Bonaiuto, M., & Bonnes, M. (2005). Environmental concern, regional identity and support for protected areas in Italy. *Environment and Behavior*, *37*, 237–257.

Chen, N., & Dwyer, L. (2017). Residents' place satisfaction and place attachment on destination brand-building behaviors: Conceptual and empirical differentiation. *Journal of Travel Research*, 0047287517729760.

Chen, N., Dwyer, L., & Firth, T. (2018). Residents' place attachment and word-of-mouth behaviours: A tale of two cities. *Journal of Hospitality and Tourism Management*, *36*, 1–11.

Cheng, T., & Wu, H. C. (2015). How do environmental knowledge, environmental sensitivity, and place attachment affect environmentally responsible behavior? An integrated approach for sustainable island tourism. *Journal of Sustainable Tourism*, *23*, 557–576.

Churchman, A., & Sadan, E. (2004). Environmental design and planning, public participation. In C. Spielberger (Ed.), *Encyclopedia of applied psychology*. New York: Elsevier/Academic Press.

De Dominicis, S., Fornara, F., Ganucci Cancellieri, U., Twigger-Ross, C., & Bonaiuto, M. (2015). We are at risk, and so what? Place attachment, environmental risk perceptions and preventive coping behaviours. *Journal of Environmental Psychology*, *43*, 66–78.

Devine-Wright, P. (2005). Beyond NIMBYism: Towards an integrated framework for understanding public perceptions of wind energy. *Wind Energy*, *8*, 125–139.

Devine-Wright, P. (2009a). Rethinking Nimbyism: The role of place attachment and place identity in explaining place-protective action. *Journal of Community and Applied Social Psychology*, *19*, 426–441.

Devine-Wright, P. (2009b). Fencing in the bay? Place attachment, social representations of energy technologies and the protection of restorative environments. In M. Bonaiuto, M. Bonnes, A. M. Nenci, & G. Carrus (Eds.), *Urban diversities, biosphere and well being: Designing and managing our common Environment*. Gottingen: Hogrefe and Huber.

Devine-Wright, P., & Howes, Y. (2010). Disruption to place attachment and the protection of restorative environments: A wind energy case study. *Journal of Environmental Psychology*, *30*, 271–280.

Di Masso, A., Dixon, J., & Hernández, B. (2017). Place Attachment, sense of belonging and the micro-politics of place satisfaction. In G. Fleury-Bahi, E. Pol, & O. Navarro (Eds.), *Handbook of environmental psychology and quality of life research*. Berlin: Springer.

Feldman, R. M. (1996). Constancy and change in attachments to types of settlements. *Environment and Behavior*, *4*, 419–445.

Fornara, F., Ariccio, S., Rioux, L., Moffat, E., Mariette, J., Bonnes, M., & Bonaiuto, M. (2018). Test of PREQIs' factorial structure and reliability in France and of a neighbourhood attachment prediction model: A study on a French sample in Paris. *Pratiques Psychologiques*, *24*, 131–156.

Fornara, F., & Caddeo, P. (2016). Willingness to pay for preserving local beaches: The role of framing, attitudes, and local identification. *Psyecology*, *7*, 201–227.

Fritsche, I., Barth, M., Jugert, P., Masson, T., & Reese, G. (2017). A social identity model of pro-environmental action (SIMPEA). *Psychological Review*, *125*, 245–269.

Gifford, R., & Nilsson, A. (2014). Personal and social factors that influence pro-environmental concern and behaviour: A review. *International Journal of Psychology*, *49*, 141–157.

Giuliani, M. V. (2003). Theory of attachment and place attachment. In M. Bonnes, T. Lee, & M. Bonaiuto (Eds.), *Psychological theories for environmental issues*. Aldershot: Ashgate.

Giuliani, M. V., & Scopelliti, M. (2009). Empirical research in environmental psychology: Past, present, and future. *Journal of Environmental Psychology*, *29*, 375–386.

Gosling, E., and Williams, K. J. H. (2010) 'Connectedness to nature, place attachment and conservation behaviour: Testing connectedness theory among farmers', *Journal of Environmental Psychology 30*: 298–304.

Haggett, C. (2011). Understanding public responses to offshore wind power. *Energy Policy*, *39*, 503–510.

Halpenny, E. A. (2010). Pro-environmental behaviours and park visitors: The effect of place attachment. *Journal of Environmental Psychology*, *30*, 409–421.

Han, J. H., Kim, J. S., Lee, C., & Kim, N. (2019). Role of place attachment dimensions in tourists' decision-making process in Cittáslow. *Journal of Destination Marketing & Management*, *11*, 108–119.

Hidalgo, M. C., & Hernandez, B. (2001). Place attachment: Conceptual and empirical questions. *Journal of Environmental Psychology*, *21*, 273–281.

Hosany, S., Prayag, G., Van Der Veen, R., Huang, S., & Deesilatham, S. (2017). Mediating effects of place attachment and satisfaction on the relationship between tourists' emotions and intention to recommend. *Journal of Travel Research*, *56*, 1079–1093.

Huber, M., and Arnberger, A. (2016) 'Opponents, waverers or supporters: the influence of place-attachment dimensions on local residents' acceptance of a planned biosphere reserve in Austria', *Journal of Environmental Planning and Management* 59: 1610–1628.

Jorgensen, B. S., & Stedman, R. C. (2001). Sense of place as an attitude: Lakeshore owners attitudes toward their properties'. *Journal of Environmental Psychology*, *21*, 233–248.

Jorgensen, B. S., & Stedman, R. C. (2006). A comparative analysis of predictors of sense of place dimensions: Attachment to, dependence on, and identification with lakeshore properties. *Journal of Environmental Management*, *79*, 316–327.

Hummon, L. (1992). Community attachment: Local sentiment and sense of place. In I. Altman, & S. Low (Eds.), *Place attachment*. New York: Plenum.

Keyes, C. L. M. (1998). Social well-being. *Social Psychology Quarterly*, *61*, 121–140.

Kim, S., Lee, Y., & Lee, C. (2017). The moderating effect of place attachment on the relationship between festival quality and behavioral intentions. *Asia Pacific Journal of Tourism Research*, *22*, 49–63.

Korpela, K. M. (2012). Place attachment. In S. D. Clayton (Ed.), *The Oxford handbook of environmental and conservation psychology*. New York, NY: Oxford University Press.

Kyle, G. T., Absher, J. D., & Graefe, A. R. (2003). The moderating role of place attachment on the relationship between attitude toward fees and spending preferences. *Leisure Sciences*, *25*, 33–50.

Larson, L. R., Cooper, C. B., Stedman, R. C., Decker, D. J., & Gagnon, R. J. (2018). Place-based pathways to proenvironmental behavior empirical evidence for a conservation–recreation model. *Society & Natural Resources*, *31*, 871–891.

Lee, J. S., & Oh, C. (2018). The causal effects of place attachment and tourism development on coastal residents' environmentally responsible behaviour. *Coastal Management*, *46*(3), 176–190.

Lenzi, M., Vieno, A., Pastore, M., & Santinello, M. (2013). Neighborhood social connectedness and adolescent civic engagement: An integrative model. *Journal of Environmental Psychology*, *34*, 45–54.

Lewicka, M. (2005). Ways to make people active: Role of place attachment, cultural capital and neighborhood ties. *Journal of Environmental Psychology*, *25*, 381–395.

Lewicka, M. (2011). Place attachment: How far have we come in the last 40 years? *Journal of Environmental Psychology*, *31*, 207–230.

Lewicka, M. (2013). Localism and activity as two dimensions of people-place bonding: The role of cultural capital. *Journal of Environmental Psychology*, *36*, 43–53.

López-Mosquera, N., & Sánchez, M. (2013). Direct and indirect effects of received benefits and place attachment in willingness to pay and loyalty in suburban natural areas. *Journal of Environmental Psychology*, *34*, 27–35.

Low, S. (1992). Symbolic ties that bind: Place attachment in the plaza. In I. Altman, & S. Low (Eds.), *Place attachment*. New York: Plenum.

Manzo, L. C. (2005). For better or worse: Exploring multiple dimensions of place meaning. *Journal of Environmental Psychology*, *25*, 67–86.

Manzo, L. C., & Perkins, D. D. (2006). Finding common ground: The importance of place attachment to community participation and planning. *Journal of Planning Literature*, *20*, 335–350.

Meloni, A., Fornara, F., & Carrus, G. (2019). Predicting pro-environmental behaviors in the urban context: The direct or moderated effect of urban stress, city identity, and worldviews. *Cities*, *88*, 83–90.

Mishra, S., Mazumdar, S., & Damodar, S. (2010). Place attachment and flood preparedness. *Journal of Environmental Psychology, 30*, 187–197.

Morgan, P. (2010). Towards a developmental theory of place attachment. *Journal of Environmental Psychology, 30*, 11–22.

Mullendore, N. D., Ulrich-Schadb, J. D., & Prokopyb, L. S. (2015). U.S. farmers' sense of place and its relation to conservation behaviour. *Landscape and Urban Planning, 140*, 67–75.

Ramkissoon, H., Smith, L. D. G., & Weiler, B. (2013). Testing the dimensionality of place attachment and its relationships with place satisfaction and pro-environmental behaviours: A structural equation modelling approach. *Tourism Management, 36*, 552–566.

Relph, E. (1976). *Place and placelessness*. London: Pion Limited.

Riley, B. R. (1992). Attachment to the ordinary landscape. In I. Altman, & S. Low (Eds.), *Place attachment*. New York: Plenum.

Rollero, C., & De Piccoli, N. (2010). Does place attachment affect social well-being?' *Revue Européenne de Psychologie Appliquée: European Review of Applied Psychology, 60*, 233–238.

Scannell, L., & Gifford, R. (2010a). Defining place attachment: A tripartite organizing framework. *Journal of Environmental Psychology, 30*, 1–10.

Scannell, L., & Gifford, R. (2010b). The relations between natural and civic place attachment and pro-environmental behaviour. *Journal of Environmental Psychology, 30*, 289–297.

Scannell, L., & Gifford, R. (2013). Personally relevant climate change: The role of place attachment and local versus global message framing in engagement. *Environment and Behavior, 45*, 60–85.

Scarpi, D., Mason, M., & Raggiotto, F. (2019). To Rome with love: A moderated mediation model in Roman heritage consumption. *Tourism Management, 71*, 389–401.

Shumaker, S. A., & Taylor, R. B. (1983). Toward a clarification of people place relationships: A model of attachment to place. In N. R. Feimer, & E. S. Geller (Eds.), *Environmental psychology: Directions and perspectives*. New York: Praeger.

Snider, A. G., Luo, S., & Fusco, E. (2018). Predicting college students' environmentally responsible behavior from personality, political attitudes, and place attachment: A synergistic model. *Journal of Environmental Studies and Sciences, 8*, 290–299.

Stoll-Kleemann, S. (2001). Barriers to nature conservation in Germany: A model explaining opposition to protected areas. *Journal of Environmental Psychology, 21*, 369–385.

Takahashi, B., & Selfa, T. (2015). Predictors of pro-environmental behavior in rural American communities. *Environment and Behavior, 47*, 856–876.

Tuan, Y. F. (1977). *Space and place: The perspective of experience*. Minnesota: The University of Minnesota Press.

Tonge, J., Ryan, M. M., Moore, S. A., & Beckley, L. E. (2015). The effect of place attachment on pro-environment behavioral intentions of visitors to coastal natural area tourist destinations. *Journal of Travel Research, 54*, 730–743.

Twigger-Ross, C., Bonaiuto, M., & Breakwell, G. (2003). Identity theories and environmental psychology. In M. Bonnes, T. Lee, & M. Bonaiuto (Eds.), *Psychological theories for environmental issues*. Aldershot: Ashgate.

Uzzell, D. L. (2003). Memorandum. *House of Commons environmental audit committee: Sub-committee on education for sustainable development: Learning the sustainability lesson, tenth report of session 2002–2003* (Vol. II). London: The Stationary Office. Online. http://www.publications.parliament.uk/pa/cm200203/cmselect/cmenvaud/472/472we42.htm (1st December 2012).

Uzzell, D., Pol, E. and Badenas, D. (2002) 'Place identification, social cohesion, and environmental sustainability', *Environment and Behavior* 34: 26–53.

Van Valkengoed, A. M., & Steg, L. (2019a). Meta-analyses of factors motivating climate change adaptation behavior. *Nature Climate Change*. https://doi.org/10.1038/s41558-018-0371-y.

Van Valkengoed, A. M., & Steg, L. (2019b). *The psychology of climate change adaptation*. Cambridge: Cambridge University Press.

Vaske, J. J., & Kobrin, K. C. (2001). Place attachment and environmentally responsible behaviour. *Journal of Environmental Education*, *32*, 16–21.

Vorkinn, M., & Riese, H. (2001). Environmental concern in a local context: The significance of place attachment. *Environment and Behavior*, *33*, 249–263.

Wilkins, E. J., & De Urioste-Stone, S. (2018). Place attachment, recreational activities, and travel intent under changing climate conditions. *Journal of Sustainable Tourism*, *26*, 798–811.

Zhang, Y., Zhang, H., Zhang, J., & Cheng, S. (2014). Predicting residents' pro-environmental behaviors at tourist sites: The role of awareness of disaster's consequences, values, and place attachment. *Journal of Environmental Psychology*, *40*, 131–146.

Chapter 13: Reattach! Practicing endemic design

Randolph T. Hester, Jr.

Attachment to place exerts the most positive influence of any force on the design of community. When values and meanings embedded in place are awakened, they remind people of their common identity and shared fate. People become more empathic toward others, more aware of their dependence on local ecosystems, and how the form of their community enriches or diminishes their lives (Hester, 1985a). The resulting design captures the distinct essence of the community, so grounded in place and culture that the form is endemic. It could only arise in that place.

I make these claims as a landscape architect reflecting on fifty years of community design work. Our Center for Ecological Democracy and the Neighborhood Laboratory achieve these ends through a robust participatory design process that includes a specific mapping procedure labeled the Sacred Structure that makes place attachment explicit, spatial, and legitimate. The Sacred Structure is a pattern of the places that people in a community most value and to which they are most likely deeply attached (Hester, 2006). If I could make only one analysis map for any community, I would create a sacred place map.

FIRST AWARENESS OF PLACE ATTACHMENT

In the early 1960s, I worked in the largest ghetto of Raleigh, North Carolina. Black activists were concerned that an Urban Renewal Clearance Project and a cross-city freeway would destroy their community of Chavis Heights. As in most American cities, Raleigh's leaders viewed the Black ghetto as a slum that should be removed. Some considered it a blight on the city, and most imagined the ghetto, once cleared, as a real-estate opportunity.

Residents of Chavis Heights considered it home. They could not imagine their homes bulldozed. Because they had lived there all their lives and had limited choices, they were likely more attached to their homes than most people (Marcus, 1995). I had not heard of "place attachment" or "Negro Removal" as these projects were called by critics in the 1960s when intentions became clear. Destroying Black people's homes simply seemed unfair, so I joined the seemingly hopeless struggle to stop the freeway and urban renewal clearance.

As the city moved ahead with its plans to bulldoze the neighborhood, we created a plan to renew the neighborhoods without residents being forced to relocate at all (Hester, 1972). I moved into Chavis Heights. Living there as the only white person, I learned first-hand why people were so attached to their community. Although racially isolated and discriminated against, Chavis Heights supported people's daily patterns, provided security and common purpose, and mitigated some of the burdens of extreme poverty (Coles, 1964; see also Fullilove, chapter 11 this volume). Civil Rights discontent was grounded in place.

The City of Raleigh's strategy was to condemn houses for building code violations. If not repaired by a designated time, the city evicted the residents and bulldozed the houses. We formed a group to make minor repairs to prevent evictions. We had been doing this for over a year when an activist contractor concluded that we had to stop the Urban Renewal Clearance and the freeway once and for all.

Rallying around our alternative plan, leaders in Chavis Heights mobilized protests against the Urban Renewal Clearance. Our plan called for block-by-block housing rehabilitation; protection of places people were most attached to like home, narrow streets, front porches, corner stores, reinvestment in community services, and no relocation of residents. By 1975, the city had abandoned the Urban Renewal Clearance Plan; I was elected to the Raleigh City Council and led the effort to allocate funds for housing rehabilitation. A year later, we cobbled together a majority vote to eliminate the freeway and road projects that were destructive to valued community places. At the time, I still did not register how central attachment to place was. I saw it as a power struggle, the oppressed rising up against injustice, but place attachment permeated every project I did during this time.

In Cambridge, Massachusetts, a street gang was so attached to Dana Park that they called themselves the Dana Park Gang. The City asked our design team to work with the community to redesign the park to resolve problems arising from the gang's control of the area. Their territory, which we mapped by degree of symbolic ownership, dictated the design outcome. The places to which they were most attached explained conflicts with other users. The gang attacked anyone who entered their hang out area. They harassed senior citizens sitting in benches along diagonal paths that divided the only grass lawn into four tiny triangles where the gang played field sports. The new design we developed with the gang eliminated these conflicts by creating a large shared central open space and placing elderly sitting at the edges removed from the gang's hang out (Hester, 1975). Similarly, in a plan for Aurora, North Carolina, a conservative City Council adopted a plan with radical land use controls to conserve ecologically sensitive areas where people hunted and fished. When we started work in Aurora, the former mayor warned me that he had personally disposed of every copy of the previous city

Land Use Plan by throwing them in nearby South Creek. In an about-face he became an outspoken supporter of our plan because, through our consideration of people's attachments to place, it saved sacred hunting and fishing grounds cherished by his constituents.

EXPLORING PLACE VALUES WITH DESIGN STUDENTS

In 1971, I started teaching a course in psychological relationships with place that I taught at North Carolina State and the University of California, Berkeley for over thirty-five years. The course always began with an exercise using self-hypnosis to uncover places most special to students. They would explore ten such places, then draw and analyze them. Consistently, this revealed that designers have cherished places that both inspire them and to which they are captive. In most cases, designers hold dear some childhood places that they try to replicate, often inappropriately. In one class, a practicing professional did drawings of places from his youth in such vivid detail you could distinguish vegetation species and sense the joy of swinging from saplings and the danger of traversing the swamp. It was the overgrown bog, snakes and all, that held him captive, constricted him, and motivated him. He laughed after he realized he continuously tried to recreate that mucky swampland, even in central city plazas. A reptilian paradise to him was a slimy nightmare of poisonous serpents to his urbane clients (Hester, 1979).

CROPPING LAND WITH SHORTY LAWSON

Teaching this course, I explored places of deepest meaning for myself, helping me understand how place attachments control my own intentions as a designer and how inextricably bound to one place I am. The land at Hester's store has been farmed by the Hesters since before the Revolutionary War. My grandson is the tenth generation. That place provides security, identity, and reciprocal caring (Relph, 1976; Tuan, 1974). North Carolina was the poor man's paradise, and the place fulfilled the Hesters. By my dad's generation, the land had been gifted to so many descendants that his parents' small farm couldn't sustain our family. We were landless. We day labored in tobacco so Dad could buy back the land he grew up on. We built barns, each marking my adolescent growth. The landscape ingrained in me my father's value of land stewardship. The cropland cut from the oak hickory forest embodied the necessity for constant attention to the most nuanced grading and drainage for soil conservation. Each field held special meaning. One field embodies Shorty Lawson, the Black sharecropper with whom I cropped tobacco for much of my youth and from whom I learned to farm (see Figure 13.1).

That field sloping down to Hyco Creek contains his spirit: simple joys, endurance, songs of resistance and faith, and a brotherhood beyond the color of skin. I learned race from Shorty. Racial justice and land stewardship have guided my work since then. I will describe the museum I am making to honor him later.

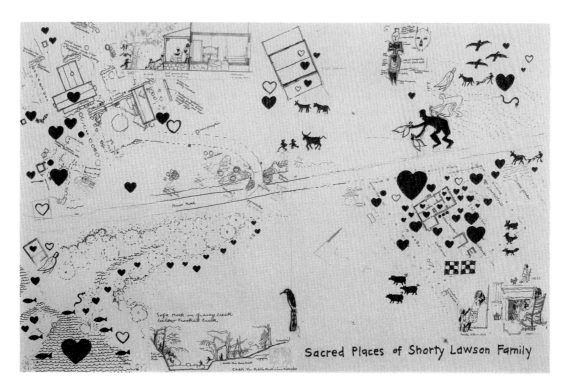

Sacred Places of Shorty Lawson Family

Figure 13.1
The sacred places of
the Lawsons resulted
from over fifty years of
mapping. The fireplace,
porch, pond, and fields
remain the same as in a
1970 drawing; other sites
are memories of spots
where life-lessons were
learned.

FIRST LESSONS EXTRACTED FROM EXPERIENCE IN COMMUNITY DESIGN

These reflections made it obvious why place attachment inspires professional work (see Figure 13.2):

1. Deeply meaningful places subconsciously define the designer's palette.
2. Place attachment seems indirectly connected to multiple values as diverse as environmental justice and child welfare.
3. Once uncovered, the community's deeply held values related to place produce exceptional plans.
4. The subconsciously held values are generally nobler, but it is difficult to separate these from conscious values (Relph, 1976).
5. Place attachment enables bold civic actions reflecting distinctive local values. Later I realized that this distinctiveness underlies endemic design.
6. Although place attachment is a positive force, the community may still be overcome by politics of real-estate speculation and other hidden interests.
7. We lacked a vocabulary for public discussion of place attachment in community design.
8. We had few methods to transform deep place values into design form.

Figure 13.2
The values that many
Black tenant farmers lived
by during Jim Crow were
expressed by outsider
artists like Buddy Snipes.

THE SACRED STRUCTURE OF MANTEO

During the revitalization of Manteo, North Carolina, these lessons came into sharp focus (Hester,1985a). Although our collaboration with Manteo has lasted forty years, the first year of the project was marked by discovery. We identified multiple techniques to uncover public attachment to place that provided legitimate data, a place vocabulary, a replicable procedure for community design to transform values of place into explicit landscape design. Manteo forced us to more systematically uncover these attachments. We combined two standard social science techniques, behavior observation and surveying, with active listening, to discover the places most essential to the community. Listening revealed an unusual commitment to values embedded in places plus hints of unique patterns of daily life. However, because we focused on economic development in the face of 22 percent unemployment, we did not ask specific follow-up questions when people mentioned place qualities. We learned to be more assertive (we called it "aggressive listening"), ask more pointed questions, probe for deep subconscious attachments to places, and challenge people to be spatially precise in the listening step, but, at that time, we were neophytes. The summary of listening interviews indicated that we were missing essential dependencies on place. To compensate, we did extensive behavior observations within the center of the city to record daily life patterns, where they occurred and how spatial form facilitated the activities. Through this, we discovered rituals like sharing local news at the post office, round table debates at the Duchess diner, and repairing boats in dilapidated sheds. Seeing these data and drawings, community leaders added places, daily and seasonal, as well as events we had not observed but that they thought were essential to their community. We compiled a master list of places that seemed to underlie Manteo's essence from which we developed a newspaper survey asking residents to make tradeoffs between protecting places and developing them to create jobs. We also asked people to add other places to the list and then rank the entire list from most essential to less so.

Listening, behavior mapping, and the newspaper survey produced distinct findings, but triangulation of data revealed consistency that is important to legitimize this type of information as evidence when compared to other more traditional inventories like traffic counts and building conditions (Appleyard, 1981). Confident of the evidence, we created a map, showing the intensity of importance of each place. One City Councilman, upon seeing the map, proclaimed it "The Sacred Structure of Manteo." We labeled the map the Sacred Structure and have used that designation, literally and metaphorically, ever since. Admittedly, it is confusing in its quasi-religious ambiguity but is useful in radical planning. Yes, it is like the sacred in that these place attachments are deeply meaningful and people are willing to sacrifice some economic gains for them; but, no, it is not explicitly religious. The label "Sacred Structure" is provocative and continues to be a source of its power in community design. It is central to the twelve-step process we have developed to make affective relationship with place a legitimate part of civic decision making (Hester, 1984).

THE CIVIC FRONT PORCH: PAST THINKS FORWARD

With the consideration of people's place values and attachments, the new Manteo took a dramatically different form than standard urban landscapes. The sacred structure told us what to protect, like daily ritual places and fragile ecosystems encircling the city, and inspired city form. As one example, the waterfront park took shape from a gestalt inspired by seemingly mundane residential porches combined with a traditional value held dear by people in Manteo: turning bold visions into reality. "Come, sit on our front porch, let us tell you of the dreams we keep" expressed the essence of everyday life and civic imagination. Based on that, we designed a series of parks connected by a boardwalk as a civic front porch with details derived from behavior observations like "hanging out at the docks." It retains today an informality that welcomes teen rowdies, elderly in wheelchairs, long-term residents, and firsttime visitors. There are places for major celebrations and quiet solitude, for strolling and power walking, for affluent boaters to dock and subsistence fishermen to launch.

The front-porch boardwalk is the spine of the design, extending over a mile with businesses connected to boat building shops and rentals, museums, wetland restoration, rain gardens, and mixed-use residential neighborhoods. The Freedman's Colony, an all-Black Life Saving community, and a performing arts center are connected by a greenway wending its way through five ecosystems. Every spot looks and is homemade. There is no catalog-specified, corporate design here. Furnishings are hand crafted in a local furniture business. Local contractors and volunteer groups made the boardwalk that expresses their idiosyncrasies. The place feels distinctive as if it grew incrementally from its previous life, but there has been a firm commitment to the visionary framework expressed in zoning and urban design guidelines, codified as *The Manteo Way of Building* (Hester et al,2005).

Former Mayor John Wilson and Planning Board Chairman Bill Parker have stewarded their plan for five decades. Their affection for the place shows in every design detail from the use of local building materials to the careful shaping and reshaping of public spaces to accommodate daily rituals. Wise place attachment is central to this precedent-setting way of designing the city. With daring intentions counter to dominant formalist trends, the design for Manteo won widespread acclaim, becoming the poster child for grassroots community design. In recent years, I question whether community design is the most accurate description of this work. However labeled, Manteo is radical design, offering hope against the forces that make every place like every other place (Hester, 1990, 2006).

INSTRUCTIONS FROM MANTEO: SOME ATTACHED SUGGESTIONS FOR DESIGNERS

Over the ensuing decades we reconfirmed the design imperatives we had learned, recalling some of the most salient ones:

1   Develop a procedure particular to community building. The twelve steps begin by listening to people individually. Listen between the lines (Hester, 1984).

2   Draw existing patterns of daily life. Note why the activity occurs where it does. Draw activities that might be added in the future.

3   Search for undiscovered resources. We call these resources "fish heads" because in fishing communities local people know that fish heads and tails are usually thrown away, considered valueless. The secret to improving a town is often in making these waste products useful. Fish heads might include buildings in disrepair, unique skills of local residents or industrial by-products that offer exceptional opportunities for new economies.

4   Determine real needs. Dig deeply into the community subconscious to understand people's desires and fears that often are interwoven with place (Gans, 1962).

5   Find natively wise people with whom to test ideas. They are a rich source of the keenest insights and most creative designs (Liu, 2001).

6   Learn from poverty. This can direct you to locally intelligent design solutions—vernacular, unnerving, or magical.

7   Combine abstract science and phenomenological knowledge as one. Do not be distracted by seeming contradictions (Abram, 1997). Do not compromise irreconcilable oppositions of theory and experience, community and privacy, the global and the hearth, neighborhood and region, or the past and the future. Maximize both. For example, history and speculation, frequent themes of attachment and detachment, can create a powerful "progressive nostalgia" borrowing from tradition to create visionary change. Combining the public and domestic, past and future in Manteo led to the civic front porch that made Manteo's waterfront unique (Hester, 2007).

8   Deploy professional skills in ways that serve community. Develop enough knowledge of many disciplines to engage in ecolate thinking. Ecolate thinking requires considering the community—its history, social structure and values, politics, land, and natural processes—as a single whole ecological system. Over-specialization of professions makes this difficult.

9   Explore places of the heart. Let deep place values inspire you to imagine the unimaginable.

10   Shape the arena for innovative community design. Play whatever roles are necessary. Encourage creative conflict as well as cooperation.

11   Commit to the place longterm. That entitles you to be an aggressive participant. Nothing is more disrespectful than withholding your point of view. Make a fool of yourself being in love with place. Topophilia, like other love, risks being hurt.

12   Design back and forth with citizens. Draw what they say. Articulate their ideas. Help people evaluate your best design ideas by showing them as choices. Be open to rejection or elaboration (Hester, 2009).

13   Believe in participatory democracy. Shaping democracy is more precious than the most precious photogenic design (Lappé, 2009).

DETACHED MONSTERS AND ATTACHED WISHES

After the first phase of Manteo was completed, our firm, led by Marcia McNally, was continually called on to "do for us what you did in Manteo." Most publicized of this has been our work in Los Angeles where, since 1985, we have worked for the Santa Monica Mountains Conservancy to create "Big Wild," a greenbelt that now largely encircles the metropolis by land purchased through bond issues and taxes.

The central focus has been helping people reconnect with the joys and ecological processes of wildlife and reacquainting them with the place from which they are alienated by fear, technology, and comfort. Helping people become native to their place, Los Angeles has achieved an almost unthinkable big vision through incremental neighborhood-based actions. We stopped freeways and rebuilt mountains to connect enough habitat for the mountain lion to roam onto Hollywood Boulevard, and bring urban nature to communities throughout the Los Angeles basin. Along the way, we have made distinctive gateway parks from a former Nike Missile base, LA 96C, high in the mountains, to Parque Natural, the first urban wilderness park in the flats of South Central LA. Each was designed to develop strong bonds between people and their landscape (McNally, 1995).

Equally instructive has been our ongoing effort to save the black-faced spoonbill (*Platalea minor*, the rarest, most endangered of all spoonbill birds) from extinction. In Tainan County, Taiwan, a lagoon was scheduled to be filled for an industrial complex. Officials of Tainan County, one of the poorest regions of Taiwan, were eager for any development. The problem was that the lagoon provided 17,000 fishing-related jobs and was key to spoonbill survival. Local people were intensely attached to the place, but because it was stigmatized by poverty, they were vulnerable to virtual capital's allure. Reversing the stigma required legitimizing the local sacred structure. This empowered local people to choose a plan that grows from its existing fishing industries, adding an overlay of tourism. Place pride replaces stigma as the region now thrives. I will detail this at the end of this chapter.

Other projects have shown us the complexity of attachment in different cultures, forcing us to smile at how little we know. In Carroll County, Maryland, we employed our sacred places mapping for the EPA trying to improve water-quality upstream from the Chesapeake Bay, but a County Commissioner proclaimed that the sacred structure would create an "unholy mess." Place attachment was delegitimized and the effort was derailed as a result of this criticism of the heart of the matter. In contrast, at Camp 4 in Yosemite National Park, rock climbers claimed every boulder strewn around the camp by cherished name and accomplishment, eventually saving the camp from demolition by the Park Service. In 2003, it was listed on the National Register of Historic Places.

These cases provided unusual insights. Place attachments are tied to four basic wishes—for security, new experience, reciprocal response, and belonging (Thomas, 1923). With each wish are associated monsters, most notably fear, superficial thrill seeking, loss of nearness, and status seeking, respectively. If these are not recognized, they can indeed create an unholy mess, blocking our awareness of how place attachments inform place making. The wishes and monsters apparently are at war within our communities subconsciously because the monsters dominate our awareness. Therefore, the deep wishes related to place attachments must first be awakened. Unleashed from the community subconscious, there is often still skepticism, so evidence must be presented verifying their utility to decision-making. Once legitimized, place values can be transformed into a land use or development plan that reflects highest values and sacrifices less important ones. Usually, this process prepares the community to organize for action. Then these attachments can be manifested through design that champions a community's collective wishes and tames monsters. In all of our design projects, citizens have expressed a longing for community structure grounded in the four wishes. Their sacred places form a center, shape boundary by some natural landscape and express the unique character of a place that provides orientation, collective pride and identity, environmental distinction, and rootedness. This allows the community to inhabit the everyday sacred (Hester & Nelson, 2019).

REFLECTIONS: ENDEMIC DESIGN RISING

Discussing discoveries about place attachments, my closest colleagues in professional practice questioned what label best describes our work. It embraces folk, vernacular, and outsider traditions. Grassroots design neglects externalities. Participatory design has been coopted and never felt complete. Community design only satisfied me when it welcomed both Aldo Leopold and Dr. Martin Luther King, Jr. as democratic design requires a nuanced reading.

Recent projects led me to "endemic design." I will briefly define this and illustrate a continuum of endemic designs with ongoing projects using projects in Taiwan and North Carolina in the US. In ecology, an endemic species is one that only lives in that region; it is landscape restrained. It is well adapted to the environmental factors from geology to climate. It fits. It has a role. In social terms, endemic refers to characteristics prevalent, distinctive, or unique to a people in a region. This may include different architecture, language, economy, skills, customs, worldview, myths, beliefs, patterns of social interaction, land use, and attachments to the landscape. The culture critiques tradition for advantages and injustices and filters global forces for appropriateness. The local pattern language explicates an endemic gestalt, not universal but idiosyncratic (Alexander, 1977). There are universal wishes for center, natural boundary, and particularness, but there is a distinctive expression of these by locality. I called this the sacred structure; the artistic expression at the heart of this structure is endemic design. Capturing both the ecological and social endemic qualities as a single phenomenon expresses the essence of a place, makes intuitive sense and touches peoples' hearts, and, thereby creates meaningful design. It shapes a way for people to become native to their future.

Dong-Kang Banyan Trees: Before I ever visited the small Taiwanese fishing village of Dong-Kang, it was described to me by John Liu, with whom I have collaborated for over two decades, as a classic example of endemic design by the people. DongKang is located at the mouth of a river flowing to the Pacific Ocean. A dike was built to protect the townspeople from floods. As the dike arose, it created unmatched views of mountains to the east, ocean to the west; the river stretched the mind's eye from mountain to sea in great sensuous curves through the agricultural plain. People of all ages gathered on the dike on hot summer afternoons, catching the ocean breeze. "But the barren dike provided no shade. Elders collectively decided to plant a double row of banyan trees along the dike. Families in the village adopted individual seedlings, competing to nurture the trees to maturity." Some ten years later, when the trees were big enough, families made hammocks from used fishing nets and hung them between the trees. Attachments to the place grew over time. The tree-lined rows of hammocks became a most cherished place within the community, "celebrated throughout Taiwan as a distinctive, comfortable, pleasing spot." John points out that the residents created this special setting from their internal native wisdom without any help from designers (Liu, 2001). Although it is a contemporary undertaking, it seems to qualify as visionary folk design. It is likely that this design is endemic; it could only have evolved in this locale, in this climate, from these people with the particular needs and resources of their local culture at that point in time.

Shin Tsen Town Revival: The second case, also in Taiwan, was a collaboration between the west coastal community of Shin Tsen and a native landscape architect Fuchang Tsai; John and I played minor roles. For several hundred years, the inhabitants harvested salt from vast flats surrounding the town. Salt was so valuable that gun towers were constructed for armed guards to protect the salt pans from theft. But by the turn of the century imported salt replaced the local industry. Salt factories, warehouses, and gun towers fell into ruin. Young people left for work elsewhere. An elementary school, enrollment declining, faced closure. The abandoned salt pans invited only subsistence fishing as well as endemic, endangered, and migratory birds.

Fuchang initiated a community process to revive his town. When they mapped sacred places, the community focused on settings of great sentiment in need of new uses. They combined resources unique to their town—a half vacant school with an energetic principal, abandoned salt lands teeming with bird life, a former Toyota engineer who returned home to open an auto-repair shop across the street from the school and who created windmills and other green energy, skilled volunteers, and the Gods—to shape a bright future amidst a seemingly dismal prospect.

First, the elementary school curriculum was revised so that almost all subjects from math to reading are taught with hands-on research about salt pan wetland ecosystems; the black-faced spoonbill, the endangered bird mentioned before; horseshoe crabs, an endemic species once abundant, now extirpated; and green energy taught by the Toyota engineer. Telescopes allow students to monitor details of never-before-studied spoonbill behavior in the adjacent salt flat. They record horseshoe crab recovery in a wet lab and participate in the experiment to reintroduce the crabs into the wetland, led by a scholar of the prestigious Academia Sinica. The latest hand-crafted windmills and bike energy products spill out from classrooms into the town.

Second, advances in the management of wetland hydrology to increase biological diversity and minimize flooding risk have attracted a new economy and international attention. Hsiao-Wen Wang, a hydrologist at National Cheng Kung University, found dramatic seasonal fluctuations in bird life in the adjacent Budai salt pan; water-quality and depth determined biodiversity. The most endangered species could only feed in water four to twenty centimeters deep. Unless water levels could be managed, some species were likely to fall into an extinction vortex, but water gates had not functioned since the salt industry collapsed. With multiple public agencies and a few old timers who remembered how to operate the gates from years of working in the salt industry, Hsiao-Wen embarked on a campaign to reenlist the water gates (Wang et al, 2018). Controlling water levels seasonally has reduced flood damage and brought thousands of birds within viewing distance of the elementary school, creating an ecotourism bonanza.

Third, to create new job opportunities in ecotourism Fuchang, with a National Taiwan University team, led a participatory process to redesign a park overlooking the Budai salt ponds adjacent to the school. The highest priority was a bird-watching station, but townspeople resisted generic blinds prevalent in Taiwan and around the world. They sought something more expressive of Shin Tsen. After much deliberation they reimagined a gun tower similar to ones that had once protected the salt ponds. The tower hides bird watchers from disturbing the wild-life and provides an unusual elevated view of birds and the wetland ecosystem. Most important it captures the essence of the town's cultural roots and advances a new economy in one single-design action. However, the God of the local temple questioned the exact location of the first tower. Through an ancient ritual the God redrew the site plan, mobilizing community volunteers to construct the tower. It was instantly cherished as a symbol of the town's rebirth. This entire effort from the elementary school to water gates and gun tower is another case of endemic design, growing out of this place and people's attachments to the landscape in a form that could not have happened anywhere else.

Shorty Lawson Museum of the Black Tenant Farmer: During the past four years, I have created a "museum" as a tribute to the sharecropper described earlier. Cornell "Shorty" Lawson was born in Caswell County, North Carolina, March 5, 1938 (see Figure 13.3). He was a tenant farmer all of his life. For most of that time, he lived in the house on the Tom Bowes Farm that became the museum. He was widely known throughout the community for his honesty, sense of good and bad, his work ethic, his strength, his endurance, his capacity to make dignified things from scrap, his manly humanity, and the way he raised his children. Race constrained his fortune, but he did not let racism define him. As noted earlier, I farmed with him every day during the most formative period of my life. He taught me more about farming, hard work, race and class, caring, and enduring values than anyone else. He dispelled every racial stereotype of our time. He was the single hardest working man I have ever known. When we pulled tobacco, he worked two rows. I worked one, and he always met me coming back, helping me with my single row. He died in 1974.

After Shorty died, his house fell into disrepair. The oak sill rotted; the south wall collapsed. I didn't want his memory erased so I started repairing the house with discarded materials I found on the farm. That was how Shorty had once improved the place. I had no expectation to do anything more. But a neighbor stopped by and asked why I was working on the house, and without thinking,

Figure 13.3
This painting after
Dorothea Lange depicts
daily life during tobacco
season and expresses the
character for which Shorty
Lawson was so widely
respected.

I responded, "I'm making a museum for Shorty." That crystallized my subconscious intention.

Shorty's daughter Carolyn and I shared stories about her father. Family and neighbors offered memories of him. A film maker undertook a documentary. I mapped the family's sacred places and drew house and site plans to reconstruct the lost places. I content analyzed all the stories from which grew a concept: each room illustrates the daily life of Shorty's family from about 1950 until his death. But instead of furnishing each space as a history museum, we use outsider art combined with the text we wrote to explain Shorty's remarkable character. To history he was just another tenant farmer, but his story should not be forgotten. He lived by the seasons so one room tells of family life in summer (tobacco, illustrated with a painting of worming rows of the cash crop), fall (selling, buying, and repairing, illustrated by an old mule collar Shorty patched), winter (hog killing, shown in a painting by memory artist Bernice Sims), and spring (plowing, planting, and mating, depicted in a tin cutout "Mr. Rooster Tending the Chicks After His Wife Left Him" by outsider artist Buddy Snipes). Other rooms focus on food production; family values and fishing; work and prejudice; and snakes, God, and the Devil (see Figure 13.4).

Most of the rooms were left or repainted "Haint Blue" to keep ghosts away. Shorty had added two rooms as he had more expendable income so we painted those rooms gallery white to better display the art depicting tenant farming. The art is primarily done by untrained African American artists who created folk, visionary or resistance works during the Jim Crow era up to the present. Many of these artists had been southern tenant farmers themselves so their paintings capture the detail and passion of Shorty's life. Works by Willie Jinks, Mama Johnson, Thornton

Figure 13.4
The Lawsons consider
these years as the best
time of their lives; the
museum contrasts
hardships and pleasures.
Fish Time by Willie
Jinks captures a joy still
reenacted each summer.

Dial, Mose Tolliver, Mary T. Smith, and Purvis Young express the essence of chores and emotions the Lawsons experienced. They make you sweat in July heat, delight when a big fish hits your hook, and fly back to Africa on the wings of an owl. Eula Parris' paintings show not only harsh everyday life but also how the landscape itself felt. Benny Grinstead carved mules at work that are more like mules at work than live mules at work. Charlie Lucas created the touching Lawson Family Portrait as a present for the museum; Joe Minter gifted a magnificent African Queen (see Figure 13.5).

Shorty's wife Annie and older daughter Carolyn cooked on both a wood stove and an electric one. They had electricity but no well. Water had to be fetched from the Big House across the Tom Bowes Road. Shorty's invention to collect rain water to wash clothes is shown in a Wringer washer, and the bucket to wash hair is depicted in a painting by Black Joe Jackson as both extreme hardship and creative solution. Many of the family's most cherished places were outside the house. In recent months, we have rebuilt the woodshed, smokehouse, outhouse and basketball goal, repaired tobacco barns, laid out garden, clothes line, hog lot, and chicken coop. This project, like those in Taiwan, exemplifies endemic design. This "museum" could not have emerged in this form under any other cultural, environmental, and personal circumstances. It testifies to deep attachments to people and place.

Black Wall Street Garden: When I lived in the Durham area forty years ago, race defined the public debate. It still does, shaping endemic design, less in terms of freeways and clearance projects and more in the memory of how racial stigma twisted attachments to place. Memory of loss encircles every new battle. Negro Removal has evolved, now removing the mostly Black underclass for downtown revitalization.

Figure 13.5
Visitors to the museum are confronted with not only daily life without running water but also Shorty's creativity to overcome the limitations.

In this context Marcia McNally and I have led the protection and redesign of a central city open space cherished by a great diversity of users and properly called the most democratic place in downtown. Among the diversity are marginal groups (e.g., homeless or near-homeless AfricanAmericans), whom the City targeted for removal. The Mayor acknowledged that he did not want "those people" in "his" downtown. To explain this attitude requires history.

Durham arose from a railroad stop to become the gritty, industrial "Cigarette Capital of the World," low wages, bluecollar, and Black. As a post–Civil War city, it is an experiment in racial negotiation. W. E. B. de Bois and Booker T. Washington praised Durham for its independent and robust Black economy largely free from racial intimidation, a place where Washington noted he had never seen so many prosperous Negroes (Brown,2008). Black and White capitalists thrived during Jim Crow segregation with support from Trinity College, Methodism, and free enterprise values. Black-owned banking, insurance, trades, and services created what came to be called Black Wall Street, remnants of which remain today. Durham hosted debates about the direction of the Civil Rights Movement featuring Martin Luther King Jr., Floyd McKissick, and Malcolm X. Dr. King was scheduled to speak in Durham the day he was murdered in Memphis. In contrast to Raleigh, Black and White leaders partnered to destroy the Black neighborhoods for a freeway and urban renewal clearance. Malcolm X Liberation was founded in 1969; the "Best of Enemies" negotiated desegregation in 1971.

At one point, over 200 billion cigarettes were produced annually in North Carolina, mostly in Durham. The city's stigma as the ugly step-sister of nearby Raleigh and Chapel Hill was exacerbated when the tobacco industry left the city (Leonard, 2015). Thousands lost their jobs, expanding a lingering divide between the haves and the have nots. Millions of square feet of brick factory buildings sat empty. Downtown businesses went belly up.

Fast forward to 2000. The corporate research economy outgrew Raleigh and the Research Triangle Park and discovered Durham's vacant tobacco factories, perfect for creative economy start-ups. Repurposing the infrastructure from the city of cigarettes, Durham reinvented itself as the "City of Medicine." Downtown Durham became "cool." A coalition of Black professionals and White progressives steered the politics of the "free-market-with-city-subsidy" reinvention, pushing the underclass out. This leads us to the battle over the park. In this half-acre oasis religious groups feed the homeless, jobless people hang out, Latino workers take breaks, residential newcomers walk dogs, and start-ups are venture capitalized. Each is attached to the place for their own use and for the diversity it represents. But a business in an adjacent building claimed the public open space for a restaurant. City officials encouraged the proposal and led a process to gain approval to replace the homeless with the upscale eatery. Marcia successfully organized opposition to the privatization, created a citizen-led process to claim the park for the public in perpetuity, and invited anyone interested to a series of on-site workshops to make a long-term plan for the park. After spirited debate the competing groups supported making the park more welcoming for all publics as an expression of Durham's deepest values. The restaurant has outdoor seating along Main Street, not in the park. The area for homeless services is expanded. Lighting encourages night use. A large free play area, a centering square, and porch swings invite new uses. Moveable chairs and tables facilitate temporary claims on shady spots created by extensive replanting. To acknowledge the painful history and present struggles of race, class, and gender inequality, the primary walkway curves north to south, east to west as the arc of the universe bending ever so slowly toward justice. Viewed as racist, what was previously called Chicken-bone Park was renamed Black Wall Street Garden. The design of Black Wall Street Garden, too, is endemic. It acknowledges racism, confronts exclusion, and turns toward inclusion in a distorted arc unique to Durham. This park, with this name, in this form, addressing these issues of history, race, and class, could only be made in Durham.

REATTACHED

The measure of place attachment in our community design practice is the sacred structure. As described in the cases, sacredness is most central to our work. Centeredness, limited extent, and particularness are the next most central factors. Each is related to place attachment, but each has multiple functions beyond attachment. Detachment from community must also be countered. Centeredness addresses retreat from civic life. Limited extent and particularness attend to critical issues of equity, community, and sustainability (Hester, 2006).

To address detachment requires both theoretical and phenomenological knowledge.

We have to keep multiple, mutually exclusive ideas firmly in our heads at once. The sun rises every day, and, of course, the sun never rises. Oppositions must be maximized, not compromised. Place attachments are critical to community because they usually mark values that cross lines of class, ethnicity, age and gender, clarify contested values, and point out community neglect.

Community building is a process that requires a setting, and the shape of that setting is critical. Design matters (Hester, 1985b). This returns me to endemic design. Of our earlier work, Chavis Heights, Dana Park, Aurora, Manteo, LA96C, and Camp 4 exemplify endemic design. Recent projects make me aware of how we strive to uncover factors that make a place most distinctive and develop futures that grow from those forces of uniqueness. The above cases suggest that endemic designs fall along several continuums. One is the degree of designer involvement. Another is the extent to which deep values rather than status or power-seeking, guide the design. A third is how attached or unattached people are to their place. A fourth is the ways conflicting values are acknowledged and resolved. Another is how completely the uniqueness of a place is expressed. There are likely others. Exploring endemic design further will be fruitful. As I do that, I am comforted knowing that deep attachment and reattachment create city form that is distinct to a region, a people, and a time. These are critical to healthy identity and joyful survival.

REFERENCES

Abram, D. (1997). *The spell of the sensuous*. New York: Vintage Books.

Alexander, C. (1977). *A pattern language*. New York: Oxford University Press.

Appleyard, D. (1981). *Livable streets*. Berkeley: University of California Press.

Brown, L. (2008). *Upbuilding black Durham*. Chapel Hill: University of North Carolina Press.

Coles, R. (1964). *Children of crisis*. New York: Dell Publishing Company.

Gans, H. (1962). *The urban villagers*. New York: Free Press.

Hester, R. (1972). Student advocacy in Raleigh and the community development process. *Landscape Architecture, 62*(4), 331–334.

Hester, R. (1975). *Neighborhood space*. Stroudsburg: Dowden, Hutchinson and Ross.

Hester, R. (1979). A womb with a view: How spatial nostalgia affects the designer. *Landscape Architecture, 69*(5), 475–481, 528.

Hester, R. (1984). *Planning neighborhood space with people*. New York: Van Nostrand Reinhold.

Hester, R. (1985a). Subconscious landscapes of the heart. *Places, 2*(3), 10–22.

Hester, R. (1985b). Landstyles and lifescapes: 12 Steps to community development. *Landscape Architecture, 75*(1), 78–85.

Hester, R. (1990). *Community design primer*. Mendocino: Ridge Times Press.

Hester, R. (2006). *Design for ecological democracy*. Cambridge: MIT Press.

Hester, R. (2007). Reciprocal and recombinant geometries of ecological democracy. *Places, 19*(1), 68–77.

Hester, R. (2009). No representation without representation. In M. Treib (Ed.), *Representing landscape architecture* (pp. 96–111). London: Routledge.

Hester, R., & Nelson, A. (2019). *Inhabiting the sacred in everyday life*. Charlottesville: George F. Thompson Publishing.

Hester, R., McNally, M., & Berney, R. (2005). *The Manteo way of building*. Berkeley: Community Development by Design.

Lappé, F. M. (2009). *Liberation ecology*. Cambridge: Small Planet Media.

Leonard, T. (July 20, 2015). North Carolina once led in cigarette manufacturing. *The News and Observer*. https://www.newsobserver.com/living/liv-columns-blogs/past-times/article27906262.html

Liu, J. (2001). A continuing dialogue on local wisdom in participatory design. *Building cultural diversity through participation* (pp. 444–450). Taipei: Building and Planning Research Foundation, National Taiwan University.

Marcus, C. C. (1995). *House as a mirror of self: Exploring the deeper meaning of home*. Berkeley: Conari Press.

McNally, M. (1995). Making Big Wild. *Places*, *9*(3), 38–45.

Relph, E. (1976). *Place and placelessness*. London: Pion.

Thomas, W. I. (1923). The unadjusted girl: With cases and standpoint for behavior analysis. *Criminal Science Monographs*, *4*, 4–32.

Tuan, Y. F. (1974). *Topophilia: A study of environmental perception, attitudes and values*. Englewood Cliffs: Prentice Hall.

Wang, H. W., Dodd, A., Kuo, P. H., & LePage, B. (2018). Science as a bridge in communicating needs and implementing changes towards wetland conservation in Taiwan. *Wetlands*, *38*(6), 1223–1232.

Chapter 14: Dynamics of place attachment in a climate changed world

Patrick Devine-Wright and Tara Quinn

INTRODUCTION

Climate change is causing significant environmental impacts across the globe as evidenced by rising temperatures, melting sea-ice, rising sea levels, coastal flooding, and an increase in extreme weather events. These are, in turn, causing significant changes to the fabric of the places where people live, work, and take leisure, and consequently to the emotional attachments associated with such places. Yet our understanding of how place attachments may be affected by climatic changes, or how they may inform an understanding of human responses to such changes remains in its infancy. Accordingly, this chapter has two aims: first, to critically review the ways in which the dynamics of place attachments have been theorized and empirically researched in the literature; second, to discuss the application of this body of knowledge about place attachment to the subject of climate change, encompassing both mitigation and adaptation.

DYNAMICS OF PLACE ATTACHMENT

Giuliani (2002) noted that place attachment refers both to a process of attachment *and* to the outcome of that process (i.e., an emotional bond). Yet despite this, most studies have adopted a theoretical perspective, and a methodological approach, which has focused upon uncovering aspects of the attachment bond itself rather than aiming to reveal aspects of the process of attaching or detaching oneself from a place(s) over time.

Hay (1998) commented that "in modern, Western society people tend to shift places often through residential mobility, and the places themselves change rapidly through economic development and migration. A mosaic of places thus influences most people over the course of a lifetime"(Hay, 1998, p.6; see also Manzo, 2005). It is becoming rare for individuals to die in the same location where they were born (see Lewicka, chapter 4 this volume) and writers on place for several decades have critically commented upon the ways that places have changed for the worse as a result of so-called "development" (e.g., Day, 2002). Despite this generalized observation of the cultural and economic context in which most place

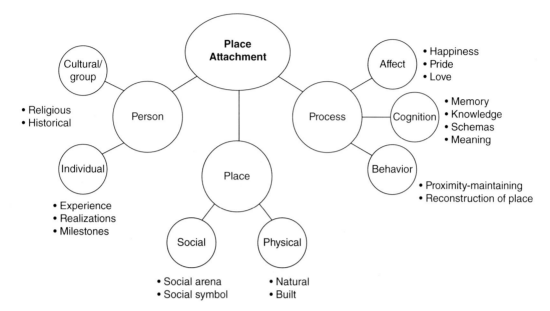

Place Attachment

Cultural/group
• Religious
• Historical

Person

Individual
• Experience
• Realizations
• Milestones

Place

Social
• Social arena
• Social symbol

Physical
• Natural
• Built

Process

Affect
• Happiness
• Pride
• Love

Cognition
• Memory
• Knowledge
• Schemas
• Meaning

Behavior
• Proximity-maintaining
• Reconstruction of place

Figure 14.1
The tri-partite model of place attachment. Source: Scannell and Gifford (2010).

attachment research has been conducted (i.e., in Western, industrialized societies), there has been a tendency to presume stasis rather than dynamism as the default when conceptualizing place attachment (DiMasso et al, 2019; Williams and Miller, this volume).

This is manifest by "structural" approaches to theorizing place attachment and related concepts. Two examples could be cited. First, Scannell and Gifford (2010) proposed a conceptual framework (see Figure 14.1) that "proposes that place attachment is a multidimensional concept with person, psychological process, and place dimensions" (Scannell & Gifford, 2010, p.2). In the framework, although "process" is identified as a relevant aspect of place attachment, it is structurally separated from "place" and "person" components, as if these latter aspects are less processual in and of themselves.

A second example is an influential elaboration of the concept of place identity that treats place attachment as a sub-component of the self-concept (Proshansky, Fabian & Kaminoff, 1983) that is distinguished by its content-specific information about everyday environmental contexts: "a sub-structure of the identity of a person consisting of cognitions about the physical world in which the individual lives. These cognitions represent memories, ideas, feelings, attitudes, values, preferences, meanings and conceptions of behavior and experience which relate to the variety and complexity of physical settings that define day to day existence of every human being"(Proshansky et al, 1983, p.59).

Although both frameworks help to identify and organize aspects of a disparate literature, they underplay the dynamism of people-place relations, saying little about how individuals and groups cope with change to the physical fabric of places or the consequences of relocation.

A similar criticism can be made of attempts to typologize place attachments or people-place relations. Lewicka (2011b) proposed multiple varieties of people-place relations encompassing types such as inherited attachment or "rootedness," active or "ideological" place attachment, placelessness, relativity, and alienation. Although the identification of types is useful to capture the diversity of ways in which people relate to place, and to call attention to neglected areas of research, they nonetheless say relatively little about whether these types are static or dynamic phenomena.

These problems with how place attachment and related concepts have been theorized are also manifest by methodological aspects of empirical research. An overwhelming majority of place attachment studies adopt a cross-sectional research design, regardless of whether they employ qualitative or quantitative methods. Studies with a longitudinal design, which arguably can allow at least temporal dynamism to emerge, are rare (see Chow & Healey, 2008; Korpela, Ylen, Tyrväinen,& Silvennoinen, 2009 for exceptional cases). To our knowledge, there have been no studies conducted to date investigating place attachment over a temporal period greater than twelve months, a point that remains true since the first edition of this book was published. Many quantitative studies infer causal relations amongst variables by measuring the strength of association between these variables using single-time data. However, single time studies are unable to reveal whether these change over time. Increased use of in-depth qualitative methods such as biographical interviews (e.g., Morgan, 2010) would help to ascertain reported change over time, as would more prevalent use of longitudinal research designs.

EXISTING THEORY AND RESEARCH ON THE DYNAMICS OF PLACE ATTACHMENT

Theoretically, processes of continuity and change lie at the root of place attachment. An ongoing dialectic between stability/change was observed by Brown & and Perkins (1992) in addressing disruptions to place attachment and by Manzo (2005) in examining mobility and connections to a range of places. Similarly, the notion of continuity with the past has been described as a "guiding principle" in studies of place-related identity processes (e.g., Devine-Wright & Lyons, 1997), referring to how individuals are motivated to maintain connections between their past, present, and future when narrating a sense of self (see Droseltis & Vignoles, 2010; Lewicka, chapter 4 this volume).

Although the predominant approach to place attachment has been static rather than dynamic, nevertheless examples can be found of studies where change has been foregrounded. These studies can be simply classified in terms of whether their focus is upon changes to people (e.g., linked to life-course development; impacts of personal mobility) or changes to places (e.g., arising from natural disasters or legal designation).

In terms of changes to people, several researchers have adopted a developmental approach, arguing that place attachment literature should be better informed about research findings on attachment that draw upon Bowlby's theory (1969). Hay (1998), for example, proposed three phases of attachments to place: embryonic (childhood to adolescent), commitment (early to mid-adulthood), and culmination (mid-adulthood to old age). Morgan (2010) used in-depth interviews to probe adults' remembrance of childhood place experience, including places deemed special to them, to reveal that "repeated enactments of the arousal-interaction-pleasure pattern generate an internal working model of the child's relationship with environment, which manifests consciously as a long-term affective bond to that environment known as place attachment" (p.18). A consistent theme of inquiry has been to elucidate ways that attachments to places may be informed by our understanding of attachments to individuals and how these change over time (see Scannell, Williams, Gifford and Sarich, chapter 3 this volume).

Studies of personal mobility have explored the impacts of residential or workplace change, with a recurrent interest in whether greater mobility leads to weaker attachments to place (e.g., Gustafson, 2001, 2014). Feldman (1990) drew on qualitative interviews to propose the concept of "settlement identity" in order to capture the ways in which frequently relocating individuals preserve a sense of continuity in their lives by opting to move between similar types of settlements (e.g., a village or a city). Yet this concept has not been markedly taken up by subsequent researchers over the past two decades.

Bailey et al (2016) shed further light on the interactions between place attachments and residential mobility through a study of individuals living in a UK rural town impacted by proposals to construct a power line. Their novel contribution was to view current attachments to the town (and responses to the power line) in light of each individual's life-course or "life-place trajectory," using in-depth interviews. Five types of trajectory were identified: (1) long-term residency in a single place, (2) return to the home place (when a person leaves their childhood place upon reaching adulthood, has a negative experience in the new place, and returns to the "home" place), (3) residential mobility with continuity in settlement type (involving moves from one place to another of a similar type, e.g., from one city to another city), (4) residential mobility with discontinuity in settlement type (involving moves from one place to another of a different type, e.g., from a city to small town), and (5) high residential mobility. Each type was associated with a different variety of attachment to the current place (Lewicka, 2011b).Trajectory types 1 and 2 were associated with "inherited" or largely taken-for-granted place attachment; type 3 was associated with "active" attachment, when the distinct characteristics of a place are intentionally sought and valued by incomers; type 4 was associated with "ambivalence" and "alienation," when individuals felt "out of place" in contrast to their settlement identities; and type 5 when attachment to a place was not relevant or important to the person.

Further understanding of how different forms of mobility and place attachment inter-relate was provided by Di Masso et al (2019) who regarded place attachment as involving a dialetical relationship between "fixity" and "flow." They propose a novel framework to better understand interactions between mobilities and place attachment, involving states of disruption, contradiction, complementarity, integration, and virtual and imaginative travel.

Places themselves can change in numerous ways, with consequent implications for emotional attachments. Legal designations change, for example, when areas become designated as environmentally protected (e.g., Bonaiuto, Carrus, Martorella, & Bonnes, 2002). Their social milieu can change, for example, arising from an influx of newcomers (e.g., Dixon & Durrheim, 2000) and their physical/material fabric can change, for example, when new developments are proposed. Of primary importance in understanding the impacts of such changes are the dimensions of extent, rapidity, and control, with changes to places of large extent, high rapidity, and low control associated with the greatest disruption to place attachment (Devine-Wright, 2009).

The literature has revealed some of the negative impacts on place attachments of changes to places. Fullilove (2004, this volume) coined the term "root shock" to describe how ill health can ensue from forced relocation. Brown and Perkins (1992) proposed the concept of "disruption" to place attachment, emphasizing the negative outcomes of events such as burglary or environmental disasters. Fried (2000) and Manzo (2008, 2014) have researched the experiences of communities experiencing forced relocation arising from the demolition of urban housing projects in the US.

Whilst the outcomes of certain forms of change are appropriately referred to as being negative (e.g., feelings of grief, Fried, 2000; loss of social networks, Speller & Twigger-Ross, 2009), the literature could be taken as suggesting that changes to places are necessarily and always disruptive to place attachment. Manzo (2014) provides an important contribution to describe some of the ways in which changes to places can have negative *and* positive impacts for people. Yet what remains overlooked is a systematic treatment of situations where changes to places are associated with positive emotional responses and outcomes. An example is Devine-Wright's (2011a) study of a tidal energy project where local residents who were strongly attached to the place expressed strongest support for the technology. Qualitative analyses of focus group discussions revealed a sense of pride that their place had been "put on the map worldwide," boosting perceptions of local distinctiveness. The study shows that place change—admittedly of a form that was neither extensive nor rapid—is not necessarily disruptive or threatening and can have place-enhancing outcomes, depending upon how it is interpreted and evaluated by those experiencing change.

Several studies have proposed conceptual frameworks incorporating stages of change over time. Brown and Perkins (1992) suggested that the process of disruption to place attachment involves stages of pre-disruption (that can include preparatory strategies of preparing oneself to become detached from a place),

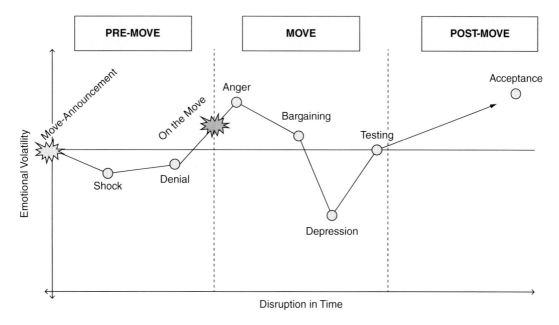

PRE-MOVE   MOVE   POST-MOVE

Emotional Volatility

Move-Announcement

On the Move

Shock

Denial

Anger

Bargaining

Testing

Depression

Acceptance

Disruption in Time

Figure 14.2
Emotional volatility
versus disruption in time.
Source: Inalhan and
Finch(2004).

disruption, and post-disruption (that can include processes of becoming attached to a new place or attempting to retain existing place attachments). Although these kinds of anticipatory and responsive processes have been corroborated by longitudinal empirical research (e.g., Chow & Healey's 2008 study of the experiences of students leaving home to go to university), the details of anticipatory and responsive processes in place attachments remain comparatively under-researched.

Inalhan and Finch (2004) proposed a conceptual framework of workplace relocation (see Figure 14.2) that is similar to Brown and Perkins (1992) in distinguishing three stages of change: pre-move, move, and post-move, but they add richness by adapting a model of coping drawn from literature on grieving that proposes a sequential order to emotional responses to change over time, encompassing shock, denial, anger, bargaining, depression, testing, and finally acceptance. The model is useful for describing the emotional correlates of physical change to places over time that are negatively perceived and suggests some similarities between the experience of workplace and residential relocation. However, the framework can be criticized regarding the presumed order in which discrete emotions are said to be felt in response to change (why depression after anger after denial, for example?) and for presuming that the normative outcome of "acceptance" of grief can be validly translated to the context of workplace relocation. Arguably, the model also underplays the politics of change to places and how collective actions can successfully obstruct attempts to relocate employees or prevent unwanted changes to the fabric of places.

A third stages of change framework was proposed to understand individual and collective responses to the siting of large-scale low carbon energy technologies (e.g., wind farms). Devine-Wright (2009) proposed five stages

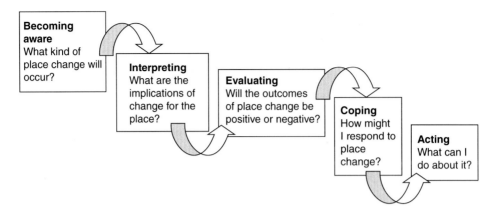

Figure 14.3
Stages of psychological response over time to place change.
Source: Devine-Wright (2009).

(see Figure 14.3) that reflect a social constructivist perspective in which understanding how proposals for change are rendered meaningful becomes an important goal of the research. Each stage is conceived at multiple levels of analysis, from intrapersonal to socio-cultural. It suggests that change can be multiply interpreted and may not be perceived as negative. The five stages include becoming aware of change, interpreting the meaning of such change for people and places, evaluating whether change will be positive or negative, coping with change (including acts of denial or avoidance), and acting (including collective acts of opposition dubbed "place-protective action").

Linking the model to place attachment specifically, it was argued that individuals holding strong attachments to a place affected by proposals for change would be more likely to attend to and respond to such changes (Devine-Wright, 2009). Empirical research has indicated significant relationships between strength of place attachment and evaluations of proposals to construct offshore wind farms, tidal energy devices, and power lines (Devine-Wright & Howes, 2010; Devine-Wright, 2011a,). Nevertheless, the model is more successful in providing a framework for representing how place changes are understood than in providing a means of better understanding the dynamics of place attachment *per se*. Place attachment is largely taken for granted within the framework, rather than something that is likely to be continually influencing and influenced by place change.

Stedman (2002, p. 577) notes that "we are willing to fight for places that are central to our identities... this is especially true when important symbolic meanings are threatened by prospective change". Yet this observation is most likely in situations where individuals feel both a strong sense of place attachment *and* feel empowered to contest proposals for change. In circumstances where individuals feel little control over how decisions are made or when individuals feel little attachment to a place, such a "fight" is less likely to occur. Once change has occurred, whether contested or not, it is possible that individuals with strong attachment to a place will be those most likely to contemplate leaving to live elsewhere if they feel that the ensuing changes have created a place that has lost its personal meaning or character. Future research can pay close attention to issues of control over place change, as well as the links between literature on strength of place attachment and varieties of people-place relations (Lewicka, 2011b). For example, alienation from a place may be the outcome of change for individuals who formerly felt strong attachments to that place. Future research that tracks both changes to a place and changes to attachments to that place over time will offer the most suitable basis for investigating these hypotheses in a systematic manner.

PLACE ATTACHMENT IN A CLIMATE CHANGED WORLD

Changes to climate will lead to changes to the places where people live, work, and take leisure. Two broad categories of change can be identified: (1) forms of change that are direct "natural" manifestations of climatic change (e.g., more frequent extreme weather events), and (2) human responses to these climatic changes. This latter category encompasses two strands: (1) responses that are designed to enable adaptation of communities and societies to climatic change (e.g., the relocation of communities away from coastal areas), and (2) responses that are designed to mitigate climate change (e.g., by developing low carbon energy technologies such as wind farms). To understand the relevance of place attachments to climate change adaptation and mitigation requires discussion of whether place attachments enable or constrain adaptation, and how place attachments are implicated in the politics of climate change mitigation.

Adger, Barnett, Chapin, and Ellemer (2011) observed disruptions to climate, culture, and livelihoods amongst communities living on Pacific Atolls such as Kiribati and Arctic communities such as the Inuit people in Alaska. Drawing upon qualitative fieldwork, Adger et al (2011) point out the ways that climatic changes have impacted upon traditional knowledge and skills (e.g., hunting and gathering of marine mammals) weakening ties to land and sea, and how the managed relocation of such communities will lead to a loss of cultural diversity as well as personal suffering. These impacts, caused by developed countries' emissions of greenhouse gases, are presented as cases of environmental injustice that are typically underemphasized or ignored by climate change policy and science. In a similar vein, a multi-method study by Cunsolo Willox et al (2012) in Rigolet, Canada, identified how disruptions to place attachment arising from changes in hunting, foraging, and traveling resulted in negative impacts on the physical, mental, and emotional health of an Inuit community. A subsequent longitudinal assessment outlined how changes in the land, snow, ice, and weather elicited feelings of anxiety, fear, and depression (Cunsolo Willox et al, 2013).

Such impacts raise important questions for research on place attachment, for example, whether individuals living in Western countries perceive climate change impacts in their own "backyards" or only in distant places such as Pacific Atolls, and what role attachments to place play in influencing whether they perceive or respond to such changes, whether local or distant. Gurney et al (2017) used a survey to study place attachment to the Great Barrier Reef in Australia amongst individuals living across Australia and internationally. Findings revealed that place attachment can stretch beyond the local to iconic places distant from the residence place. The study used cluster analysis to identify four types of community ("Armchair enthusiast," "Reef connected," "Reef user," and "Reef disconnected") that differed in their attachment to the reef, and that span physical distance from and types of interaction with the Great Barrier Reef. The findings demonstrate how people can feel attachments to distant places and suggests that place attachments could play a role in developing global stewardship of areas vulnerable to climate change.

Scannell and Gifford (2013) used a quasi-experimental design to investigate the impacts of place attachment and diverse spatial framings ("local" impacts vs. "global" impacts) on participants' levels of climate change engagement. The study involved the distribution of different versions of a questionnaire with images and texts conveying either "local" or "global" framings of climate change, or a control condition in which no information was presented. Regression analysis revealed that heightened levels of climate engagement were explained by the following explanatory factors: stronger place attachment, the presentation of information about local climate impacts, the interaction between these two factors, longer length of residence, and female gender.

These findings suggest the importance of future climate change studies to capture not just "localized" attachments to place, but also attachments at non-local scales from national to global (Devine-Wright, 2013b). Devine-Wright, Leviston, and Price (2015) and Devine-Wright and Batel (2017) used a survey method to study the relationship between attachments at local, national, and global levels (i.e., attachment to the Earth or planet as a whole) and people's views about climate change and energy transitions in Australia and the UK. Findings show an inverse relationship between national and global attachments in relation to climate change. Individuals with stronger national attachments were less likely to accept climate change as a human-caused phenomenon, in contrast to individuals with stronger global attachments.

Research investigating the role of place attachment in adaptation to climate change raises important questions, particularly whether place attachment should be regarded as disabling or preventing coping with changes to a place. Such a viewpoint has been expressed by Marshall, Fenton, Marshall, and Sutton (2007) and Marshall et al. (2012) arising from studies investigating resource-dependent communities in Eastern Australia. Findings indicated that people with strong levels of place attachment were less willing to learn new employment related skills or to be willing to relocate elsewhere (Marshall et al, 2007,2012). This refers not only to place attachments but also to occupational roles and identities, since both are inter-woven for these communities in ways suggesting some similarities with the atoll and Arctic communities researched by Adger et al (2011).

Marshall and colleagues' critical evaluation of place attachment is at odds with a longstanding tendency amongst place attachment scholars to view attachments to place as self-evidently a "good thing" (e.g., Relph, 1976; although see Manzo,

2003, 2005 for a contrary view). Clearly there are other ways of viewing place attachment and its implications, most notably the exclusionary practices noted by Fried (2000) when referring to tendencies for place attachments to be associated with distinctions between "us" and "them" and who has a rightful claim to live in a place. This is also suggested by Dixon and Durrheim's (2000; see also Di Masso, Dixon and Durrheim, this volume) research in post-apartheid South Africa where white residents evoked attachments to place when complaining about an influx of black people. Given these findings, future research could put more emphasis upon ways that attachments are implicated in exclusionary or maladaptive practices.

The Intergovernmental Panel on Climate Change (IPCC) describes adaptation as the "process of adjustment to actual or expected climate and its affects. In human systems, adaptation seeks to moderate or avoid harm or exploit beneficial opportunities" (IPCC, 2014, pp.117–130). Using the IPCCs definition, if the action people and communities take to adapt result in avoided or reduced harm, the adaptation action can be regarded as successful. Conversely, this means that any ways in which place attachments prevent optimal avoidance of harm means that they act to constrain adaptation. The ways in which people and societies are adapting are manifold, and we know that place attachment shapes predisposition to take adaptive action: constraining mobility in the face of environmental stress (Adams,2016), shaping support for infrastructure that reduces flood risk (Quinn et al, 2019), and in some cases reducing willingness to diversify livelihoods in the face of changing weather patterns (Marshall et al, 2016).

The necessity for adaptation to climate change can result in extensive changes to the fabric of local places (e.g., the construction of defenses such as flood walls, altered household living arrangements, changing land use, resettlement away from coastal areas), raising questions about whether such change is socially acceptable. Harries (2017) suggests that the reason why some people do not adapt their living spaces or businesses to potential hazard risk is because they are perceived as threats to ontological security, defined as the belief that life will continue much as it always has. Adaptation to climate hazards such as floods or fires require changes to everyday life such as changed flooring, altered doors, bolted furniture, and so on. Such alterations to familiar places challenge ontological security and are a constant reminder that one's home place is insecure. Therefore, from an everyday wellbeing perspective it may be rational to *not* adapt, in order for a place to continue to feel fundamentally secure. Harries suggests that when considering adaptation interventions, it is important that such measures be designed to not emphasize awareness of hazards. Such tradeoffs between managing hazard risk and everyday wellbeing will become more pertinent with increasingly severe climatic changes. How much change are we willing to see in our local areas to adapt to climate risks before such place change drastically undermines wellbeing? Who gets to determine when a threshold of unacceptable change has been reached? And, going forward, how can such change processes be managed?

As the contribution of place attachment to wellbeing becomes better defined (Scannell & Gifford, 2017), we are better able to understand how climate change will impact psychological health. In his 2005 study, Knez (2005) outlined how local climate contributes to place related meaning, highlighting its role in place continuity, and shaping one's memory of a place over the lifecourse. In a climatically changing world, such continuities will be challenged. For example, research on the impact of changing weather patterns on farmers' wellbeing in Australia found that shifting weather patterns challenged farmers' sense of self-identity, contributing to cumulative and chronic forms of place-based distress and mental health issues, including depression (Ellis & Albrecht, 2017). Walker-Springett et al's (2017) work on flood events and wellbeing in England identified how attachment to one's home-shaped residents' wellbeing in the eighteen months after the floodwaters had receded. Participants in the study described how evacuation, staying in unfamiliar accommodations, and dealing with builders during the recovery collectively undermined feelings of home and security in the period after the floods.

Climate change mitigation involves actions to reduce the emission of greenhouse gases into the atmosphere, notably avoiding the use of fossil-fuel energy resources (i.e., coal, gas, and oil) and replacing them with renewable energy resources (e.g., solar, wind, hydro). While such actions are vital for collective response to climate change, mitigation produces unintended consequences that have significant implications for place attachments. Proposals to site low carbon energy infrastructure, from wind farms to high voltage power lines, have been associated with social conflict in many locations around the world. In such contexts, changes to place arise directly from human decision-making and are open to contestation and outright opposition. Such opposition, often simplistically referred to as "NIMBYism" (Devine-Wright, 2005), should not be easily presumed to be a maladaptive response to climate change, since it is possible that technology proposals are poorly thought through (Bauer, 1995) and the act of pejoratively labeling those who protest merely serves to close down debate and overlook potentially important, place-relevant values (Devine-Wright, 2011b).

Devine-Wright (2013a) has shown that in such contexts, the variety of place attachment (see Lewicka, 2011b) held by local residents can influence their willingness to accept energy technologies in that place. A study of responses to power line proposals in the town of Nailsea in South West England showed no association between "inherited" place attachment and responses to the power line, but a significant and negative association between "active" place attachment and levels of acceptance. This was manifest not only in residents' attitudes to the power line, but by their behavioral responses as well—actively attached individuals were more likely to report attending meetings organized by a local protest group and making donations to the group (Devine-Wright, 2013a).

Similar findings were obtained by Bailey et al (2016) in a follow-up study in the same location. Interviews revealed that long-standing residents who expressed "inherited" or taken-for-granted place attachment were more likely to accept the new power line, viewing it as similar to other infrastructure that had already been in the landscape for decades. By contrast, recent incomers who were also strongly attached to the place, but who expressed a more "active," conscious form of attachment to the place were less likely to accept the power line, viewing it as spoiling or "industrializing" the natural landscape of the area. Finally, the study revealed that individuals with ambivalent or alienated relationships to the local area were also likely to object to the power line but differed from the "actively attached" residents by using arguments that were not about negative impacts to the place, but were instead about the fairness of decision-making.

These findings point to an important political dimension to processes of place change that is often overlooked in the literature on place attachment, aspects that are much more visible in writings by human geographers who for many years have been interested in documenting imbalances of power between local residents and development companies or decision-makers (see, e.g., Dalby & Mackenzie, 1997). These concerns relate to the notion of environmental justice, specifically issues of procedural and distributional justice (Walker, 2012), and raise wider concerns about whether emotional bonds with a place are taken into account in land-use planning. For example, Escobar (2001) theorized about the role of place attachment in motivating local resistance to globalization and noted that such protests are rarely parochial, being often founded upon relations between protestors across local, regional, or national boundaries.

Garavan's (2007) research on a controversial gas pipeline in the West of Ireland documented how local residents' objections were founded upon place attachments. Interviewees spoke of their love of the place and how this had been made salient and transgressed by the technology proposals, leading Garavan to conclude that the pipeline "forced the community to reflect on the nature of their cultural identity and the value of the place … the key to the mobilization of these actors was the perception that their locality was under threat from the company proposal" (Garavan, 2007, p.855). These findings point to ways that place attachment can motivate collective actions on behalf of a place, as noted by Manzo and Perkins (2006), and suggest that future studies of the dynamics of place change should pay closer attention to the politics of such contexts and the ways that multiple and diverse place meanings are rhetorically propagated by different actors to legitimate "development" or to oppose place change.

Research on community responses to offshore wind energy projects have emphasized the role of place meanings. Bidwell (2017) found that beliefs about the sea were crucial in understanding acceptance of a proposed US offshore wind farm. He argued that taking account of symbolic meanings associated with the coast or sea was an important basis for future wind energy deployment. Similar findings were reported in a study that compared pre-installation and post-operation opinions about an offshore wind farm amongst island and coastal residents in the US (Firestone et al, 2018). The broader context of energy policies has also been shown to be important, with stronger support if a proposal was seen as part of a wider program of technology deployment beyond the specific project under consideration (Firestone & Kempton, 2007).

Devine-Wright and Wiersma (2019) showed that the same project proposal (e.g., number of turbines, ownership model) can produce significantly different community responses depending on which offshore location was selected. Coastal locations considered to be "natural" and "pristine" were consistently considered less suitable for an offshore wind project by local residents. Locations already considered to be industrialized were consistently considered more suitable. The relevance of place-related meanings to community acceptance of low carbon energy projects supports the findings of previous studies (e.g., Batel et al, 2015; Wolsink, 2010).

However, the study raises difficult questions about place attachments, climate change mitigation, and justice. Communities that already live with a "locally unwanted land-use" (e.g., a land-fill site) are more likely to be asked to live with new infrastructures by comparison to communities living in less-developed, more "pristine" areas. Given that these infrastructures benefit everyone, regardless of living place, and that poorer socio-economic groups tend to live closer to unwanted infrastructures (Walker, 2012), it is imperative that the needs of impacted communities are fully recognized, taken into account by decision-makers and, if necessary, compensated for to ensure a just and fair process of low carbon energy transition.

CONCLUSIONS

The relevance of place attachment to the study of human understandings of, and responses to, climate change is increasingly well recognized. Nevertheless, this subject brings to the fore a wider set of questions concerning the dynamics of place attachment that this chapter has attempted to critically review. We would argue that developing a more dynamic perspective on place attachment can help to better understand two underlying questions that are crucial to a deeper understanding of this topic: (1) whether place attachments enable or obstruct the ability of individuals to adapt to change—and the evidence indicates that both outcomes are possible depending on the circumstances (Harries, 2017; Marshall et al, 2016); and (2) how place attachments are embedded within and reflect the politics of place change, notably acts of resistance.

This chapter has critiqued a persistent tendency in the literature to underplay the inherently dynamic nature of place attachment processes, and to consider how a more dynamic view of place attachment would better help to explain human responses to climate change. Whilst research on mobilities (see Lewicka, chapter 4 this volume) is beginning to address some of these aspects, and there have been some important attempts to capture the dynamics of relocation (notably contributions by Fullilove, chapter 11 this volume; Manzo, 2014), there remains a general neglect of research on how place attachments change over time. Responding to these criticisms will require new ways of theorizing about attachment processes and openness to novel methodologies. Finally, generating a better understanding of the inter-relations between place attachment and climate change challenges the primarily "localist" focus of much place attachment research, requiring more investigation of attachment to distant places (e.g., Gurney et al, 2017) and to attachments at different scales, from local to global (e.g., Devine-Wright & Wiersma, 2017).

REFERENCES

Adams, H. (2016). Why populations persist: Mobility, place attachment and climate change. *Population and Environment*, *37*, 429–448.

Adger, W.N., Barnett, J., Chapin III, F. S., & Ellemer, H. (2011). This must be the place: Under-representation of identity and meaning in climate change decision-making. *Global Environmental Politics*, *11*, 1–25.

Bailey, E., Devine-Wright, P. and Batel, S. (2016) Using a narrative approach to understand place attachments and responses to power line proposals: The importance of life-place trajectories. *Journal of Environmental Psychology*, 48, 200–211.

Batel, S., Devine-Wright, P., Wold, L., Egeland, H., Jacobsen, G., & Aas, O. (2015). The role of (de-)essentialisation within siting conflicts: An interdisciplinary approach. *Journal of Environmental Psychology*, *44*, 149–159.

Bidwell, D. (2017). Ocean beliefs and support for a wind energy project. *Ocean and Coastal Management*, *146*, 99–108.

Bauer, M. (1995). Resistance to new technology and its effects on nuclear power, information technology and biotechnology.In Bauer, M. (Ed.), *Resistance to new technology: Nuclear power, information technology and biotechnology* (pp. 1–41). Cambridge University Press: Cambridge, UK.

Bonaiuto, M., Carrus, G., Martorella, H., & Bonnes, M. (2002). Local identity processes and environmental attitudes in land use changes: The case of natural protected areas. *Journal of Economic Psychology*, *23*, 631–653.

Brown, B., & Perkins, D. D. (1992). Disruptions to place attachment. In I. Altman, & S. Low (Eds.), *Place attachment* (pp. 279–304). New York: Plenum.

Chow, K., & Healey, M. (2008). Place attachment and place identity: First-year undergraduates making the transition from home to university. *Journal of Environmental Psychology*, *28*, 362–372.

Cunsolo Willox, A., Harper, S. L., Ford, J. D., Landman, K., Houle, K., Edge, V. L., Rigolet Inuit Community Government (2012). 'From this place and of this place': climate change, sense of place, and health in Nunatsiavut, *Canada. SocSci Med*, *75*, 538–547

Cunsolo Willox, A., Harper, S. L., Ford, J. D. *et al*. (2013). Climate change and mental health: an exploratory case study from Rigolet, Nunatsiavut, Canada. *Climatic Change 121*, 255–270. https://doi.org/10.1007/s10584-013-0875-4

Dalby, S., & Mackenzie, F. (1997). Reconceptualising local community: Environment, identity and threat. *Area*, *29*, 99–108.

Day, C. (2002). *Spirit and Place: Healing our environment*. Architectural Press: London.

Devine-Wright, P. (2005). Beyond NIMBYism: Towards an integrated framework for understanding public perceptions of wind energy. *Wind Energy*, *8*, 125–139.

Devine-Wright, P. (2009). Rethinking Nimbyism: The role of place attachment and place identity in explaining place protective action. *Journal of Community and Applied Social Psychology*, *19*, 426–441.

Devine-Wright, P. (2011a). Place attachment and public acceptance of renewable energy: A tidal energy case study. *Journal of Environmental Psychology*, *31*, 336–343.

Devine-Wright, P. (2011b). Public engagement with large-scale renewable energy: Breaking the NIMBY cycle. *Wiley Interdisciplinary Reviews: Climate Change*, *2*, 19–26.

Devine-Wright, P. (2013a). Explaining 'NIMBY' objections to a power line: The role of personal, place attachment and project-related factors. *Environment and Behavior*, *45*, 761–781.

Devine-Wright, P. (2013b). Think global, act local? The relevance of place attachments and place identities in a climate changed world. *Global Environmental Change*, *23*, 61–69.

Devine-Wright, P., & Lyons, E. (1997). Remembering pasts and representing places: The construction of National Identities in Ireland. *Journal of Environmental Psychology*, *17*, 33–45.

Devine-Wright, P., & Howes, Y. (2010). Disruption to place attachment and the protection of restorative environments: A wind energy case study. *Journal of Environmental Psychology*, *30*, 271–280.

Devine-Wright, P., & Batel, S. (2017). My neighbourhood, my country or my planet? The influence of multiple place attachments and climate change concern on beliefs about energy infrastructure. *Global Environmental Change*, *47*, 110–120.

Devine-Wright, P., Leviston, Z., & Price, J. (2015). My country or my planet? Exploring the influence of multiple place attachments and ideological beliefs upon climate change attitudes and opinions. *Global Environmental Change*, *30*, 68–79.

Devine-Wright, P., & Wiersma, B. (2019). Understanding community acceptance of a potential offshore wind energy project in different locations: An island-based analysis of 'place-technology fit'. *Energy Policy*, *137*, 111086.

Di Masso, A., Dixon, J., & Durrheim, K. (Chapter 5, this volume).Place attachment as discursive practice: The role of language, affect, space, power and materiality in person-place bonds. In L. Manzo, & P. Devine-Wright (Eds.), *Place attachment: Advances in theory, methods and applications*, 2nd ed.

Di Masso, A., Williams, D. R., Raymond, C. M., Buchecker, M., Degenhardt, B., Devine-Wright, P., & vonWirth, T. (2019). Between fixities and flows: Navigating place attachments in an increasingly mobile world. *Journal of Environmental Psychology*, *61*, 125–133.

Dixon, J., & Durrheim, K. (2000). Displacing place identity: A discursive approach to locating self and other. *British Journal of Social Psychology*, *39*, 27–44.

Droseltis, O., & Vignoles, V. (2010). Towards an integrative model of place identification: Dimensionality and predictors of intrapersonal-level place preferences. *Journal of Environmental Psychology*, *30*, 23–34.

Ellis, N.R., Albrecht, G. A. (2017). Climate change threats to family farmers' sense of place and mental wellbeing: a case study from the Western Australian Wheatbelt. *SocSci Med* 175, 161–168

Escobar, A. (2001). Culture sits in places: Reflections on globalism and subaltern strategies of localization. *Political Geography*, *20*, 139–174.

Feldman, R. (1990). Settlement Identity: Psychological bonds with home places in a mobile society. *Environment and Behavior*, *22*, 183–229.

Firestone, J., & Kempton, W. (2007). Public opinion about large offshore wind power: Underlying factors. *Energy Policy*, *35*, 1584–1598.

Firestone, J., Hoen, J., Rand, J., Elliott, D., Hübner, G. & Pohl, J. (2018) Reconsidering barriers to wind power projects: community engagement, developer transparency and place, *Journal of Environmental Policy & Planning*, *20*, 370–386, DOI:10.1080/1523908X.2017.1418656

Fried, M. (2000). Continuities and discontinuities of place. *Journal of Environmental Psychology*, *20*,193–205.

Fullilove, M. T. (2004). *Root shock: How tearing up city neighborhoods hurts America and what we can do about it*. New York: Ballantine Books.

Garavan, M. (2007). Resisting the costs of 'development': Local environmental activism in Ireland.*Environmental Politics*, *16*, 844–863.

Giuliani, V. (2002). Theory of attachment and place attachment.In M. Bonnes, T. Lee, & M. Bonaiuto (Eds.), *Psychological theories for environmental issues* (pp. 137–170). Aldershot: Ashgate.

Gustafson, P. (2001). Meanings of place: Everyday experience and theoretical conceptualizations. *Journal of Environmental Psychology*, *21*, 5–16.

Gustafson, P. (2014). Place Attachment in an Age of Mobility. In L. Manzo, & P. Devine-Wright (Eds.), *Place attachment: Advances in theory, methods and applications*, Oxford: Routledge, pp. 37–48.

Gurney, G. G., Blythe, J., Adams, H., Adger, W. N., Curnock, M., Faulkner, L., James, T., Marshall, N.A. (2017) Redefining community based on place attachment in a connected world. *Proc Natl AcadSci USA* 114:10077–10082

Harries, T. (2017). Ontological Security and Natural Hazards.In *Oxford research encyclopedia of natural hazard science* (Vol. 1). Oxford: Oxford University Press. DOI:10.1093/acrefore/9780199389407.013.279

Hay, R. (1998). Sense of place in developmental context. *Journal of Environmental Psychology*, *18*, 5–29.

Inalhan, G., & Finch, E. (2004). Place attachment and sense of belonging, *Facilities*, *22*, 120–128.

IPCC. (2014): Annex II: Glossary.InK. J. Mach, S. Planton, & C. von Stechow; core writing team, R. K. Pachauri, & L. A. Meyer (Eds.), *Climate change 2014: Synthesis report. Contribution of working groups I, II and III to the fifth assessment report of the intergovernmental panel on climate change* (pp. 117–130). Geneva, Switzerland: IPCC.

Knez, I. (2005). Attachment and identity as related to a place and its perceived climate. *Journal of Environmental Psychology*, *25*, 207–218.

Korpela, K. M., Ylen, M., Tyrväinen, L., & Silvennoinen, H. (2009). Stability of self-reported favorite places and place attachment over a 10-month period. *Journal of Environmental Psychology*, *29*, 95–100.

Lewicka, M. (2011a). Place attachment: How far have we come in the last 40 years? *Journal of Environmental Psychology*, *31*, 207–230.

Lewicka, M. (2011b). On the variety of people's relationship with places. *Environment and Behavior*, *43*, 676–709.

Manzo, L. C. (2003). Beyond house and haven: Toward a revisioning of emotional relationships with places. *Journal of Environmental Psychology*, *23*, 47–61.

Manzo, L. C. (2005). For better or for worse: Exploring multiple dimensions of place meaning. *Journal of Environmental Psychology*, *25*, 67–86.

Manzo, L. C. (2008). Experience of displacement on sense of place and well being.In Eyles, J., & Williams, A. (Eds.), *Sense of place, health and quality of life* (pp. 87–104).London: Ashgate Publishing, London.

Manzo, L. C. (2014). Exploring the shadow side: place attachment in the context of stigma, displacement, and social housing. In L. Manzo, & P. Devine-Wright (Eds.), *Place attachment: Advances in theory, methods and applications*, Oxford: Routledge, pp. 178-190.

Manzo, L. C., & Perkins, D. (2006). Finding common ground: The importance of place attachment to community participation in planning. *Journal of Planning Literature*, *20*, 335–350.

Marshall, N., Fenton, D. M., Marshall, P. A., & Sutton, S. G. (2007). How resource dependency can influence social resilience within a primary resource industry. *Rural Sociology*, *72*, 359–390.

Marshall, N. A., Park, S. E., Adger, N. E., Brown, K., & Howden, S. M. (2012). Transformational capacity and the influence of place and identity. *Environmental Research Letters, 7,* 034032 (9 pages).

Marshall, N. A., Crimp, S., Curnock, M., Greenhill, M., Kuehne, G., Leviston, Z.,...& Ouzman, J. (2016). Some primary producers are more likely to transform their agricultural practices in response to climate change than others. *Agriculture, Ecosystems and Environment, 222,* 38–47.

Morgan, P. (2010). Towards a developmental theory of place attachment. *Journal of Environmental Psychology, 30,* 11–22.

Proshansky, H., Fabian, H. K., & Kaminoff, R. (1983). Place identity: Physical world socialisation of the self. *Journal of Environmental Psychology, 3,* 57–83.

Quinn, T., Bousquet, F., Guerbois, C., Heider, L., & Brown, K. (2019). How local water and waterbody meanings shape flood risk perception and risk management preferences. *Sustainability Science, 14f,* 565–578.

Relph, E. (1976). *Place and Placelessness.* London: Pion.

Scannell, L., & Gifford, R. (2010). Defining place attachment: A tripartite organizing framework. *Journal of Environmental Psychology, 30,* 1–10.

Scannell, L., & Gifford, R. (2013). Personally relevant climate change: The role of place attachment and local versus global message framing in engagement. *Environment and Behavior, 45,* 60–85.

Scannell, L., & Gifford, R. (2017). The experienced psychological benefits of place attachment.*Journal of Environmental Psychology, 51,* 256–269.

Speller, G. M., & Twigger-Ross, C. L. (2009). Cultural and social disconnection in the context of a changed physical environment. *Geografiska Annaler: Series B, Human Geography, 91,* 355–369.

Stedman, R. (2002). Toward a social psychology of place: Predicting behaviour from place-based cognitions, attitude, and identity. *Environment and Behaviour, 34,* 561–581.

Walker-Springett, K., Butler, C. and Adger, N. (2017) Wellbeing in the aftermath of floods. *Health and Place, 43,* 66–74.

Walker, G. (2012). *Environmental justice: Concepts, evidence and politics.* London: Routledge.

Williams, D. R., & Miller, B. A. (Chapter 1, this volume). Metatheoretical moments in place attachment research: Seeking clarity in diversity. In L. Manzo, & P. Devine-Wright (Eds.) *Place attachment: Advances in theory, methods and applications,* 2nd ed.

Wolsink, M. (2010). Near-shore wind power—Protected seascapes, environmentalists' attitudes, and the technocratic planning perspective. *Land Use Policy, 27,* 195–203.

Chapter 15: The agency of place attachment in the contemporary co-production of community landscapes

Deni Ruggeri

INTRODUCTION: THE NECESSITY OF PLACE ATTACHMENT IN THE SUSTAINABLE CITY

The local places of everyday lives, including our nearby nature, are essential life-supports for both individuals and communities. Our interactions with these home landscapes and their people constitute a "daily ballet" (Seamon, 2012, see also chapter 2 this volume) through which place attachments develop. Further, these attachments and identities take on a social dimension, reinforcing mutual bonds of trust among community members, and an action dimension motivating sustained, collective stewardship of place (Ruggeri, 2018). As a landscape architect who regularly engages communities in participatory design projects, I have seen how place attachment and identity are intertwined and mutually constituted in our interactions in community spaces. It is these interrelationships that are the focus of this chapter.

Throughout their lives, people's identities are renegotiated and revealed through place-based experiences. The bond between place and self-identity is a pre-requisite for the emergence of place attachments that can instill in residents a desire to engage in stewardship and foster resilience. But for these bonds to become resources for greater long-term sustainability, planning and design must become increasingly participatory, inclusive, generative of the shared sense of community, and mutual trust that can instigate actions to improve everyone's livelihoods and capabilities (Ganz, 2011; Nussbaum, 2011).

In urban redevelopment and placemaking processes, participation is not only a tool for building consensus but also a way to make places common grounds for cultivating civics and stewardship (Manzo & Perkins, 2006). By working together and imagining new futures for their community spaces, residents lay the foundations for a collective sense of urgency and commitment to both the place and the people who inhabit them that is critical to their survival. Further, place attachment plays a crucial role in promoting ecological democracy because it helps to channel individual bonds and feelings toward practices of bottom-up, inclusive place transformation and renewal (Hester, 2006).

When integrated into participatory design, research, and education efforts, place attachment and identity help bring to the surface shared values, feelings, ambitions, and visions for the future, thus dissolving and disentangling their otherwise bundled-up existential insideness (Relph, 1976; Seamon, 2014). Whatever challenges a community may face—limited access to nature, mental and public health concerns, or social isolation—revealing the infrastructure of local place attachment is essential to achieving any sustainable and resilient change (Hester, 2006, see also Hester, chapter 13 this volume).

This chapter reflects on the nature, quality, and intensity of the transformation generated by processes of redevelopment that deliberately sought to engage place attachment questions as windows into the community's deeply held feelings toward the future, their shared fears, ambitions, and values. It focuses on two case studies—Giske, Norway, and Zingonia, Italy—communities where the author has been engaging in participatory action research and service-learning efforts (Bose et al., 2014). While different in scale and challenges faced, Giske and Zingonia are windows into the nature and qualities of residents' place attachment at times of change illustrate the consequences of a renewed sense of identity and connection to the landscape on their visions for sustainable development.

Both stories suggest that as powerful as place attachments may be in facilitating change, tackling the wicked challenges of our time requires long-term investments in place-based participatory processes and in practices of community building that can foster greater engagement. As cities and neighborhoods transform, the impact of these changes on people/place relationships, self-doubt, discouragement, and frustration may inhibit socially responsive progress. It is precisely at a time of change that the sharing of residents' stories of place attachment and identity can inspire continued commitment to place, tenacious stewardship, and impactful action (de la Peña et al., 2017; Ganz, 2011).

BACKGROUND: PLACE ATTACHMENT CHALLENGES FOR THE TWENTY-FIRST CENTURY CITY

Worldwide, cities have invested great resources into becoming denser, better connected, and more energy-efficient, but they continue to lag behind in livability, affordability, and social equity (Adloff & Neckel, 2019). As urban lifestyles have become more palatable to young professionals and the upper class, gentrification has undermined the identification and attachments of long-time residents as they get displaced from their neighborhoods leading to significant disruptions to place attachments (see also Fullilove, chapter 11 this volume).

In the contemporary city, owning a home in an affordable, livable neighborhood has become a luxury. Working class families are looking for affordable housing in ex-urban and rural areas, shifting the boundaries of world mega-cities (Pojani & Stead, 2015). Traffic jams and longer commutes take a toll on their ability to engage in social life and physical activity leading to a marginalization that is further exacerbated by digital technologies. For children, seniors, and the differently abled, social isolation and disconnect from the landscape (Louv, 2008) translates into poorer physical and mental health and feelings of isolation (Ward Thompson and Aspinall, 2011). Such shifts in the landscape and the way we live on it also shift our relationships and attachments to place.

In response to displacement, advocates for the "right to landscape" suggest that providing all human beings—especially the marginalized—with access to the natural and cultural resources of our cities is a fundamental human right and may be the most pressing human rights emergency of our time (Egoz, Jørgensen & Ruggeri, 2018; Egoz, Makhzoumi & Pungetti, 2011). This notion implies citizens' responsibility to participate in envisioning the future of their place and contributing to its stewardship (Mattijssen et al., 2017). Community participation can function as the platform for practicing of democratic life and the sharing of civic values that can ensure that redevelopment is not only sustainable but resilient and empower communities to take ownership of their futures (Manzo & Perkins, 2006; Seamon, 2014).

Alongside such shifts, in 2000, the Council of Europe unveiled the European Landscape Convention (ELC) a landscape-based redevelopment approach that recognizes social ties and place attachments as a way to mitigate displacement and re-ground people in place. The approach is grounded in a definition of the landscape as "perceived by people, whose character is the result of the action and interaction of natural and/or human factors" (Council of Europe, 2000, p. 30). The convention relies on full, meaningful participation as an essential tool for strengthening "the identities of populations, which recognize themselves in their surroundings" (p. 46). The ELC calls for urban redevelopment to include processes that are democratic, informed by local knowledge, pedagogical of new and positive relationships between people and place, and sensitive to place-specific contexts and needs rather than generalizable trends. It also demands new models of design/planning practice, whereby educators and researchers act as partners and collaborators rather than experts in promoting positive landscape change. Furthermore, it serves as a reminder that when it comes to places, it is residents who possess "the empirical knowledge (local and naturalistic knowledge) that may be useful in completing and contextualizing specialist knowledge" (p. 47). That knowledge is grounded in place identities and attachments.

THE MULTIFACETED, SOCIALLY CONSTRUCTED NATURE OF PLACE ATTACHMENT

In order to more fully appreciate the potential of place attachment and identity for community participation in design and planning, it is helpful to consider how these have been understood in the literature, where the concepts continue to be "fuzzy" and mean different things to different people (Markusen, 2013).

Researchers tend to agree that sense of belonging and place attachment either results from positive experiences people entertain in their locales in their daily lives (Hernandez et al., 2007; Lewicka, 2011) or it can be the byproduct of a deep awareness and identification with the places that makes us feel fulfilled (Korpela, 2012; Proshansky, Fabian, & Kaminoff, 1983). Place attachment is not only the result of individual cognitive and emotional processes of place identification but also of collective processes of meaning-creation (Mihaylov & Perkins, 2014) informed by and representative of socially produced values, norms, behaviors, and social identities (Appleyard, 1979; Di Masso, Dixon & Durrheim, 2014; Schein, 2009). Through the ritualistic performance of community life in public settings (Hester, 1993, 2006; Milligan, 1998), residents merge their personal attachment into a gestalt-like shared awareness of their uniqueness that move individuals to take collective action (Ganz, 2011; Uzzell, Pol, & Badenas, 2002).

PLACEMAKING, STEWARDSHIP, AND COMMUNITY

The constantly evolving nature of people's place attachment and identity and the complex nature of their relationships with place contribute to making environmental design a "wicked" problem for those engaged in urban development (Brian, 2008). Additionally, an endless number of plausible actions, the inability to claim ultimate success, or the fact that once initiated, environmental transformations may have unpredictable consequences (Rittel & Webber, 1973) determine the wicked, complex nature of place making. How, then, does one ensure that future transformations of local places continue to improve the relationship between people and place, by supporting their place attachment and identity, and fostering long-term resilience? Research shows that active and meaningful participation in placemaking, redevelopment, and conservation processes in a person's community lead to stronger place attachment, identity, and social cohesion (Hou & Rios, 2003; Manzo & Perkins, 2006; Putnam, 2007). When individual emotional connections with place are revealed and shared through participation, they become a shared resource and foundation for the future of the community.

Seamon (2014, this volume) identifies six processes that can either strengthen or undermine place attachment in any particular context: (1) place interaction—the ability to use and engage with the place, (2) place identity—to associate and identify with a place, (3) place release—to be challenged and intrigued by place, (4) place realization—to embody a community's values and ambitions, (5) place intensification—to reflect its vibrancy and resilience, and (6) place creation—to inspire collective creativity and vision. These processes have the potential to instigate a "spectrum of emotional engagement that ranges from appreciation, pleasure, and fondness to concern, respect, responsibility, care, and deep love of place" (Seamon, 2014, p. 21), with consequences on their long-term resilience and sustainability. Unleashing that potential requires framing participation as the act of researching-by-design which of Seamon's processes may be most effective in instigating democratic, resilient change.

Just as place identities are continually evolving, place attachment can fluctuate between states of preservation (i.e., desires for continuity) and desires for change and transformation. Whether it is through place interaction, identity, release, realization, creation, or intensification, place attachment can instigate a "spectrum of emotional engagement that ranges from appreciation, pleasure, and fondness to concern, respect, responsibility, care, and deep love of place" (Seamon, 2014, p. 21). When these emotional bonds are integrated into participatory, inclusive forms of citizen engagement, these bonds can become a collective resource, and cultivate of a shared sense of responsibility for one's community, because "processes of collective action work better when emotional ties to places and their inhabitants are cultivated" (Manzo & Perkins, 2006, p. 347).

THE TRANSFORMATIVE AGENCY OF PLACE ATTACHMENT

Investigating the relationship between places, people's identities, their socially constructed meanings and symbols, and their consequences on attachment requires "thick description" (Geertz, 2008). Place attachment methods should be sensitive to each community's uniqueness and nuanced in their representation of their devotion to place (Manzo & Devine-Wright, 2014; see also Manzo and Pinto de Carvalho, this volume; Southworth & Ruggeri, 2011). Traditional surveys, interviews, observations, and cognitive mapping are now being complemented by alternative methods like photo-voice, oral histories, role-playing (Bowman, 2010; Cooper Marcus, 1995; Rishbeth, this volume; Ruggeri, 2014; Sandberg, 2003;), socially engaged performance (Cohen-Cruz, 2012), placemaking through public art (Redaelli, 2016), gaming, and virtual reality (Oleksy & Wnuk, 2017; Ruggeri and Szilágyi-Nagy, 2019). Researchers are deliberately addressing global challenges related to public health, biodiversity, climate adaptation, resource depletion, energy, livability, social capital, and social justice (Low, 2017; Manzo & Devine-Wright, 2014; Seamon, 2014), engaging in transdisciplinary Participatory Action Research processes with a humanitarian focus (Egoz et al., 2018; Stokols, 2006).

In the remainder of this chapter, I introduce evidence of the transformative function of place attachment as a shared focus of two participatory processes led by the author and designed by a diverse group of graduate and undergraduate students of landscape architecture and planning in Norway and Italy acting as researchers. While each community is unique, they share a similar disconnect between people and their places and with each other, a fundamental landscape democracy struggle. In both cases, the research challenge became the imagining of meaningful landscape transformations that could motivate people to work together for a more sustainable future.

Story 1: Giske

On the west coast of Norway lies Giske, a municipality established in 1908 to incorporate the islands of Vigra, Valderøya, Giske, and Godøya into one administrative unit. Beginning in the 1950s, the communities' historic reliance on farming, grazing, and fishing for survival was challenged by urbanization (Figure 15.1, left). The late 1950s creation of a small regional airport in Vigra, and the 1987 opening of a complex system of underwater tunnels further redefined Giske's identity. As

Figure 15.1
Satellite photo of Giske
Municipality in Western
Norway, with the islands
of Valderøya, Vigra, Giske,
and Godøya (left) and view
of the Island of Valderøya,
the administrative center
of Giske Municipality,
showing the sprawl along
the water's edges (right).

commuting became a matter of minutes, rather than hours, Giske residents began to leave their farms and fisheries in for less demanding occupations and more comfortable lifestyles in the nearby mainland city of Ålesund.

As housing began to sprawl on productive farmland and along the islands' waterfronts (Figure 15.1, right), the historic districts emptied out, with businesses moving to the automobile-oriented town center of Valderøya. Here, a new City Hall, big box stores, and a new, centralized high school campus served the daily needs of the entire municipality, requiring residents to converge here by car for their daily needs. Bound to their automobiles, residents distanced themselves from the landscape and from each other, with deleterious consequences on community life and social capital as well as place attachments. Aside from churches and schools, supermarkets are the only loci of socialization.

In 2014, Giske participated in a nationwide pilot research project named Barnetråkk, which aimed to gather information on residents' place-identity, attachments, and preferences of children of 60 Norwegian municipalities (Aradi, 2010). The resulting maps of pleasant/unpleasant and activity-rich places that young people encountered on their way from home to school helped to give spatial definition to the community's place attachment and identity challenges. However, there was a lack of information about the how and why of children's choices, and about the qualities and multifaceted nature of their attachment. To fill this gap, student-researchers from the landscape architecture department at the Norwegian University of Life Sciences (NMBU) joined the Barnetråkk project and engaged young residents in participatory workshops to dive deeper into children's perceptions of their community places. Once identified and discussed collectively, the children's most beloved places would be integrated with their wishes and ambitions into visions for a system of new hubs and trails that would support a renewed, richer public life.

The community redevelopment process began in September of 2015 with a workshop held at the municipal building involving a group of thirty 10th graders from the local junior high school. Before the community meeting, NMBU student-researchers held focus groups with politicians and community leaders to gain some clarity about the challenges Giske municipality was facing as it attracted a growing population of families from all of Norway and the world. Questions of place attachment played a central role in the workshops that began with a role-playing exercise called "Typical Us" where student-researchers put on a performance where they characterized, often humorously, the sub-identities of the Giske municipality.

Role-playing was an opportunity to reflect on differences in place identity and acknowledge possible biases and misconceptions. The activity continued with an exercise that used "pictograms"—artistic images to allow participants to role-play as they engaged in a critical identity politics discussion. In the process, they revealed their perceptions vis-à-vis the values and attitudes that Giske residents shared, and the idiosyncratic place identity of each island community. Children saw residents of Vigra, the flattest and largest island, as kind, semi-boring farmers, and people of Valderøya as friendlier, more social yet somewhat divided. Giske's residents were depicted as lonely, religious, and conservative farmers blessed with the best natural landscapes and views. Finally, participants described Godøya residents as wealthy, antisocial, blessed with beautiful nature, and outspoken about their values. Through participation, student-researchers were able to uncover differences in the intensity and qualities of the communities' place attachment. Their research confirmed that while residents felt relatively secure in their attachment to broader natural landscape, they desperately longed for more social interactions and for new neighborhood and civic places to be proud of and spend time in.

The project also sought to understand how essential nature was to Giske residents. Stakeholders blamed the time they spent driving every day for an impoverished social life and the limited interactions children and their families had in and with the landscape. To investigate these issues further, NMBU student-researchers used a triangulation of methods, including photo-elicitation, a digital survey, and participant observation in social media communities. The "A Giske for All" survey, which inquired about infrastructural needs and attitudes toward their place, received 351 responses. The publicly accessible results revealed a great deal about residents' feelings about their community. Three out of four residents did not feel united, and only one out of two was satisfied with the services and public life Giske offered them. The survey also revealed that 41 percent of the respondents had never engaged in community-based activities or participated in volunteering— evidence of the disappearing cultural practice of *dugnad*, a Norwegian ritual that involves neighborhood-based upkeep and beautification efforts required of all residents at the start and end of the warm season, like the assemblage of street furniture, street cleaning, or the planting of flowers (Amundsen, 2012).

Figure 15.2
The #Vårtgiske method, which employed Twitter posts to elicit information about place attachment in Giske municipality (left) and the "Google review" activity, which asked children to imagine the qualities of their ideal future community space (right).

Explorations of place attachment also engaged digital media. NMBU student researchers collected pictures of people's favorite places in the community through Instagram using the hashtag #Vårtgiske ("Our Giske") to identify the physical expressions of their place attachment, which would serve as foundations for the new vision of Giske they would help to give form to (Figure 15.2, left). A content analysis of the pictures provides a window into residents' place attachments and their strong biophilic bond with the landscape. This then gave the design students directions about the qualities that made particular places special to locals. The vast majority of images depicted views of the distant horizon and the sea. As a resident explained, the horizon was an integral part of their daily lives as residents of a small island, serving as a frame of reference in their otherwise shifting place identity. Giske residents saw in it stability and perspective to help them deal with the physical and socio-cultural consequences of the dramatic changes they are facing in terms of identity, values, and outlook on the future, further underscoring Korpela's (2012) understanding of place attachment and identity as self-regulating mechanisms.

In the Fall of 2017, NMBU student-researchers organized a second participatory workshop at Valderøya Elementary School, during which 40 pupils would co-design and envision strategies for initiating the changes in some of the vital community places identified in 2015. The primary goal was to gather ideas for the redesign of a new public landscape adjacent to the Municipal headquarters in Valderøy, and envision new connections to the island's most beloved beaches and water access points. Municipal leaders additionally asked NMBU student-researchers to explore the possibility of integrating a "smart city" perspective into their work to tap into newly available public funds for policies and interventions surrounding digital media. This requirement inspired the team to think of methods that would engage new technologies and innovation as both a window into children's creativity and as tools for communicating place attachment and identity.

Central to the 2017 workshop was the "Google Review" activity, which began with a brainstorming session to visualize, through collaging and sketching, the experiences and qualities that would characterize Giske's future public places. Using a template that mimicked a Google Review, children identified key places, narrated their unique attributes, and assessed with a five-star rating system the quality of the experiences and perceptions these places would afford (Figure 15.2, right). The digital metaphor served as both an introduction into their current place attachment and identity, and a tool to overcome their frustrations, "restructure interactions and relationships of power" and imagine "opportunities that are qualitatively different from life outside of the game" into a new, imaginary place identity (Baldwin-Philippi & Gordon, 2014, p. 726).

Engaging their vision of a future place identity empowered local children to explore the unconventional and the unknown, freeing their creativity. Paradoxically, their out-of-the-box thinking became a source of intense disagreement for NMBU student-researchers about the need to balance ambition and realism in their design proposals. Filtered through the skepticism of the NMBU team, the idealized, virtual places that local students had imagined were translated into neighborhood-scale tactical urbanism[1] interventions that community could seed, implement, and nurture through stewardship. Their designs included IKEA-like booklets to illustrate how community members might begin to activate public life by decorating their places with flower boxes, platforms, and benches built by the community, one screw, and wooden board at a time (Figure 15.3).

Three years from the conclusion of the workshop, Giske has slowly taken steps toward a better future. Thanks to the knowledge and visions co-created in partnership with locals, NMBU student-researchers have helped raise awareness about the community's place attachment and identity assets, calling for their preservation and integration into the new development. This awareness has resulted in stricter approval processes for new projects and new requirements for preserving and enhancing the community's most sacred spaces of attachment. The next challenge would be to tackle the social isolation and identity conflicts between members of each island community.

Story 2: Zingonia: Digital mapping and the sacred structures of identity

Beginning in 1965, a Modernist New Town emerged from the economically depressed agricultural fields between Milan and Bergamo in Northern Italy (Figure 15.4, left). Its vision was the dream of Renzo Zingone, a private developer with the ambition to found a city that would embody the innovativeness and dynamism of the Italian economic boom of the 1960s. He created a community strikingly at odds with the traditional image of the Italian city, with wide arterial roads replacing narrow medieval streets, and a landscape to be viewed from the perspective of the automobile driver rather than pedestrians. The Modernist city of

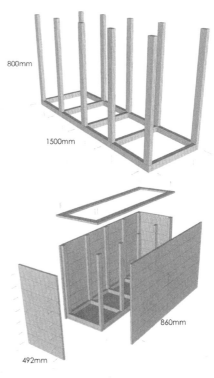

Figure 15.3
NMBU students designed street furniture and a handbook with instructions and graphic illustrations to facilitate the implementation of children's visions.

residential towers and monumental fountains served as a theatrical backdrop for the success, entrepreneurship, and hard work of its residents. The business node of Piazza Affari featured a Grand Hotel, and an open-air galleria inviting visitors and locals to participate in the urban spectacle of modernity and wealth of the thriving businesses fronting the space.

By the start of the second millennium, Zingonia and its Piazza had become the breeding ground for petty crime, drug dealing and prostitution, resulting in the sharp decline of real estate values. Fueled by predatory lenders, immigrant families began to purchase housing units from original Italian families, only to find themselves unable to pay for mortgages and management fees. In 2007, at one of the lowest moments in Zingonia's history, residents began to voice their disagreement with the public image as a dilapidated urban ghetto on social media. Through the "Quelli Della Zingonia" Facebook group, residents coalesced together to counter public discourses of decline with images of past and present attachment and community life. Beginning in 2008, against this backdrop of new hope and commitment for change, the Zingonia 3.0 project brought together politicians, planners, policemen, social workers, NGOs, community organizers, and residents with the intent to re-write the story of the place and ignite bottom-up processes of regeneration drawing on local place attachment to instigate local transformations, both physical and personal (Ruggeri, 2018).

 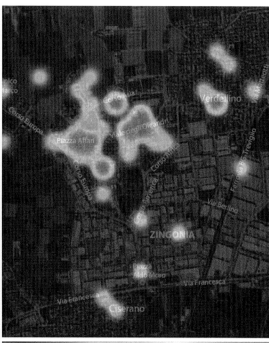

Figure 15.4
Skyline of Zingonia with
the residential towers of
Piazza Affari (left) and a
heat map illustrating the
community's most beloved
places (right).

The project partners used the name Zingonia 3.0 as a digital metaphor to suggest a focus on renewal in the software (social infrastructure), rather than hardware (physical infrastructure), of the community. The name also referred to three eras of Zingonia's history, from its initial founding as a New Town (1.0) to the renewal efforts of the late 1990s and 2000s (2.0). The partnership's first action-item was a detailed inventory of the community's physical and social landscapes, performed by housing and landscape experts in cooperation with social workers and other community activists. These efforts revealed a grim reality of degradation and decline, due to property management irregularities that left the poverty-stricken residents no choice but to default on their mortgages and maintenance fees. In collaboration with the author, Zingonia 3.0 partners designed a digital questionnaire to investigate place attachment and identity (Ruggeri, 2009). Questions related to emotional attachment, imageability, distinctiveness, social imageability, and social capital. It also included an innovative mapping interface that allowed residents to click on a digital aerial photo of the territory to mark the places that they would be sorry to leave behind if they were to leave tomorrow.

The results shed light on the community's place attachments, highlighting landscapes that in the views of residents held the most significant potential for the future. A heat map translated into visual evidence the degree of attachment residents felt for key community spaces (Figure 15.4, right). Just as its founder had intended, the monumental fountains, piazzas, schools, churches, community centers, and soccer fields of the original plan of Zingonia had resonated in people's hearts, constituting a sacred infrastructure of meaningful places, primed to become fertile ground for the performance of a new covenant between people and their landscape.

Countering a decades-old core story of decline and marginality, Zingonia 3.0 project partners employed a diversified strategy to communicate the value and transformative potential of the places identified as meaningful by the digital survey respondents and gave residents a chance to reclaim their pride in the community. They began with organizing a PARK(ing) day event in Piazza Affari, and street festivals, showcasing Zingonia's diverse offering in terms of culture, food, the arts, and manufacturing. Armed with a renewed awareness and confidence in the regeneration of the community, municipal leaders began by repairing *Piazza Affari's* monumental fountain, which had sat inactive for years. The water jets, the improved maintenance, and the planting of annuals flowers and fruit trees became evidence of new vitality and community pride. Zingonia 3.0 partners also placed a lot of importance on the hiring of a young artist to produce a coloring book celebrating the city's past, present, and future (Figure 15.5, left) and initiating new after school programs focusing on creative writing, music, and the arts. This coordinated, diversified strategy helped renew awareness of place attachments and identity, offering residents new platforms onto which to build positive stories of place and community identity.

The unpacking and revealing of the attachments that community members of all ages and ethnicities felt for Zingonia initiated by the participatory workshop proved transformative for the community, eventually empowering residents to take on the revitalization of spaces within the housing towers—stairways, basements, apartments, and guardhouses—and the nearby parks, playgrounds,

Figure 15.5
The "Zingonia da Colorare" coloring book (left) and a visual storyline, which helped clarify Zingonia's social imageability and shifting public narrative (right).

and promenades. At a 2017 workshop organized to evaluate the impact of the project, a "visual timeline" tested whether the transformations it initiated had resulted in new shared stories (Figure 15.5, right), while a social network analysis mapped the quantity and intensity of social links established through its concerted activities. A survey of 33 project partners and stakeholders reveals that on a scale from 1 to 6, they would rank its impact in terms of empowerment at 5.22, and at 5.36 for its effectiveness in engaging new residents.in its activities.

Zingonia's story illustrates the power of place and awareness as agents of sustainable, democratic change. Project partners integrated personal feelings of attachment toward their community into a shared place identity and helped reveal positive perceptions that transformed a narrative of despair toward one of hope for the future. Through participation, the residents channeled their nostalgia and attachment into transformative actions—many revolving around the public landscape—that reaffirmed the relevance of these places to their future together. The opening of new retail stores in Zingonia's Piazza Affari and the improvements of the semi-public residential landscapes are tangible evidence of the gradual construction of a new and stronger place-identity, respectful of the past but oriented toward resilience and adaptability.

DISCUSSION: PLACE ATTACHMENT AS THE IMPETUS FOR SUSTAINABLE TRANSFORMATIONS

In every community, positive expressions of place attachment and identity co-exist in a delicate balance with negative perceptions that in the worst cases can lead to alienation, despair, and hopelessness. In Giske, Zingonia, inadequate policy, economic instability, and changes in lifestyles, employment opportunities, and socio-economic conditions had led to places that are unable to support the residents' most basic functions of community life: walking to and from school, feeling safe, and socializing, and nurturing pride in the community. As the social and physical fabric of their communities deteriorated, and in the absence of a positive core story to unite around, residents of Zingonia reacted with discouragement or nostalgia for a long-lost past (evidenced in Zingonia's Facebook group postings), or in Giske's case, with social inertia resembling a state of "living on autopilot" (Ganz, 2011, p. 277).

In both communities, participation has challenged residents to act upon their place attachment and identity through collective action and revealed the visual, cultural, and emotional prominence of many community spaces in the lives of residents. Yet, awareness of place attachments in itself is insufficient to achieve sustainable and resilient change. As Seamon (2014) suggests, a synergy of processes ought to be active for the full, transformative potential of place attachment and identity to be unleashed. The stories offered here, provide evidence of the dynamic nature of the bonds between people and place and the necessity to reveal and cultivate them through participation and collective action. While the Italian community has dramatically expanded opportunities for place interaction, release, realization, and creation, it has yet to feel intensification benefits of policies and large-scale investment that would ensure the resilience of these transformations.

In Giske, participation has strengthened its place identification and uncovered place attachments. It has shown the promise of collective creativity in place creation. Still, it has yet to generate more significant place interaction and realization that would empower them to abandon their auto-oriented lifestyles. Whereas Zingonia residents have begun improving their favorite places with the new community gardens, playgrounds, and the renewal of old spaces through artistic performances, Giske's progress has been slow and barely noticeable. Without physical interventions to remind them of the agency of their place attachment and identity, residents have proved reluctant to join in, waiting by the sidelines for municipal staff and volunteers to set new place and community-making processes into motion (Romslo & Stordalen, 2016).

The participatory design efforts in Zingonia and Giske offered all those involved—academics included—the opportunity to reflect on their responsibility as citizens and their bonds to the landscape and one another. In both communities, our efforts were facilitated and enriched by the participation of children, and in return, it empowered them to demand sustainable changes. Their willingness to open up, share their daily pains and pleasures, and participate in challenging the status quo with new, ambitious visions has been transformative of the designers and researchers, who, in return, have learned about the power of collective creativity. It has also offered them the ideal opportunity to test abstract theories and methods on real-world examples of the disruption and re-building of positive relationships between people and places.

However, awareness alone is insufficient to unleash the full benefits of place attachment. In Giske, learning about the loss of a sense of community has revealed deep wounds that the municipality has committed to healing through participation. In Zingonia, awareness of their shared place attachment has ignited pride and hope for change, resulting in processes of place-keeping, urban agriculture, creative placemaking, and cultural programming. Yet the effects of these efforts are not yet fully evident and will require much energy and continued commitment to succeed. More work and case studies are needed to better understand how place attachments and identity can lead to mobilization versus inertia.

Through the sharing of these stories of place attachment, this chapter illustrated how a shared awareness of the bonds between residents and their places could motivate positive transformations in all those involved. In both Zingonia and Giske, the sharing of people's attachment in a participatory setting has leveled the field, giving all residents reasons to coalesce around new visions for their local places. Both case studies have led to a deeper understanding of the nuanced, evolving relationships in these communities, and has informed and enriched both the designs and the education of the student-researchers involved, preparing them to become better practitioners. It also revealed to all those involved that this kind of change is indeed wicked, requiring long-term efforts and investments.

Traditional bonds between people and place are under threat due to changing lifestyles, climate uncertainty, the skyrocketing cost of living, the influence of technologies, and ideological polarization. Zingonia and Giske offer those of us interested in improving the relationship between people and their places a yardstick against which to better comprehend the place attachment and identity tradeoffs and the challenges many communities face as they move toward becoming more sustainable and resilient. Their stories also offer reasons to hope and illustrate how the integration of these fundamental questions may help us come together as citizens sharing a common bond with the landscape.

ACKNOWLEDGEMENTS

The author is grateful to Zingonia and Giske residents for their willingness to share their feelings toward their community places and to the many students who participated in the community engagement efforts described in this chapter for their thoughtfulness, creativity, and rigor.

NOTE

1 Landscape architect John Bela (2015) founder of the annual PARKing Day, a yearly event that aimed to transform for one-day parking spaces into parks, describes tactical urbanism as a placemaking practice of involving community-generated forms of beautification and occupation of public space.

REFERENCES

Adloff, F., & Neckel, S. (2019). Futures of sustainability as modernization, transformation, and control: A conceptual framework. *Sustainability Science*, *14*(4), 1015–1025.

Amundsen, H. (2012). Illusions of resilience? An analysis of community responses to change in Northern Norway. *Ecology and Society*, *17*(4), 46–60.

Appleyard, D. (1979). The environment as a social symbol: Within a theory of environmental action and perception. *Journal of the American Planning Association*, *45*(2), 143–153.

Aradi, R. (2010). Kartlegging av barns bruk av plass: Erfaringer fra Fredrikstad, *Norge. Kart og Plan*, *70*, 295–310.

Baldwin-Philippi, J., & Gordon, E. (2014). Playful civic learning: Enabling reflection and lateral trust in game-based public participation. *International Journal of Communication*, (8), 759–786.

Beatley, T. (2011). *Biophilic cities: Integrating nature into urban design and planning*. New York: Island Press.

Bela, J. (2015). User-generated urbanism and the right to the city. In J. Hou, B. Spencer, T. Way, & K. Yocom (Eds.), *Now urbanism: The future of city is here* (pp. 149–164). New York: Routledge.

Bose, M., Horrigan, P., Doble, S., & Shipp, S. (Eds.) (2014). *Community matters: Service-learning in engaged design and planning* (pp. 189–209). New York: Routledge.

Bowman, S. (2010). *The functions of role-playing games: How participants create community, solve problems and explore identity*. Jefferson, NC: McFarland.

Brian, W. (2008). Wicked problems in public policy. *Public Policy*, *3*(2), 101–118.

Cohen-Cruz, J. (2012). *Engaging performance: Theatre as call and response*. New York: Routledge.

Cooper Marcus, C. (1995) *House as a mirror of self: Exploring the deeper meaning of home*. Berkeley: Conari.

Council of Europe. (2000). *European landscape convention and reference documents*. Strasbourg: Directorate of Culture.

de la Peña, D., Jones Allen, D., Hester Jr., R. T., Hou, J., Lawson, L. L., McNally, M. J. (Eds.) (2017). *Design as democracy: Techniques for collective creativity*. New York: Island Press.

Di Masso, A., Dixon, J., & Durrheim, K. (2014). Place attachment as discursive practice. In L. Manzo, & P. Devine-Wright (Eds.), *Place attachment: Advances in theory, methods, and applications* (pp. 75–86). London: Routledge.

Egoz, S., Jørgensen, K., & Ruggeri, D. (Eds.) (2018). *Defining landscape democracy: A path to spatial justice*. Glos, UK: Edward Elgar Publishing.

Egoz, S., Makhzoumi, J., & Pungetti, G. (Eds.) (2011). *The right to landscape: Contesting landscape and human rights*. Farnham, UK: Ashgate Publishing.

Ganz, M. (2011). Public narrative, collective action, and power. In S. Odugbemi, & T. Lee (Eds.), *Accountability through public opinion: From inertia to public action* (pp. 273–289). Washington, DC: The World Bank.

Geertz, C. (2008). Thick description: Toward an interpretive theory of culture. In T. Oakes, & P. Price (Eds.), *The cultural geography reader* (pp. 41–51). New York: Routledge.

Hernandez, B., Hidalgo, M. C., Salazar-Laplace, M. E., & Hess, S. (2007). Place attachment and place identity in natives and non-natives. *Journal of Environmental Psychology*, *27*(4), 310–319.

Hester, R. (2006). *Design for ecological democracy*. Cambridge, MA: MIT Press.

Hester, R. (1993). Sacred structures and everyday life: A return to Manteo, North Carolina. In D. Seamon (Ed.), *Dwelling, seeing, and designing* (pp. 271–297). New York: SUNY Press.

Hou, J., & Rios M. (2003). Community-driven place making. *Journal of Architectural Education*, *57*(1), 19–27.

Kahn, P. H., & Hasbach, P. H. (Eds.) (2012). *Ecopsychology: Science, totems, and the technological species*. Cambridge, MA: MIT Press.

Korpela, K. (2012). Place attachment. *The Oxford handbook of environmental and conservation psychology* (pp. 148–163). Oxford: Oxford University Press.

Lenzholzer, S., Duchhart, I., & Koh, J. (2013). Research through designing in landscape architecture. *Landscape and Urban Planning*, *113*, 120–127.

Lewicka, M. (2011). Place attachment. *Journal of Environmental Psychology*, *31*, 207–230.

Louv, R. (2008). *Last child in the woods: Saving our children from nature-deficit disorder*. New York: Algonquin Books.

Low, S. (2017). *Spatializing culture: The ethnography of space and place*. New York: Routledge.

Manzo, L., & Devine-Wright, P. (Eds.) (2014). *Place attachment: Advances in theory, methods and applications*. London: Routledge.

Manzo, L., & Perkins, D. (2006). Finding common ground: The importance of place attachment to community participation and planning. *Journal of Planning Literature*, *20*(4), 335–350.

Markusen, A. (2013). Fuzzy concepts, proxy data: Why indicators would not track creative placemaking success. *International Journal of Urban Sciences*, *17*(3), 291–303.

Mattijssen, T., Van der Jagt, A., Buijs, A., Elands, B., Erlwein, S., & Lafortezza, R. (2017). The long-term prospects of citizens managing urban green space: From place making to place-keeping? *Urban Forestry and Urban Greening, 26*, 78–84.

Mihaylov, N., & Perkins, D. (2014). Community place attachment and its role in social capital development. In L. Manzo, & P. Devine-Wright (Eds.), *Place attachment: Advances in theory, methods and applications* (pp. 61–75). London: Routledge.

Milligan, M. J. (1998). Interactional past and potential: The social construction of place attachment. *Symbolic Interaction, 21*(1), 1–33.

Nussbaum, M. (2011). *Creating capabilities*. Cambridge: Harvard University Press.

Oleksy, T., & Wnuk, A. (2017). Catch them all and increase your place attachment! The role of location-based augmented reality games in changing people-place relations. *Computers in Human Behavior, 76*, 3–8.

Putnam, R. D. (2007). E Pluribus Unum: Diversity and community in the twenty-first century, the 2006 Johan Skytte Prize Lecture. *Scandinavian Political Studies, 30*(2), 137–174.

Pojani, D., & Stead, D. (2015). Sustainable urban transport in the developing world: Beyond megacities. *Sustainability, 7*(6), 7784–7805.

Proshansky, H., Fabian, A., & Kaminoff, R. (1983). Place-identity: Physical world socialization of the self. *Journal of Environmental Psychology*, 3(1), 57–83.

Redaelli, E. (2016). Creative placemaking and the NEA: Unpacking a multi-level governance. *Policy Studies, 37*(4), 387–402.

Relph, E. (1976). *Place and placelessness*. London: Pion.

Rittel, W., & Webber, M. (1973). Dilemmas in a general theory of planning. *Policy Sciences, 4*(2), 155–169.

Romslo, I., & Stordalen, T. (2016). *Memories of tomorrow: Reconnecting community and landscape in Roald through participation. Master's Thesis*, Norwegian University of Life Sciences, Aas, Norway.

Ruggeri, D., & Szilágyi-Nagy, A. (2019). Exploring the use of digital technologies in participatory landscape planning processes. In K. Bishop, & N. Marshall (Eds.), *The Routledge handbook of people and place in the 21st-century city*. London: Routledge.

Ruggeri, D. (2018). Storytelling as a catalyst for democratic landscape change in Modernist utopia. In S. Egoz, K. Jørgensen, & D. Ruggeri (Eds.), *Defining landscape democracy: The search for spatial justice*. Glos, UK: Edward Elgar Publishing.

Ruggeri, D. (2014). The 'My Mission Viejo' project: Investigating the potential of photovoice methods in place attachment and identity research. *Journal of Urban Design, 19*(1), 119–139.

Ruggeri, D. (2009). *Constructing identity in master planned utopia: The case of Irvine New Town, PhD Dissertation*, University of California, Berkeley, USA.

Sandberg, A. (2003). Play memories and place identity. *Early Child Development and Care, 173*(2–3), 207–221.

Seamon, D. (2012). Place, place identity, and phenomenology: A triadic interpretation based on JG Bennett's systematics. In H. Casakin, & F. Bernardo (Eds.), *The role of place identity in the perception, understanding, and design of built environments* (pp. 3–21) [online], United Arab Emirates: Bentham Ebooks.

Seamon, D. (2014). Place attachment and phenomenology. In L. Manzo, & P. Devine-Wright (Eds.), *Place attachment: Advances in theory, methods and applications* (pp. 12–22). London: Routledge.

Schein, R. H. (2009). A methodological framework for interpreting ordinary landscapes: Lexington, Kentucky's Courthouse Square. *Geographical Review, 99*(3), 377–402.

Southworth, M., & Ruggeri, D. (2011). Place identity and the global city. In T. Banerjee, & A. Loukaitou-Sideriss (Eds.), *Urban design: Roots, influences, and trends: The Routledge companion to urban design* (pp. 495–510). New York: Routledge.

Stokols, D. (2006). Toward a science of transdisciplinary action research. *American Journal of Community Psychology, 38*(1–2), 79–93.

Uzzell, D., Pol, E., & Badenas, D. (2002). Place identification, social cohesion, and environmental sustainability. *Environment and Behavior, 34*(1), 26–53.

Ward Thompson, C., & Aspinall, P. A. (2011). Natural environments and their impact on activity, health, and quality of life. *Applied Psychology: Health and Well Being, 3*(3), 230–260.

Index

Note: Page numbers in *italics* and **bold** refer to figures and tables respectively; and pages followed by "n" indicate notes.